THE WORKS OF WILLIAM H. BEVERIDGE

Volume 4

THE EVIDENCE FOR
VOLUNTARY ACTION

T0271956

THE EVIDENCE FOR VOLUNTARY ACTION

Being Memoranda by Organisations and Individuals and other Material relevant to Voluntary Action

Edited by
LORD BEVERIDGE AND A. F. WELLS

Routledge
Taylor & Francis Group
LONDON AND NEW YORK

First published in 1949

This edition first published in 2015
by Routledge
2 Park Square, Milton Park, Abingdon, Oxon, OX14 4RN

and by Routledge
711 Third Avenue, New York, NY 10017

*Routledge is an imprint of the Taylor & Francis Group, an informa
business*

British Library Cataloguing in Publication Data
A catalogue record for this book is available from the British Library

ISBN: 978-1-138-82643-4 (Set)
eISBN: 978-1-315-73730-0 (Set)
ISBN: 978-1-138-82828-5 (Volume 4)
eISBN: 978-1-315-73818-5 (Volume 4)
Pb ISBN: 978-1-138-82882-7 (Volume 4)

Publisher's Note
The publisher has gone to great lengths to ensure the quality of this
reprint but points out that some imperfections in the original copies may
be apparent.

Disclaimer
The publisher has made every effort to trace copyright holders and
would welcome correspondence from those they have been unable to
trace.

THE EVIDENCE FOR VOLUNTARY ACTION

Being Memoranda
by Organisations and Individuals
and other Material
relevant to Voluntary Action

Edited by

LORD BEVERIDGE

and

A. F. WELLS

LONDON
GEORGE ALLEN AND UNWIN LTD
Ruskin House, Museum Street

PRINTED IN GREAT BRITAIN
in 10-*Point Plantin Type*
BY THE BLACKFRIARS PRESS LIMITED
SMITH-DORRIEN ROAD, LEICESTER

PREFACE

by Lord Beveridge

IN submitting my Report to the Government in 1942 on Social Insurance and Allied Services, I accompanied my own Report by a volume of Memoranda from Organisations which had given evidence to the Committee of which I was Chairman. In making my Report on Voluntary Action as a Means of Social Advance it has equally appeared convenient to accompany that by a Supplementary Volume, setting out some of the material on which the Report is based and amplifying the Report by expressions of views and statements of fact submitted by experts in the field covered by my Inquiry.

Organisations for Voluntary Action should be allowed to speak for themselves, as they act according to their own inspiration in serving society. I hope that many who read my Report on Voluntary Action will proceed to the Evidence contained in the present volume.

The Supplementary Volume begins with the results of two investigations commissioned for the purpose of the Inquiry and conducted by Mass-Observation and by Research Services respectively. It was extremely valuable to be able to use both these organisations, applying different methods of study to similar or related fields of investigation.

The Mass-Observation Inquiry is qualitative rather than statistical, though a certain number of statistical tables emerge from their work. The Mass-Observation reports represent on the one hand information gathered by personal interviews by expert investigators in selected areas of different kinds in Britain and on the other hand, replies to questions from a panel of individuals who have agreed to answer questions. Mass-Observation made altogether six reports for the purpose of the present Inquiry, extracts from five of these being Part I of the present volume. From the sixth report on "The People and the Co-op." no extracts are printed in this volume but some quotations from it have been used in *Voluntary Action*. All six Mass-Observation Reports are available for consultation by students.

The Research Services' investigation is essentially statistical, being based on a questionnaire put personally to a number of individuals chosen so far as possible to be a random sample of the whole population and sufficiently numerous to let reasonable inferences as to the general population be drawn from them. The main results of this investigation are given in Part II in a series of tables with brief accompanying letterpress. In addition to the tables printed in the Supplementary Volume, a number of other tables were prepared by Research Services and are available for consultation by students.

Part III of the present volume includes Memoranda on the Finance of Voluntary Action. One is a statement of central government grants to voluntary agencies based on information specially obtained for the purpose of the Inquiry from the various departments by the Treasury. The second consists of notes on the taxation of voluntary agencies.

Part IV includes in whole or in part Memoranda submitted by Organisations which in most cases appeared before the Assessors and myself to give oral evidence and discuss the points raised in their Memoranda. Two Memoranda, relating to the Red Cross and the St. John Ambulance Brigade were not the subject of interviews ; the former was prepared in the first instance in the office of the Inquiry but has been seen and approved as a statement of its work by the organisation concerned. All the Memoranda in Part IV have been seen and checked in proof by the organisations concerned.

In two cases Memoranda in Part IV as originally submitted are supplemented by additional information. The representatives of the British Association of Residential Settlements were asked to obtain information as to the individual settlements and a summary of this information is attached as an Annex to the Memorandum of the Association. It illustrates the variety of the work of the settlements and also the variety of social service.

The Memorandum from the Central Association for the Care of Cripples has also an Annex ; this is a summary of actual cases dealt with by the Surrey Association for the Physically Handicapped.

There follow in Part V a series of Memoranda on special topics by individuals, all of whom with the exception of Mr. Roger Wilson were engaged in the work of the Inquiry itself. One Memorandum which it had originally been intended to include here on "The Physically Handicapped," by Mrs. Joan Clarke, has been omitted, since the problem appears to deserve treatment in a separate volume of its own which the author hopes to publish shortly. The Memorandum had been drawn on freely in the preparation of Chapter VIII of *Voluntary Action*.

Part VI includes on the one hand a complete list of the voluntary agencies which furnished information on request to the Inquiry, and on the other hand, summary data as to some of these agencies, chosen not so much for their individual importance, as to illustrate the nature of Voluntary Action. These summaries have been seen by the agencies and corrected by them in some cases, but the responsibility for them rests on the Inquiry.

Finally, it has seemed worth while to give in Part VII an informal Bibliography listing all the works consulted in preparation of the Report in sequence related to the different topics. It is hoped that as many of those who study the Report and this volume will wish to follow up the references made to them.

In the preparation of this Supplementary Volume I have been assisted by Mr. A. F. Wells who in fact did the greater part of the editing, in particular of the Mass Observation and Research Services Reports and of the Memoranda submitted by Organisations. He was responsible for the Directory of Social

Service Agencies and Bibliography ; in the former of these tasks he was assisted by Miss M. S. Weiner, who had also done for me much valuable work on the main volume.

Since Mr. Wells, through his absence in the West Indies, was not able to assist in seeing this rather complicated volume through the press, that has been undertaken by Mrs. Lucia Turin. Her help has been indispensable.

BEVERIDGE

December, 1948

CONTENTS

THE EVIDENCE FOR VOLUNTARY ACTION

Part V. MEMORANDA BY INDIVIDUALS ON SPECIAL
TOPICS

Part VI. SOCIAL SERVICE AGENCIES

Part VII. SELECT BIBLIOGRAPHY ON VOLUNTARY
ACTION

TABLES

TABLES

Finance of Voluntary Action

14

PART I

MASS-OBSERVATION REPORTS

It was stated in the prefatory Acknowledgments to the Report on Voluntary Action that the Voluntary Social Service Inquiry had been fortunate in securing the help of Mass-Observation, who made for it a number of valuable studies on some of the topics treated in that Report. The particular merit of these studies was, first that they produced a volume of information on the attitudes of the man in the street towards Mutual Aid and the Voluntary Social Services; and in the second place, that the field work of the investigators permitted us some illuminating insights into the actual working of some of the voluntary groups. In these fields the studies of Mass-Observation formed a valuable supplement to the other work of the Inquiry, as did those of Research Services Ltd., which are dealt with in Part II of the present volume.

Space, unfortunately, does not permit of their quotation in full; but substantial extracts follow. In all cases these have been quoted verbatim; passages omitted are indicated by dots; where it has been necessary to add some connecting passages, these are printed in italics, usually at the beginning of a section or sub-section. Italics are used also for headings and cross-headings and also for passages in the original Reports underlined by their writers for emphasis.

The first section deals with the Friendly Societies, which figure more largely in the Report on Voluntary Action than any other single class of agency. The findings here are disquieting, and the picture given of ignorance and apathy on the part both of members and of non-members of Friendly Societies will repay study by officials of those bodies. But in judging of the public attitude to Friendly Societies as shown in this section, regard must be had to the confusion in the public mind between the Friendly Societies proper, based on Mutual Aid, and the collecting businesses which legally are still permitted to call themselves Friendly Societies. (See *Voluntary Action*, p. 295.) In the Mass-Observation Reports, as by the mass of the people, these two very different types of organisation are not distinguished.

The second section deals with some of the less formal aspects of Mutual Aid, a subject to which the Inquiry was otherwise able to devote little attention. The third section treats of the voluntary social services in general : it includes a general study of public attitudes to the voluntary social services ; of the extent of public participation in these services ; and of the opinions of the public on the need for new social services.

The fourth and fifth sections again deal with particular aspects : the former with the public's attitudes towards Charity, and the latter with the question of Holidays.

Readers will note the degree of general accord between the findings of Mass-Observation in this Part, and those of Research Services in Part II, on matters which both treat, despite the differences of technique of these two research organisations.

I. THE FRIENDLY SOCIETIES

I. OPINIONS OF THE GENERAL PUBLIC ON FRIENDLY SOCIETIES

Although the Trade Unions* can, in a limited sense, be regarded as Mutual Aid organisations, their political and industrial activities assume first importance, and it is these aspects of Trade Unionism which are most commonly stressed by people in general. The activities and policy of the Friendly Societies are nothing like as complex; and consideration of attitudes towards the Friendly Societies reveals a picture which—if interpreted simply in terms of approval—disapproval—disinterest—is superficially somewhat similar to the Trade Union attitude-pattern, though more likely to be valid because of the greater simplicity of the Friendly Society.

Thus, about two-fifths of the people who were asked how they felt at present about the Unions and the Friendly Societies expressed a generally favourable opinion. Rather fewer people disapproved of the Friendly Societies than of the Unions, fewer were disinterested. The main point of divergence—something which was a specifically Friendly Society "reaction" —was the question of lack of knowledge. Approximately two out of five had no knowledge of the meaning of the term "Friendly Society."

General approval of Friendly Societies was very slightly more marked among women than among men, among people of working class and artisan background than among middle-class people, among people over forty as compared with people under forty. The whole number of those expressing any kind of approval was rather more than double the number of those who were in any way hostile.

Of the smaller number expressing disapproval, men were apt to be more critical than women, and, to some extent, middle-class people rather than working-class people. (Too much stress should perhaps not be laid upon middle-class opinion here; the Friendly Society was not designed to cater for middle-class needs, and middle-class attitudes are less likely to be based on actual contact with Friendly Society organisation.)

Disapproval of Friendly Societies was not to any appreciable extent conditioned by age. What does most importantly emerge from this whole consideration of attitudes, however, is the fact that such a comparatively large proportion of people under forty are unaware of the existence and nature of the Friendly Societies to the extent of confusing them, in some cases, with

---

* For the Trade Unions, see Section 3, "Voluntary Services," pp. 36-37. (Editors' Note.)

social clubs, political organisations, debating clubs, and, in one case, with some sort of company for selling cigarettes ! A woman in a northern town remarked :

"I have had no dealings with them, but I should imagine they would be very good. During the war, the Americans had nowhere to go, had they ?"

Another in East London :

"I tell you I have nothing against them, but I think that if people want to be friends they will be, without any old society." (Working-class man, aged 45.)

As with the use of such a phrase as "Social Services," which proved on occasion quite incomprehensible to people, allowance must be made here for confusion in terminology. Investigators reported, for instance, that a small number of those who were questioned about the Friendly Societies did, in later conversation, reveal that their ignorance was not as complete as at first appeared. Even so, their numbers were not sufficiently large to assume much significance ; and if due allowance be made for confusions of this kind, we are still left with a proportionate figure which suggests that one person in three, and nearly twice as many younger as older people, are unaware even of the existence of the Friendly Society.

Returning to those people whose attitude towards the Friendly Societies is a positive one, and to the way in which they express their approval : clearly opinion which is unqualified, intensive opinion, is, in the assessment of the degree of *willing* good feeling which attaches to an organisation, more valuable than the qualified opinion which may be indicative of a changing viewpoint. Where expression of opinion about the Friendly Societies is concerned, unqualified approval typifies the answers of a majority of those people whose attitudes towards the Societies are positive. This is the attitude of rather less than one person in two.

What sort of reasons do people advance for their support of the Friendly Societies ?

Appreciation is, as one might anticipate, largely based on the sense of security which the Societies provide :

"I am a member of one of them. They look after sick people at ours. I've been a member for twenty years. I don't go to the meetings very often but they pay sick benefit when I'm ill." (Working-class man, 50.)

"They're very good. You must put away something for a rainy day, if you're working-class." (Housewife, 40.)

"They're all right. If there's anything you need you get it." (Working-class housewife, 45.)

"I myself believe in insurance. I mean there must be insurance. My husband didn't believe in 'em, but he died, so it was a good thing I had insured." (Working-class housewife, 55.)

In the majority of spontaneous comments the Friendly Societies appear exclusively as a convenient mechanism for "putting by for a rainy day." Only an occasional person takes, at this level of approach, a more personalised view, describing his attitude in terms of co-operation with others or, in any sense, showing that he *feels* himself part of a mutual aid movement :

"It is a safeguard against sickness, and another thing that appealed to me and still does, is, in a Friendly Society, there's not a lot thrown away on management. What money you pay into the Society is practically your own. You don't pay any big salaries to officials, just a nominal sum to the secretary. If there's not a lot thrown away you can reap all the profits." (Middle-class man, 75.)

or : "It's a good idea. Helps to create a sense of thrift in the individual." (Middle-class man, 45.)

Criticism of the organisations, although representative only of a minority opinion is often strongly felt. Of the reasons given for disapproval of the Friendly Societies these were the ones most frequently advanced :

(*a*) *The Friendly Society should not really be necessary :*
"They're all right if you haven't got a good State Health System." (Artisan housewife, 40.)

(*b*) *The benefits given by the Societies are not given for a sufficiently long period :*
"If I had my time over again, I'd never belong to one. Yes, I've been a member for thirty years, and they're no good. They say they'll pay you when you're ill, but they don't ! They paid me for three weeks, and then they stopped. I used to go to meetings, but never again." (Working-class man, 63.)

(*c*) *The Friendly Societies have no future :*
"Up to now they have filled a much-needed want. But in the new scheme of 1948 they will be implemented, and then they will have served their purpose." (Middle-class man, 45.)

(*d*) *They make money out of the working classes :*
"A lot of profiteers, and it's time the Government took them over." (Working-class man, 70.)

(*e*) *They should be nationalised :* Here, people do not apparently feel it necessary to elaborate their remarks, nationalisation being regarded as an all-embracing solution.

It is not our intention in this section of the Report to do more than draw attention to the complex of attitudes which surrounds the Friendly Society and other voluntarily-run groups. The feelings of the members of particular Friendly Societies, and the points of view of those who have some responsibility for local branches will be considered at a later stage. In conclusion, however, we may mention here that there is a tendency among those who have been members of Friendly Societies for some considerable period to look back with regret to the time when the Society was very much more than a useful vehicle for "a rainy day," when, through the provision of opportunities for social contacts it built up for itself a "group" loyalty . . .

2. MEMBERS' ATTITUDES

A survey was also made of the opinions of some one hundred and fifty people who stated that they were members of Friendly Societies. A significant point emerged here. Out of the twenty-one insurance bodies to which these people belonged—all of which were stated by them to be "Friendly Societies"—no less than nine were afterwards identified as being, not Friendly Societies proper, but Collecting Societies or insurance companies. The fact throws an interesting light upon the general ignorance of what a Friendly Society is ; it is a notable reinforcement of Mass Observation's other findings. Fortunately the actual number of informants who made this mistake was not large, and conclusions are therefore not much vitiated.

These members were asked how they felt about their Society, whether, on the whole, they approved or disapproved of the way in which it was functioning at present, why they had joined the Society, how long they had been members, whether they knew or wished to know any of the other members of their group. They were asked, also, how they felt about attending meetings and taking part in the election of officials of their Society ; and, finally, whether they had any suggestions to make about ways in which the Friendly Society could contrive to serve a useful purpose in view of the wider provision for insurance now to be made by the State.

No formal questionnaire was used in this more intensive study, nor were Friendly Society members selected on a specified age, sex and class basis. Some of the older and some of the newer members of particular Friendly Societies were visited after an interview with the secretary of the Society, but apart from this, members were selected at random. Classification of comment, however, revealed that although rather more men than women members of Friendly Societies had been approached, age differences were sufficiently well balanced for roughly proportionate inferences to be drawn.

(a) *Why People join Friendly Societies*

The reasons most commonly given for membership of Friendly Societies are :

Economic security	Death and Sickness Benefits
	Benefits for dependents
	General provision for the future
Family influence	Members of family have "always belonged"
	Parents obtained membership for children
Friends and work influence	Membership taken up on advice of friends or workmates
Friendly Society administers State Health Insurance ..	Membership a convenient way of obtaining National Health Benefit
Social Amenities	Society had a "club" appeal.

Economic security reasons were advanced about twice as often as the "family influence" argument, and both these reasons were far more often given than any others. Only a very few people appear to have joined a Friendly Society with the idea of participating in the social functions which it might provide. A small number of people said they had joined because they believed that it was compulsory to do so, but this was almost invariably, a "younger member" attitude, as, to a large extent was the assumption that the main object of the Friendly Society was to administer National Health Insurance. . . .

(b) *Attendance at Meetings*

The membership of Friendly Societies today, judged in terms of attendance at meetings, in lack of interest in the election of officials, in lack of desire for contact with other members of the Society, is very largely a passive one and, while there have, no doubt, always been a number of purely passive members of Friendly Societies, expression of feeling and opinion among older members suggests that in the earlier days of the societies, there were proportionately far more people actively interested in the movement than at present. It is rare today to find a Friendly Society which has much more than the nucleus of an active membership, or attracts to itself anything like the group loyalty which has in the past characterised such organisations.

One indication of a more active type of membership is attendance at meetings. Of the one hundred and fifty Friendly Society members with whom we came into contact, only three people said that they attended any sort of meeting (branch or general meeting) *regularly* ; not more than twenty-five attended any sort of meeting *occasionally* ; the remainder never attended meetings, and merely paid their subscriptions. Branch secretaries invariably stressed the present irregularity of attendance at meetings ; and even where there was an increasing branch membership, the increase was not reflected in meeting attendances. The secretary of a Friendly Society in a northern town, for example, stated that in spite of an increasing membership, at an annual meeting where provision would be made for four hundred members, twenty might come. The secretary of a London branch of one of the Affiliated Orders, a group with a fairly steady membership, at present one hundred and fifty adults and fourteen juniors, expected about thirty to attend the annual meetings and about ten or twelve at fortnightly meetings. In the latter case the "ten or twelve" includes committee members.

With some Friendly Societies, meetings have ceased altogether for lack of support ; with others, committee meetings and ordinary pay-in meetings are still fairly well attended, but increasingly fewer members are attending annual meetings or monthly meetings of a more general character.

The majority of the Friendly Society members whose opinions we recorded were clearly uninterested in the idea of attending meetings . . .

In the majority of comments there was the feeling that :

"I'm just a member, that's all. I don't take part in anything." (Working man, 32.)

And it was only minority opinion which even suggested that people might consider the idea of attending meetings, and then, for various reasons—lack of time, concern with work and living problems, remoteness from branch headquarters—reject it. Sometimes, it also appeared that people might have attended meetings, but lacked the initiative to find out when and where they were held . . .

(c) *Election of officials*

Although people who had at some time held an official position in a Friendly Society spoke of the activities and organisation of the Society with more interest than the average member and appear to attend meetings more regularly, even today, the majority of members were no more interested in the election of branch officials or delegates than in attending meetings. To our question, "Are you interested in taking a more active part in the direction of your local branch, and in elections of local and national officials ?", the first response was most often a surprised "Oh, no !" sometimes developing later into comment which suggested, as with attendance at meetings, that passivity was related to personal and post-war problems, was an indication of satisfaction with the society, or expressive of the feeling that "It's only an Insurance, you know." As an inverse measure of satisfaction with Friendly Society organisation, passivity was more marked in replies to this question than to the enquiry about attendance at meetings . . .

(d) *Acquaintance with other members*

Friendly Society members were asked whether they knew or wished to know any of the other members of their particular Society. Almost invariably, the answer to both questions was "No" . . .

Acquaintance was restricted to the family, a few neighbours, or a small group of workmates, and there was no particular indication that membership of the same Society was regarded as any bond between them. Some older members, and even occasionally younger members, who before the war had taken a more active part in their Society, spoke of their enjoyment of the social occasions on which it had been possible to meet other members, but this was not a usual attitude . . .

(e) *The Age Factor*

The majority of Friendly Society members stated that they did not attend meetings ; felt no desire to take part in the election of officials ; knew very few members of their society and had no wish to meet others. In other words, the attitude of the individual member towards active participation in Friendly Society organisation is negative and resistant.

So far as the immediate future of the Friendly Societies is concerned these results are not encouraging. They are less so, the more obvious it becomes that, on the whole, these negative attitudes are more pronounced among younger people, and that Friendly Society membership today tends towards the older age-groups. Most Friendly Society secretaries stressed the fact that younger members were not now joining the Societies to the extent necessary to balance the older membership, most of them believing that younger people were less interested in saving at the present time than they had ever been . . .

Some Friendly Societies still hold their ordinary meetings in pubs. An Investigator, attending a meeting of one such Society in East London, found points of similarity in age and member attitudes between this and other Friendly Societies. Thus it has *more older than younger members*, meetings are now held fortnightly instead of monthly, and attended only by a few older people who live nearby, and the committee members ; annual general meetings are sparsely attended ; most of the Society's business is now done through the post. "Only the officials," said the secretary, "are in any sense active members today."

An Investigator attended a paying-in meeting of a Society in its pub head-quarters where payments are collected, but usually only about a dozen members turn up and they are in the main members of the committee. The meeting, which lasted from seven until nine, was held in a small room, used also for storage, leading off the bar. During two hours less than a dozen members came in, the youngest of them a woman of fifty, the others between sixty and seventy. Two were officials. The only real business of the meeting on this occasion was to receive subscriptions, but the members obviously knew each other well and talked freely to the Investigator and among themselves :

"I like this Society," said one member of seventy, "because it is small and personal. We make our own rules, and we only pay ninepence a week. I've been in it for over fifty years. 'Course, today, we don't get the support of the younger generation, and it seems to me that they have got some very funny ideas."

And another, also over seventy :

"My feelings have not changed about it. I've moved out of the district now, but I still come back every month to pay my subscription and meet my friends. I still enjoy coming because I have got many friends. I do feel that we could do with more members and particularly of the younger generation."

A woman of fifty, paying in for her husband, also described how she liked coming to pay in because :

"It's no trouble to pay in here. I know the people and they have been very good to me. I think it's wonderful really. You see, as my husband is in an asylum, and I have a little boy at home I can only take a part-time job. With this insurance money I can keep going."

These older members, like the older members of other Friendly Societies, while enjoying the small "personal" meetings which take place in the pub back room, still speak nostalgically of the social gatherings of the past, and would welcome their survival :

"It used to be more fun then, in the good old days when we 'ad sheepshead suppers 'ere, and perhaps a hundred of us together. 'Appy days, 'appy days !"

Except for this feeling, and a realisation that younger members are needed, the members who came to this particular meeting were satisfied with the way in which the Society was working. The branch secretary also felt that it was "working smoothly and efficiently," although he remarked that "there does not seem to be any future for people like me, does there ?"

The future of the Friendly Societies, as we have elsewhere emphasised, could partially depend upon the attractions provided by group membership. A group such as that described above, while "working smoothly" as a business concern, and in a very limited way providing social satisfaction for a small number of people, has no certain ground on which to base its appeal to the younger people whose support is clearly needed.

3. THE FUTURE OF THE FRIENDLY SOCIETIES

(a) Views of Members

Members of Friendly Societies were asked if they had any suggestions to make about ways in which the societies could continue to be useful to people after they had ceased to function as Approved Societies. From their replies to this question there emerged the same pattern of majority passivity, and minority active interest that characterised most comment and attitude towards the Friendly Societies. Many of the members had not previously understood what the position of the Societies would be : they seemed fairly certain that they would continue to pay their own contributions, but were otherwise confused and disinterested in their attitude, and had no constructive proposals to offer. Nor did minority interests produce a very wide spread of suggestions. The "wishful" attitude was clear—the feeling that the Friendly Societies *must* continue because payments were likely to be made more promptly and individuals receive more sympathetic attention ; but apart from this, the only suggestions made were that the Societies could function more extensively as short-term Loan and Thrift Clubs, help people to save for holidays, finance long-term loans for house purchase, help members to get jobs, reduce contributions after a term of years to help Old Age Pensioner members, increase sick benefits and help unemployed members financially. The fact that Friendly Societies do, for the most part, already serve some of these purposes, was, apparently, unappreciated . . .

(b) Views of Officials

However favourable the environment itself may be to the successful emergence of groups, much will also depend upon those who have some responsibility for group organisation. If the Friendly Societies are again to become more locally active, the attitude of the branch secretary becomes more important. In our experience, most organisers of local lodges are worried about decrease in attendance at meetings, by the amount of postal work they are now called upon to deal with, by the greater difficulty in getting voluntary helpers today and, sometimes, by the inadequacy of their own "token" remuneration, but are not unduly worried about the future of the Friendly Society movement itself. On the whole, it is the organisers of those Friendly Societies which have, in the past, been most interested in social activities and counted upon a more active membership who are most pessimistic, and here problems such as those just described are stifling initiative. Once again, we feel that classification is required on questions of the type of membership desired, and of activities and methods of organisation best calculated to attract that type of member, if local officials are to act without confusion.

All Friendly Society officials, and by far the greater majority of members, were convinced of the value of Mutual Aid as exemplified by the groups to which they belonged; in their attitude to the future of the Friendly Society movement generally, they were uncertainly optimistic . . .

4. A GROUP STUDY

Mass-Observation concludes its survey of the Friendly Society Movement by a study of one particular Society, "to illustrate the way in which diminishing membership, increasing average age, cessation of social activities, can together combine to produce deterioration in group feeling and purpose."

This Friendly Society is one which in terms of membership, activities and enthusiasm, in everything but inexacting goodwill and financial security, is in process of decay; a group which looks backwards over a period of fifty years when it was a live social organism, and forward, with faint hope, to an uncertain future.

Three-quarters of its members are over forty-five years of age. Twenty years ago there were 120 members; today there are 85. No one is quite sure how many came to general meetings in the early days of the Society, but it is believed that nearly all the members did so. In 1930, forty people would come: immediately before the war, a dozen; today, none. During the war, the hall previously hired for meetings remained unblacked-out, and so unused. No effort is now being made to hold general meetings, because, says the secretary:

"Although, according to the rules, we should have meetings on the first and third Wednesdays of every month . . . all the members know that they can come to my house if they want to hold a meeting. A lot of them have moved away from the district, and they send their contributions by post; I only see them when they want anything or when they are sick."

The Society has, naturally, a management committee: seven people who constitute the only people taking an active part in affairs. Even these, it seems, are not *very* active, and, in fact, the Secretary and the Treasurer do most of the work. No ordinary member now has any say in the election of officers. Again, "according to the rules," officers should come up for election at the annual general meeting. But as no general meetings have taken place since the war, members of the Management Committee remain officials as long as they wish; if one dies, another, "one of the older members," says the secretary, is co-opted in his place.

In the early days of the group, there were all kinds of social events, and some of the older members look back regretfully to the heyday of the Society. Said one of the older members, though he does not blame the Society for this:

"The Government's cutting out all that friendliness. They're cutting out the sociabilities of meetings, and it'll soon be just a cypher. Meetings? Cor, no! We don't have none of them now. There was thirteen attended the last general meeting. We used to make a bit of conversation and we had socials and little concerts . . . Ah, yes, we used to have cricket matches between the different sections, and the two would join together to play one another."

The secretaries of this and other Friendly Societies say, and often, that although at one time more people used to come to meetings, they "never took much part in them." The possibility that attendance at the meetings was looked upon by the ordinary member as part and parcel of his *being* a member, even if he did take little active part in the proceedings ; the idea that his participation in social gatherings was a reinforcement of his interest as a member, was not anywhere considered. If this "reinforcement" be dropped, perhaps it is little wonder that one more recent member with no experience of the social side, coming into the group at a time when meeting attendance was declining, can say :

"Although I did go to a few meetings, I was bored stiff and came away each time. I dare say it was the way they ran it ; but all the members were mainly older people, and no one seemed particularly interested. All the committee members had been sitting for years. The only way a change is made is when one of them dies. They had annual general meetings, but nobody ever nominated anybody new, because of the feeling of, oh well, so-and-so's been a member for so long now, we mustn't hurt his feelings !"

Less, perhaps, that an even more recent member, a young engineer with no experience even of meetings, sees the Society simply as a provider of financial benefits :

"I'm just a member you know. I pay my subscriptions and that's all. It's a sort of insurance with me. I've never had a look at the books and I've never been to a meeting. The secretary lives near me. I've never seen the books but I know it's all right !"

This young man was "signed up as a Junior Member" by his father. Today Friendly Society membership, of whatever Society, leans towards the older age groups. If the financial inducement is the only one offered by the Friendly Society, and a National Insurance Scheme offers wide benefits at a *compulsorily* increased rate, what are the chances that younger people will join and revive the movement? It does seem that something more than the additional insurance benefit will be required, and certainly something more than a mere *wish* for new and younger members, such as is felt by the secretary of this particular group, who told us that :

"We lost a lot of members through the war. Of course, we always *hope* for new members. The head office has put forward different schemes for increasing membership but I'm not very clear about them. Twenty years ago we ran a series of dances to try and attract new members, but although we didn't lose any money on them, we didn't get any new members."

And even if someone did respond to this *hope*, he would not it seems, be made to feel that he was joining a group which had any but financial benefits to offer him, for :

"We don't have initiation ceremonies any more. We just get a doctor's certificate for them, and I inform the committee, and that's that !"

2. MUTUAL AID AND THE PUB

An account of the mutual aid movement would be incomplete without some reference to the rich variety of more or less informal unregistered benefit societies, frequently connected with public houses. The following extracts give an account of some of these societies. The materials were collected by intensive investigation in two localities—in a workers' estate in Southern England, and in the East End of London. Pseudonyms have been used throughout to replace actual names of public houses.

I. THE UNICORN

(a) *Reason for selecting the "Unicorn" for special study*

The *Unicorn* is a square, solid building, sixty years old, the only pub in a specialised community of some 800 people in southern England. The pub, two shops, a Works Sports Ground and a Workmen's Institute are the only amenities on an estate where blocks of barracks converted into flats and houses surround a large open space of green. The estate is one and a half miles from a small town in one direction ; in the other, it verges upon open country.

The *Unicorn* is not in all ways a "typical pub"—no pub is. From the present viewpoint it probably differs from the "average" pub in that it houses rather more organisations than is usually the case. It was selected for the following main reasons :

It is situated in a totally working-class area.

Many of its regular customers work for the same industrial concern, most at fairly heavy manual labour.

There is no church on the estate, and as a centre for group interests the pub has no rival.

As a building, the pub with its extra room for dances and meetings, is well designed for group activities.

The reports of an Investigator living at the *Unicorn* and mixing with the people of the district show that these factors *were* important in the function of the pub as a community centre, and suggest a relationship between the broad delineation of the total group as determined by environment and the character of smaller groups more consciously organised.* Background community of interest no doubt accounts in part for the positive feelings which the people of the estate have about their pub, the landlord and his wife, and

---

* The question of what type of environment is most likely to be conducive to the formation of what types of groups is a subject in which M-O has for some time been interested. The implications of the question are so vast, however, that at present we can, as above, hazard the most tentative of conclusions.

the pub groups of which they are members, but the picture is peculiar in its intensity rather than in the broad lines of communal interest and mutual aid which it exemplifies.

(b) Groups at the "Unicorn"

Almost all local organisations of whatever type have their headquarters at the *Unicorn*. The Buffaloes meet there regularly. The Slate Club, the Help-out Club (a women's Holiday and Christmas Club), Cricket and Football Clubs, the Ramblers' Club, the Darts Club, and the Horticultural Society are among the varied groups organised from the *Unicorn*. The pub has between seventy to eighty regular customers, and as many more who come in more casually ; groups such as the Help-out Club, the Darts Club, and the Horticultural Society have been spontaneously organised by the regulars, and all groups draw largely upon the regulars but also on the more casual customers for their membership. The non-regulars may come to the pub simply on paying-out or meeting nights (in the opinion of the landlord they are not interested in drinking and buy drinks simply so that they may be acceptable as club members), but it is interesting to find that both regulars and casual customers of this pub show more consistent interest in their group organisations—as measured by attendance at meetings and willingness to support other activities—than is usually the case among pub groups.

Club membership inclines to be large both in relation to the total number of people living in the district and in relation to the number of people who are regular customers of the *Unicorn*. The Darts Club, for example, has seventy-eight members, the Slate Club sixty, the Women's Group thirty. The secretaries or organisers of groups report an active membership of something near two-thirds of the total membership. They do not, as is sometimes the case with organisers of non-pub groups, complain of lack of support from the rank and file or the difficulties which they experience in getting voluntary help from their members.

What sort of Mutual Aid practices take place at the *Unicorn*, formally and informally ? At what age do people show most interest in the various groups ? How willing, generally, are pub-goers to help each other ? Regulars tend to be more interested in group activities than non-regulars, but there is also an age-interest factor. Among the customers of the *Unicorn* there is a fairly wide age spread although there are more regulars over than under forty, and, with the exception of cricket and football clubs, it is the older rather than the younger people who become group members. Here, the pub follows the pattern of the non-pub organisation.

Mutual Aid organisations at the *Unicorn* divide as elsewhere, into those which provide specified individual benefits along Friendly Society lines, and those which aim to give their members more generalised benefits, the outings arranged by the Help-out Club, for example, or the bulk buying of seeds at a cheaper rate by the Horticultural Society. The Club with the largest membership—seventy-eight persons—at the *Unicorn* is the Darts Club.

This merits detailed description as an organisation which began simply as a sports club, developed a most decided group-consciousness and is now in process of change into something which in some respects resembles a Friendly Society! A resident investigator reports :

"The Darts Club has seventy-eight members, men and women. Each member pays sixpence weekly to the Club. Some weeks they have a quarter week when the subscription is ninepence. If payments get five weeks in arrears the member is suspended.

"This group which originally grew out of the interest which people felt in the playing of what has now become perhaps the most popular of pub games, has now become formalised and developed a number of activities which have little to do with playing darts but a good deal to do with the mutual aid spirit which seems to arise in any group where people get to know each other well."

The Darts Club now provides for its members :
1. Darts Matches
2. Home and Away Outings
3. Christmas Party for Children
4. Party and Dinner for Members
5. Christmas Pay-out. Last year what you paid in you got back. Raffles covered the rest
6. Darts Club Banking Account
7. Derby Day Outing. (Members paid seven shillings and sixpence, the Club the rest)
8. If a member is ill over six weeks, the Club gives financial assistance, has a Benefit Darts Match, etc.

The groups at the *Unicorn* are made up of people who know almost equally well the members of their own circle and members of other groups—there is, of course, some overlapping of membership too—and the picture of organisations here is a picture of compact, friendly and not too highly formalised groups. It was not surprising that in this particular district the pub would become a headquarters for organisations. What was at first less clear, though it later became increasingly so, was that the mutual aid motive, basic to the success of voluntary organisations, was so much a part of the everyday behaviour of people in the pub . . .

Pub attitudes and behaviour are always to some extent influenced by the landlord. Another interesting facet of the Mutual Aid pattern at the *Unicorn* was the close, almost "family" relationship which existed between the landlord and his wife and their customers.

"In the *Unicorn* all the regulars refer to the landlord as "Pop" and his wife as "Ma" or "Mummy" ; regulars or not, people come to them when they are in any sort of trouble. "Mummy" gives five shillings to the parents of any new-born baby, and they often come to her for advice. About once in every two months "Pop" buys drinks all round for the regulars."

Pop and Ma are together, or singly, members of all the groups which meet in the pub. Ma is Treasurer of the Women's Club, Pop is an official of the Darts Club. Pop, even if not attached in any official capacity to any particular group, takes charge of their funds and gives advice and assistance to any groups as required. Their identification with the group interests of their customers, besides being good for business, undoubtedly has the additional effect of helping to create and canalise enthusiasm for the clubs ; further, it provides a guarantee of financial security for the various groups. That Pop and Ma do exert a stabilising influence on the groups is amply illustrated from an investigator's monthly record of chance incidents observed in the *Unicorn.* The following is one of many which could be quoted to prove the point :

"On Wednesday night members of the Darts Club were becoming more than a little heated over the question of pay-out following a special game. Members argued hotly over the best way of sharing out the money. One of them then saw the landlord coming over and immediately turned and said to the others :

"It's O.K. Hold on, you chaps. Here comes Pop. He'll settle it. He'll know what's the best thing to do."

(c) Conclusions

What then emerges from this account of activities at the *Unicorn* ? Briefly, a picture of the influences bearing upon the formation of groups in a single selected area.

The layout of the estate, identity of work interests among the people of the estate, the favourable position of the pub, the personality and influence of the landlord and his wife, all these have combined to build up :

(*a*) A larger number of groups than is usually to be found concentrated on a single pub.

(*b*) Within these groups, a larger percentage of active members than is normally to be found in non-pub organisations.

(*c*) (Here the conclusion is more tentative), an intensity of group attachment feeling which appears to be greater than is usual among present-day groups.

(*d*) A general inclination towards neighbourliness and voluntary service for which the pub is, as it were, a distributing centre . . .

2. THE EAST END GROUPS

Let us take the East End Loan Clubs next. Investigators have personally visited such clubs and have judged from casual conversation with people in the streets and in their homes, that knowledge of such clubs is widespread—more widespread incidentally than knowledge of Friendly Societies proper.

Two such clubs are those run from the *Nelson* and the *Masons' Arms* in an East London district. Financial arrangements in both clubs are similar. The Secretary of the *Nelson* club describes the way his club works as follows :

"We've 140 members now. It's a very old club. We really started it about twenty-five years ago, but we broke up during the war and we've only started running again last year. The aims of the club are these—we give loans to our members when they need them, and we have a payment at Christmas time. Members buy shares at 6d. each, and they can have as many shares as they like. Suppose they buy ten shares, then they have to pay five shillings each week. Each member pays a quarterly charge of 3d. which covers expenses like printing the payment cards and ink, and that sort of thing. We also have a system of fines. Members have to pay a ½d. fine each week for each share if they don't make the weekly payment. If a member has ten shares and doesn't pay for one week he is fined 5d., for the second week 10d., and so on."

The investigator asked if members often fell behind with their payments. The secretary replied :

"No, they pay quite regularly. It does happen sometimes because of illness, but not often. All members can get a loan to the amount they have to their credit. But we don't stick to that as a hard and fast rule. If we know a man's all right, we let him have a loan even if he hasn't got the security in the club. Nearly all the members have been in the club before the war, so we know they're all right. Loans are repaid at a shilling a week for each £ borrowed. If they fall behind with payments we fine them 1d. per £ each week. At the end of the year we stop 1s. in the £ from every member who hasn't borrowed at least £1. That goes into the fund for the next year."

The secretary then went on to explain that the club met on Monday nights for payment, that they had two auditors to examine the books every quarter, that the licensee guaranteed the funds. The average weekly amount saved by members was 6s. and the amount loaned varied from £2 to £5.

Two general points which were made by the organisers of this and other loan clubs was that membership had fallen because of the war but was now steadily increasing again, and that groups such as these could only be run successfully "if you know all your members personally." Said the secretary of the *Nelson* club :

"The whole idea is to keep it local. If it was on a large scale you'd have to make it so that they could only borrow as much as they had paid in and then you couldn't help anyone out of a jam like we can now because we know the people. There's been lots of times when someone wanted money in a hurry and we've let him have it. You can't do that unless you know who you're dealing with."

Investigators attended pay-out meetings at the *Nelson* and the *Masons' Arms,* and their reports of these meetings emphasise the intimate and local character of the groups. Members were greeted by their Christian names and there was a good deal of talk about jobs and families. Some of the members told investigators how they felt about the Loan Clubs ; "Charley," for example, who is a docker of 35, with two children, says :

"It's a very good way of saving money for Christmas and holidays. Another fing, John. If you get art of work for long you 'ave got a bit be'ind you. If you got a family like I 'ave, you got to save for 'olidays and fings. You can't just take it art of the wage packet. I got forty shares, and that mounts up. You got ter keep goin' wiv it though. See, if I mike a bit extra I only spend it 'ere, so I might as well put some by for the time even if we 'ave to go a bit short. Getting together like this is the only way people like us can keep goin' in 'ard times."

And Bill, a shrivelled old working-man of 60, after he has made his payment of 5s. remarks :

"This is the best way of doin' fings. There's na charity abat it. You all pay in, and if yer need a bit o' money, you can get it . . . I used to belong to a Friendly Society once, but I gave it up . . . all a bloody swindle. I paid in for years, and then because I was ill for a while they stopped my sick benefit. I got noth' out of 'em. Paid me for a few weeks an' that was all."

There is some evidence to suggest that the various Loan Clubs are beginning to acquire younger members again, but on the whole their membership is an older one. A count of the first twelve people who came to pay in at the *Nelson* gave the following results :

		paid	
Man—60 years		paid	5s.
„ 50 „	„		5s.
„ 45 „	„		£1 6s. 9d.
„ 50 „	„		4s.
„ 55 „	„		8s.
„ 65 „	„		4s.
„ 45 „	„		5s.
Woman 40 „	„		£1 2s. 6d.
„ 50 „	„		8s.
„ 35 „	„		£1 5s. 0d.
„ 60 „	„		4s.
„ 50 „	„		8s.

Investigators were detailed to check up on this by talking to people under 35 selected at random in the streets near the pubs, and these recorded conversations again make it clear that it is the exception rather than the rule for the younger person to belong to such a club. In general, though there may be people like Sam, who at thirty years is earning "easy money" and does not belong to a Loan Club because :

"I did once where I worked, and we doubled up every week and the bloke wot was running it did a bunk wiv' the dough and plonks it on a dog. The dog don't turn up and that's the last I see of me money. I 'aven't belonged to one since !"

It is safe to say that the younger people of the district are not much interested in the idea of saving through associations of this kind. This is particularly true of young, single people, the young marrieds being rather more, though even not very determinedly, interested, in saving "for a rainy day."

One important sidelight on the organisation of loan clubs in pubs is the brewers' interest. As the landlord of one such pub remarked :

"It's a case of money circulation, see. I mean there's the Christmas pay out. Well, what do they do with some of the money they get ? Buy drinks of course ! So the brewers see the money or some of it, back again. Pays them to do it, don't it ?"

From the customer's point of view the fact that the brewery is "in" on the club offers a guarantee of financial security. A docker of 35 said most emphatically when asked what he thought about the idea of that sort of thing being done through the brewery :

"It's a good idea. Yus, it is ! You 'ave got a safeguard for yer money, 'aven't yer ? See, if the landlord did a bunk wiv it the brewery would still pay wot you 'ave in. There's a lot of money arand Christmas time, yer know !"

So far as can be judged the brewers are certainly interested in encouraging the formation and continuance of such clubs, and with the pub playing the part that it does in the lives of the people of the area, there is a possibility that the membership of such groups will return to their pre-war strength, that is, to a membership about a third greater than it now is. The problematical factors are, as with so many voluntary groups of varying types, the attitude of the younger people and the extent to which State insistence on compulsory insurance contributions will prove a financial drain.

Comments such as this from a woman of 30 with two children :

"I ain't got no time to go to no loan clubs. My time's taken up 'ere wiv' this lot !"

and from a young man of 20 :

"Look, I 'aven't fought abart it. Look, I gotta go now. I gotta date," are characteristic of the viewpoint of the younger people in the district.

Investigators did not find many other kinds of voluntary groups associated with East End pubs. Darts Clubs and Shove Ha'penny Clubs are popular, but membership fluctuates a good deal. Occasionally a Friendly Society holds its meetings in a pub. In our report on the Friendly Societies, we describe one such society and its pub associations in rather more detail ; here, it will suffice to say that the pub connections of the Friendly Societies are not as close as is the case with Loan Clubs, though the fact that some Friendly Societies meet in pubs appears, to members, to be a point in their favour.

There is no such clear connection between the Friendly Societies and the brewers as in the case of Loan Clubs, but it often happens that the licensee of a particular pub is also the treasurer for the Friendly Society that meets there. This arrangement is, as the secretary of one Friendly Society put it, "convenient and economical." Meeting in a pub is more economical than hiring a hall or room and the amount paid to the landlord for the privilege is usually small, in the region of £5 yearly. Meeting in a pub is convenient because if the secretary is unable to be present the members can simply hand their subscriptions across the bar to the landlord.

3. VOLUNTARY SERVICES

The preceding Reports dealt with agencies, formal or informal, for mutual help and relief. The subject of the present study is the Voluntary Social Services in general.

The extracts are arranged under the following main heads :

    I. What does Voluntary Social Service mean to people ?

    II. Who belong to Organisations ?

    III. Penetration of Organisations

    IV. New Social Services

The material for this report, as for its forerunners, was obtained largely through informal contacts and conversation with people in various parts of the country, and by observation ; the informal approach was stressed throughout. Information from Mass-Observation's Panel of Voluntary Observers was also made use of. Mass-Observation's Panel i: a largely middle-class group widely representative of professional and technical interests.

WHAT DOES VOLUNTARY SOCIAL SERVICE MEAN TO PEOPLE ?

(i) *Participation in Voluntary Social Service*

No matter in what sort of area they lived, whether in the East End of London, in the industrial north, or in a small village, only a minority, less than a third, of the people with whom investigators came into contact, were found to be giving any sort of fairly regular voluntary help to people outside their own families. Rather less than half of these were doing so as private individuals ; the remainder in connection with some type of organisation. People who preferred to give help as private persons were almost all of them over forty years of age ; though apart from this there was no appreciable sex or age difference in attitudes.

The picture of voluntary services provided by members of Mass-Observation's National Panel was one of more conscious and intensive activity. Even so, rather less than half the Panel Members who gave details of their activities and attitudes towards voluntary work undertook any special form of voluntary service. Among the "active" members of the Panel, slightly more men than women are to be found engaged in voluntary work, and in comparison with the general sample, there are more Panel people who view voluntary social service as something which entails group membership.

Further conversation with people who did not at first admit to doing much to help others made it clear that many more did so occasionally and in times of emergency ; that they "would be prepared to do so if need arose." It was men rather than women who replied simply, "No, I don't do anything like that," in response to questions about voluntary activities ; and women rather than men who tended to be defensive in their attitudes and produce excuses for themselves . . .

33

C

To what extent do the attitudes revealed by Mass-Observation's Panel Members correspond to those of people in general ? An analysis of the written opinions of Panel observers shows that of the men and women not engaged in any voluntary activities (more women than men), the outstanding difference between the sexes is again that men seldom offer excuses or qualify their answers. Women, on the other hand, are more generally inclined to say that they have neither the time nor energy to cope with extra work. Thus, the views expressed by the more articulate of the community in this case correspond very closely to the views of those less easily able to explain why they do and do not do certain things.

Consideration of negative attitudes towards social service among people in general and among members of the Panel thus leads one to the conclusion that most of those who do not go out of their way to help their neighbours—this being especially true of women—are somewhat guiltily conscious of the fact that they do not do so. As incipiently positive attitudes, these feelings should be considered together with the fact that "only a minority of people are doing any sort of fairly regular work to help people outside their families." There is therefore a reserve of willingness to be drawn upon if ways and means of dealing with people's more immediate material needs can be devised.

(ii) *Range of Voluntary Activities*

The range of activities mentioned by people interested in doing voluntary work outside their own homes is wide. Giving advice to neighbours, selling flags, helping with youth clubs and canteens, looking after children for neighbours and relatives, shopping for other people, contributing to the hospitals, acting as a Borough Councillor, doing odd jobs for people in the same trade in one's spare time : all these and many other activities are interpreted as voluntary social service. In comparison with members of the middle-class Panel, the street sample takes a more active interest in voluntary work for the more purely Mutual Aid organisations, such as Friendly Societies, and for religious organisations, but otherwise their range of activities is equally varied.

The number of activities which Panel Members view as voluntary social service is again large, and their nature varied ; and any work which is undertaken without remuneration, whether such work is done individually or as a member of a group, tends to be regarded as voluntary social service . . .

(iii) *Knowledge of Social Services*

Over half of all the people who were asked for information about the social services in their district, whether run by voluntary aid organisations or by the Borough Council, failed to name any. Whether the area was, in fact, well provided with social services appeared not to have much bearing on the matter ; though the fact that people in rural areas knew more about the social services of the area made it clear that the size of the district was an important factor.

Among those who did have some knowledge of the social services of their

34

district, the order of frequency in which different kinds of organisations were mentioned was as follows :

Youth Clubs
Maternity and Baby Welfare Centres
Hospitals
Sick Clubs
W.V.S.
Old Age Pensioners' Associations or Clubs
British Legion and S.S.A.F.A.
Settlements (in an East London area only)

Miscellaneously mentioned were such organisations as :

Society for the Blind
The Citizens' Advice Bureau
Mass X-Ray
Blanket Fund
Community Council
Catholic Fund

In rural districts the activities of the W.V.S. were more often alluded to than those of any other organisation ; in other districts, the work of hospitals, and Maternity and Child Welfare Clinics.

Over half of the people in all districts failed to name any social services. A consideration of the answers given by those people classified as having some knowledge of social service makes it clear, however, that "knowledge of social services" very often means simply knowing the names of two or three organisations or giving detailed information about one organisation in particular.

Middle-class people were slightly more knowledgeable about the social services of their district than working-class people, but the distinction was not sufficiently obvious to assume any great importance . . .

Even a local Councillor in one London district, which is particularly well supplied with officially-organised and with voluntarily-run social services of varied types, failed to name more than five of the services existing in the district.

For some people, especially in an entirely working-class district, social services and the Assistance Board are identical. For others, voluntarily-run social services and charities are identical. Others again, and this is particularly the case in towns, assume that any sort of social service must have something to do with the local council. Two of the questions we set out to answer before trying to arrive at any sort of conclusion about the possible future of the voluntary social services were : "What do the Voluntary Social Services mean to people ?" and "What sort of knowledge have people at present of the social services provided in their district ?" The fact that people showed so little knowledge of the social services locally provided does to some extent additionally answer the first of these queries. Some people, men in particular, appear from their further comments to appreciate the difference in principle between voluntarily-run and state-or municipally-organised services, but the prevailing lack of knowledge of existing social services, organised on whatever

35

basis, suggests that Voluntary Social Services, though they may mean much to those people who have had personal dealings with particular organisations, have only the barest significance for people in general.

Members of Mass-Observation's Panel were not specifically asked what knowledge they had of the social services existing locally. They were, however, asked for suggestions about the future of the social services, and then how they felt such services could best be run ; and while their answers do not show, with any exactitude, how much they know of the social services of their own district, it is clear that their knowledge of existing social services and the ways in which they are run is far more extensive than among the population generally. Over three-quarters of Panel Observers are representative of educated middle-class interests ; less than a quarter have a working-class background. A wide spread of professional interests is represented, and the more highly-skilled technical, clerical and commercial fields. Those of the Panel, who are attached to social service organisations of any kind, incline to hold positions of responsibility in their groups ; incline, in fact, to be the people who organise and "give" rather than those who "receive" and are organised. Thus it is not perhaps surprising to find that Panel Observers show a greater social awareness than is ordinarily the case.

(iv) *Attitudes to Particular Social Services*

Mass-Observation points out that people may hold ideas about individual organisations quite different from their views on voluntary social service or mutual aid in general. Accordingly, some study was undertaken of particular organisations. Of these, the Friendly Societies were reported on in an earlier section : the following paragraphs treat of the Trade Unions, and of organisations for the welfare of the Young and the Old respectively.

(a) *Trade Unions*

Trade Unions are not at present receiving anything like wholehearted "attitude" support. Under half (40 per cent.) of people talking about Trade Unions expressed any sort of feeling which could be interpreted as approval, and at least a third of those who did express approval qualified their answers in some way. This figure applies to both men and women ; considered separately, nearly twice as many men as women approved of Trade Unionism.

Taking the whole sample, for two-thirds of those who without equivocation made some such remark as :

"I agree with them. I think working men couldn't get on without them." (Working-class man, 42),

a third qualified their approval with some such remark as :

"Well, I think they're a good thing in their way but they go too far sometimes." (Artisan housewife, 45.)

The number of those who disapproved of or were disinterested in the whole question were almost equally balanced. Reasons for disapproval of the Unions varied. People often felt that the original purpose of Trade Unions had now become obscured :

"I think they were good when they started, but they're not being used as they're meant to be." (Working-class man, 30) ;
that the "Closed Shop" principle was unacceptable :
"Like going back to school, isn't it ? As regards Trade Unions—I mean, take the transport. If you don't join the Union you are thrown out of work. In that way it seems a dictatorship." (Working-class man, 30) ;
that they were gaining too much power, not putting national interests first, not taking a sufficiently firm line with unofficial strikes, or "becoming too much like Russia."

Only a small number of men had nothing to say either approvingly or disapprovingly about the Unions. Lack of interest was, however, far more obvious among women. Two out of three women were not sufficiently knowledgeable or interested to give any opinion at all. Not that there is anything surprising about this ; on any survey women are commonly found to be less interested than men in questions of industrial organisation and there are, of course, fewer women than men in the Trade Union movement.

These were the attitudes towards Trade Unionism among people generally ; *but* class and age proved of some importance in the determination of opinion. For example, the greater measure of approval and of interest in the Unions comes from the over rather than the under-forties, and from the skilled rather than the unskilled working man. Younger people (the under-forties) were more often and more decidedly disapproving in their viewpoint. Proportionately, people with a middle-class background continue to be more critical of Trade Unionism than any kind of non-professional worker . . .

(b) Young People's Welfare

The desirability of further provisions to meet the needs of youth was given first consideration by those people who were asked if they considered that there was any call for new social services in their district. This was particularly the case in an East End area, but the demand was also marked in other areas. Almost half of all the people who had suggestions to make about new social services were, in fact, concerned that, as far as they knew, there were either no organisations in their neighbourhood for looking after children and young people, or too few of them. One point frequently made was that even if there were youth clubs in the district, membership was not usually open to the younger children, and people asked not only for many more clubs for adolescents, both boys and girls, but for children's clubs, play centres, organisations for looking after children during school holidays, more playing fields and parks, more youth hostels, day nurseries and, occasionally, night nurseries also.

A distinction must, however, be drawn between what people have to say about the organisations which are needed in their own district and their feelings about what is being done for youth generally. On the latter subject, nearly a third felt that a "good deal" was now being done for young people, and only one in six that too little was being done. How do general attitudes of this kind link with particular statements about localised social service needs ? The confusion—or what appears to be a confusion of feeling—may be partially

37

explained by the fact that (as we have so often found to be the case in any neighbourhood study) people's knowledge of the amenities of their districts are apt to be strictly limited. Thus, the fact that people emphasise the need for more youth clubs in their locality does not necessarily imply that they have any knowledge of the numbers of clubs which are already in existence there. It may be remembered also, that before people were asked if there was a need for any new social services in their neighbourhood we enquired if they could name any of the social services already provided; few people were able to name more than one such service. Here again is a further indication of the lack of knowledge which may condition the "local" attitude. Those people who approve of the interest they feel is now being taken in youth, mention often the opportunities for further education, and the work of the youth clubs in "keeping them off the streets," and providing the kind of environment which will make young people both more socially inclined and more thoughtful of future responsibilities . . .

Where there is a feeling that too much consideration is now being shown to young people, the two criticisms most frequently made are that the young are benefiting at the expense of the old, and that they are being "spoonfed"! . . .

Sex and class differences in attitudes to youth have not yet been referred to. Briefly, the picture is that two-thirds as many women as men approve of the interest which is being taken in the welfare of youth, and that the greatest measure of approval comes from working-class people.

(c) Old People's Welfare

Naming the social services which they thought should receive priority provision, people placed the needs of old people second on the list, the needs of the young getting first consideration. The welfare of the young and the old were both mentioned far more frequently than the needs of any other section of the community, and in particular, the necessity for making greater provision for old people was more often stressed in urban than in rural districts, in particular, in the "Blacktown" district of a Midland industrial town.

On a further occasion, people were asked how they felt generally about the work which was being done for old people; only one person in four considered that sufficient attention was being given to the old, and only two in a hundred that too much was being done. Nearly half of all those who were asked for their opinions on this subject considered that existing arrangements for the welfare of old people were inadequate.

Men appeared to be more conscious of and more interested in the needs of the old than women and, not surprisingly, the over rather than the under-forties adopted a more clearly critical attitude, more younger people feeling that the old were now receiving about the right amount of attention. Class divergencies on this question were not striking, though working-class people did allude rather more often to the need for a wider recognition of the difficulties experienced by old people at the present time . . .

The special problems of the old, the inadequacy of their rations and pensions, the possibility that they might be neglected if they were ill, the loneliness of the old, were often mentioned. A variety of improvements was suggested : cheap tobacco, more food, especially milk and eggs, free transport and entertainment, bigger pensions generally, and pensions for women at an earlier age, more superannuation schemes, flats or houses specially designed for old people, cheaper meals. It was generally felt that existing institutions for old people were badly run . . .

As opposed to those who feel so strongly that more should be done for old people one person in four feels that they are adequately provided for at present. Here, however, feeling is noticeably less intense. People usually contented themselves with a brief expression of opinion, their remarks more often suggesting a cursory interest in the problem than a considered attitude . . .

(v) *Attitude towards Voluntary Organisation of Social Services*

We have, so far, been concerned with attitudes towards selected voluntary organisations, and with opinions about the attention now paid to the welfare of two sections of the community, the young and the old. It remains to consider what is the general feeling about the desirability of social services being undertaken by voluntary organisations. The implications of the question for the future of the voluntary social services will be discussed in more detail in a later section of this report, but brief reference to prevailing "attitudes" is desirable at this point.

Members of Mass-Observation's Panel were asked to describe their feelings about the voluntary organisation of social services generally rather than to discuss the merits and demerits of individual organisations. Their attitudes towards particular organisations did sometimes appear, but as this was incidental to the main consideration—which was one of principle—there was little point in attempting to relate Panel opinions to those of the general public. Comparison *is* possible on the question of the acceptability of the voluntary *principle* and in this final section of our report on "Attitudes to Voluntary Social Service," Panel opinion will again be drawn upon.

It is interesting to note first, that whereas in an earlier survey only one person in three had anything to say approvingly about charity or charities,* one person in two expressed a general approval of the voluntary organisation of social services. Rather less than a third were disapproving of voluntary organisation, as compared with nearly half of those who gave their opinions about charity. Thus, broadly speaking, and without taking class, sex or age difference into consideration, proportionate attitudes towards charity and towards voluntary organisation of social service are reversed. (This is not to say that people appreciate to any extent any difference in principle between the two ; indeed, some confusion is evident here. It could mean that where the *idea* of charity is associated with any organisation more people will say they disapprove than if what may, in fact, be the same type of work, can be considered a voluntarily-run social *service*.)

---

* Where reference is made here and later to charity, further details of attitudes to charity may be found in Section IV (pp. 55 *seq.*).

Just over twice as many women as men were ready to speak approvingly of the idea of people being helped by voluntary organisation of social services; this was especially the case with working-class women, and here comparison with attitudes to charity can again be made, more working-class people (that is, those more likely to have been *receivers* of charity) disapproving of charity, more approving of voluntary organisation of social services; in general, a larger proportion of working-class people approving of voluntary social service organisation than artisan or middle-class.   There was a very slight tendency for approval to be more marked among the over than the under-forties, but too much significance should not be attached to this.

Apart from saying that helping people through voluntary organisations was "a good thing," the reasons most commonly given for approval were that organisations of this type were in a good position to know who really needed help, that they were "more human" and could be more economical than a State system.   Approval was sometimes based on personal contact with voluntary organisations, or with a Mutual Aid Society, but this did not appear to be usual . . .

We have already suggested that people's attitudes may be conditioned by the very use of the word "charity."   The two main reasons given for disapproval of the voluntary organisation of social services were that any kind of voluntary aid was bound to be charity, and that in any case, provision of social services was the responsibility of the State.   The latter of these two arguments was much more frequently advanced by men, and by the skilled worker more often than by middle-class or more strictly working-class people. Typically representative of these viewpoints is :

"I don't think there should be any ; the State should have more scope for bringing people what's asked for." (Artisan, 40.)

Other arguments which were not as strongly represented as the above were that the financial resources of voluntary organisations were too restricted, that they are not likely to be as well organised as a centralised service, that their workers were sometimes inefficient, and that the people who were helped might feel humiliated if they did not receive that help as "right."

A very small number of people confessed to mixed feelings on the question ; and would say, for example, something like :

"I think all voluntary assistance is rather fine.   But I regard this as a national duty.   There should be adequate machinery apart from voluntary organisations which should only provide some extra form of benefit or service." (Middle-class man, 45.)

This minority opinion was almost invariably expressed by middle-class people.

MASS-OBSERVATION PANEL ATTITUDES

The attitudes of the predominantly middle-class Panel on the subject of voluntary social service proved difficult to summarise, because of the mass of reservations which most members attached to their replies.   In brief, they may be expressed as follows :

(a) Proportionately, approval of the voluntary social services is greater among the general public than among the Panel ; greater, that is, among those who are more likely to be "organised" than among those more likely to become the "organisers."

(b) Among women generally, and among women Panel Members who take part in the work of the voluntary services, approval is more often expressed than it is by men in either category.

(c) Similarly, there was among men generally, and among the male Panel Observers who were participating in some form of social services, a more decided tendency to criticise the work of the voluntary associations, and to favour State control . . .

II. WHO BELONG TO ORGANISATIONS?

The present section deals with the membership of organisations, and the way in which it is affected by age, sex, class, marital status, occupation, etc. It must be borne in mind that this section covers a wider range of organisations than did previous ones : not merely voluntary social service bodies in a narrow sense, but cultural, recreational, political and other bodies as well.

The results summarise material collected in four different Mass-Observation Surveys :

(a) 1941 survey of the leisure activities of youth in two London districts.

(b) 1947 survey of the leisure activities of youth in one of these same districts.

(c) 1946 survey of adult leisure activities and attitudes in the "Blacktown" division of a large industrial town in the Midlands.

(d) Analysis of information about themselves given by new members of Mass-Observation's National Panel, recruited through the *New Statesman* at the beginning of 1947.

(i) *The Organisations ; range and extent :*

(a) *Amongst adults.* In "Blacktown," a poor working-class district, two people out of every five belong to some kind of organisation. But this figure is an outside estimate ; it is based on a wide interpretation of the word organisation, including not only political clubs and associations, but also Trade Unions. It is clear that from the point of view of Voluntary Associations, the latter at least ought often to be discounted ; economic considerations and the "closed shop" system prevailing in some industries, combine to make belonging to a Trade Union meaningless from the point of view of active and spontaneous membership of a social organisation, at least. A high proportion of the members both of political associations and Trade Unions are often more or less completely inactive ; a parallel of an extreme kind is provided by Co-op statistics, which show that *only about 1 per cent. of all members take any sort of active part in co-op. affairs* . . .

Discounting Trade Unionists, only 28 per cent. are left of the original 39 per cent. who claimed membership of some organisation. Further discounting political associations (a high proportion of whose members are likely to be inactive, even though they have at least spontaneously taken the initial step of joining, and are less concerned with personal economic motives), only 25 per cent. of the sample remain organised. To put this in a clearer form :

Table E.1

MEMBERSHIP OF ORGANISATIONS IN "BLACKTOWN"

---

39 per cent. belong to some sort of organisation

28 per cent. belong to some sort of organisation *excluding* Trade Unions

25 per cent. belong to some sort of organisation *excluding* Trade Unions and political clubs and associations

(and 61 per cent. belonged to no organisation at all)

This is a minimum estimate in so far as our interviews were made in a poor working-class district ; there are indications that the higher people are in the social scale, the more likely they are to belong to some organisation. On the other hand, we are concerned here with town habits ; in the country people are even less likely to be members of anything. These figures, then, are probably more or less accurate in so far as the general population is concerned. To get an idea of organisation as it *can* be it is only necessary to compare the "Blacktown" figures with those for Mass-Observation's National Panel ; the very fact that the latter have voluntarily put themselves on the Panel indicates that this group is self-selected through its tendency to join organisations. It represents, then, the peak of organisation-mindedness :

Table E.2

MEMBERSHIP OF ORGANISATIONS

"Blacktown" and Panel compared

Number belonged to	"Blacktown" general sample, %	Mass-Observation National Panel, % *
None	61	14
One	26	28
Two	8	40 ⎱
Three	3 ⎱ 5	12 ⎱ 18
Four	2 ⎰	6 ⎰

*The difference between these two groups is in reality even greater than this table shows ; "Blacktown" figures refer to *numbers of organisations* belonged to, and Panel figures to *numbers of sorts of organisations*. Many Panel members belong to several of the same type. An earlier analysis of a different but similarly constituted Panel group revealed that 30 *per cent. were members of six or more organisations*.

Of this group of middle-class and more than usually intelligent and well-educated adults, more than half are members of two or more sort of organisations, and only one in seven belongs to none at all (other than Mass-Observation Panel). But these organisations are of very different type to those mentioned by the general sample :

Table E.3

Type of Organisation mentioned	Percentage belonging to this type of organisation amongst:		Mass-Observation National Panel
	"Blacktown" general sample		
Religious	15		9
Trades Union and Occupational	16		38
Purely Social Club	11		5
Political and Social	10		41
To do with Hobbies or Amusements	4	Arts and Cultural	27
		Sport	6
		Holiday and Travel	11
		Educational, Scientific	15
Others	7	Youth	7

(N.B.—Percentages do not add to 100 as many people belong to more than one sort, and many others to none at all.)

. . .

It seems fairly clear that the 39 per cent. organised figure for "Blacktown" does not represent a very active body. Probably the clubs most frequently attended are the sociable and recreational ones, possibly also the political associations. But this rules out the very organisations which are most frequently mentioned. On the whole, the picture is by no means one of a vigorously organised community . . .

(b) *Organisations amongst youth.* The figures for youth are very similar to those for adult organisation membership. In 1947, a Mass-Observation survey of youth in a London district showed that *between one-third and half—44 per cent.—belonged to some organisation or other.* This is a 19 per cent. increase on 1941 when, however, the dislocating effect of Blitz conditions must be taken into account. In 1941, of the combined youth of two London districts, only 17 per cent. belonged to anything at all. Table E.4 shows the effect of return to peace-time conditions, and perhaps also of the later war-time direction of youth into organisations :

Table E.4

	Percentage belonging to youth organisations in :	
	1941	1947
First London district ..	25	44
Second London district ..	10	—
Total	17	44

That the present figure of 44 per cent. organised youth represents a genuinely active membership is indicated by the next table. Of those who do belong to organisations, only one in eight say they go *less* than once a week ; rather more than a third go three times a week, or more.

Table E.5

	Percentage of boys and girls who say they go as often as :		
	Males %	Females %	Total %
Three times a week or more ..	44	25	37
Twice a week	16	25	19
Once a week	28	38	32
Less than once a week ..	12	12	12

Here again as in the case of the adult general sample, these are mostly non-intellectual organisations. The chief club activity mentioned was games, or sport of some kind or other ; in the second place came dancing. Semi-social physical activities are clearly the most important. Table E.6 lists the activities in their order of frequency of mention :

Table E.6

CLUB ACTIVITIES IN YOUTH CLUBS

In order of Frequency of Mention

1. Games
2. Dancing
3. Sports, P.T.
4. Parade, Drill, Scout Training
5. Discussion, Social
6. Handicraft
7. { Vocational Training
Official Meetings
Cycling and Hiking

(ii) *Who belong to organisations*
(a) *Effect of Sex*

1. *Adults.* It is clear that men are far more organised than women. In "Blacktown," 55 per cent. of the men are members of something, against only 24 per cent. of the women. This difference is somewhat smaller, however, when Trade Unions are excluded from the final figure, as in our sample no women at all were Trade Unionists ...

2. *Youth*

Sex differences in the nature of club activities chosen are just as marked. Whilst both boys and girls prefer some outlet for physical energy, their activity takes different forms. Dancing is much more popular than anything else amongst girls, as games and sports are amongst boys. Even so, discussion ranks surprisingly high in both sexes. The following lists give the order of preference for both sexes :

Table E.7

YOUTH CLUB ACTIVITIES

Table of Preferences : Each Sex separately

Boys	Girls
1. Games	1. Dancing
2. Sports	2. Games
3. Parade, Drill	3. Discussion
4. Dancing	4. { Handicraft / Parade, Drill
5. Discussion	5. Vocational Training
6. Cycling, Hiking	6. Meetings
7. { Official Meetings / Handicraft / Vocational Training	7. (none mentioned) { Sport / Cycling / Hiking

Evidently sociability, and the company of the opposite sex is more important to girls than to boys. Sex difference in choice of activity may be one reason why girls belong to organisations to a lesser degree than boys. Dancing, and male company is more easily obtainable outside clubs than are games and the more sporting forms of physical exercise.

(b) *Effects of age*

Age differences are as marked as those between men and women. Older people belong to organisations considerably more than the under-forties. *Of the latter, in "Blacktown," three out of every ten mention themselves as members of some sort of organisation, compared with five in ten of the over-forties* . . .

Amongst the semi-intellectual Panel group, on the other hand, age differences are negligible in respect of the number of organisations belonged to by each person. The only differences lie in the *type* of organisation preferred. Younger Panel members tend to belong more to sports clubs, holiday and travel associations, and youth organisations ; older people mention more often the social and political type. This difference is in line with the "Blacktown" results, but since in the latter case younger people belong to organisations less often than the older group the conclusion can perhaps be drawn that *working-class club facilities are especially inadequate in so far as the under-forties are concerned* . . .

(c) *Effect of class*

Comparison of the "Blacktown" (working-class) and the Panel (middle-class) results, indicates a pronounced difference between the classes. This difference is too marked to be more than partially accounted for by the fact that the Panel is an unusually serious-minded group, and selected in the first place through its willingness to join the Mass-Observation organisation. Of the Panel, more than half belong to two sorts of organisations or more ; of the "Blacktown" general sample, on the other hand, only two out of every five belong to even one. How far this difference is a question of choice, or how far of the facilities available, it is difficult to judge ; no doubt both are influential factors. It does at least seem clear, however, that organisations of the intellectual and cultural type, likely to have a greater appeal for the more adequately educated sections, abound more than the clubs and associations preferred by the working classes . . .

(d) *Marriage. Service Experience*

So far as the Panel was concerned, no significant relation was found between either marital status or service experience, on the one hand, and membership of organisations. The question was not asked of the general sample.

(e) *Occupation*

Mass-Observation finds occupation to have only an indirect effect on organisation membership : while certain jobs are associated more than others with membership of some body, these jobs are ones more likely to attract the middle classes.

III. PENETRATION OF ORGANISATIONS

(i) *Introduction*

Mass-Observation undertook a further study, this time not of the individual but of the organisation. In all, some seventy organisations were approached : the aim in doing so was "to discover through question, conversation and observation what was the present standing of the particular group, so far as it could be measured in terms of its present and past membership and activities ; the average age of members ; the reasons they gave for first joining the group ; in general what satisfactions were to be gained from group membership."

Group vitality, Mass-Observation finds, is related to :

(a) The appreciation by members of the initial purpose of the group. Where these aims have been lost sight of, the group tends to deteriorate. This was the case with some of the Friendly Societies with which we came into contact, and some of the political groups.

(b) The age of the members, and, where the membership is an older one, the interest shown by group organisers in attracting new members, and the willingness of present members to accept them.

(c) The extent to which the group provides satisfaction for some basic *age* needs, as with Youth and Old Age Pensioner Clubs.

(d) The fact that the group has an easily understood "focussing" aim. For example, sports clubs or social service groups like St. John's Ambulance.

(e) The opportunities that are given to members to participate both in the organisation of the group (to do committee work, etc.), and in its general activities.

(f) Its neighbourhood, or district community basis, i.e., the extent to which a particular district favours the emergence of groups.

Some of these findings are illustrated in the report on the Friendly Society in decay, appearing on Section I above. A contrasting example, this time of groups owing their success to an appeal to basic age needs, is found in Old Age Pensioners' Associations.

(ii) *Old Age Pensioner Associations*

These associations are, in our opinion, largely successful as groups providing for the fulfilment of a basic need. Some of the reasons for this conclusion are now given :

A very large, sometimes almost full, attendance at meetings of branch associations which numbered two to three hundred members ; every indication that the sociability value of the meetings was enormously appreciated ; every indication that here were groups of people closely bound together by a strong interest in two common problems, the inadequacy of their pensions, the inadequacy of their normal opportunities for social contact ; enthusiasm among the organisers, competition among the Pensioners to undertake the various small jobs which the meetings involved : these were the things which were stressed in the reports of all the Investigators who joined in with the activities of the groups. Total : a picture of an organisation which is being largely successful in at least one of its aims as expressed by an organiser ; "to bring a bit of interest into their lives," whether equally so in another, "Justice for the Aged," is not of present consequence.

A common interest in sociability ; a common interest in the cost of living ; it is interesting to see how at Pensioners' meetings these two considerations prove ways of overriding interest. Speakers at meetings, if they touch upon topics of personal interest, or if they give talks illustrated with films, may be listened to with interest ; Branch Secretaries, if they talk about members who are ill, about the distribution of free cinema tickets, or about plans for holiday outings, or a proposal, for example, to distribute leaflets at a penny each, receive an equal degree of attention. It does not seem that the average Old Age Pensioner is particularly anxious, as one councillor put it :

" . . . to know what is happening. That's what they want. You see my branch is different from most of the clubs. The members are practically all Labour people and they are more curious than most."

And a visit to a meeting of his branch certainly did not prove his point.

Extracts from Investigators' descriptions of meetings illustrate these various points. The following is part of an account of an afternoon meeting in a London district. Nearly two hundred old people were present, nearly twice as many women as men :

" . . . there was a majority of women, and they quickly established themselves into little gossiping groups. The men, for the most part, came alone, but later some joined together and moved towards the seats in the front of the hall. They were rather weary and worn, more, perhaps, than the women who all seemed intensely interested in the subject matter of their conversation.

"The meeting began. The lady secretary called the meeting to order with 'Friends, Friends, Friends . . .' and she announced that there would be a draw for some cinema tickets at the end of the meeting. Chatter arose again, mainly, it seemed, because another Pensioners' Branch managed to get tickets for 'all their members.'

"The secretary announced the death of a member, and asked everyone to stand. They rose, with much scraping of chairs, and chattered again. 'Shh !' she said, and everyone stood for half a minute with bowed head.

"After they had sat down : 'Now,' said the secretary, 'about our annual picnic.' This caused an expectant hush, and everyone strained to hear the details of the plans . . . They continued to listen as a little later they were told about a tea which was soon to be given.

"Then the minutes were read. During this procedure, the audience embarked on a little flurry of conversation which effectively drowned the voice of the speaker, so that this time the secretary felt compelled to say, 'Now, please, no talking. Please reserve your talking for later.' But her plea was useless. The audience went on as before . . .

"Soon after this, there was some reading of correspondence. Seemingly, the audience again took little notice, but when an item about the system of payment of dues to the Old Age Pensioners occurred, the meeting was suddenly silent and attentive.

"Next came the tea break, and the helpers busily passed round tea and scones. Someone began to play the piano, and the audience acknowledged the music by raising their voices above it . . .

"After tea, a talk entitled 'How I became a Pauper.' The audience was amused by the title, inattentive during an account of the origins of the Poor Law, but finally listening intently and applauding and laughing at revelations of workhouse procedure in the 1890's . . . At the end of the talk, the lady chairman, who appeared to have been much moved by it, rose, and coming to the front of the stage, held out her arms to the audience and said :

" 'Friends ! Today they are offering us all sorts of charity. Well, we don't want their charity ! We want them to give us enough to get the things we need for ourselves. That's the real reason for these meetings. To organise ourselves into a fighting brotherhood and sisterhood, to get these things. That's what we want, a decent pension, not charity !'

"There was a burst of prolonged applause, and then the meeting closed with the draw for cinema tickets and the singing of Auld Lang Syne. People did not seem very anxious to go, and there was much lingering before the final good-byes were said."

An almost identical picture appears in other reports of Pensioners' meetings ; the groups are successful because of cohesion of aims, and because they provide for the fulfilment of a real need. If this is not so with all Old Age Pensioner groups, it is certainly so with those we have studied.

As a footnote, here are the remarks of two Old Age Pensioners, one of whom belongs to an organisation, and who feels that doing so has made a difference to her life, the other of whom does not belong to any group :

"I come every week, you know. It's ever so nice, something to look forward to, and you can meet people. I don't like being with young people much now, not even my daughter. And then they would visit you if you were ill. There's talk of a holiday home, too, where all us old people could be together. I mean, if you could afford to go away private, there's no one to look after you and you might be ill. See what I mean ; then, sometimes you might get a cinema ticket.

"I joined the club when it started four years ago. Just happened to see a crowd so I followed them. It's a great advantage for outings, too. You pay a little each week, and there's the outings paid for, and the same at Christmas. Last Christmas we had a wonderful meat tea.

"Last time there was a pianoforte and a violin and with the holidays, the children gave performances, tap dancing and that. Oh, there's always something." (Working-class woman, 67.)

and, from another Pensioner, a man of seventy-six :

"There's a lot of old people in our street, and no one ever comes to see us, no, not even from the church where we was brought up to go. There are enough committee men in the district. You'd think they'd do something. The Lord Mayor runs a meeting in other parts. They don't 'ave to pay an extra shilling for tobacco there. I think they ought to 'elp the old folk nowadays. I've been 'ere forty years, and no one come to see whether you're dead or alive."

(iii) *Neighbourhood Groups*

This is a description of "groups" rather than a "group," but the groups are inter-related by environment. The scene is a council estate of some 2,000 small, working-class houses, fairly well planned, with wide streets, schools and shops, though without public houses. The whole estate, though in close proximity to a town, is an appreciable neighbourhood unit.

In our report on "Mutual Aid and the Pub" we showed how a pub in a small, closely-knit community became the centre of active group interests. This was, very largely, a spontaneous development, and not, as was the case on this housing estate, the result of any organised decision to promote different kinds of group activities. Nevertheless, in both instances, the community is small, and it is, environmentally, a unit ; these facts have undoubtedly helped to secure the successful development of groups within a group.

Investigators who met people living on the estate describe how well they know each other, and how aware they are of the different events which take place within the area. Everyone is, simply by virtue of living on the estate, a member of the Tenants' Welfare Association. Other groups which have been formed as offshoots of the Association cater for different age groups, and their membership is therefore to some extent limited by the interests for which they are intended to cater. Nevertheless, group membership represents a fairly wide age spread, group members are active, a section-organisation links the different groups together, and we met with no complaints at all about the unwillingness of members to attend either general or committee meetings.

The Secretary described the aims of the Association as :

" . . . the creation of social activity throughout the estate, and helping the tenants if they come on hard times. Every tenant on the estate is treated as a member and can join in if he wishes. There is a general and an executive committee, twenty-eight on the general committee, which is

49

D

elected at an annual general meeting. The general committee represents the different groups we run ; it meets once a month, and every section has its own representative. All officials and helpers are voluntary."

Among the various activities promoted by the Association are a cycling club, a horticultural section, an entertainments group, a discussion circle, whist drives, sports, baby shows, an annual "Mums' and Dads'" day. Special events are organised to collect money for an Old Age Pensioners' Fund, and the general fund for tenants who may be in distress.

People spoke especially of the big events which, naturally, attracted larger numbers than the individual groups, and the secretary gave details of attendance at functions :

"On the 'Mums' and Dads'" Day we had nearly 2,000, and on the Children's Day we had 599 entrants. On Monday we had a baby show with 93 entries. When we have the children's sports we start getting ready for it in February ! It needs a tremendous amount of organisation, but people seem to like doing it. With the sections, the committees will organise things, and if they are running a certain event, they will co-opt and bring in all sorts of people to help. There's never any difficulty for helpers."

Obviously, this secretary was an enthusiast in his work, but even so, his enthusiasm did not appear to give rise to overstatement. Membership of all groups, with the exception of the discussion group, was increasing. (The discussion was non-political, and people were found "not to be attending quite so well at present.") The secretary was generally optimistic, too, about the future of voluntary groups.

A point of particular interest was that he put the age of the most interested members as "something between 20 and 35." The age groups were from 18 upwards, the average age round about 30. There are a number of young people, and a number of young married people on the estate, which would account for the low average age ; what is important is that here, organised into various groups, are people of just those age-groups, which, unless they are of educated middle-class extraction, are not usually found to be much interested in group membership.

There is a general tendency today to accept the fact that people between say, 25 and 35, are not, on the whole, as commonly members of groups as younger and older people, as proof that they do not wish to be organised, or as non-organisable because of family responsibilities, or are more interested in commercial entertainments. No doubt this is so in some cases, and, as we have earlier shown in our survey of reasons people give for not joining groups, they themselves certainly believe it to be so. On this housing estate, younger people are not cut off from any form of commercial entertainment ; they have plenty of family responsibilities ; and in spite of this, a good proportion of them are still interested in joining groups. Interested enough, in fact, for many of them to think that even greater facilities for community interest are needed, in particular, the community centre which the neighbourhood now lacks.

Clearly, the whole question of "neighbourhood" feeling, its relation to the social character of the community and to its environment, is of first importance in any attempt to discover what makes for active membership of groups . . .

Their study of groups leads Mass-Observation to the following general conclusions about the vitality of groups, so far at any rate as this is reflected in the age-composition of members and in attendance at meetings :

1. Large general meetings do not appear to be popular at present in any type of group. Even if membership is increasing, the increase is not always reflected in increased attendance at general meetings.

2. The small branch meeting is more popular. With the exception of youth groups, sports clubs, an occasional Choral or Dramatic Society, attendance even at these meetings inclines, however, to be a gathering of the older members.

3. This was particularly the case with Friendly Societies or political groups, especially the women's sections of political groups.

4. The more intellectually biassed cultural or political group (an Art Circle, Fabian Society, etc.) and the occasional religious organisation, mostly report either a static or decreasing membership at present.

5. Those organisations which in all districts reported an increasing membership and interest were Youth Groups, Old Age Pensioner Associations, Rotary Clubs, British Legion, Allotment Associations (unless meeting with such practical difficulties as lack of space), St. John's Ambulance.

6. Almost all groups with a decreasing membership stressed the anti-group feeling which they claimed was obvious today among people between the ages of 21 and 35. It did generally transpire that not very much had been done to make the membership of the organisation attractive to people of these ages.

7. A final point which emerges is one relating to active and passive membership of organisations. There was, especially among the organisers of groups, a *tendency* to assume that active membership would express itself in good attendance of meetings and that this was the *first* test of group interest and loyalty. This is a natural enough organiser viewpoint. Talking to members, however, and especially to members of those groups which offered a varied selection of activities, we found that non-attendance at more formal meetings was sometimes equally an expression of a feeling of trust in the organisers and the way in which they were running the group . . .

(iv) *New Social Services*

People in all areas where we were working were asked whether they considered there was any need for any new social services in their district. Roughly half had some suggestions to make. This does not mean, and we re-emphasise a point already made, that their answers were based upon any great *knowledge* of the services already existing in the district : when asked to name some of the services already in existence, a large number of people, in this case over half, were not able to name any. *It does mean, however, that* the suggestions made represent the needs uppermost in people's minds at the present time.

The list of suggestions was not extensive. The services suggested were:

> Youth Service
> Old People's Welfare
> Mother's and Children's Welfare (including Day Nurseries and Play Centre)
> General Enlargement of the Health Services
> Provision of Social Centres
> Provision of Cheap Meals
> Information Bureaux
> Legal Advice Bureaux
> Enlarge existing services
> Everything is needed

Of these, the need for youth services was mentioned almost twice as often as Old People's Welfare—next in frequency of mention. Both were mentioned far more often than Mothers' and Children's Welfare, which came next on the list. The remainder represent minority mention only. Of those who had no suggestions to make for improvements, the majority were simply disinterested or incomprehending in their attitude, exceeding by more than half the numbers of those who stated that no new services were needed in their area.

We have already pointed out that the largest demand for more extensive provision for youth came from an East London area, and for old people from "Blacktown." Apart from this, no clear area difference emerged at all, though it was interesting to note that the need for Information Bureaux came exclusively from another London district, where, in fact, such a centre has quite recently been established! No area difference was obvious either when in further conversation with people about the future of the social services, we asked whether *apart from young and old people* they felt that there were any groups of people who could be helped in any way at present. Again, many people were vague in their answers, but again more than half had suggestions to make. This time the groups which were mentioned were—in order of frequency:

> Cripples, and disabled people generally
> Blind
> Ex-service men
> Widows
> The poorer classes
> The very young
> Spinsters
> Unemployed
> Mothers with young children
> Young married people (Nurseries, etc.)
> Clearance of slum area.

Cripples and disabled people generally were mentioned three times as often as blind people, but otherwise, there was no outstanding difference.

Where the future of the voluntary services was in question, it was necessary to know who people considered should be responsible for the organisation of help where it was needed. Here, a point of some importance to the present survey arose, for of those making suggestions for the provision of new, or the extension of existing social services, more than half recommended either the local council or the "government" as the appropriate authority. Less than a third thought that such work could be left to voluntary organisations. A few said they would prefer a voluntary organisation running the services under the supervision of the State, and a few were of the opinion that a new, separate body would be required on which both the State and the voluntary organisations could be represented.

We had previously found that among all sections of the population there existed a clear feeling of goodwill towards the work of the *existing* voluntary organisations. It now appeared that goodwill feeling did not of necessity imply any active optimism about the future of the voluntary services. One person in two, could, in a general way, express approval of the voluntary organisation of social services ; but if people were asked specifically to suggest new social services, and state who should run them, the numbers of those supporting voluntary organisation of such services dropped considerably. Superficially, a mildly paradoxical result, in fact, this apparent contradiction is more likely to be a reflection of the varied influences which at one and the same time condition public opinion. It is in keeping with the social climate of our time to *expect* the State to take the initiative in the creation of social services ; equally, people can—and without logically relating one thing to the other—express general approval of the *type* of service for which the voluntary organisation stands. During the whole course of the present survey it became increasingly clearer, for instance, that in speaking of the voluntary organisation of social services, people thought rather of the nature of these services than of their practicability for the future.

Thus, the voluntary social services in any consideration of their possible future will have to balance general approval against general expectation on the part of the public. Clearly, there is a demand for those qualities in administration *now* associated in people's minds with the voluntary services ; humanity, the individual approach, rightly or wrongly, people do not associate the personal touch with an official service ; equally clearly, there is a general expectation that centralisation of authority will increase.

MASS-OBSERVATION PANEL OPINIONS ON THE NEED FOR NEW SOCIAL SERVICES

It will be remembered that on the question of approval or disapproval of the voluntary organisation of social services, it was possible to suggest an approximate opinion grouping into three categories, "pro" and "anti" voluntary organisation, and a "mixed" group uncertain in their present attitude and more appreciative of the arguments for either side. We suggested, further, that if the "qualified" answers of Panel Members in the "mixed" group be considered as indicative of general goodwill towards the voluntary social services, then the volume of approval expressed by people generally, and by the more "socially-conscious" middle-class Panel approximates very closely.

The keyword here is *approval* : the controversial point, the extent (as with people generally) to which approval is linked with expectation.

"Mixed" approval was more marked among Panel Observers who were better able to enlarge upon the reasons for their opinions, than among the general public ; and on a further analysis opinion in this group gives points in "approval" to the voluntary organisation of social services, in "expectation" to State direction. This is not to say that no one in this group approves of State control even if it is anticipated, but that the sympathy balance, the emotional argument, lies with the voluntary organisation.

On "expectation," whether accompanied by approval or not, it becomes obvious that a majority of Panel members expect, and that on a considered, rational basis, many of them prefer that social services of the future should be State financed, and under the direction of trained and paid workers. At the same time, it was felt that the value of the contribution made by voluntary workers in terms of enthusiasm and warmth of approach could not be under-estimated, and for this reason volunteers should always be part of a well-organised social service. (As we have previously stressed, strong criticism of the personnel of *all* social services is to be found in all Panel opinion groups.) In brief, the ideal which many of the Panel feel is the one to be aimed at is "a system of social services so organised that the spirit of the old voluntary social services may be retained, but supported financially by the Treasury."

What suggestions for new social services are made by Members of the Panel ? Fewer people were interested in making suggestions for new services than in discussing their attitudes towards the organisation of social services. Of those who did make some suggestion, however, a minority considered that the existing social services were adequate, and of the remainder, almost as many suggested that an extension of the existing services should take precedence over the creation of new ones. The suggestions which were made are :

For Extension of Existing Social Services :

> Day Nurseries and Nursery Schools
> The Home Help System
> Revival of Citizens' Advice Bureaux
> Birth Control Clinics
> Old People's Welfare Associations
> Children's Playgrounds in cities
> Community Centres
> More frequent review of the cost-of-living index
> More British Restaurants
> More Family Clubs on the lines of the Peckham Health Centre
> Extension of Vocational Guidance Schemes
> More Convalescent Homes, and

For New Social Services :

A Legal Aid Service (on different basis from Poor Man's Lawyer)
Bureaux for organising interchange of homes in holiday season
Holiday Homes for Workers—on Butlin model
State Boarding Schools for low income groups
Hostels for Children from ten upwards, run on family lines
Blind Workshops and Libraries in all towns
A "younger brother" to the W.E.A. to cater for adolescents
Information Bureaux
Health Centre in all towns

Most of these services are visualised as State or Borough controlled, and detailed suggestions about organisation are often given . . .

4. ASPECTS OF CHARITY

The purpose of this fourth study was to discover current attitudes to charity, reasons for giving to charity, and whether or no people considered that charity was necessary in the world of tomorrow.

Besides using some material collected for other purposes, it was based on long informal interviews with a large variety of people ; these interviews were carried out in two London districts, a working-class district of a Midland industrial town, and in a Northern industrial town. Mass-Observation Panel Observers provided additional information.

(a) Meaning of Charity

In their investigations, Mass-Observation found that most people today appear to have two or three clearly defined but opposed conceptions of "charity." These conceptions appear most clearly among the National Panel whose written statements are naturally more considered and thought out than those of people "interviewed," either formally or informally.

About one-fifth of both men and women Panel members describe charity in its Biblical sense of love or as a general attitude of tolerance, kindness, and sympathy.

Particularly clear among this group—and implied to a greater or less degree among most of the others—is the feeling that the word "charity" has decayed in its meaning, that once it meant any sort of generous or kindly action but that now it simply means giving money. Technically, this is not so, but the misconception is very widespread among Panel members.

A majority of the Panel regard "charity" not in its Biblical sense but as aid given in money or goods by one individual to the other or as aid given to organised bodies dependent for the continuation of their work upon voluntary aid :

"I presume that by charity is meant donations to charitable institutions such as Dr. Barnardo's, the Cancer Fund, the Soldiers', Sailors' and Airmen's Families Association, etc." (Research chemist, male, 23.)

"The word 'charity' has a dreary sound these days, but if it means giving what you can spare to people who seem to need it, I don't think that any State social security will obviate the need for it because of the uncertainty that you may refuse someone genuinely in need." (Housewife, 26.)

Nearly half the replies from the Panel regard charity in the restricted sense of giving aid, mainly monetary, to *organised* bodies ; about three in ten (more women than men) as giving aid to all in need, and one-fifth, as we have seen, in its Biblical sense of love and kindness. But very frequently people say that they have more than one mental picture of charity :

"Charity has two connotations. The one is another name for brotherly love, another carries with it pictures of the workhouse, collecting boxes, and the Salvation Army." (Man, 40.)

Among street samples, it was to be expected that there would be hazier mental pictures of what the word means. Their comments bring out very clearly this confusion ; very few take the Biblical meaning of charity but there is a far greater variety of definition within the aspect of charity as "giving money to supposedly good causes."

Thus a woman in Bristol stated at length to an investigator that she didn't believe in charity at all, but subsequently said with surprise that of course she gave to all flag days as they were "good causes." Or again :

"No, I don't believe in charity, I've got a delicate husband with a delicate spine, and I hardly ever see any money at all." (Asked if she gave to flag days) "Oh, yes, I always buy a flag when they come out, it's only like a penny, it's neither here nor there. I couldn't tell you why really. *I don't think it's charity, it's just to help the poor things up a bit.*" (Sweep's wife, 55, Middlesbrough) . . .

But among the random sample it is as clear as among the Panel that charity has come to be associated exclusively with the giving of alms and of food, *not* of personal services. Any sort of generous action that involves time and labour, rather than the simple effortless provision of money, is "voluntary aid" and not "charity."

(b) General Attitudes and Group Differences

If people's general conceptions of what constitutes charity have appeared vague, there is certainly no greater clarity apparent in attitudes they express towards it. Thus among the general sample little more than one in four say that charity is a good thing, while one in five disapprove. The remaining 55 per cent. have no opinion, have not made up their mind, or express simultaneously reasons why charity should be supported and why it should not. Among the National Panel, with far more time to pass a reasoned judgment, the vagueness is equally evident. A clear majority—53 per cent.—state that although there are some aspects of charity of which they approve there are others that they disapprove ; of the remainder about three-quarters disapprove of charity with no qualifications at all.

There are, however, significant sex, age and class differences which can be summarised as follows :

(a) Middle-class people almost invariably discuss the effect of charity on the giver, working-class people the effect on the recipient.
(b) Women approve of charity to a far greater extent than men.
(c) Older people are more opposed to charity than younger people.

(c) *Reasons for Approval of Charity*
There was little specific in the reasons given for approval of the idea of charity. The most frequent were the following :

Panel :	Street Sample :
It is a fundamental principle	It is a good thing
It is a valuable personal service	It helps genuine cases
Charity is always needed	Every help is good

Indeed, among the general sample the three categories above are the *only* ones listed by more than one per cent., while analysis of Panel answers shows no other major idea among reasons for approval . . .

(d) *Reasons for Disapproval*
In all groups there is a far clearer feeling about the *bad* aspect of charity—and a far greater variety of reasons are given for disapproval.

Overwhelmingly, among both Panel and general samples, the main feeling against charity derives from the belief that there should no longer be any need for it, at any rate in its organised form ; that the State should be responsible for providing relief wherever it is required. This argument on its own accounts for over one-third of all reasons given for disapproving of charity in each group. Comments on this point, however, are almost invariably linked with others on the future of charity, and the question of State control is discussed in Section (f) of this report.

Apart from this argument, the main criticisms of charity are as follows :

Panel :	Street Sample :
Bad for the recipient	A bad thing
Bad for the giver	A racket
Hindrance to social reform	Bad for the recipient
A racket	

There was, of course, a large body of people with mixed feelings, who, while "they regard charity as a bad thing" feel that "while it still exists and does work that would not otherwise be done, then it must be supported as a necessary evil."

This has much bearing on the practice of charity, for among general samples, although nearly one person in three says that he *disapproves* of charity, only one in twenty says that he never *gives* to charity, while over a third say that they give something every time that they are asked.

Yet if people give, none the less they give under protest and their reasons for *giving* to charity are by no means the same as their reasons for approving of it. Thus, among a general sample, one person in twelve says that he gives to charity solely to prevent being pestered on flag days ; no other reason except "it's for a good cause" is mentioned as frequently . . .

57

Even if "a good cause" is more often mentioned than "to stop being pestered," the former reason is usually produced hesitantly as if it had only just entered the speaker's mind, the latter with a great deal of fervour as if it is one of the aspects of charity in which he shows real feeling :

"I give to charity when they catch me. They push a little box under my nose and make me buy a flag. That's the reason why I give. They're very good at that in Middlesbrough." (Man, 25, wholesaler's apprentice.)

The emphasis on the "blackmail" and compulsory aspects of charity collection is rather stronger among the middle-class Panel and is related to almost every form of charity-giving.

This negative reason, however, cannot account for all the money that is given to charity, as the success of wireless appeals testifies. On these, Mass-Observation was able to collect little information. There was some indication that the attitude to flag days was the result of a combination of embarrassment plus ignorance of the object for which the money was being sought. Success of wireless appeals is perhaps due to the fact that personal sympathy can be generated through a skilful broadcaster, as is indicated by an analysis of wireless appeals for 1946. Speaking on behalf of a very wide range of causes, regular broadcasters— Uncle Mac, Tommy Handley, Howard Marshall, etc.—brought in *over four times as much money per charity* as did those who were heard on the air but rarely.

(e) Relative Popularity of Charities

It is not within the general purpose of the present survey to discuss in detail the relative popularity of various charities. Nevertheless, in the course of it, there has been some indication of the *types* of organisation to which people give most willingly.

All results show a very clear tendency for hospitals and funds for disabled people to be regarded as the most praiseworthy causes ... In a street sample questioned early this year, hospitals and disabled were mentioned most frequently, followed by causes for children, old people, and such sectarian interests as the Church Army and the Salvation Army. Cultural and educational charities were barely mentioned at all.

Among hospitals, cancer hospitals are most often mentioned as deserving. Among the disabled, the blind are discussed in all surveys far more often than any other type.

(f) The Future of Charity

(i) The Present Situation

As charities have grown bigger, have had to deal with more and more people and to collect more and more money, inevitably they have lost the "personal touch" ; nowadays the giver is pestered into giving, as we have seen, while the receiver as often as not has to fill in forms or be interviewed by apparently heartless minor officials in an effort to obtain relief. It is this soullessness, rather than the effect on the people concerned or the possibility of a racket, that is one important reason why people feel that charity would be better organised by the State.

During the war and again shortly after its cessation, Mass-Observation conducted a survey into the general attitudes of people in certain areas towards a well-known charitable organisation. Particularly in the latter survey there was a very strong emphasis on the fact that although this particular organisation did a lot of good in a great many ways they were by no means helped by the business methods by which they collected their funds . . .

When charities turn into "business propositions" with large offices and advertising campaigns, then inevitably they come to be compared with the Ministries that are also dispensing monetary aid to those in need. And the feeling grows that the latter could do the job more efficiently and with less overlap, as well as ensuring that the amounts to be given were as rightly apportioned as the amounts received . . .

Possibly more important than this reason is the very general belief that to an increasing extent personal misfortune is not necessarily the fault of the individual but of the State. As such it is a State responsibility to look after him not as a favour but as a *right* . . .

(ii) *The Future Need for Charity*

If then it is very widely felt that the functions now performed by charitable organisations could better be handled by the State, has "charity" in its present sense any future significance ?

To the general sample it has little. Only about one person in one hundred and fifty mentions that even under State organisation there may be need for some sort of individual charity, to the others the problem is apparently completely solved by Government intervention . . .

Yet this is *not* the situation among the Panel—the *givers* of charity. *The need for personal charity even under a Government system is mentioned in nearly two out of three answers of those who approve of State control.*

The lines which this personal charity will take roughly divide into two types. First, there are those organisations—hardly ever mentioned by the general sample—over which there is still some doubt as to their value. There would be little disagreement if the blind, the disabled, the sick, the old, became the responsibility of the State, but equally it would be impossible at the present stage to use taxpayers' money for such causes as anti-vivisection, or sectarian church work, or help to one side in a foreign war.

Secondly, there is a strong feeling that, however efficient State charity becomes, there will still be some deserving cases which will not be covered by any scheme. These should be helped by *direct* personal charity :

"Charity in general should be rendered less and less necessary by State organisation of hospitals, pensions, insurance, etc. But there will always be plenty of gaps and individual hard cases to be provided for by private charity . . . If any of one's fellows are ill or suffer some misfortune it is a pleasure to contribute something to help them." (Inspector of Taxes, 46.)

Occasionally the feeling is that not merely will certain people be more easily helped by private charity, but that *small* organisations will be more efficiently run if that personal touch is there :

"For years I have refused to give to hardly any charity because I claimed that there should be no need for it. Hospitals, orphanages, etc., should be run by the State. While still agreeing with this principle, I have, in the last few months, come to realise that a large number of undertakings are so much better when run voluntarily. Management by national or local boards always means such a large increase of red tape and officialdom." (L.A.C., 21.)

If this situation were to exist, with the State running the major organisations that now depend on charity and with voluntary effort filling in the inevitable gaps, then there would again be a closer approach to the older and finer meaning of charity—people would not give for patronage or because they were pestered but because they wanted to give :

"There is room for organised charity in this far-from-perfect world, but there is also still plenty of room for vicarious charity and often one feels 'There but for the grace of God go I' and gives out of thankfulness. St. Paul's words on the subject have never been bettered." (Housewife, 41.)

5. HOLIDAYS

The following section reports a study of preferences and practices relating to holidays. The study was based mainly on informal interviews with 309 persons in West Country villages, two London districts, a working-class district of a Midland industrial town, and two fairly large towns in the North of England, in June, 1947. Use was also made of material previously gathered.

(a) HOLIDAY BASIS

A "holiday," for the vast majority of Britons today, essentially implies getting away, not only from work but from home and from familiar surroundings generally. As we shall see (Section (b)) a clear majority of the population nowadays feel they can, and want to, get away ; and, despite every imposed difficulty and inconvenience, probably about half have managed to go somewhere different from their 51-week-per-annum environment during the current year. Because of the suspension of holidays by war, and because of the differentiation between the many who now get paid during holiday-time and the few who still don't, the great bulk of the population today falls into two groups—the majority whose holiday-memories are very near, and the minority for whom they are very distant, or do not exist at all. All but 7 per cent. in our sample had either been away less than two years ago, or had not been away for more than eight years. Of the 71 per cent. who had been away during the previous 24 months, all but 5 per cent. had been during the preceding 12. Those who had not been away since before the war consisted of 4 per cent. of the middle class, 13 per cent. of artisans, 19 per cent. of working-class ; and, of the latter, a quarter said they had never had a holiday at all.

If we suppose that anticipated external inconveniences within the holiday resorts rather than their own economic problems or lack of desire to get away decided some 10 per cent. of those who made no holiday plans for 1947 to stay at home, then the pre-war situation is already reversed. Ten years ago two-thirds of the population stayed at home; today, if it were not for inconveniences which did not obtain in pre-war years, two-thirds of the population would go away.

The very fact that so many *do* go away despite every inconvenience shows that a holiday from home can be far from ideal, and yet seem preferable to staying in the familiar environment. But although 71 per cent. of our sample had had a holiday of sorts since the war, the proportion who had had what they considered a "real" holiday during this period was only 32 per cent. Five per cent. of middle-class people; 27 per cent. of artisan class; and 31 per cent. of working class said they had *never* had a real holiday in their own, usually not very ambitious, sense of the term. *One woman in every three said she had never had a real holiday.*

Three problems face those concerned with the planning of holiday amenities today:

  1. The provision of *new* permanent amenities to meet the greatly increased demand.
  2. The provision of interim facilities to bridge the gap.
  3. The improvement of existing facilities to meet the criticisms of those who use them.

Of these, we would say from the evidence of this survey, that the second is by far the most important. For the most part people *demand* very little of a holiday except that it must be away from the workday environment; there are many things they would like, and dream of, but the basic essentials are simple enough to provide. Moreover, the subjective importance of a holiday lies in far more than the seven days' experience which it objectively embodies. It is something to look forward to, talk about, and idealise during the months before; and something to look back on, romanticise and idealise, during the months after.

We would, therefore, emphasise in introducing this report, that, if these are the alternatives, it would be of far more value during the next several years of readjustment for many people to have a makeshift holiday than for only a slowly mounting number to have a more "real" one, with amenities more ambitiously planned and slowly executed.

The National Council of Social Service has emphasised, and post-war developments, in the holiday-camp movement especially, confirmed, a drift away from the mass-resort. In our pre-war studies of Blackpool, where observers worked for many months, our attention was inevitably drawn to the extent to which people holidaying in a big popular resort aim at getting away from it—from the crowds into the country; from the beach into or onto the sea.

(b) HOLIDAY DEMAND

People were asked when they last had a holiday. Among our sample, 66 per cent. had had some sort of a holiday away from home during the previous twelve months. While it was not the intention of this survey to obtain precise national statistics, but rather a rough impression of the size of numerical majorities and minorities as background to more detailed descriptive data, this result may be compared with a national poll by B.I.P.O. published last May. At that time 41 per cent. of the population had already fixed their holidays ; 16 per cent. had not yet succeeded in making arrangements ; and 43 per cent. intended to stay at home. Thus those who *intended* to try to go away this summer (when the B.I.P.O. poll was taken before the beginning of the holiday season), amounted to considerably over half the population ; and those in our sample who said they *had* been away during the preceding twelve months (when asked between mid and late June), amounted to two-thirds. But a substantial proportion (16 per cent.) in Mass-Observation's sample had already returned from early holidays *this* season. If instead of the twelve months, June, 1946-7, we attempt an estimate for the holiday season of 1946 alone, our figure for those who had a holiday *last* season will be close to the B.I.P.O. figure for those who *intended* to have one in 1947.

Taking both these results into consideration—the accomplishments of 1946 and the intentions of 1947—it would appear that, as a conservative estimate, at least half the population of Britain now actively plan to go away for a holiday in any one year, and that all but a few of these active holiday-planners somehow or other achieve their aim. They do this despite almost every conceivable form of discouragement—high prices, crowded conditions, difficulties in booking rooms, food difficulties, travel difficulties, and a barrage of newspaper stories which have constantly laid emphasis on the discomforts of holiday-making . . .

In the peak pre-war year for holiday-making, 1937, it has been estimated* that 15,000,000 people spent a holiday of a week or more away from home. This is roughly one-third of the population of Britain. The National Council of Social Service estimated in 1945 that the immediate post-war demand resulting from holidays-with-pay agreements maturing during the war years, would raise the total to at least 26,000,000, or some 58 per cent. of the population. That estimate is actually identical, within 1 per cent., of the proportion who said they *intended* to go away this year, according to B.I.P.O. ; and very close to the proportion who in fact managed to get away last year, among Mass-Observation's more localised sample . . .

As we shall see later, most people are very easily *fairly* satisfied with their holiday, provided they get away at all. Their basic demands are not difficult to meet, though improved facilities would no doubt rapidly make them more exacting. But they are insistent and definite. They centre on a desire for contrast. People want a reversal of the normal routines of the rest of the year, not only of factory and shop but of family, household and physical environment as well . . . *A holiday away from home under physical conditions far less convenient, far more strenuous, cramped, and objectively irksome, than those obtaining in the holiday-maker's household and home town, is still, for the majority*

---

*"Holidays." A Study by the National Council of Social Service. (Oxford, 1945)

of ordinary men and women, subjectively a "real holiday." A holiday spent at home is not a "real holiday." . . .

(c) HOLIDAY IDEAL

We asked people what was their idea of a *real* holiday. Investigators were instructed to continue informally, after the first spontaneous response had been made, encouraging people to describe their holiday ideal. Completed interviews showed that not all the attributes people associate with a "real" holiday came up immediately in response to such direct questioning. Accordingly, the full interview was taken into consideration, irrespective of the exact point at which any factor was mentioned . . .

When we come to look at the actual words people use in describing it, the most striking thing is how *little* they demand, on the "positive" side, from this vitally important break in the year's routine. Here are some typical comments :

"I like a nice quiet holiday, sitting, talking and knitting." (Widow of 69.)

"I like a laze round the seaside." (County Council workman of 30.)

"At my age I like a nice rest, sitting about knitting, just lazing. I don't want to see scenery or anything like that. I like entertainment in the evening." (Woman of 47 with two boys.)

Relaxation and rest, plain and simple, is the keynote of many of the answers. Many ask for complete change, a reversal of the usual daily routine . . . There is no suggestion that any appreciable number of people value a holiday as an opportunity to spend time on interests or hobbies for which a working-day allows inadequate leisure. Gardening, carpentry, collecting in all its forms, reading, sketching, embroidery, music—none of these or anything of the work receives any mention at all. As hobbies, many of these activities are widespread ; but clearly they are not felt to form any part of the "Holiday." Indeed a "real holiday" requires contrast to the hobby-routine of the working year just as much as a reversal of work-routine and household-routine.

This then is the main feeling about the ideal holiday—that it should afford relaxation and change of more or less unspecified character. The *positive* demands people make on a holiday are slight ; the "negative" ones (absence of familiar occupations ; a thoroughly different environment) very much to the fore.

(d) PROBLEMS AND DIFFICULTIES IN HOLIDAY PLANNING

(i) No "Real Holiday"

Altogether, just over half of the sample said they had experienced at some time what they had previously described as their idea of a "real holiday." One in three said they had had it since the end of the war. This again indicates a readiness to be very easily satisfied, provided one can get away at all. About a fifth were vague or ambivalent in their ideas on this question, but group differences in the proportions who say definitely that they have *never* had a "real" holiday show a clear trend.

There is a considerable increase in the proportion who have never experienced their conception of a real holiday as we go down the income scale. Fewer women have had a "real holiday" than men, and rather fewer young people than old. As evidenced in other parts of this survey it is the young working-class housewife who emerges as the most dissatisfied figure.

(ii) *Money*

A broadly optimistic outlook is again shown in the fact that only one person in three say they have any particular difficulties in holiday planning . . .

Young people and the two lower-class groups raise more difficulties than the older generation and the middle class. Financial difficulties are raised twice as often by the young as the old, and more than twice as often by the unskilled working class as by the artisan class (middle-class people barely raise them at all).

Asked specifically about their methods of paying for their holidays, 61 per cent. of the working class, 51 per cent. of the artisan, but only 14 per cent. of the middle class, said they saved up during the year. Conversely, 36 per cent. of the working class, 29 per cent. of the artisans, and 24 per cent. of the middle class said they sometimes had difficulty in getting together enough money for a holiday . . .

As we have mentioned, the lowest income groups, on whom these difficulties press hardest, go to the greatest lengths to make sure of their summer holidays. Methods of saving show a wide variety of ingenuity and a high degree of perseverance :

"My husband puts so much away—always had to. Couldn't manage it otherwise. It's not very easily done—but he doesn't say much to me. He has to save twice as much now—but he doesn't smoke or drink. He doesn't spend much on himself—don't go to the pictures or anything, so it makes saving a bit easier." (Working-class married woman, two children.)

"If we want some luxury we think first and then say 'no' and put it away for the holiday instead. We don't scrimp too much you know, but we think before we squander anything." (Young married woman.)

"My sister-in-law holds a 'didlum' in which we all put money. We start with a certain figure and then add bits every week till the holiday comes round. We pool the money in our family." (Married man earning under £5.)

"I laid off smoking and drinking for a while—saved in no time after that." (Builder, 21.)

Correlation of people's saving habits with their difficulties in getting together enough holiday money shows, not surprisingly in view of the relation between saving and income, that roughly five non-savers experience no money difficulties for every three savers who experience none. In other words, people tend to save because they haven't enough money to budget for a holiday without saving, not because they can spare enough money to save. Holiday saving is related to lack of money, and naturally enough those without enough money get into more difficulties, despite saving, than those who don't need to save.

(iii) *Accommodation and Children*

Family-income figures unrelated to family-budgeting realities are an inadequate guide to spending power. In all five income groups the proportion of people who have had a "real" holiday since the war differs by only 7 per cent. Over the £9 a week level there are fewer people who say they have *never* had a real holiday, but between £4 and under and £9 there is virtually no difference.

However, when we relate the experience of a "real" holiday to the presence of children (under 16) in the family, differences are striking :

Table E.8

Number of children in family	Percentage of people with this number of children who do not recall ever having had a "real" holiday
Single	29%
Married, no children	18%
Married, one child	31%
Married, two children	45%
Married, more than two children ..	50%

· · ·

Lodging problems, second most frequently mentioned of all holiday planning difficulties, most often centre on the difficulty of finding accommodation for children . . .

(iv) *Other Complaints and Suggestions*

Suggestions for making holiday-planning easier were made by just half the sample. They covered some thirty topics, only the first three of which were mentioned by more than 5 per cent. The following are all the suggestions made by more than 1 per cent. in any group, in rough order of frequency :

> Better transport
> Staggered holidays
> Facilities for early preparations
> Easier, better accommodation
> Holiday saving schemes
> Encouragement to people to keep away from popular resorts
> Allow wider choice of holiday period
> More holiday advertisements
> Cheaper accommodation
> Spread local attractions
> Make it easier to earn holiday money
> Free holiday passes

Grumbles and suggestions may be taken together from the point of view of holiday-dissatisfactions. But when we consider that three out of five say they have no trouble over holiday arrangements and half have no suggestions for making their own planning easier, the contrast between holiday moods and

E

workday moods is again emphasised. Indeed, several people refer with some self-satisfaction, almost smugness, to their lack of difficulties . . .

General grumbles about *travelling conditions* are, not surprisingly, among the most frequent holiday complaints at present. In view of the circumstances, however, the striking thing is not that they were mentioned as frequently as they were, but that they were not more often, and more vehemently, raised. While, when people were asked whether they had any ideas for making holidays easier to arrange, the most frequent suggestion was for less-crowded, cheaper and better transport, this was only raised by 12 per cent. . . .

Financial assistance for those too poor to afford holidays is not a very frequent suggestion—no one idea appears frequently—but is generally rather clearly formulated, as if people had given it some thought :

"Some people never get a holiday. They can't afford it. There should be a government scheme to help them, the firm should pay so much as in National Insurance." (Youth, 20.)

"I think if the Government was able to arrange evacuation during a war it could arrange holidays on the same basis for the poor people." (Married working-class woman, four children.)

. . .

Mostly financial assistance is thought of as coming from the Government, but a few people suggest Savings Clubs of various kinds . . .

The co-operation of employers in giving workers longer notice of the date of their holidays is part of the general desire to be able to plan well ahead . . .

Other suggestions, though sometimes expressed in considerable detail, come from only a very small number of people. The idea of some sort of *agency to bring together landladies and potential holiday-makers* is occasionally put forward :

"Well, setting up a sort of—you get them—Cook's Travelling Agencies— say each borough set up one of those in its locality, people could apply to them any time of the year. And these agencies could make arrangements. Some people won't go on holiday because of difficulty in arranging accommodation." (Married man, 24.)

And mothers occasionally suggest an extension of the idea, already in practice at Butlin's holiday camps and elsewhere, of *day-nurseries* where the children can be left while the parents go off together . . .

(e) HOLIDAY CAMPS

Holiday camps on the present scale are a rapid post-war growth. Most people have heard many, often contradictory, things said about them. Relatively few have been to one. Among our sample only 8 per cent. had been at a camp at any time, but 82 per cent. were willing to express some generalised or specific opinion of them. It is not surprising then that these opinions are often flatly contradictory in regard to factual detail.

Juxtaposed, some remarks show the general confusion about what a holiday camp is really like. Thus, one person complains that enjoyment of a holiday camp depends on the weather being good . . . Another approves of holiday camps on the very grounds that you are *not* dependent on the weather . . . Many comment favourably on the way children are catered for . . . On the other hand, several complain that children are *not* adequately catered for . . .

The following table shows all points raised by people in discussing their views of holiday camps :

Table E.9

Attitude	Percentage expressing this attitude	
	Favourable	Unfavourable
Good thing, would like to go..	27%	—
Don't like them	—	19%
Heard they are nice, know others who like them	16%	—
Nice if you are young	11%	—
Indifferent, not interested in them	—	7%
Too much organisation	—	5%
Too much of a crowd	—	4%
Good if you have children	3%	—
Plenty to do, sport, entertainment	3%	—
Too expensive, cheaper elsewhere	—	3%
Good for some	3%	—
Not good if you have children	—	2%
No privacy	—	2%
Miscellaneous favourable comments	5%	—
Miscellaneous unfavourable comments..	—	7%
Vague, don't know ..	— 18% —	

There are major class differences in the proportion of people saying that they have heard the camps are nice : that they are a good thing : and that they do not like them :

Table E.10

Opinion	Percentage expressing this opinion among :		
	Middle-Class	Artisan Class	Working-Class
Do not like holiday camps	62%	24%	12%
Camps are good things ; would like to go ..	5%	31%	30%
Have heard the camps are nice ; know others who like them ..	5%	19%	16%

Young people say unreservedly that holiday camps are a good thing and they would like to go to one considerably more than older people (35 per cent. as against 20 per cent.), just as old people often say they are good for the young . . .

(*f*) GOING ABROAD

When asked how they felt about going abroad rather more than half of the sample said immediately that they would like to go. But this must be compared with the much smaller number who *spontaneously* mentioned going abroad as their idea of a real holiday. The latter figure (6 per cent.) is an index of the existing unsatisfied demand; the former (55 per cent.) of the potential demand.

Sex differences were negligible, but there were major class and age differences : 81 per cent. of the middle class said they would like to go abroad for a holiday ; 67 per cent. of the artisan class ; only 47 per cent. of the working class ; 47 per cent. of the over-forties said they would like to go ; 62 per cent. of the younger generation . . .

PART II

RESEARCH SERVICES' REPORT: A SELECTION OF TABLES

A SPECIAL survey was undertaken for the Inquiry in July and August, 1947, by Research Services Limited. This was concerned both with the Friendly Societies and with other forms of Mutual Aid and Voluntary Service. In respect of the Friendly Societies, the survey provided information on such matters as present membership; the activity or passivity of membership; the assurances and other benefits provided, and the use made of these services; opinions on the services provided, and members' views on the possible continuance of their membership after the National Insurance Act came into operation. It provided data also upon the numbers and proportions in the sample who belonged to various other classes of association for Mutual Aid and Voluntary Service; together with the form which this participation took, the degree of activity of membership, and other matters.

The results were presented statistically in a large number of Tables, which revealed a great deal of most valuable information. A selection from these Tables is printed below, with short notes added by the editors. A complete list of the Tables submitted is attached. Those not printed here can be consulted on application to Research Services Ltd., 91 Shaftesbury Avenue, London, W.1.

The sample totalled 3,000 persons. Tables E.11 and E.12 below show its composition by age, sex, region and town size, and Table E.13 lists the areas from which the sample was drawn.

Table E.11
COMPOSITION OF SAMPLE
(Age by Sex)

All informants (base for percentages)	Total		Sex			
			Men		Women	
	3,000		2,088		912	
	No.	%	No.	%	No.	%
Age :						
16—24	570	19.0	234	11.2	336	36.8
25—44	1,480	49.3	1,066	51.1	414	45.4
45—64	872	29.1	710	34.0	162	17.8
65 and over ..	78	2.6	78	3.7	—	—
TOTAL	3,000	100.0	2,088	100.0	912	100.0

NOTE.—All men and women interviewed were drawn from the working population.

69

Table E.12

COMPOSITION OF SAMPLE

(Town Size by Region)

All informants (base for percentages)	Total		Region							
			Southern England		Midlands and Wales		Northern England		Scotland	
	3,000		1,223		637		837		303	
	No.	%	No.	%	No.	%	No.	%	No.	%
Town size :										
Conurbations	1,596	53.2	680	55.6	272	42.7	505	60.3	139	45.9
Other Towns	802	26.7	310	25.3	307	32.5	215	25.7	70	23.1
Rural Areas	602	20.1	233	19.1	158	24.8	117	14.0	94	31.0
TOTAL	3,000	100.0	1,223	100.0	637	100.0	837	100.0	303	100.0

NOTE.—Conurbations = Towns or conglomerations of towns with a population of 115,000 or over

Other Towns = Towns with a population of less than 115,000

Rural Areas = Areas administered by a Rural District Council

RESEARCH SERVICES' REPORT

Table E.13

LIST OF TOWNS INCLUDED IN SAMPLE

Region	Conurbations	Other Towns	Rural Areas
Southern England ..	Greater London	Cheltenham	Bishop's Stortford R.D.
	Bristol	Chichester	Cheltenham R.D.
	Portsmouth	Reading	Reading R.D.
Midlands and Wales ..	Birmingham	Lincoln	Lincoln R.D.
	Nottingham	Kettering	Derby R.D.
	Derby	Crewe	Wrexham R.D.
	Cardiff	Wrexham	
Northern England ..	Manchester	Leyland	Preston R.D.
	Leeds	Castleford	Beverley R.D.
	Merseyside	Beverley	
	Tyneside		
	Teesmouth		
	Hull		
Scotland	Glasgow	Falkirk	Uphall R.D.
	Edinburgh		Dunfermline R.D.
	Dundee		

All the men and women interviewed were gainfully occupied. The distribution of gainfully occupied persons as between men and women and as between the various age groups was derived from estimates published in the *Monthly Digest of Statistics* and the *Ministry of Labour Gazette* (May, 1947). The Armed Forces were excluded and certain other allowances were made, e.g., for persons of 14 and 15 years of age at work, for men of 65 and over and women of 60 and over at work, for domestic servants, and for persons in part-time employment. The distribution of interviews in the sample corresponds to the distribution of gainfully occupied persons in the population arrived at on this basis.

Interviews were distributed among regions and town sizes according to the distribution of the population as a whole by region and town size. Figures were derived from the Registrar-General's estimate of population.

Most Friendly Societies have undertaken State Insurance as Approved Societies, either directly or by forming a separate Approved Society. The Tables distinguish accordingly between those belonging only to the Approved Section of a Friendly Society and those contributing to it for voluntary benefit.

The term Friendly Societies here, as in the Report itself, excludes Collecting Societies.

71

Table E.14

SUMMARY OF PURPOSES FOR WHICH MEMBERS BELONG
TO FRIENDLY SOCIETIES

(by Sex and Age)

All informants (base for percentages)	Total		Sex		Age		
			Men	Women	16—24	25—44	45 & over
	3,000		2,088	912	570	1,480	950
Informants who :	No.	%	%	%	%	%	%
Belong for other than Approved Section ..	743	24.8	30.0	12.7	14.2	25.6	29.9
Belong for Approved Section only ..	400	13.3	12.0	16.5	17.9	11.8	12.9
Do not belong to a Friendly Society ..	1,857	61.9	58.0	70.8	67.9	62.6	57.2
TOTAL ..	3,000	100.0	100.0	100.0	100.0	100.0	100.0

Table E.14 shows the proportion of the sample who (*a*) were members of the voluntary section of a Friendly Society (in the Table referred to as those who "belong for other than Approved Section"); (*b*) were members of the Approved Section (State Insurance) only ; and (*c*) did not belong to a Friendly Society. Those described as belonging for other than Approved Section might of course belong also to the Approved Section.

Where any doubt as to the informant's membership of a Friendly Society was conveyed in his answer to the question ("Do you belong to a Friendly Society ?"), the interviewer followed up the question by mentioning a few of the better-known Societies as examples, and by going on to ask whether the informant made any provision for sick benefit, savings or insurance and who dealt with it, asking also of informants who would be insured for N.H.I. where they sent their cards. The great bulk of those shown as not belonging to a Friendly Society, would be subject to compulsory health insurance and would belong to an approved society sponsored by an Industrial Life Office or a Trade Union.

For present purposes, interest attaches mainly to those informants who were voluntary members. Slightly under a quarter of the sample were voluntary members of a Friendly Society. This refers to persons of 16 years of age and over. No data were collected on younger persons, and there are no up-to-date figures of their membership available from official sources.

The Table shows clearly how voluntary membership increases with age. In the lowest age group the proportion of members is much lower than in the middle one, and less than half that in the oldest. As the proportion of voluntary members rises the proportions in the other two divisions of the Table fall. Some of those who belonged only to the Approved Section join for voluntary benefits also ; some of those who did not belong to a Friendly Society join it. To some extent lack of members in the lowest age group is

72

due to their smaller responsibilities, and thus their smaller need for extra insurance. But it is clear that on the whole the appeal of Friendly Societies to young people is less than it used to be.

It will also be seen that only 12.7 per cent. of women, as against 30 per cent. of men, were voluntary members. Out of all the women who were members of a Friendly Society, only a little more than two-fifths belonged for other than Approved Society business. In contrast, five-sevenths of male Friendly Society members were Voluntary members. The Friendly Societies still remain largely men's societies.

Table E.15

NAMES OF FRIENDLY SOCIETIES TO WHICH MEMBERS BELONG
(by Sex and Age)

Members of Friendly Societies other than those for Approved Section only: (base for percentages)	Total		Sex		Age			Total Membership in 1945
			Men	Women	16—24	25—44	45 & over	
	743		627	116	81	378	284	
Friendly Societies :	No.	%	%	%	%	%	%	%
National Deposit Friendly Society ..	159	21.4	19.6	31.0	30.9	25.7	13.0	18.3
Oddfellows (all Orders)	141	19.0	21.1	7.8	17.3	18.0	20.8	11.2
Hearts of Oak Benefit Society	72	9.7	9.1	12.9	8.6	9.5	10.2	4.9
Ancient Order of Foresters	56	7.5	8.3	3.4	4.9	7.1	8.8	5.9
Rechabites	45	6.1	5.7	7.8	3.7	5.8	7.0	5.7
Ancient Shepherds ..	30	4.0	4.1	3.4	3.7	3.2	5.3	2.7
Gloucester Conservative Benefit Society ..	24	3.2	3.3	2.6	4.9	2.4	3.9	0.3
Druids (all Orders) ..	18	2.4	2.7	.9	2.5	2.9	1.8	1.0
Ideal Benefit Society ..	14	1.9	1.1	6.0	3.7	1.8	1.4	1.6
Sons of Temperance ..	12	1.6	1.6	1.7	2.5	1.6	1.4	2.1
Other Societies ..	201	27.0	27.6	24.1	18.5	26.0	31.0	46.3

Table E.15 shows the distribution of the 743 voluntary members among the principal Friendly Societies.

Interviewers were provided with a list of the principal Friendly Societies. They were also provided with a list of the principal collecting Friendly Societies and Industrial Assurance organisations, which together with Trade Unions were to be excluded from the scope of the enquiry. Questionnaires were subsequently scrutinised in the office and unlisted organisations included therein as Friendly Societies were rejected if they were found not to be so in fact.

To the Table, as submitted by Research Services, a column has been added based on the Chief Registrar's statistics for 1945 showing the percentages of the total membership belonging to the societies named. It will be seen that the sample under-represents the smaller societies grouped as "all others." Relatively to these it over-represents the larger societies. This over-representation is less with the National Deposit Friendly Society than with most of the others, no doubt owing to the fact that the sample is drawn from the working population, while the National Deposit has relatively more family members. The exceptional over-representation of the Gloucester Conservative Society is due to the choice of particular localities for the sample, as is shown in Table E.13. Apart from this the sample gives a not unreasonable representation of the different societies.

The relatively greater strength of the National Deposit Friendly Society among young people and among women is a sign of its exceptional recent growth. The same features appear for the Ideal Benefit Society.

Table E.16

MEMBERSHIP OF ONE OR MORE FRIENDLY SOCIETIES
(by Sex and Age)

Members of Friendly Societies other than those for Approved Section only : (base for percentages)	Total		Sex		Age		
			Men	Women	16—24	25—44	45 & over
	743		627	116	81	378	284
Informants who are :	No.	%	%	%	%	%	%
Members of one Society ..	715	96.3	95.8	98.3	98.8	96.0	95.8
Members of two Societies ..	27	3.6	4.0	1.7	1.2	4.0	3.9
Members of three Societies..	1	.1	.2	—	—	—	.3
TOTAL	743	100.0	100.0	100.0	100.0	100.0	100.0

Table 16 requires little comment. It furnishes a useful addition to official statistics, which give figures of *memberships* only, and makes possible an estimate of the number of individuals belonging to Friendly Societies. Thus the 743 individual members in the sample represent 772 memberships. It can be inferred that the 8,720,000 memberships of 1945, given in the official statistics of the Registrar of Friendly Societies, probably thus represent some 8,392,000 individuals.

The number of individuals who are members of more than one society is small, particularly among the lowest age-groups, and among women.

Table E.17

REASONS FOR JOINING A FRIENDLY SOCIETY
(by Sex and Age)

Members of Friendly Societies other than those for Approved Section only : (base for percentages)	Total		Sex		Age		
			Men	Women	16—24	25—44	45 & over
	743		627	116	81	378	284
Reasons :	No.	%	%	%	%	%	%
For benefits other than N.H.I.	461	62.1	64.0	51.7	39.5	65.1	64.4
For N.H.I. benefits ..	325	43.7	43.2	46.5	45.7	43.4	43.7
Parents joined for him ..	85	11.4	10.8	14.7	23.4	11.6	7.7
For social activities ..	14	1.9	2.1	.9	2.5	1.3	2.5
Other reasons	48	6.5	7.3	1.7	—	5.0	10.2
Don't know, can't remember	73	9.8	8.8	15.5	17.3	9.8	7.7

Table E.17 shows the reasons advanced by voluntary Friendly Society members for joining the Friendly Society movement. Informants could offer more than one reason, so that 1,006 reasons in all are noted for 743 informants, and the percentages add up to more than 100.

As would be expected, the largest proportion joined primarily for the benefits provided by the voluntary section ; what is of considerable interest is that over 40 per cent. gave as a reason for joining the voluntary section that they were, or were about to become, members of the State section. Since informants could offer more than one reason, this one need not have been in all cases the most important ; nevertheless, it brings out clearly the importance of the State section as a recruiting ground for voluntary members. It will be seen that there is little difference here as between sexes and ages.

The number of persons giving the social activities of the Friendly Societies as grounds for their becoming members was minute in all age-groups and among both men and women.

The comparatively large proportion of younger people (17.3 per cent.) who did not know, or had forgotten, why they had become members may perhaps be another indication of the lack of interest in Friendly Societies among the young.

*Table E.*18

REASONS FOR JOINING PARTICULAR FRIENDLY SOCIETY
(by Friendly Society)

Membership of Friendly Societies other than membership for Approved Section only :	Total		Friendly Society				
			Odd-fellows	Nat'nal Deposit F.S.	Hearts of Oak	Fores-ters	Other Societies
(base for percentages)	772		141	159	72	56	344
Reasons :	No.	%	%	%	%	%	%
Parents' influence, parents joined	334	43.3	51.8	48.5	50.0	53.6	34.3
Friends', workmates' influence	156	20.2	19.2	17.6	13.9	14.3	24.1
Relatives' influence ..	88	11.4	10.6	12.6	12.5	14.3	10.5
Society offered better benefits..	73	9.5	5.7	9.4	9.7	7.1	11.3
More convenient ..	37	4.8	3.5	2.5	1.4	7.1	6.7
Has good reputation ..	17	2.2	.7	1.3	2.8	3.6	2.9
Compulsory at work ..	15	1.9	.7	—	—	—	4.1
Social reasons ..	5	.6	1.4	—	—	—	.9
Other reasons ..	27	3.5	1.4	3.1	6.9	1.8	4.1
No particular reason ..	26	3.4	5.0	5.0	2.8	—	2.6

Table E.18 shows the various reasons advanced for joining the *particular* Friendly Society of which the informant was a member. The reasons given for joining in all cases put the influence of parents in the first place, with friends and workmates second, and relatives as the next important cause.

Parental influence appears stronger in the case of the two largest orders than with the other named Societies or the sample as a whole; while personal choice based on expectation of "better benefits" is relatively more marked with the two centralised societies shown in the Table than with the Oddfellows and Foresters.

Table E.19

EXTENT TO WHICH MEMBERS ATTEND BUSINESS MEETINGS
(by Sex and Age)

Members of Friendly Societies other than those for Approved Section only :	Total		Sex		Age		
			Men	Women	16—24	25—44	45 & over
(base for percentages)	743		627	116	81	378	284
Informants attending :	No.	%	%	%	%	%	%
Regularly	40	5.4	6.2	.9	—	5.3	7.0
Occasionally	88	11.8	13.4	3.4	1.2	10.3	16.9
Never	615	82.8	80.4	95.7	98.8	84.4	76.1
TOTAL	743	100.0	100.0	100.0	100.0	100.0	100.0

This Table fully bears out the remarks made by Mass-Observation (see Part I, Sec. 1) as to the lack of active interest shown by members in the business of their societies. Little more than a sixth of members ever attend meetings at all; little more than one in twenty attend regularly. The proportions are even smaller among women and the young.

Table E.20

EXTENT TO WHICH MEMBERS HAVE HELD OFFICE IN A
FRIENDLY SOCIETY
(by Sex and Age)

Members of Friendly Societies other than those for Approved Section only :	Total		Sex		Age		
			Men	Women	16—24	25—44	45 & over
(base for percentages)	743		627	116	81	378	284
Members who :	No.	%	%	%	%	%	%
Have held office	64	8.6	9.9	1.7	—	6.6	13.7
Have not held office	679	91.4	90.1	98.3	100.0	93.4	86.3
TOTAL	743	100.0	100.0	100.0	100.0	100.0	100.0

The extent to which the burden of office is shared among members is probably a very fair indication of active participation in membership. If so, this Table reinforces the lesson of the preceding one : only 8.6 per cent. of the members in the sample had at any time held office in a Friendly Society. The proportion of women who have held office is less than 2 per cent., as compared with nearly 10 per cent. among men.

Table E.21

EXTENT TO WHICH MEMBERS WILL CONTINUE MEMBERSHIP
OF FRIENDLY SOCIETIES WHEN NATIONAL INSURANCE ACT
COMES INTO FORCE
(by Sex and Age)

Members of Friendly Societies other than those for Approved Section only : (base for percentages)	Total		Sex		Age		
			Men	Women	16—24	25—44	45 &over
	743		627	116	81	378	284
Members who :	No.	%	%	%	%	%	%
Will continue membership ..	444	59.8	60.8	54.3	54.3	57.7	64.1
Will not continue member-ship	95	12.8	13.5	8.6	7.4	16.1	9.9
Don't know	204	27.4	25.7	37.1	38.3	26.2	26.0
TOTAL	743	100.0	100.0	100.0	100.0	100.0	100.0

The wording of the question on which Table E.21 was based was altered from "Do you think you will still be a member of your Friendly Society ?" to "Do you think you will still go on paying to your Friendly Society ?" when this made the meaning clearer.* Otherwise the interviewer did not go beyond the full wording of the question as set out in the questionnaire. It was felt that it would not be possible in the course of the interview to give informants a complete account of the scope of the new Act if they were ill-informed about it, and that any partial account might produce biassed answers.

Just under 60 per cent. of informants had decided that they would continue their voluntary membership of a Friendly Society after the coming into force of the National Insurance Act. Only about one-eighth had decided not to do so. The very large proportion—27.4 per cent.—who were undecided is a fact of considerable interest, indicating a field for propaganda on the part of the Societies themselves.

It will be seen that among women, and in the youngest age-group, the proportion of the undecided was much higher than among the others. An

---

* The full question was "When the National Insurance Act comes into force with higher contributions and higher benefits, Friendly Societies will no longer pay out National Health Insurance *i.e.* they will no longer be Approved Societies. Do you think you will still be a member of your Friendly Society ?"

analysis was made of the reasons given for being undecided. The analysis was made, not in respect of voluntary members only, but of approved and voluntary members combined ; however, it is significant that among women, and in the lowest age-group, the proportions stating that they were not interested, or had never thought about the matter, were considerably higher than in other groups. This analysis is given in one of the tables (No. 19 in Research Services classification) which is not printed here but can be consulted on application to Research Services.

Table E.22

VOLUNTARY SOCIAL SERVICE ORGANISATIONS TO WHICH
INFORMANTS BELONG
(by Sex and Age)

Informants belonging to a Voluntary Social Service Organisation (base for percentages)	Total		Sex		Age		
			Men	Women	16—24	25—44	45 & over
	1,982		1,451	531	329	993	660
Organisation :	No.	%	%	%	%	%	%
Hospital Contributory Scheme, H.S.A., Medical Scheme, Home Nursing	1,840	92.9	91.6	96.1	82.1	93.4	97.4
British Legion, Ex-Service Organisations	242	12.2	15.9	2.3	4.6	12.2	16.1
Societies for Helping Members of Services	89	4.5	5.7	1.1	4.9	5.6	2.6
Religious Organisations ..	82	4.1	3.4	6.2	5.5	4.3	3.2
British Red Cross, St. John's Ambulance	67	3.4	3.3	3.6	2.1	4.1	2.9
Boys' or Girls' Clubs ..	64	3.2	3.0	3.8	11.2	2.2	.8
Social Organisations ..	49	2.5	2.5	2.3	3.3	2.1	2.6
Blind Welfare Organisations ..	44	2.2	2.4	1.7	.3	1.7	3.9
Boy Scouts, Girl Guides, Cadets	41	2.1	1.8	2.8	4.3	2.0	1.0
Professional and Trade Organisations	40	2.0	2.3	1.3	1.5	2.2	2.0
Educational and Cultural Organisations	32	1.6	1.6	1.7	2.4	1.6	1.2
Philanthropic Organisations ..	29	1.5	1.3	1.9	.3	1.5	1.9
Other Organisations ..	82	4.1	4.7	2.6	2.4	3.9	5.3

Philanthropic Organisations include : Care of Aged Committees, Council of Social Service, Personal Service League, Societies for the Care of Children, Women's Voluntary Services, etc.

Religious Organisations include : Church Organisations, Student Christian Movement, Toc H, Y.M.C.A., Y.W.C.A., etc.

Cultural Organisations include : Workers' Educational Association, Dramatic Clubs, Workers' Travel Association, etc.

Other Organisations include : Local Benevolent Funds, Blood Transfusion Service, Ramblers' Association, Women's Institutes, etc.

Table E.23

ANALYSIS OF MEMBERSHIP OF VOLUNTARY SOCIAL SERVICE ORGANISATIONS

	Total		Number of organisations to which informant belongs											
			Hospital Schemes				Ex-Service Organisations				Other V.S.S. Organisations			
			None	One	Two	Three or more	None	One	Two	Three or more	None	One	Two	Three or more
	No.	%	No.	No.	No.	No.	No.	No.	No.	No.	No.	No.	No.	No.
All informants (base for percentages)	3,000		1,309	1,572	98	21	2,759	240	1	—	2,497	411	76	16
Informants who are members of:														
Hospital Contributory Schemes only	1,298	43.4	—	1,208	69	21	1,298	—	—	—	1,298	—	—	—
Ex-Service Organisations only	72	2.4	72	—	—	—	—	72	—	—	72	—	—	—
Hospital Schemes and Ex-Service Organisations only	109	3.6	—	106	3	—	—	108	1	—	109	—	—	—
Hospital Schemes and other V.S.S. Organisations	253	8.3	—	227	26	—	253	—	—	—	—	205	45	3
Ex-Service Organisations and other V.S.S. Organisations	29	1.0	29	—	—	—	—	29	—	—	—	27	2	—
Hospital Schemes, Ex-Service Organisations and other V.S.S. Organisations	31	1.1	—	31	—	—	—	31	—	—	—	25	4	2
Other V.S.S. Organisations only	190	6.3	190	—	—	—	190	—	—	—	—	154	25	11
None	1,018	33.9	1,018	—	—	—	1,018	—	—	—	1,018	—	—	—
TOTAL	3,000	100.0	1,309	1,572	98	21	2,759	240	1	—	2,497	411	76	16

Tables E.22 and E.23 together give some information on the membership of Voluntary Social Service organisations. The data on which these and the following Tables are based were obtained thus :

Interviewers did not attempt a definition of a Voluntary Social Service Organisation. They showed informants a list of organisations, agreed upon by Research Services and the Inquiry. Having given informants time to read through the list, interviewers asked whether they belonged to any of those listed, or to any other voluntary social service organisations, using the list as showing the types they had in mind.

Interviewers were instructed not to accept membership of political or trading associations or sports clubs, or simple attendance at a place of worship, as membership of a Voluntary Social Service organisation.

Of the sample of 3,000, 1,982 (66.1 per cent.) belonged to some kind of Voluntary Social Service organisation, and 1,018 (33.9 per cent.) stated that they belonged to none.

Table E.22 shows the classes of body to which the 1,982 members belonged, and the numbers belonging to each. As many belonged to more than one society, the total of memberships is much greater than 1,982, amounting to 2,701.

Hospital Contributory Schemes account for much the larger part of the total memberships shown in Table E.22, and represent a form of insurance or mutual aid rather than voluntary service to others. Table E.23 shows that, of the 3,000 informants, 1,298 or 43.4 per cent., belonged to a Hospital Contributory Scheme and nothing else ; 393 or 13.1 per cent. belonged to a Hospital Contributory Scheme in combination with some other organisation ; 291 or 9.7 per cent. belonged to some other organisation without belonging to a Hospital Contributory Scheme ; and 1,018 or 33.9 per cent. belonged to no organisation at all.

One hundred and nineteen persons out of the 1,691 members of Hospital Schemes were members of more than one ; this represents 7.0 per cent. of such members. It is of interest that this percentage is almost twice as great as the percentage of Friendly Society members belonging to more than one Society (see Table E.16).

Next to the Hospital Contributory Schemes the largest membership is found in the Ex-Service Organisations, which also to some extent are organisations for mutual aid. Seventy-two or 2.4 per cent. of all informants belonged only to these ; 169 or 5.6 per cent. to these bodies in combination with others.

The total number of individuals belonging to any type of organisation other than a Hospital Scheme or an Ex-Service Organisation is shown in Table E.23 to be 503, or 16.7 per cent. of all informants. This last percentage agrees closely with the finding of Mass-Observation that "less than a third of the people with whom investigators came into contact were found to be giving any sort of regular voluntary help to people outside their own families" ; of whom a little more than half were doing so "in connection with some type of organisation." (See p. 33.)

Table E.24

PART TAKEN BY MEMBERS IN WORK OF VOLUNTARY SOCIAL SERVICE ORGANISATIONS
(by Organisation)

Members of Voluntary Social Service Organisations (base for percentages)	Total		Organisation						
			Hospital and Medical Schemes	Ex-Service Organisations	Youth Organisations	Philanthropic Organisations	Religious Organisations	Other Bodies
	2,701		1,840	242	105	229	82	203
	No.	%	%	%	%	%	%	%
Part taken:								
Subscribe only	2,386	88.3	97.1	86.8	48.6	74.2	45.1	64.5
Officer	116	4.3	.9	4.1	26.6	7.0	22.0	13.8
Committee Member	89	3.3	.6	4.6	11.4	9.2	9.7	12.8
Field Worker	60	2.2	.8	2.9	6.7	6.6	14.7	1.9
Other activities	50	1.9	.6	1.6	6.7	3.0	8.5	7.0
TOTAL	2,701	100.0	100.0	100.0	100.0	100.0	100.0	100.0

F

Table E.25

BASIS OF PARTICIPATION IN WORK OF VOLUNTARY SOCIAL SERVICE ORGANISATIONS

(by Organisation)

Members of *Voluntary Social Service Organisations* (base for percentages)	Total		Hospital and Medical Schemes	Ex-Service Organisations	Youth Organisations	Philanthropic Organisations	Religious Organisations	Other Bodies
	2,701		1,840	242	105	229	82	203
	No.	%	%	%	%	%	%	%
Basis:								
Voluntary ..	301	11.1	2.6	13.2	50.5	25.3	53.7	32.5
For Expenses only	6	.2	—	—	.9	.4	1.2	1.5
For Wage or Salary	8	.3	.3	—	—	—	—	1.5
No participation ..	2,386	88.4	97.1	86.8	48.6	74.3	45.1	64.5
TOTAL ..	2,701	100.0	100.0	100.0	100.0	100.0	100.0	100.0

Organisation

Table E.26

EXTENT TO WHICH MEMBERS ATTEND MEETINGS OF VOLUNTARY SOCIAL SERVICE ORGANISATIONS
(by Organisation)

Members of Voluntary Social Service Organisations (base for percentages)	Total		Hospital and Medical Schemes	Ex-Service Organisations	Youth Organisations	Philanthropic Organisations	Religious Organisations	Other Bodies
	2,701		1,840	242	105	229	82	203
	No.	%	%	%	%	%	%	%
Frequency of attendance :								
Once a week	197	7.3	.1	11.6	53.3	13.5	41.5	22.7
Once a month	162	6.0	.3	15.3	21.9	13.5	20.7	23.7
Once a quarter	87	3.2	.6	12.4	6.7	4.8	7.3	11.3
Less often than once a quarter	155	5.7	1.4	28.1	5.7	10.1	12.2	10.8
Never	1,735	64.3	79.8	31.8	9.5	48.5	14.6	28.1
No Meetings held	365	13.5	17.8	.8	2.9	9.6	3.7	3.4
TOTAL	2,701	100.0	100.0	100.0	100.0	100.0	100.0	100.0

Table E.27

LENGTH OF TIME SINCE MEMBERS OF VOLUNTARY SOCIAL SERVICE ORGANISATIONS LAST ATTENDED A MEETING

(by Organisation)

Members who attend Meetings (base for percentages)	Total		Hospital and Medical Schemes	Ex-Service Organisations	Youth Organisations	Philanthropic Organisations	Religious Organisations	Other Bodies
	601		44	163	92	96	67	139
	No.	%	%	%	%	%	%	%
When last attended:								
Up to and including one week ago ..	140	23.3	2.3	14.1	33.7	25.0	38.8	25.2
More than one week ago, up to and including one month ago ..	144	24.0	15.9	22.1	28.3	26.1	19.4	26.6
More than one month ago, up to and including three months ago ..	129	21.4	20.4	19.0	27.2	20.8	16.4	23.7
Longer ago than three months ..	188	31.3	61.4	44.8	10.8	28.1	25.4	24.5
TOTAL	601	100.0	100.0	100.0	100.0	100.0	100.0	100.0

Table E.28

WEEKLY CONTRIBUTIONS MADE BY MEMBERS OF VOLUNTARY SOCIAL SERVICE ORGANISATIONS

(by Organisation)

Members of Voluntary Social Service Organisations (base for percentages)	Total		Organisation					
			Hospital and Medical Schemes	Ex-Service Organisations	Youth Organisations	Philanthropic Organisations	Religious Organisations	Other Bodies
	2,701		1,840	242	105	229	82	203
Weekly contribution :	No.	%	%	%	%	%	%	%
Up to and including 3d.	1,207	44.6	38.2	86.0	45.7	60.7	28.0	42.9
4d. to 6d.	1,004	37.2	49.3	4.5	16.2	8.7	17.1	17.2
7d. to 1s.	107	4.0	3.8	1.2	3.8	1.3	4.9	11.3
1s. 1d. to 2s.	46	1.7	.8	1.7	1.0	1.3	4.9	9.4
2s. 1d. to 5s.	10	.4	.1	1.2	—	.4	3.6	.5
Over 5s.	3	.1	.1	—	—	—	1.2	.5
Nothing	94	3.5	.3	1.7	19.0	10.1	23.2	10.8
Irregular amounts	51	1.9	.5	.4	8.6	6.1	11.0	4.4
Don't know	179	6.6	6.9	3.3	5.7	11.4	6.1	3.0
TOTAL	2,701	100.0	100.0	100.0	100.0	100.0	100.0	100.0

The five Tables E.24 to E.28 relate to the extent and nature of participation in Voluntary Service Activities.

In these Tables, certain organisations shown in the fuller list in Table E.22 have been grouped. Thus :

Youth Organisations include Boys' and Girls' Clubs, Boy Scouts, Girl Guides, Cadets ;

Philanthropic Organisations include societies for helping members of the Services, Blind Welfare Organisations, and British Red Cross and St. John, as well as the "philanthropic organisations" of Table E.22.

Other Bodies include social organisations, professional or trade organisations, educational and cultural organisations and "other organisations" as in Table E.22.

Table E.24 shows the proportion of those whose participation is limited to mere subscribing, and of those in whom it is more active.

Hospital and Medical Schemes have been included, but there is naturally little room in them for active membership on the part of any but a handful of staff. This Table would also appear to show a passive membership on the part of nearly six out of seven members of Ex-Servicemen's Associations; but the figures are probably somewhat misleading as they stand. Thus Table E.26 shows that over one-quarter of the members attend their meetings once a month or oftener ; and it may be surmised, though there are no figures to support the surmise, that a good proportion attend regularly for "social intercourse and rational recreation."

Youth organisations and Religious organisations (the latter including such bodies as Toc H and the Y.M.C.A.) each show, in Table E.24, the active participation of more than half of the membership.

Philanthropic organisations, which include Councils of Social Service, the Red Cross, St. John, Blind Welfare organisations and others, occupy an intermediate position.

The "other bodies," including as they do a miscellany of professional and trade organisations, educational and cultural bodies, benevolent funds, women's institutes and ramblers' associations, cannot usefully be commented on here.

Table E.25 shows that of the 315 members who take an active part in the work of their organisations, nearly all (301) do so voluntarily, that is, without pay. Six do so for expenses only ; nowhere but in the Hospital Schemes and the mixed group of "other bodies" are there workers who do so for a regular wage or salary.

Table E.26 shows a wide variety in the frequency of attendance at meetings. In the case of Hospital Schemes regular attendance is confined to a handful, probably officers who attend committee meetings. At the other extreme, three-quarters of the members of youth groups attend at least once a month, and over half do so weekly. It was said above that "Religious organisations" include the Y.M.C.A. and other youth groups ; this no doubt partly accounts for their relatively good showing.

A broadly similar picture is given in Table E.27 which shows the length of time elapsed since members last attended a meeting.

Table E.28 shows the amount of weekly contributions paid by members. Leaving aside the Hospital Contributory Schemes, it is clear that for the majority the financial outlay is small. In all other classes over a half pay nothing or less than threepence per week. Even in Hospital Schemes, with their insurance function, very few pay more than sixpence a week.

COMPLETE LIST OF RESEARCH SERVICES' TABLES

Following is a complete list of Tables in which the results of Research Services' Study were presented. The numbering used by Research Services is shown for ease of reference. Students desirous of consulting any of these Tables should apply to Research Services Ltd., 91 Shaftesbury Avenue, London, W.1.

Tables to which an asterisk has been prefixed appear in the foregoing selection of Tables

TABLE

*A   Composition of sample (age by sex)
*B   Composition of sample (town size by region)
 1   Membership of Friendly Societies (by sex and age)
*Supp. 1   Summary of purposes for which members belong to Friendly Societies (by sex and age)
 1A   Membership of Friendly Societies (by region and town size)
Supp. 1A   Summary of purposes for which members belong to Friendly Societies (by region and town size)
 2   Names of Friendly Societies to which members belong (by sex and age)
*Supp. 2   Names of Friendly Societies to which members belong (by sex and age) (Members for other than Approved Section only)
 2A   Names of Friendly Societies to which members belong (by region and town size)
Supp. 2A   Names of Friendly Societies to which members belong (by region and town size) (Members for other than Approved Section only)
 3   Membership of one or more Friendly Societies (by sex and age)
*Supp. 3   Membership of one or more Friendly Societies (by sex and age) (Members for other than Approved Section only)
 3A   Membership of one or more Friendly Societies (by region and town size)
Supp. 3A   Membership of one or more Friendly Societies (by region and town size) (Members for other than Approved Section only)
 4   Age at which members first joined present Friendly Society (by sex and age)
 4A   Age at which members first joined present Friendly Society (by region and town size)
 5   Reasons for joining a Friendly Society (by sex and age)
*Supp. 5   Reasons for joining a Friendly Society (by sex and age) (Members for other than Approved Section only)
 5A   Reasons for joining a Friendly Society (by region and town size)
Supp. 5A   Reasons for joining a Friendly Society (by region and town size) (Members for other than Approved Section only)
 6   Reasons for joining particular Friendly Society
*Supp. 6   Reasons for joining particular Friendly Society (Members for other than Approved Section only)
 7   Services which Friendly Societies are known to provide (by sex and age)
 7A   Services which Friendly Societies are known to provide (by region and town size)

87

RESEARCH SERVICES' REPORT

TABLE
26 Membership of Voluntary Social Service Organisations (by sex and age)
26A Membership of Voluntary Social Service Organisations (by region and town size)
*27 Voluntary Social Service Organisations to which informants belong (by sex and age)
27A Voluntary Social Service Organisations to which informants belong (by region and town size)
28 Membership of one or more Voluntary Social Service Organisations (by sex and age)
28A Membership of one or more Voluntary Social Service Organisations (by region and town size)
*Supp. 28 Analysis of membership of Voluntary Social Service Organisations
29 How members came to join Voluntary Social Service Organisations
*30 Part taken by members in work of Voluntary Social Service Organisations
31 Financial outlay of members of Voluntary Social Service Organisations
*32 Weekly contribution made by members of Voluntary Social Service Organisations
*33 Basis of participation in work of Voluntary Social Service Organisations
*34 Extent to which members attend meeting of Voluntary Social Service Organisations
*35 Length of time since members of Voluntary Social Service Organisations last attended a meeting
36 Nature of last meeting of Voluntary Social Service Organisation attended by members
37 Extent of "group" attendance at meetings of Voluntary Social Service Organisations
38 Summary of purposes for which members belong to Friendly Societies (by sex and age)
38A Summary of purposes for which members belong to Friendly Societies (by region and town size)
39 Membership of Friendly Societies and Voluntary Social Service Organisations (by sex and age)
Supp. 39 Membership of Friendly Societies for different purposes and of different types of Voluntary Social Service Organisations (by sex and age)
39A Membership of Friendly Societies and Voluntary Social Service Organisations (by region and town size)
Supp. 39A Membership of Friendly Societies for different purposes and of different types of Voluntary Social Service Organisations (by region and town size)

89

PART III

MEMORANDA ON FINANCE OF VOLUNTARY ACTION

I. GOVERNMENT GRANTS TO VOLUNTARY AGENCIES

TABLE E.29, below, which was furnished to the Inquiry by H.M. Treasury, shows the financial assistance given by Government Departments to voluntary bodies in 1946-1947. The term "voluntary" here indicates the possession of a substantial income from other than public sources.

The scope of the Table is wider than social service as narrowly understood (for instance, it includes agencies for general education and research—not merely social research). Public grants to bodies primarily concerned with defence, trade and industry are, however, excluded. The exclusion is not always easy to apply ; grants for educational purposes being included, it is sometimes difficult to distinguish money spent on, say, industrial research, and that spent on general educational purposes. Grants to universities are a case in point, since these are not allocated to particular purposes.

Indirect contributions are also excluded. Again the distinction is not an easy one to make : but, while expenditure from the Education (Scotland) Fund or the Development Fund is regarded as direct, that by the Arts Council or the British Council is looked on as indirect.

Assistance to bodies outside Great Britain is excluded ; but not assistance to bodies in Great Britain for work done abroad.

Contributions of under £100 are ignored.

The assistance included consists in every case of *grants*, not loans, except where otherwise stated.

Column 4 ("Whether Government represented on Governing Body") should be read with some caution. The arrangements for liaison between the Government and the grantee vary a good deal, and the answer "no" may not be incompatible with fairly close control, while "yes" may refer to a representative with a mere watching brief.

In Table E.29 a "voluntary" agency means one having a substantial income from sources other than public funds. This has resulted in the exclusion from that Table of a number of interesting and important bodies whose work otherwise resembles to some degree the agencies which have been included. Among these bodies are the Medical Research Council, the Agricultural Research Council, the Arts Council of Great Britain, the British Council and the Council of Industrial Design. They do not, of course, exhaust the list of bodies excluded on this ground.

The *Medical Research Council*, whose Royal Charter dates from 1920, was set up under the general authority of the Ministry of Health Act, 1919. It operates under the direction of a Committee of the Privy Council,

Table E.29

GOVERNMENT GRANTS TO VOLUNTARY AGENCIES

Department responsible	Voluntary Body or Class of Voluntary Body assisted	Amount granted 1946-47 £	Whether Government represented on Governing Body	Remarks
Treasury	23 Universities and Colleges ..	6,336,583	No	Including £566,996 non-recurrent and £477,500 for teaching hospitals
	2 Royal Societies	52,300	No	
	2 Royal Geographical Societies	1,700	No	
	4 Royal Schools of Music ..	26,200	No	
	Royal Academy of Dramatic Art	2,000	No	
	British Academy	2,500	No	
	2 Schools of Archaeology Abroad	5,000	No	
	National Central Library ..	7,500	No	
	Scott Polar Research Institute	1,800	No	
	Solar Physics Observatory ..	3,000	No	
	Empire Parliamentary Association	11,750	No	
	Inter-Parliamentary Union ..	700	No	
Ministry of Education ..	Schools for normal children: 240 Direct Grant Grammar and other Schools Asstd. Gr. Reg. 2	1,646,090	No	
	Schools and Institutions for special educational treatment : 168	7,330	No	Grant on employers' contribution to teachers' superannuation
	22	31,000	No	For maintenance expenses
	12	62,000	No	For accommodation and equipment

Table E.29—continued

Department responsible	Voluntary Body or Class of Voluntary Body assisted	Amount granted 1946-47 £	Whether Government represented on Governing Body	Remarks
Ministry of Education (cont.)	38 Technical and Arts Schools and Colleges .. .. :	109,760	No	
	Adult Education :			
	47 Responsible Bodies .. :	198,067	No	
	27 Vacation Courses .. :	6,800	No	
	6 Residential Colleges .. :	11,880	Yes	
	3 National Associations .. :	5,350	No	For local classes
	Youth Organisations :			
	442 Local Organisations .. :	116,350	No	
	3 National Organisations .. :	151,186	Yes	
	Adult Recreative Organisations :			
	61 Local Organisations .. :	80,155	No	
	3 National Organisations .. :	20,000	Yes	
	52 Voluntary Training Colleges .. :	1,202,000	No	Including £14,000 capital
	Miscellaneous :			
	National Foundation for Educational Research in England and Wales .. :	1,500	Yes	
	English-Speaking Union .. :	2,750	Yes	For interchange of teachers with U.S.A.
	Nursery School Association of Great Britain :	1,500	Yes	
	Council for Promotion of Field Studies :	1,350	Yes	
	Chelsea Physic Garden :	150	No	
Scottish Education Department ..	Scottish Universities .. :	60,000	No	
	Central Institutions* .. :	260,038	No	
	Training Colleges for Teachers :	149,658	Yes	
	Voluntary Secondary Schools* :	230,499	No	
	Residential Special Schools* .. :	27,788	No	Including £8,010 capital

* Also receive indirect assistance, i.e., grant is paid on contributions by Education Authorities

Table E.29—continued

Department responsible	Voluntary Body or Class of Voluntary Body assisted	Amount granted 1946-47 £	Whether Government represented on Governing Body	Remarks
Scottish Education Department (cont.)	Technical Training Institutions	4,372	No	
	Orphanages*	3,886	No	
	*Voluntary Continuation Classes	6,954	No	
	Approved Schools	148,534	No	
	Bodies engaged in Educational Research and Development*	1,379	In some cases	
	Bodies engaged in Provision of Social and Physical Training*	53,000	In some cases	
	Certain Institutions employing Teachers	16,982	No	Proportion of employers' superannuation contributions
Ministry of Health	Voluntary Hospitals	1,247,300	No	Pending introduction of National Health Service
	Central Council for Health Education	15,000	Yes	
	National Association for Mental Health	45,306	No	
	National Council of Social Service	8,000	No	For headquarter expenses on Citizens' Advice Bureaux
	National Council for the Unmarried Mother and her Child	500	No	
Department of Health for Scotland	Scottish Council for Health Education	1,910	Yes	
Ministry of Labour and National Service	Blood Transfusion Association	30,505	Yes	
	17 Bodies training and employing Disabled Persons	79,166	No	
	After-care Association (Physically handicapped youth)	2,000	No	
Assistance Board	National Council of Social Service	45,700	Yes	For clubs, etc., for unemployed, since discontinued

* Also receive indirect assistance, i.e., grant is paid on contributions by Education Authorities

Table E.29—continued

Department responsible	Voluntary Body or Class of Voluntary Body assisted	Amount granted 1946-47 £	Whether Government represented on Governing Body	Remarks
Ministry of Pensions	Royal Patriotic Fund Corporation	1,212	Yes	For grants to ineligible widows
Ministry of National Insurance ..	Medical Expenses Fund for Silicosis	2,500	Yes	
General Post Office	King Edward Hospital Fund	500	No	
	Institution of Post Office Electrical Engineers ..	250	No	
Stationery Office	Printers' Pension Corporation	157	Yes	
Board of Trade	British Standards Institution ..	25,000	Yes	
	Institute of Management ..	12,000	Yes	
	Design Centres	500	No	
Department of Scientific and Industrial Research	Research Associations and other bodies engaged in industrial research	860,000	Yes	£200,000 non-recurrent
Development Fund	Rural Community Councils ..	21,000	No	
	National Council of Social Service :		Yes	
	(1) Erection of Village Halls ..	120,000	No	Loan free of interest
	(2) Rural Development ..	8,000	No	
	Women's Institutes	8,160	No	
	Society of Friends	2,000	No	For Allotments Scheme
	Land Settlement Association ..	2,000	No	For Welfare Secretaries
	Scottish Gardens and Allotments Society	750	No	
	Fishery Institutions	63,400	No	For research
	Liverpool University	24,000	No	For research

Table E.29—continued

Department responsible	Voluntary Body or Class of Voluntary Body assisted	Amount granted 1946-47 £	Whether Government represented on Governing Body	Remarks
Ministry of Agriculture and Fisheries and Department of Agriculture for Scotland	Colleges and Institutions for Agricultural Education	495,373	No	Including £168,650 capital
	Research	966,836	No	Including £508,217 capital
	Y.M.C.A.	14,500	No	For training town boys in agriculture
	Agricultural Organisation Societies	9,200	No	For research
	Scottish Association of Young Farmers' Clubs	1,500	No	
Forestry Commission ..	Colleges and Institutions for Education	7,800	No	
	Research	7,300	No	
Home Office	Central Committee for Refugees	345,000	No	
	Women's Voluntary Services*	148,000	No	
Lord Chancellor's Department ..	Law Society	210,000	No	(for 1947–8) For organising legal aid under Poor Persons Rules
Prison Commission	Borstal Association..	15,981	No	
	Central Association ..	5,854	No	
	Aylesbury After-care Association	4,518	No	For female prisoners and Borstal inmates
	National Association of Discharged Prisoners' Aid Societies	15,223	No	Part of this grant was paid to Local Authorities
Scottish Home Department ..	Voluntary Bodies concerned with Physical Training and Recreation	21,000	No	

*The Ministry of Works pays the rent of accommodation occupied by W.V.S., which also receives free stationery. Payments were also made by certain Departments (Ministry of Food, Board of Trade and War Office) for administrative services rendered.

Table E.29—continued

Department responsible	Voluntary Body or Class of Voluntary Body assisted	Amount granted 1946-47 £	Whether Government represented on Governing Body	Remarks
Scottish Home Department (cont.)	Discharged Prisoners' Aid Societies	1,300	No	
Ministry of Transport	Royal Society for Prevention of Accidents*	100,000	No	
Foreign Office ..	Council of British Societies for Relief Abroad and Voluntary Societies who are Members of the Council	159,398	No	In respect of expenditure incurred in supplying workers to administer relief abroad
Colonial Office	Bureau of Hygiene and Tropical Diseases	3,000	Yes	
	Colonial Department, Institute of Education, University of London	1,000	No	
	Various voluntary bodies in respect of welfare of colonial students in this country	980	No	
Dominions Office (as it then was) ..	Six Voluntary Societies concerned with Overseas Settlement	5,693	No	
War Office	Sailors', Soldiers' and Airmen's Families Association	236,285	Yes	
	Incorporated Soldiers', Sailors' and Airmen's Help Society	25,000	Yes	
	Council of Voluntary Welfare Work	4,000	No	
	First Aid Nursing Yeomanry	3,000	No	

*Also received payments from General Post Office in respect of entrance fees of drivers for Safety First competition.

Table E.29—continued

Department responsible	Voluntary Body or Class of Voluntary Body assisted	Amount granted 1946-47 £	Whether Government represented on Governing Body	Remarks
Admiralty	Sailors' Homes	2,350		
	Hospitals and District Nurses at three Home Ports and Malta	1,540		
	National Association for Employment of Sailors, Soldiers and Airmen	480		
	Royal Naval Lay Readers' Society	300		
Air Ministry	Royal United Services Institution	325	Yes	
	National Association for Employment of Soldiers, Sailors and Airmen	320	Yes	

"with a view to facilitating the holding of, and dealing with, any money provided by Parliament for medical research and any other property."

The Agricultural Research Council, whose Charter dates from 1931, is also responsible to a Committee of the Privy Council.   It operates
"with a view to facilitating the holding of and dealing with any money provided by Parliament and any other property real or personal available for those objects and with a view, further, to encouraging the making of gifts and bequests in aid of the said objects."

The Charter of the *Arts Council* dates from 1946, although this, as Council for the Encouragement of Music and the Arts (C.E.M.A.), was working for some years prior to this, its income being derived in part from grants from the Pilgrim Trust.   In 1946 it was created a body corporate on the advice of the Chancellor of the Exchequer,
"to improve the standard of execution of the fine arts and advise and co-operate with our Government Departments, local authorities and other bodies on any matters conceived directly or indirectly with those objects, and with a view to facilitating the holding of and dealing with any money provided by Parliament and any other property, real or personal, otherwise available for those objects."

The *British Council* was given its Charter in 1940.   It had been set up in 1934 at the instance of the Foreign Office, supported by a number of other Government bodies.

The *Council of Industrial Design* was appointed by the President of the Board of Trade in December, 1944,
"to further the establishment of design centres, advising the Board of Trade on grants to them, to advise on the training of designers and the design of articles to be purchased by public bodies and to be a centre of information and advice for industry and for Government departments."

Table E.30, below, shows the amount of grants from public funds received by each of these bodies in the financial years 1946-47 and 1947-48, together with the accounting department in each case.   The increase in the amounts of the grants in the later year is in each case noteworthy.

Table E.30

SOME GRANT-RECEIVING BODIES WITH NO SUBSTANTIAL
INCOME FROM NON-GOVERNMENT SOURCES

Grant Receiving Body	Amount of Grant 1946-47 £000	Amount of Grant 1947-48 £000	Accounting Department
Medical Research Council	465	748	Treasury
Agricultural Research Council ..	300	400	Treasury
Arts Council of Great Britain ..	350	428	Treasury
British Council	2,454	2,913	Foreign Office
Council of Industrial Design ..	100	164	Board of Trade

2. NOTES ON THE TAXATION OF VOLUNTARY AGENCIES

I. FRIENDLY SOCIETIES

1. *Exemption of Societies from Tax.* A registered Friendly Society which is precluded by Act of Parliament or by its rules from assuring to any person a sum exceeding £500, or an annuity exceeding £104, the limits fixed by the Friendly Societies Acts—is entitled under Section 39 (1) of the Income Tax Act, 1918 (a Consolidation Act—the exemption is much older) to exemption from income tax under Schedules A, C and D.   The limits of £500 and £104 were fixed in 1948 to accord with the increase allowed by the Industrial Assurance and Friendly Societies Act, 1948.   From 1910 to 1948 the insurance limit was £300 and the annuity limit £52, and for the previous seventy years they were £200 and £30.

An unregistered Friendly Society whose income does not exceed £160 per annum is entitled to total relief from tax.

Any income of a Friendly Society which is exempt from Income Tax is also exempt from Profits Tax.

2. *Subscriptions to Registered Friendly Societies.* The ordinary life insurance relief under Section 32 of the Income Tax Act, 1918, is given to members in respect of payments for life insurance to a *registered* society.   Where the member pays a composite subscription to cover other benefits, e.g., relief in certain circumstances of distress, the relief is allowed in respect of so much of the composite subscription as is attributable to the insurance element.

Life insurance relief is also allowed in respect of payments to a *registered* society to secure a deferred annuity where the contract was entered into before 23rd June, 1916, or was made under certain superannuation or bona-fide pension schemes, including schemes for the employees of any employer or for persons engaged in a particular trade, profession or business.

The relief does not apply to other types of payment to a registered society, or to payments of any kind to an unregistered society.

3. *Payments by Friendly Societies.* Contractual annuities are income of the recipients and are liable to Income Tax, as are also sickness or disability benefits which have continued for at least 12 months prior to the commencement of the year of assessment.   Other benefits received by the members are not regarded as income for Income Tax purposes.

4. It is to be noted that under the same section of the Income Tax Act as grants exemption to Friendly Societies, exemption is granted, subject to the same insurable limits, to registered trade unions in respect of interest and dividends for the purpose of provident benefits.

2. BUILDING SOCIETIES

1. Under the ordinary law a building society would, like a company, be liable to tax at the standard rate on the whole of its income.   Thus the society would suffer tax by deduction at the source on the interest it received on advances to its borrowing members, and on income from other investments,

and would be directly assessed on any interest from 3½ per cent. War Loan or other investments not taxed at the source. Having paid on its total gross income the society would be entitled to deduct tax at the standard rate on the interest and dividends paid or credited to its investing members (depositors and shareholders), and would be left bearing tax at the standard rate on the undistributed balance of each year. It would then be for any shareholder or depositor, who was liable to tax at a rate less than the standard rate or was altogether exempt, to claim from the Revenue the repayment of tax to which he was entitled.

2. The non-statutory Arrangement with the building societies, which came into being in the nineties, was designed to avoid the mass of repayment claims by the persons of small means who then formed the main part of the societies' investors. A society which enters into the Arrangement pays tax at the full standard rate on its undistributed income and pays on its distributions by way of dividends and interest to shareholders and depositors tax at a "composite rate" (which is the same for all societies) without deducting any tax from the dividends and interest, and the shareholders and depositors individually do not obtain any repayment of tax from the Revenue. The "composite rate," which is based on samples supplied by the societies and other statistics, is fixed so as to yield approximately the same amount of tax as would be obtained through the normal procedure of deduction at the full standard rate and repayment by the Inland Revenue to the recipients where they are not liable to tax at that rate. Its yield represents approximately the *net* tax due from the shareholders and depositors after taking into account any personal allowances, etc., which they would otherwise have been entitled to claim by repayment from the Revenue against their income from the society.

It is also part of the Arrangement that the borrower from a building society pays interest on his loan without deduction of tax. If the borrower is liable to tax, he is given tax relief in respect of the interest paid by an allowance in any direct assessment made upon him (normally the Schedule A assessment on the mortgaged property).

3. Building Societies are liable to Profits Tax, but there are special provisions in the Profits Tax legislation limiting the amount of the tax chargeable. As from 1st January, 1947 (the date from which Profits Tax is charged at the rates of 25 per cent. on the distributed profits of an ordinary trading company and at 10 per cent. on profits which it does not distribute) the Profits Tax chargeable on building societies is limited to 6 per cent. on the profits computed without allowing any deduction for interest paid on loans from members or depositors.

3. CHARITABLE COVENANTS

Under the law in force prior to the Finance Act of 1946, the Revenue gave relief from both Income Tax (standard rate) and Surtax in respect of the annual payment which a taxpayer covenanted under a seven-year deed to make to a charity. On making the annual payment to the charity the taxpayer deducted tax at the standard rate from the payment so that the actual cash payment made by him to the charity represented the annual payment less tax, and the tax so deducted was repaid by the Revenue to the charity. If the taxpayer were liable to Surtax, the amount of the annual payment was a deduction in computing his total income for Surtax purposes, and he thus obtained direct relief from Surtax in respect of the payment. On every pound paid under the seven-year deed to a charity the Exchequer lost both Income Tax and Surtax, and in the case of the largest incomes the effect was that the actual sacrifice to the taxpayer involved in making the annual payment might be no more than 6d. in the £. Thus, assuming a covenanter with an income of £25,000 who covenants to pay £1,000 to a charity for a period of seven years, he would, taking 1946-47 rates of tax, pay the charity each year £550 in cash (£1,000, less standard Income Tax at 9s. in the £); and the £1,000 would be deducted in computing his total income for Surtax with the result that his Surtax bill would fall by £525 (tax on £1,000 at 10s. 6d. in the £, the rate of Surtax applicable to income in excess of £20,000). The final result was that the charity received £1,000, of which £975 (£450 Income Tax repaid and £525 Surtax lost) was at the cost of the Exchequer and the Surtax payer bore £25, i.e., 6d. in each £ on his gift.

The general effect of Section 28 of the Finance Act, 1946, is to disallow the payment under a seven years' covenant as a deduction for Surtax purposes, while leaving undisturbed the existing position as regards Income Tax, under which a payer can deduct Income Tax from his payments and a charity can recover from the Revenue the tax so deducted.

The Section is drawn in wider terms than would be required merely to forbid deduction of annual payments to charities. It applies to annual payments to non-charitable bodies, which clearly should not receive more favourable treatment than payments to charities. It also applies to the income from capital which has been temporarily transferred to a charity or other body, the income in such a case continuing to be treated for Surtax purposes as income of the settlor.

The Section does not apply where income under a settlement is payable to an individual for his own use, as in the case of settlements for dependants.

PART IV

MEMORANDA BY ORGANISATIONS

1. Registry of Friendly Societies
2. National Conference of Friendly Societies
3. Building Societies Association
4. National Federation of Housing Societies
5. British Association of Residential Settlements
     Annex : Notes on Certain of the Settlements
6. National Federation of Women's Institutes
7. Women's Voluntary Services
8. British Red Cross Society
9. St. John Ambulance Brigade
10. National Old People's Welfare Committee
11. Nuffield Foundation : The Needs of Old People
12. National Institute for the Blind
13. Central Association for the Care of Cripples
     Annex : Cases from the Surrey Voluntary Association
       for the Care of Cripples
14. Nuffield Foundation : Provident Associations
15. Liberal Party Organisation

In Part IV are printed Memoranda submitted mostly between March and October, 1947, by Organisations which also in most cases appeared before the Inquiry to give oral evidence. To these are added annexes containing further information bearing upon the subject of the Memorandum to which they are annexed.

The Memoranda are given either in full or in copious verbatim extracts. Where omissions have been made, these are indicated by dots. In one or two cases Organisations which submitted Memoranda preferred that these should not be published in the present volume.

I. THE REGISTRY OF FRIENDLY SOCIETIES

Note on the Functions of the Registrar of Friendly Societies and Industrial Assurance Commission

THE principal work of the Department may be summarised under the following main heads :

A.—*Judicial*

(i) *Disputes between Societies and their Members*

Broadly speaking, a dispute between a friendly society, an industrial and provident society or a building society and one of its members may be referred to the Registrar if the rules so direct or if both parties agree to the reference. In practice such disputes form only a very small proportion of the disputes with which the Registrar deals, for the rules commonly provide for settlement by arbitrators appointed within the society.

(ii) *Disputes between Industrial Assurance Policyholders and Collecting Societies or Industrial Assurance Companies*

Under Section 32 of the Industrial Assurance Act, 1923, either party may refer such disputes to the Commissioner without consent of the other provided the amount claimed does not exceed £50 and provided the legality of the policy is not questioned and fraud or misrepresentation is not alleged. If both parties agree, such disputes may be referred without restriction as to the amount claimed or the issues involved. Before the war more than 2,000 disputes were referred for hearing by the Commissioner or his Deputy in each year. This figure fell rapidly during the war, but had begun to rise again by 1946 when the number of disputes referred was 669. The disputes fall into two main classes : those in which liability to pay part or whole of the sum assured is disputed, e.g., on the grounds of misstatement as to health, and those in which the company or society does not dispute liability but is uncertain which of two or more rival claimants it should pay.

Besides its convenience and cheapness to the policyholder, this procedure for arbitration gives the Commissioner some insight into the practical working of industrial assurance. Further, it is reasonably certain that any widespread grievance among the policyholders of a particular company or society will sooner or later reach the Commissioner in the form of a dispute, and if the company or society is at fault the Commissioner's decision in a single dispute may at least point the way to corrective action.

(iii) *Disputes relating to Savings Banks and Savings Certificates*

Under the Trustee Savings Bank Acts any dispute between a savings bank and any depositor or rival claimant to a deposit must be referred to the

Registrar. This jurisdiction has been extended by Acts and Regulations to cover similar disputes relating to deposits in the Post Office Savings Bank, Railway Savings Banks and the Birmingham Municipal Bank, and to Savings Certificates and other investments made through the Post Office. Because of the high proportion of savings invested in the Post Office Savings Bank and in Savings Certificates these form the subject of the majority of the savings bank disputes with which the Registrar deals. The jurisdiction is of growing importance. The number of disputes referred in 1938 was 211 and by 1946 the number had risen to 431.

The Registrar or Commissioner when hearing any of the above disputes has a general power to compel the attendance of witnesses and to examine them on oath. Except when no material question of fact is in dispute, it is the practice to insist on oral evidence from the parties and their witnesses. If these live at any distance from London, a hearing is arranged at the nearest convenient centre. Regulations prescribe a small fee on the reference of an industrial assurance dispute and on the award in a savings bank dispute, but apart from this the parties need incur no expense beyond that of travelling to the place of hearing.

(iv) *Complaints under the Political Fund Rules of Trade Unions*

Under Section 3(2) of the Trade Union Act, 1913, any member of a trade union may complain to the Chief Registrar if he considers that he is aggrieved by a breach of any of the rules governing the political fund of a trade union, and the Registrar after hearing both sides may, if he considers that a breach has been committed, make such order as he thinks just for remedying it. In practice few such complaints are made, and most of these are settled satisfactorily after an exchange of letters. The object of the provision in the 1913 Act was to provide a simple means of enforcing the rules governing the political funds of unions, under which no member may be compelled to contribute to the political fund or victimised if he fails to do so.

The Registrar has no functions as arbitrator between trade unions and their members except on questions arising under the political fund rules.

B.—*Administrative*

(i) *Registration of Rules and Amendments of Rules*

When a society applies for registration it has to submit the whole of its proposed rules. These are examined primarily with a view to seeing that they include all the provisions which the law requires and nothing contrary to the law, and this strictly is still the limit of the Registrar's authority in dealing with applications to register under most of the Acts he administers. In practice he has and uses the opportunity to check inconsistencies and ambiguities, to draw attention to practical difficulties or inequities which may arise under the proposed rules, and to see that the society has made some attempt to relate proposed benefits to contributions. The same functions are exercised whenever the society subsequently amends its rules. Model rules are issued by the Registrar for most of the common forms of association with which he is concerned, and these have been widely adopted. In 1939 the number of new registrations was 278 and of amendments of rules 2,988. In 1946 the corresponding figures were 335 and 1,921.

(ii) *Receiving and Examining Accounts and Valuations*

The form of Annual Return is in most cases prescribed by the Registrar. It comprises a balance sheet, income and expenditure accounts and such other accounts as are appropriate to the particular type of society.

If the accounts have been properly audited a report by the auditor should draw attention to any such irregularities as incorrect accounting, misapplication or wrongful investment of funds, expenditure on management exceeding the amount allowed by the rules, defalcations, inadequate records, unvouched expenditure, over-statement of assets, etc. In societies where the audit is conducted by laymen such irregularities can usually only be deduced from the information or lack of information in the return, and from a comparison of the figures with those in previous returns or in the accounts issued to members. In such cases, explanations are called for and the returns may be sent back for correction. In the case of irregularities of a type which cannot be set right by amendment of the return, the Registrar takes all steps possible to require the officers to rectify them and to ensure that no further irregularity occurs. Where a statutory offence has been committed the Registrar may prosecute the society and the officers responsible, but if the return correctly sets out the society's financial dealings for the year and discloses nothing contrary to law, the Registrar cannot generally speaking take legal action should the return show that the society's affairs have been wastefully or negligently managed.

In the case of friendly societies, the results of quinquennial valuations are of course the surest guide to a society's soundness, besides providing some of the most valuable statistical information on the movement as a whole. Although the Registrar has little power to compel, he can often assist in persuading a society to adopt the recommendations of its valuer.

(iii) *Prosecutions*

The Registrar undertakes prosecutions for offences under the various Acts which are punishable by summary process. Most prosecutions are for failure to send Annual Returns, but proceedings are also taken from time to time for false statements in or omissions from returns, for withholding or misapplication of funds, and for offences by collectors and others under the special provisions governing industrial assurance business. Where serious defalcations come to light and the society has not itself taken proceedings, it is usual to submit the papers to the Director of Public Prosecutions.

(iv) *Inspections and Investigations*

In general the Registrar can only institute inspections at the request of a certain proportion of the members of a society, but there are two important exceptions to this rule. The Industrial Assurance Act, 1923, empowers the

Commissioner to inspect any industrial assurance company or collecting society where he has reason to think that an offence has been or is likely to be committed. These powers were widely used in the decade following the passing of the Act, and the inspections then conducted by the Commissioner resulted in the liquidation of many disreputable industrial assurance offices. Under the Prevention of Fraud (Investments) Act, 1939, the Registrar may, in certain circumstances, investigate the affairs of an industrial and provident society or of a building society ; in the former case he may cancel the registry of the society or compel it to wind up or transfer to the Companies Acts, and in the case of a building society he may forbid the society to invite further investment from any quarter. The disclosures in any type of inspection may of course be brought to the notice of the Director of Public Prosecutions and criminal proceedings may result.

(v) *Amalgamations, Transfers of Engagements, Dissolutions, etc.*

On these matters the Registrar's principal function is to see that the conditions laid down in the Acts have been fulfilled, that resolutions have been passed after properly convened meetings, that the necessary consents of members and persons having claims on the funds have been given and, so far as he may, that the rights of minorities are protected. On an amalgamation or transfer of engagements he has also the quasi-judicial function of deciding after hearing representations by interested parties, whether the proportion of consents normally required by the Acts may be dispensed with. Where two large societies merge, though there may be no substantial opposition to the merger, it may in practice be extremely difficult to obtain all the requisite consents. In such cases, if satisfied that no minority is being unfairly dealt with, the Registrar can use his discretion in allowing the merger to take place. The number of amalgamations, transfers and dissolutions (including cancellings) dealt with by the Registrar in 1939 was 480 and in 1946, 370.

The Registrar has power under all the principal Acts which he administers to cancel a society's registry in certain circumstances. Generally, these circumstances are (a) if the society exists for an unlawful purpose, or has wilfully and after notice violated any provision of the Act, or (b) if it has ceased to exist, or (c) if the society so requests. But if a society has assets the power of cancellation needs to be used with discretion, since one result of cancellation is to remove such control as the Registrar has over the distribution of funds on the dissolution of a registered society.

(vi) *Recording of Documents*

Besides rules and amendments of rules, returns and valuations, notices of amalgamation, transfer or dissolution, etc., there are many other documents which societies are required to send to the Registrar and which are recorded by him and available for public inspection. The most important are notices of appointments of trustees, of changes of registered office, and of change of name (the last requiring the Registrar's approval). The number of miscellaneous notices recorded in 1939 was 5,151, and in 1946 4,811.

(vii) *General Correspondence*

Finally, the Registrar receives each year up to 60,000 letters from societies, their members and others, many of them seeking advice or raising questions of law or practice.

C.—*Reports to Parliament*

Until the outbreak of war the Registrar prepared an annual report to Parliament summarising the work of the Registry during the year, drawing attention to any significant developments and giving statistics of membership, funds, etc., of the various classes of registered associations. These reports were suspended during the war, and their publication has not yet been resumed. The Registrar's report is in five parts, Part 1 dealing generally with all associations in the Registrar's purview, and Parts 2, 3, 4 and 5 dealing in detail with Friendly Societies, Industrial and Provident Societies, Trade Unions and Building Societies respectively. A separate report is prepared by the Industrial Assurance Commissioner on activities within his sphere. Additional research and statistical work is undertaken by the Registrar's staff to meet the special needs of official committees and others concerned with problems of voluntary insurance and associations for thrift.

Apart from its immediate use to the societies themselves and to others interested in their activities, the statistical material collected in the Reports and elsewhere may be of considerable value to social historians of the future. *April*, 1947.

2. NATIONAL CONFERENCE OF FRIENDLY SOCIETIES

. . .

Problems Facing Friendly Societies

(i) *Administrative*

During the course of the past thirty-five years friendly societies have extended their operations and have moulded their constitutions for the purposes of providing adequately for the administration of National Insurance jointly with their voluntary activities.

With the divorcement of State from Voluntary insurance a policy of retrenchment has now to be adopted which will inevitably be involved by the dislocation of closely-woven administrative functions and whilst it is true that societies will be relieved of much detailed administrative work for which they are at present responsible, the consequential relief from necessary expenditure for management will be much less than the administrative income now received under the National Insurance Act which will cease. The economy resulting from joint administration is lost to both parties and whereas the State will experience no difficulty in raising the monies required by compulsory contributions, the cost of the sole administration of the voluntary benefit will be a relatively higher burden for the voluntary sections, necessitating in most cases an increase in contributions for management purposes, payable by members voluntarily insured.

As an illustration of the extent of this problem we estimate that the amount of the reduction in the friendly societies administration income will approach £2,000,000 per annum. Moreover, a serious temporary difficulty will be caused by the loss upon transfer to the Government of trained and experienced staffs.

A further consequence of the abolition of joint administration is the need for separate medical evidence of incapacity in support of a claim for sickness benefit which, subject to any special arrangements conceded by the Government, would involve additional charge to members for medical certificates . . . The matter is at present the subject of negotiations between the Executive and the Government.

(ii) *Effect upon Benefit Funds*

The Actuary advising the Conference on this issue (Mr. Victor A. Burrows, F.I.A., of Messrs. R. Watson & Sons, Consulting Actuaries), reported to the Conference on January 29th, 1946, in supplementation of his Reports on the effects upon Friendly Society Finance and Practice in the following terms :

"Referring to our conversation over the telephone you will remember that in my preliminary report to the National Conference dated 23rd February, 1943, I stated in paragraph (10) that an increase of 12½ per cent. in the level of sickness claims would result in an increase in the total capital liability of all registered friendly societies of roughly £12,650,000. Having regard, however, to the fact that this estimate can only be considered a rough approximation, I expressed the additional liability in the succeeding paragraph as being of the order of ten million to fifteen million pounds.

"If the anticipated increase of 12½ per cent. assumed by the then Government Actuary were increased to 20 per cent., which is the revised percentage adopted in the case of males by the present Government Actuary, as indicated in paragraph 15 of the Appendix to his Report on the Financial Provisions of the National Insurance Bill, 1946, the additional liability falling upon friendly societies would be increased to a corresponding extent. Ignoring for this purpose the larger percentage assumed in the case of women—a reasonable course to adopt having regard to the relatively small female membership amongst friendly societies—this would increase the primary estimate of £12,650,000 to £20,000,000 and the broad estimate given in paragraph (ii) to a liability of the order of sixteen million pounds to twenty-four million pounds."

The Actuary sees no means of meeting the anticipated increases in sickness claims without increasing contributions or reducing benefits. In this connection it is noted that the Chancellor of the Exchequer stated in the House of Commons that the combined compulsory contribution under the new Social Insurance Acts will be allowed as a set-off in the assessment to income tax of corresponding contributions for the insured person concerned. If a similar concession could be granted in respect of voluntary insurance the Actuary advises that this would go some way towards meeting the anticipated increase in the cost of voluntary benefits.

(iii) *Loss of Contact with Insured Persons*

The value of the past personal contact between friendly societies and the State-insured person is indicated by the 25 per cent. increase of voluntary membership which occurred between 1910 and 1937. This contact will be lost and one of the greatest problems which the friendly societies have to face is that of finding an alternative ready means of bringing to the notice of the public the advantages of supplementation by voluntary insurance which, as stated in paragraph 13 of the Government White Paper (see paragraph vii below), will make available "a standard of comfort and amenity which it is no part of a compulsory scheme of social insurance to provide."

(iv) *Effect upon Juvenile Membership*

One of the essential features of friendly society activities is that of association with the young life movement of the country and much attention is paid to the encouragement of juvenile membership. In the past this has been facilitated by the provision of medical, sickness and funeral and other benefits for children. In the future the need for such provision will to a great extent be met by the comprehensive character of the National Health Service and by the death grant under the National Insurance Act in respect of children born after the appointed day. To meet these changes a policy of extension and adaptation of the present practices, particularly in endowment insurances, could be followed. To achieve a steady flow of adult members an active juvenile organisation is a cardinal feature and permits the inculcation of the friendly society outlook and the principles of thrift at an early age.

(v) *Effect on Adult Membership*

Until such time as the general public has assessed the values of the benefits under the new Social Insurance Scheme in relation to the high contributions compulsorily payable and as a cumulative effect of the changed conditions referred to in the earlier paragraphs it is to be expected that there will be not only a reduction in the number of new entrants to friendly societies of persons desiring to effect supplementary insurance but also an increase in the lapse ratio of those who have already made such provision.

(vi) *Government Present Money Policy*

By far the greater number of tables of contributions and benefits in use by societies are based on an assumed interest income of 3 per cent. or over per annum, and it will be clear that a prolonged money policy reducing interest rates as low as those currently obtainable must in due time have an adverse effect upon the financial structure of such societies. Stable financial conditions and full employment however must necessarily be beneficial to friendly societies.

Prospective Policy

(vii) *Benefit Provisions*

There must be development and adaptation within the several systems practised by friendly societies of the terms of contract of membership in order to meet changed demand for supplementation of social insurance benefits by voluntary benefits. As was stated in paragraph 13 of the Government White Paper on Social Insurance (Cmd. 6550) :—

"The Government therefore conclude that the right objective is a rate of benefit which provides a reasonable insurance against want and at the same time takes account of the maximum contribution which the great body of contributors can properly be asked to bear. There still remains the individual's opportunity to achieve for himself in sickness, old age and other conditions of difficulty a standard of comfort and amenity which it is no part of a compulsory scheme of social insurance to provide. And in reserve there must remain a scheme of National Assistance designed to fill the inevitable gaps left by insurance and to supplement it where an examination of individual needs shows that supplement is necessary."

Different types of society will necessarily select varying forms of supplementation. As additional features the provision for a sickness benefit for a short period only of each illness will appeal to some and a comparatively small unit of sickness benefit, coupled with a more extensive death or endowment insurance, to others.

The extent and conditions of the new retirement pensions will clearly render it undesirable for any society to undertake insurance to provide sickness benefit for illnesses occurring after the age of 65 or 70. Experience in fact shows that the only provision for members after those ages should be annuity, death and endowment benefits . . .

(viii) *Extension of Relief during Sickness, etc.*

To the limited extent possible under the National Health Insurance Acts, friendly societies have assisted their members in the determination and prosecution of their claims to Workmen's Compensation and under Common Law. The Industrial Injuries Act, 1946, will, in the main, replace Workmen's Compensation provisions but in the wide field of third party risks and actions at Common Law there will remain a necessity for protection as in the past. The friendly society is in a unique position to be able to assist members in this respect and equally will be able to help by looking after their interests generally when claiming to be entitled to benefits under the new schemes of social insurance. In most cases the members will no doubt be willing to pay any increased contributions which may be necessary to provide this benefit.

(ix) *Relief in Old Age*

The powers of friendly societies in this respect have in the past mainly been used in the provision of a small cash benefit though there have been instances where friendly societies have built and maintained homes for their aged members. This latter might well be extended, in the case of the larger societies, and by the smaller societies in combination, and thus assist in the alleviation of the growing problem of provision for the aged. It is felt that such provision should not be of an institutional character, but whilst allowing for communal recreation and some organised form of amenity, such as catering, should achieve the greatest measure of freedom for the individual and foster a spirit and feeling of independence. In view of the more adequate State provision of pensions it may be possible for organisations to be so formed which will be economically self-supporting.

(x) *Rehabilitation*

. . . The practice of friendly societies to provide a Convalescent Home Benefit, which does not involve any particular form of treatment, is a useful ancillary (to State benefit) and should be continued and encouraged in order to provide facilities for rest and recovery.

(xi) *Extension of Powers under Friendly Societies Acts*

All the foregoing supplementary benefits are possible of provision under existing powers contained in the Friendly Societies Acts and as matter of policy it seems to be undesirable to suggest any extension of the powers under those Acts, such suggestions being used officially as reasons for proposing modification of the privileges extended to friendly societies under the Income Tax Acts. It is probable, however, that it would be an advantage if societies, by the formation of subsidiary bodies, such as are contemplated by Section 8 (4) of the Friendly Societies Act, 1896, would to a greater extent than at present make suitable provision for mutual helpfulness, mental and moral improvement and rational recreation for their members.

(xii) *Determination of Needs*

. . . In the event of any future legislation dealing with the present Poor Law providing for a form of assistance which is based upon a Needs Test, it is recommended that the whole of the individual's income arising from friendly societies' sickness or annuity benefit shall be disregarded.

30th June, 1947

3. THE BUILDING SOCIETIES ASSOCIATION

Historical

The building society movement has a history which extends over a period of at least 166 years, the first known building society having been established at Birmingham in 1781 and there may have been earlier societies of which no record exists. By 1836 societies had become sufficiently numerous to obtain statutory recognition in the Building Societies Act passed in that year, which applied to them certain provisions of the Friendly Societies Act, 1829. There are nine societies in existence which were established more than one hundred years ago.

The Royal Commission on Friendly Societies of 1870 dealt with building societies in its Second Report which was presented in 1872 and this led to the passing of the Building Societies Act, 1874, which is still the main Act under which building societies operate. This Act gave them the privilege of incorporation and, by clarifying and extending their powers, provided a considerable stimulus to the movement, as may be judged by the fact that their total assets grew from £18 millions in 1870 to £51 millions in 1890. Six amending Acts have been passed between 1875 and 1940.

From 1890 to 1914 building societies have a record of useful service and of steady but unspectacular growth. The war of 1914-18 provided the first severe test of their financial soundness and this was surmounted without any difficulty whatever.

The end of that war provided them with a great opportunity of service to the public, which they may claim to have grasped to the full. During the twenty years between the two wars rather more than four million new houses were built, of which three million were provided by private builders. Over two million of these were bought for occupation by their owners with the help of building societies.

Their total assets, which in 1890 were £51 millions, had risen by 1919 to £77 millions, but by 1939 that figure had increased tenfold to £773 millions. During the twenty years to 1939 the building societies lent for the purchase of houses almost £1,500 millions, the amount lent during 1938 being £137 millions . . .

The building societies emerged from the second world war with greater resources than when they entered it. The following preliminary figures issued by the Chief Registrar of Friendly Societies relate to the position at 31st December, 1946 :

Total assets	£876 millions
Reserves	£56 millions
Number of share investors	2,055,000
Number of depositors	731,000
Number of borrowers	1,336,000
Amount advanced during 1946 ..	£187 millions

The last figure may be compared with the figure of £137 millions which was lent in 1938, mainly on new houses, whereas the advances in 1946 were made almost entirely on houses built in 1939 or earlier, in many cases to enable tenants to become owner-occupiers. Some allowance must, of course, be made for the increased prices of houses, but this is offset by the fact that the building society's valuation (which forms the basis of the advance) is a conservative estimate of the real value and discounts the exaggeration in prices which has resulted from scarcity.

Present Organisation

There are in Great Britain 796 permanent building societies and 78 terminating societies. The latter are based on the earliest form of building society and are wound up when each of their members has received and repaid an advance. The growth in the assets of building societies has been accompanied by a steady decrease in the number of societies, which in 1890 amounted to no less than 2,795 . . .

The representative body of building societies is The Building Societies

Association, which was founded in 1869. Its membership includes 383 societies and the total assets of these societies amount to 96 per cent. of the total assets of all societies . . .

Structure and Objects

A building society receives the savings of the public in the form of shares or deposits, but it has no fixed capital. Shares are either fully paid or subscription shares, the latter of which carry an obligation to subscribe a regular amount per month. Depositors, unlike shareholders, are not members of the society but are creditors much in the same way as depositors in any bank. The power to accept deposits is limited by statute and some societies will not accept any deposits. Both shares and deposits can be for small sums upwards and can be repaid at short notice, which is normally one month and is indeed often waived where good cause is shown.

The funds invested in a building society by shareholders and depositors are used in one way only, viz., in making advances on first mortgage of freehold or leasehold property, mainly on dwelling houses for owner-occupation but also on houses to let and to a limited extent on other properties. Any surplus funds are required by statute to be invested in trustee securities . . .

The advances made are in almost every case repayable by monthly instalments over a period which varies but which may be as long as 25 years. There is, however, no statutory requirement that advances must be repaid in this way. In addition, societies will accept complete or partial repayment in a lump sum, e.g., through the operation of a will or the sale of a property, with the result that the average life of a mortgage is only about ten years . . .

The rate of interest which must be paid by borrowers on their advances is governed almost entirely by the rates of interest which the societies must pay to attract and retain shares and deposits and also by the rates earned by the societies' investments in trustee securities.

The current rate charged for mortgages is 4 per cent. (gross) and, though they are under no legal obligation to do so, many building societies have voluntarily reduced the rate of interest payable on existing mortgages granted at a time when higher rates prevailed. Out of this 4 per cent. the building society must meet interest to investors, income tax on such interest and also on the society's taxable profits and expenses of management and provide some contribution to its reserves. Expenses of management are low, amounting on the average only to 11s. 11d. per £100 of assets . . .

Social Policy

The average held by each investor, whether in shares or deposits, is £291 and before the war the great majority of advances were for sums of less than £700, while a considerable proportion were less than £500. These amounts have, of course, increased with the rise in prices of houses, but the building societies still find their main supporters among the people of moderate incomes . . .

Suggestions have been made from time to time that building societies should extend the scope of their activities. One of the suggestions most frequently made is that they should themselves undertake the building of houses, which in fact was done by a few of the very early societies more than 100 years ago. The Association ventures, however, to doubt whether this development would in fact be to the public advantage and it thinks that the public is best served by the separation of the two functions which at present obtains.

Societies do, however, give a great deal of service to their borrowers after purchase and this has been developed to an enormous extent in connection with cases of war damage, where societies have (apart from making large contributions under the War Damage Act, 1943) undertaken on behalf of their borrowers a great deal of work in connection with claims and the maintenance of their legal rights. At the same time societies have voluntarily extended the most considerate treatment to those borrowers whose homes have been destroyed by enemy action. . . .

Criticisms of Building Societies
"Building Societies are Monopolies"

They are far from being monopolies. Apart from competition among themselves (there are 874 separate societies), advances for house purchase are made by insurance companies, banks, friendly societies and other bodies, private persons and also by local authorities under subsidised conditions . . . While suggesting that building societies are too powerful, none of their critics has produced any evidence that they have misused such power as they are alleged to possess. This criticism is to some extent cancelled by the other criticism that there are too many building societies. As already mentioned, the number of societies is declining steadily and a case could be made out for prohibiting the creation of further societies unless it could be shown that the creation was necessary in the public interest.

"Building Societies Restrict the Mobility of Labour"

The suggestion was that, because a man owned a house, he would not be so willing as a tenant might be to accept employment in another part of the country. The societies never accepted that there was any real validity in this argument and there can be no justification whatever for it now. Indeed it may be argued that the only mobile person is one who has a house to sell and can therefore afford to buy another one in the district required and that the least mobile person is a tenant. However, building societies do not normally make advances to persons in the mobile labour groups. It should be remembered, too, that a mortgage can easily be transferred if a house is sold and there must be thousands of cases of borrowers who have been prepared to move their home in the pursuit of their career. . . .

"Building Societies encourage people to buy houses they cannot afford"

If there were any truth in this allegation it would soon be the end of building societies, for a society cannot gain, though it may well lose, if a borrower should be unable to keep up his repayments. It has, however, been suggested, even by those who should know better, that a building society which sells the property of a defaulting borrower can retain any surplus which may be realised. This is the opposite of the truth ; building societies are required by law to send an account of the transactions to the borrower together with any surplus realised.

The more important point is, however, that societies take great pains to impress upon prospective borrowers the full extent of their future commitments (including particularly their responsibility for repairs) and discourage them from undertaking too heavy an obligation. If, however, the circumstances of a borrower change and it becomes difficult for him to keep up his repayments, societies invariably do their best, by accepting modified payments for a period or in other ways, to assist the borrower to continue in ownership. This policy was most fully tested during the recent war when the hundreds of thousands of borrowers whose houses were rendered uninhabitable through war damage found that their building society was prepared to deal most sympathetically with the resultant financial hardship. Had it been otherwise, there would, of course, have been a great public outcry : as it was, the number of cases in which the Association was consulted by the Treasury during the six years of war because the borrower was not satisfied with his society's treatment was six, all of which were disposed of without difficulty.

The extent of this problem can be gauged from the official figures published by the Registrar which show :

(a) Cases in which the property has been more than 12 months in the possession of the society, and

(b) Cases where the repayments are more than 12 months in arrear.

The figures given below, which represent percentages of the total value of all building society mortgages, show how very small is the proportion of such cases :

Year		Cases in Possession	Cases in Arrear
1938	..	0.16 per cent.	0.10 per cent.
1946	..	0.23 per cent.	0.96 per cent.

"Building Societies encourage Jerry-Building"

. . . From the strict point of view, a building society is concerned with the value of a house as security for the money to be lent and it must also be borne in mind that a house is usually finished before the building society is approached.

However, building societies have no desire to rest upon their strict legal responsibilities and they recognise their ability to assist in the improvement of standards of construction. To this end they have, from the first, taken a prominent part in the establishment of the National House-Builders' Registration Council which has received the statutory approval of the Minister of Health and the Treasury. Its activities have recently been commended to local authorities by Mr. Aneurin Bevan.

To be admitted to the register established by the Council, a builder must agree to build only "certified" houses, which the Council inspects five times during the course of construction and, after completion to its satisfaction, the Council issues a certificate that the house complies with the standards laid down in the Council's model specification. The certificate carries with it a guarantee by the builder to make good any defects which appear within two years and which are consequent upon non-compliance with the standards of construction laid down in the model specification.

"Building Societies charge high rates of interest to borrowers"

Their present charge is 4 per cent. (gross) which can hardly be considered extortionate. . . .

When a borrower executes a mortgage he almost invariably agrees to pay a certain rate of interest throughout the period of the mortgage. Between the two wars this rate was for some time 5 per cent. and even higher but, although under no obligation to do so, building societies have voluntarily reduced the rate, in some cases to the current rate of 4 per cent. . . .

3rd June, 1947

4. NATIONAL FEDERATION OF HOUSING SOCIETIES

Name

The National Federation of Housing Societies was founded in 1935 . . . It was incorporated under the Board of Trade in June, 1935, with a membership of 35 affiliated societies and it is recognised under Section 96 of the Housing Act, 1936, as the "central association" of the Voluntary Housing Societies as defined in Section 188 of the same Act . . .

Objects

The purpose of the Federation was and is to co-ordinate the work and policy of its member societies, and to promote new societies, to represent their interests to the various Government Departments and to watch all legislation which affects them.

Membership

The membership of the Federation is confined to Housing Societies within the meaning of Section 188 of the Housing Act, 1936 . . . There is also a class of subscribing or associate members without voting rights. These are interested individuals, who, for a subscription of 10s. per annum, receive the Federation's literature and notices of all conferences and meetings.

At the present time the Federation has a membership of 320 affiliated societies in England, Scotland, Wales and Northern Ireland. This number is increasing month by month.

Regional Organisation

In 1946 the membership was grouped into regional organisations, and there are now six regions in operation . . . There is also a grouping of the Welsh Societies under the Welsh Town Planning and Housing Trust, Cardiff. The

London Societies (some 76 in number), being so close to headquarters, have no special regional machinery—but meet from time to time for the exchange of news and ideas.

A small grant from headquarters is made to each region to cover expenses, but all the regional officers are voluntary, and at present each region enjoys the hospitality of the office of a member society.

Administration

Council. The Federation is governed by a Council of 21 members, 15 of whom are elected in annual meeting, with six co-opted members. Each member of the council is a representative member of a member housing society. One-third of the members retire annually and are eligible for re-election. Members of Council are entitled to travelling and out-of-pocket expenses only . . .

Member Societies. The Housing Society movement is over 100 years old and housing societies have been on the statute books since 1919. Up to the beginning of the war they had built or reconditioned some 50,000 houses and flats. The Ministry of Health monthly returns for 30th April, 1947, are as follows :

Permanent Houses—Housing Associations

The number of houses on licences issued or in respect of which approval has been given and the number of houses completed to the end of March and April, 1947, respectively, are as follows :

	31st March, 1947	30th April, 1947
Number of houses on licences issued ..	481	520
Number of houses on approvals given ..	749	1,033
Houses—construction begun	718	757
Houses under construction at end of period ..	573	586
Houses completed	145	171

(Since January 1st, 1946)

When building houses to let and working in co-operation with their local authorities, housing societies are eligible for the same subsidies and the same priorities as the local authorities themselves.

The member housing societies are usually registered under the Industrial and Provident Societies Act or under the Companies Act, 1929. Out of the present total membership of 320, 95 per cent. are registered under the Industrial and Provident Societies Act, and a considerable proportion of these have, by amendment of their rules, acquired charitable status. All of them, in conforming with the definition in Section 188 of the Housing Act, 1936, are prohibited from trading for commercial profit and the rate of interest on their capital is restricted by the Treasury rate for the time being (at present 5 per cent.). Generally speaking, housing societies pay interest and dividend between $2\frac{1}{2}$ per cent. and 4 per cent. per annum . . .

Finance

The Federation is maintained by the annual affiliation fees of its member societies, the scale being a minimum of three guineas and the maximum 25 guineas. Between these limits the subscriptions are based on 0.2 per cent. of gross rents plus subsidy from the ordinary societies, and 0.1 per cent. from the charitable societies. The estimated income from this source for 1947 is £1,250. There is in addition a small income of about £30 from associate members' fees, and a further small grant of £500 for services rendered to, and a survey for, another organisation. There is also a certain income from registration fees. The estimated expenditure for 1947 is £5,548.

During the first five years of its existence the Federation had an annual grant of £1,000 from the Ministry of Health and the Department of Health for Scotland. During the war this was discontinued, and there were given instead small deficiency grants. Arrangements are being made to go back to the basis of an annual grant—but the amount is to be fixed each year in accordance with the Federation's programme of work, and ability to increase its own income from its member societies. This at present is extremely difficult as there is comparatively little building, and the progress of work is slow, except for the smaller reconditioning schemes—which are not, of course, eligible for Exchequer subsidy, and whose subscriptions are in the lowest category.

The amount received last year from the Ministry and the Department was £1,500. The balance sheet for 1946 showed an excess of income over expenditure of £138 0s. 10d.

The financial position of the Federation has at all times been precarious, and there is no doubt at all that the work could expand in many directions if it were more secure. The Federation desires to publish a number of pamphlets, to organise more conferences, to do more research (for which additional staff would be required) and to develop in many ways—but it has to cut its coat according to its cloth . . .

The present administrative machinery is adequate and representative—but the financial structure is a great problem. A great deal more field work could be done if the Federation could employ a bigger staff, both at headquarters and in the regional organisation. As regards the future, much will depend on the general housing situation and the allocation of labour and materials to housing societies, whose schemes rank second to those of local authorities which at present are the chosen instruments of the Government for the production of houses.

During the last two years the Federation has received growing recognition by the Ministry of Health, and its liaison with the Ministry of Works, Ministry of Town and Country Planning, and the Board of Trade, over housing matters, has been greatly strengthened . . .

Legislation

The Federation awaits with some concern the clarification of the position with regard to exemption for housing societies from development charges under the Town and Country Planning Bill. It is also concerned with the revision of the Rent Restriction Acts—as unlike those of local authorities—housing society houses come within the scope of the Acts. It is therefore impossible to increase rents where necessary, to meet increased costs and maintenance charges.

Conclusion

There is a wide field for housing society expansion—particularly in the housing of industrial workers and of old people. Some housing societies, working on Peckham Health Centre lines, have very big schemes for mixed development. A few of the societies are able to work by direct labour, and these schemes are making good progress. The Minister of Town and Country Planning has stated on several occasions that he hopes to receive the co-operation of housing societies in the development of the new towns . . .

June, 1947

5. BRITISH ASSOCIATION OF RESIDENTIAL SETTLEMENTS

At the present time the Association represents 48 Settlements (some with subsidiaries) in England and Scotland. In their affiliations, constitutions and work, they vary considerably as the neighbourhoods in which they are situated also vary. But they have certain characteristics in common. Thus :

(1) They are all voluntary organisations depending for their existence on voluntary enterprise.

(2) All base their work on the neighbourly relationships made possible by residence in the area served.

Needs change. The preoccupation of Settlements with material needs which was characteristic of earlier days has largely disappeared as material conditions of life have improved, and the State has developed common provision for social well-being. Today Settlements are mainly concerned to promote happier social relationships and a fuller use of possibilities opened to the individual by a more equitable distribution of means, a better education, more free time for the development of personal interests. They are increasingly concerned to stimulate the growth of clubs or other neighbourhood groupings which are self-led and self-supporting rather than those of an earlier pattern which were often managed and financed by the Settlement ; and this principle of increasing self-support is evident in almost all Settlement activities . . .

The gradual change of emphasis is reflected in the personnel of the governing body ultimately responsible for maintaining the Settlement, rather than in any change of formal constitution. Thus, while most Settlements have one or more members of the governing body who are also members of the local authority, it is only in a very few instances that such authorities have been given the right to appoint such representatives. More frequently the university, college or other organisation with which the Settlement is associated is given representation . . .

...The great majority of Settlements are in receipt of local grants in aid of specific pieces of work, such as youth clubs and community centres. Most, if not all of the Settlements, have a recognised and respected place in the local community. In most cases their work is steadily expanding, and would expand more rapidly if the difficulties of building and premises were not so great.

The fact that the existence of the Settlements depends on voluntary support —no case is known where a grant from the local authority is made towards the general work of the Settlement—has the advantage that they are free to initiate experiments and to criticise public provision without embarrassment, and this freedom has always been one of their principal assets . . .

The finance of the Settlements not only reflects in this way their relationship with local authorities. It also illustrates very clearly the change of relationship with those taking part in Settlement activities . . .

Of a total income of £10,000, something like one-third may come from grants and something under one-third from voluntary subscribers. The rest is likely to be met from contributions by "users" and other miscellaneous income from activities. In one of the more active provincial settlements 60 per cent. of the Settlement turnover comes from its members and users, and this condition is not uncommon . . .

The change in material conditions is also reflected in a change in voluntary workers. Few people today can give full-time, unpaid service and where the nature of the work makes full-time service necessary, paid workers must be engaged. But the growth of paid work does not imply any decline of the spirit of voluntary service, for the number of voluntary workers giving part-time service has vastly increased. The change is indeed a healthy one for two reasons. First, it is evidence that serious social service needs skilled technical direction. Second, it has made it possible to draw on a reservoir of service which was formerly untapped. It is indeed commonly true to say that every addition to the number of paid workers results in a correspondingly larger number of unpaid helpers.

It is difficult to generalise about the nature of Settlement activities, but the following are characteristic of the majority.

(1) They fulfil the office of adviser and friend to the people of their neighbourhood.

(2) They provide informal education through clubs catering for all age groups with special emphasis on children and young people. In these clubs there is observable an increasing measure of democratic control. In most cases such clubs are now aided by grants from the Ministry of Education or the Local Education Authority. In a growing proportion a considerable share of the cost is met by members' contributions, but most still depend largely on other voluntary sources of income.

(3) They provide opportunities of training and experience to large numbers of men and women who are taking up social service as a career either with a voluntary organisation or in a public service. No comparable opportunity is

obtainable apart from the Settlements. In view of the growing number of official appointments for which such training and experience are desirable and of the growth in the social science departments of the universities there is room for a further extension of this side of Settlement work.

(4) The study of local conditions and needs and the initiation of experimental work are important functions of some of the Settlements.

Almost all Settlements feel the need for expansion but are handicapped by insufficient funds, although the proportion of expenses borne by "users" is increasing and grant aid from public funds helps to finance specific pieces of work.

. . .

ANNEX TO MEMORANDUM 5

NOTES ON CERTAIN OF THE SETTLEMENTS

The following information was supplied by the British Association of Residential Settlements. It consists of brief notes on 39 of the Settlements comprising the Association. The information includes, in each case, the founder and date of foundation ; to what denomination, if any, the Settlement is confined ; whether there is residential accommodation now available (the war, amongst other things has affected their facilities), the activities which they provide for their members ; and the accommodation provided on their premises for other associations. Perusal of these notes will indicate the numerous contacts which the Settlements have with their neighbourhoods.

The present-day needs of the Settlements, financial and other, are often urgent, and a brief statement of them is appended to these notes.

Two of the London Settlements—Toynbee Hall and the Mary Ward Settlement, being included in the Directory of Some Leading Agencies in Part VI, are omitted from this Annex.

A.—LONDON SETTLEMENTS

1. BEAUCHAMP LODGE, WARWICK CRESCENT, PADDINGTON
Date of Foundation : 1940.
Founded by : Two or three Paddington residents who formed a Voluntary Committee.
Denomination : None.
Residential Accommodation : Four staff, 13 residents.
Adult Activities : Men : Indoor Games, Football, Toc H Group. Women : Handicrafts, Old Time Dancing. Mixed : Drama, Games, Talks, Poultry Club.
All men taking part in the above are, with the exception of the Poultry Club, under 30.
Children's Activities : Mixed : Crafts, Drama, Dancing. Play Centre : 7-13. Dramatics, Dancing, Indoor Games, Woodwork, Outdoor Games.
Accommodation provided for other Social Agencies : Toc H, Paddington Poultry Club, Paddington Society, Children's Clothing Committee, I.C.A.A.
Special Activities : Communal Feeding Centre catering for 120 daily. Twenties Club, formed by a group of young men and women returned from the Forces.
Country or Seaside House : None.

2. BEDE HOUSE, 351 SOUTHWARK PARK ROAD, BERMONDSEY, S.E.16

Date of Foundation : 1939. (But the group responsible for starting Bede House Association was the one in charge of the Princess Marie Louise Settlement, Jamaica Road, founded by Princess Marie Louise in 1908.)

Denomination : Definitely a Christian Community of all denominations.

Residential Accommodation : For 14 men and women.

Adult Activities : No clubs (but see below, Bede House).

Children's Activities : Clubs in Clare College Arch, Raymouth Road.

Lady Gomm Youth Centre : Rebuilding should be completed in six months, and will be an up-to-date Youth Centre.

Clare College Arch : Has been handed over to National Association of Boys' Clubs for three years. Opened in September this year.

Convent in Jamaica Road : Being converted. Architect's plans already out. Boy Scout Headquarters.

Bede House : Linked up with Student Christian Movement, which has a representative on the Council. Used as a Transit Camp during the summer for overseas visitors to "Oslo" (Christian Youth) World Federation of Youth, Works Camps, etc., etc. Is practically self-supporting. At the moment, Leaders' salaries less than £500 per annum. Architect, lawyer, technical adviser, accountant, etc., give their services. Urgent need for money to supplement various schemes.

3. BERMONDSEY SETTLEMENT, FARNCOMBE STREET, S.E.16

Date of Foundation : 1889.

Founded by : Dr. Scott Lidgett.

Denomination : The Methodist Conference appoints.

Residential Accommodation : For seven men, six women (reduced by war damage).

Adult Activities : All mixed : University Extension Lectures, Choral Society, Dramatic Society, Insurance Societies.

Children's Activities : Boys' Brigade, Old Boys' Association, Play Centre. Nursery School now taken over by Local Authority.

Accommodation provided for other Social Agencies : Various Societies. Since the war has provided accommodation for two bombed-out Schools.

Special Activities : Runs Lidgett Hall, Rotherhithe (formerly Alice Barlow House). Youth Centre, Children's Clinics, Women's Holiday Fund.

Country or Seaside House : Fairhaven, Holmbury St. Mary, Dorking. Since 1936, 364 children have had holidays there as well as many older men and women.

4. BERNHARD BARON ST. GEORGE'S JEWISH SETTLEMENT

Date of Foundation : 1919.

Founded by : West London and Liberal Jewish Synagogues.

Undenominational.

Connected with : National Association of Boys' Clubs, National Association of Girls' Clubs and Mixed Clubs, Association of Jewish Youth.

Residential Accommodation : For 16.

Adult Activities : Men : Old Boys' Club, Synagogues Guild. Women : Old Girls' Club, Synagogue Women's Guild.

Children's Activities : Three Clubs for groups from 11-18, 350 members. Three Clubs for groups from 10-18, 250 members. Play Centre. (Slowly recovering).

Accommodation provided for other Agencies : N.S.P.C.C. Offices, Citizens' Advice Bureau, Poor Man's Lawyer, L.C.C. Minor Ailments Clinic, Care Committees, National Association of Boys' Clubs Selection Boards, Society for the Blind.

Special Activities : Closed Board of British Legion. Progressive Synagogue housed in the Building. Settlement Players' Dramatic Society. Annual Camps for 500.

5. BISHOP CREIGHTON HOUSE, LILLIE ROAD, FULHAM, S.W.6

Date of Foundation : May, 1908.

Founded by : The wife and family of the late Bishop Creighton and his friends.

Denomination : Church of Egland.

Residential Accommodation : For 10 in House ; students sleep out.

Adult Activities : Mixed : Old People's Club, Parents' Club, Adult Club. Women : Women's Fellowship.

Children's Activities : Youth Club for Boys, Youth Club for Girls, Play Centre every day.
Accommodation provided for other Social Agencies : W.E.A., Social Workers' Lunch Club, Child Guidance Clinic, Care Committee Work (with its own Office), Scouts, Cubs, L.C.C. (just opening classes for maladjusted children).

6. CAMBRIDGE HOUSE, 131-139 CAMBERWELL ROAD, LONDON, S.E.5
Date of Foundation : 1897.
Founded by : Trinity Court Settlement (founded 1889) and a Public Meeting of the University of Cambridge, presided over by the Vice-Chancellor.
Denomination : Non-denominational. "Any house conducted by the Society shall be conducted on a basis as wide as that of the University of Cambridge."
Connected with : Cambridge University.
Residential Accommodation : For 19.
Adult Activities (over 18 years) : Community Centre including the Corner Club, Old People's Club, Mothers' Club, Camberwell Model Parliament, South London Film Society and Camberwell Centre Rural Music Schools' Association.
Children's Activities (under 18 years) : Sidney Sussex Boys' Club (10-14 years), Magdalene and Jesus Girls' Club (14-18 years), Magdalene and Jesus Boys' Club (14-18 years).
Accommodation provided for other Social Agencies : Cambridge House Free Legal Advice Centre, L.C.C. Children's Care Committee, Red Cross Emergency Help Committee, Hospital Savings Association, Camberwell and District Marriage Guidance Council, Children's Country Holiday Fund, Women's Holiday Fund, Provisional Committee Arts Council (Camberwell).

7. CANNING TOWN WOMEN'S SETTLEMENT, CUMBERLAND ROAD, LONDON, E.13
Date of Foundation : 1893.
Founded by : Miss Cheetham.
Connected with : Congregational Union.
Denomination : None.
Residential Accommodation : For three, plus staff.
Adult Activities : Women : Family Club, Sisterhood, Wellington Guild.
Children's Activities : Mixed : Junior and Senior Clubs, Toddlers' Club (once weekly), Nursery School, Play Centre.
Accommodation provided for other Social Agencies : S.S.A.F.A., Citizens' Advice Bureau, Hospital Savings Association.
Country or Seaside House : Loughton Lodge Convalescent Home, Essex.

8. CAXTON HOUSE, 112 FONTHILL ROAD, N.4
Date of Foundation : January, 1944.
Founded by : Combined efforts of group of local social workers, clergy, etc., under auspices of B.A.R.S.
Denomination : Non-sectarian.
Residential Accommodation : Staff only (four or five).
Adult Activities : Darby and Joan Club, Religious Meeting, Women's Own Club, Make Do and Mend Class, Mixed Youth Club up to 20 years.
Children's Activities : Boys' Club (12-14), Girls' Clubs (8-10 and 11-14), Brownie Pack, Infant Welfare Clinic.
Accommodation provided for other Social Agencies : Children's Country Holiday Fund, Old People's Welfare Committee, Working Men's Club Fund Meeting.
Country or Seaside House : None.

9. CHRIST'S COLLEGE AND KATHERINE LOW SETTLEMENT, HIGH STREET, BATTERSEA
Date of Foundation : 1924. (Christ's College Boys' Club, 1904.)
Founded by : Katherine Low and Christ's College, Cambridge.
Denomination : Church of England.
Connected with : Christ's College, Cambridge ; St. James, Malvern ; Abbots Hill, and West Hill Girls' Schools.
Residential Accommodation : For eight.
Adult Activities : Women : Make Do and Mend, Social Club. Mixed : One Club, Old People's Club.

Children's Activities : Boys : Youth Club, P.T., Boxing, Painting, Handicrafts. Junior : Ditto. Girls : Youth Club, Painting, Needlework, Dancing and Ballet Class. Junior : Ditto.

Special Activities : Monthly Meeting of Social Workers and Teachers, Free Legal Advice Bureau, Hospital Savings Association.

10. DOCKLAND SETTLEMENT NO. 1, CANNING TOWN, E.16
Date of Foundation : 1905.
Founded by : Sir Reginald Kennedy-Cox of the former Malvern Mission.
Denomination : Church of England.
Connected with : The London-over-the-Border.
Residential Accommodation : For 20 men, 18 women.
Adult Activities : Clubs : Grandfathers', Married Men's, Men's, Women's. Total membership well over 1,000.
Children's Activities : Boys : Senior, Middle and Junior. Girls : Ditto. Nursery School, 30 children.
Accommodation provided for other Social Agencies : British Legion, Citizens' Advice Bureau (until November), Free Church Organisations which have been bombed out.
Special Activities : Swimming, Theatricals, Carpentry, Plastic Work, Language Classes, two Gymnasia.
Country or Seaside House : One at Herne Bay, one at Margate, one at Maidenhead ; also two Holiday Camps.

11. DOCKLAND SETTLEMENT NO. 2, EAST FERRY ROAD, ISLE OF DOGS
Date of Foundation : 1923.
Founded by : Sir R. Kennedy-Cox.
Denomination : Church of England.
Connected with : University College School.
Residential Accommodation : For four.
Adult Activities : Men : Clubs, P.T., Music, Drama, Discussion Groups, Crafts. Women : P.T., Music, Needlework, Drama, Religion. Mixed : Music, Drama, Religion.
Children's Activities : Boys : Junior and Senior Groups, Sports. Girls : P.T., Music, Drama, etc.
Accommodation provided for other Social Agencies : Army Cadets.
Country or Seaside House : Fifield, Berks.

12. DOCKLAND SETTLEMENT NO. 8, HEATHWAY, DAGENHAM, ESSEX
Date of Foundation : 1937.
Founded by : The Dockland Settlements.
Denomination : Church of England.
Connected with : Brentwood School, Essex.
Residential Accommodation : For five.
Adult Activities : Men's Club, Football and Cricket. Women's Club : Make and Mend and Keep Fit Classes. Mixed : Recreational.
Children's Activities : Boys' Clubs, Girls' Clubs, Play Centre.
Accommodation provided for other Social Agencies : Magistrates' Interviewing Room, Red Cross Interviewing Room, H.S.A., Coal Club, Cadets.
Special Activities : Red Cross After-Care, Mental Welfare, Own Chapel.
Country or Seaside House : Use of Holiday Home at Herne Bay, Camp Site at Nazeing.

13. LADY MARGARET HALL SETTLEMENT, 131 KENNINGTON ROAD, LONDON, S.E.11
Date of Foundation : 1897.
Founded by : Bishop Talbot and Members of Lady Margaret Hall, Oxford.
Denomination : Church of England.
Connected with : Lady Margaret Hall, University of Oxford.
Residential Accommodation : For 24 persons.
Adult Activities : Women : Townswomen's Guild, 40 members ; Old People's Club, 25 members. Mixed : Community Centre, 105 members ; Gardens Guild, 50 members ; A.R.P. Wardens' Club, 30 members ; Senior Club Pensioners, 25 members.

Children's Activities (under 18 years) : Boys' Junior Club, maximum 40 members ; Mixed Open Club (14-18), maximum 100 (shortly re-opening) ; Children's Library (5-14), 150 members (run by the children themselves, with their own Librarians).

Accommodation provided for other Social Agencies : Lambeth Invalid Children's Aid Association, Family Welfare Association Sub-Office.

Special Activities : An important function of the Settlement is to act as a meeting place, formally or informally, of Church Workers of the neighbourhood.

Country or Seaside House : Hut for Youth Club at Cudham. The Settlement helps to support and organise the South London Family Camp at Deal. Agent for South London for Princess Mary Home for Women at Bognor and organises Children's Country Holiday Fund for North Lambeth.

14. OXFORD HOUSE IN BETHNAL GREEN (INC.), MAPE STREET, E.2
Date of Foundation : 1884.
Founded by : Oxford Graduates.
Denomination : Church of England.
Residential Accommodation : For 20 to 25.
Adult Activities : Oxford House Club, Oxford House Loan Club, Oxford House Players, Friendly Club, Oxford House Advisory Committee, Discover Your Neighbour Training Course.
Children's Activities : Webbe Club for Boys (14-18) ; Oxford House Girls' Club (14-18).
Accommodation provided for other Social Agencies : British Legion, Welsh Club, Trade Unions, Friendly Societies, Political Groups.
Special Activities : London Agent for Free Holidays for Old Age Pensioners at Westcliff.
Camps : Sites for Adults at Brentwood, for Junior Boys at Dorking, and for Senior Boys at Upminster.

15. PILGRIM HOUSE, DACE ROAD, LONDON, E.3
Date of Foundation : 1931.
Founded by : St. Margaret's House, E.2.
Denomination : None.
Residential Accommodation : For the Warden.
Adult Activities : Men : Football Club. Women : Club, and L.C.C. Classes in Dressmaking and Dancing.
Children's Activities : Boys' Club, Girls' Club, Mixed Dancing Class, Play Centre (4-6 p.m., 160 children), Dramatics, Dancing, Percussion Band, etc.
Special Activities : Citizens' Advice Bureau, 110 Bow Road ; Two Hospital Savings Association Groups, S.S.A.F.A. ; Care Committee of Local School.
Country or Seaside House : None.

16. PRESBYTERIAN SETTLEMENT, EAST INDIA DOCK ROAD, POPLAR, E.14
Date of Foundation : 1899.
Founded by : Women of the Presbyterian Church of England.
Denomination : Presbyterian.
Residential Accommodation : For 10 men and women.
Adult Activities : Women : Afternoon Meetings, three times weekly. Mixed : Parents' Evenings.
Children's Activities : Boys (11-15), Girls (11-14), Mixed Youth (14-20), Play Centres (separate ones for Boys and Girls).
Accommodation provided for other Social Agencies : Hospital Savings Association, Federation of Social Workers, Care Committee of two schools.
Special Activities : Citizens' Advice Bureau, open Monday to Friday.
Country or Seaside House : Darmers, Nazeing, Essex.

17. RATCLIFFE SETTLEMENT, E.14
The Settlement was not founded but grew naturally out of the life and efforts of two or three women who made the neighbourhood their home.
Residential Accommodation : For eight women.
Undenominational.

127

Activities : Only activity at present is Loan Club. This paid out £16,000 at Christmas, 1947.
Country or Seaside House : Ratcliff Cottage, Epping Forest.
All classes came to an end in 1939 but will be restarted when we get help.

18. St. Francis House, Church Hill, Woolwich

Date of Foundation : 1918.
Founded by : Bishop Hough (late Bishop of Woolwich), Canon Hutchison, Miss Alice Green and others.
Denomination : Church of England.
Connected with : Southwark Diocese.
Residential Accommodation : For 10 residents.
Activities : All the work of the Settlement is in connection with the Churches, and though there are Women's Meetings in the House, they are all Parish Meetings.
Accommodation provided for other Social Agencies : Moral Welfare Office ; Local Church Workers' Meeting.
Country or Seaside House : Two houses, which give a week's holiday to about 630 people annually.

19. St. Hilda's East, 3 Old Nichol Street, Bethnal Green

Date of Foundation : 1889.
Founded by : Guild of Cheltenham Ladies' College.
Denomination : Interdenominational.
Residential Accommodation : For 20.
Adult Activities : Women's Fellowship, Young Mothers' Club.
Children's Activities : Junior Boys' Club (8-13), Girl Guides, Youth Club (14-20), Junior Girls' Club, Play Centre for Children (3-8).
Accommodation provided for other Social Agencies : Shoreditch and Bethnal Green Marriage Guidance Council ; Bethnal Green and Shoreditch Skilled Employment Committee ; Soldiers', Sailors' and Airmen's Help Committee ; Children's Country Holiday Fund ; Bethnal Green Hospital Savings Association ; Care Committee Work for two Schools ; Training Centre for Students.
Country or Seaside House : None.

20. St. Margaret's House, 21 Old Ford Road, Bethnal Green

Date of Foundation : 1889.
Founded by : A group of Oxford women in response to a request by the Rev. A. Winnington Ingram to do work for women and girls similar to that done by Oxford House for boys.
Denomination : Church of England.
Connected with : St. Hilda's College, Oxford.
Residential Accommodation : For 24.
Adult Activities : Women : Three Afternoon Clubs and one Evening Club. Mixed : Young People's Clubs (16-25) six evenings per week. Old Age Pensioners' Club, once per week.
Children's Activities : Boys : Two evenings per week. Girls : Four evenings per week. Play Centre one evening and Saturday morning.
Accommodation provided for other Social Agencies : Hospitals Savings Association, St. John Ambulance Brigade. L.C.C. has use of buildings in new house for Occupational Centre for defective children.
Special Activities : Citizens' Advice Bureau for Bethnal Green, Children's Care Committee for two local Schools, Women's Holiday Fund, Children's Country Holiday Fund.
Country or Seaside House : None.

21. Talbot Settlement, 14 Bromley Hill, Bromley, Kent

Date of Foundation : 1900.
Founded by : Supporters of Cambridge House, to provide for the Women's Work.
Denomination : Church of England.
Residential Accommodation : For nine women.
Adult Activities : Women's Club, Senior Section, Youth Club.
Most of the work with adults is done in connection with local churches.

MEMORANDA BY ORGANISATIONS

Children's Activities : Boys (8-11, 11-14, 14-18) : Boxing, Football. Girls (8-11, 11-14, 14-18) : Drama, Dressmaking. Play Centre.
Accommodation provided for other Social Agencies : Hospital Savings Association Office.
Special Activities : Club for Mentally Defective Girls still at school, Training of Club Workers. Daughter House on new isolated Housing Estate at Horn Park, S.E.12. Resident Worker. Hut for Church on Sunday used for Clubs during the week.

22. TIME AND TALENTS, 187 BERMONDSEY STREET, S.E.1
Date of Foundation : 1895.
Founded by : Time and Talents Guild.
Denomination : Interdenominational.
Residential Accommodation : For Resident Housekeeper and two Guests.
Adult Activities : Women : Singing Group Meeting once a week. Mixed : Borough Club and two Industrial Social Clubs. Girls : Clubs for four age groups.
Accommodation provided for other Social Agencies : Borough Council of Social Service, permanent office ; large Clubroom available for letting for neighbourhood activities.
Special Activities : Hospitals Savings Association one night per week, Lunch Club for Social Workers.
Country or Seaside House : Thatched Cottage, Godden Green, Sevenoaks. The House is open to everyone except children under five.

23. TIME AND TALENTS, DOCKHEAD HOUSE, 225 ABBEY STREET, S.E.1
Date of Foundation : 1895.
Founded by : Time and Talents Guild.
Denomination : Interdenominational.
Residential Accommodation : For two Staff and Students.
Adult Activities : Men : Football, Team and Coaching, P.T. Women : Dressmaking, Handicrafts and Singing Classes. Mixed : Dancing Class, Discussion and Social Group, Veterans' Club. There is a Canteen at each Club.
Children's Activities : Boys : P.T., Football. Girls : Handicrafts, Drama. Dancing Class for Boys and Girls. Play Centre. Saturday morning.
Accommodation provided for other Social Agencies : S.S.A.F.A. Office.
Special Activities : Wednesday afternoon Mission Group.

24. QUEENS HOUSE, ROTHERHITHE, 53 ROTHERHITHE STREET, S.E.16
(Branch of Time and Talents)
Date of Foundation : 1941 (Queens College, Cambridge, Mission, 1907-39).
Founded by : Miss G. E. Richards and Mr. S. Smith.
Denomination : Interdenominational.
Connected with : Time and Talents Association, Bermondsey Street, S.E.1.
Residential Accommodation : For five Students and Staff.
Adult Activities : Parents' Association (of Youth Club Members), Veterans' Club, in co-operation with Local Council of Social Service.
Children's Activities : Boys : Junior Club (11-14) ; Girls : Junior Club (11-14) ; Mixed : Junior Club (14-20) ; Play Centre.
Accommodation provided for other Social Agencies : 7th Bermondsey Troop Boy Scouts.
Country or Seaside House : Thatched Cottage, Godden Green, Sevenoaks ; Holiday Home of Time and Talents Association.

25. UNION OF GIRLS' SCHOOLS SETTLEMENT, STAFFORDSHIRE STREET, PECKHAM, S.E.15
Date of Foundation : 1896.
Founded by : Girls' Schools, with Canon Veazey as the first missioner.
Denomination : Settlement is undenominational but U.G.S. Mission is Church of England.
Connected with : Union of Girls' Schools for Social Service.
Residential Accommodation : For 15.
Adult Activities : Women : Community Club Class, Mothers' Club, two Mothers' Classes. Mixed : Youth Club (15-20), Community Club (Young Married), Old People's Club. Old People's Dinner Club forms large part of activities.
Children's Activities : Boys : Clubs for three Groups. Girls : Clubs for three Groups. Play Centre, Saturday mornings. Nursery School (2-5), 30 children.

I

Accommodation provided for other Social Agencies : Servers of the Blind, fortnightly ; R.A.F. Association once a week ; London Association of Girls' Clubs, S.E. Area Division.

Special Activities : Old People's Dinner Club provides Dinner from Monday to Friday at 8d. per head for Old Age Pensioners. Children's Library. Survey is being carried out to determine the need for Community Centre or Association. Children's Country Holiday Fund and Women's Country Holiday Fund. Hospitals Savings Association Branch, 1,000 members. Care Committee.

26. WOMEN'S UNIVERSITY SETTLEMENT, 44 NELSON SQUARE, BLACKFRIARS, S.E.1
Date of Foundation : 1887.
Founded by : Mrs. Barnett, later Dame Henrietta Barnett.
Denomination : Undenominational.
Connected with : Girton, Newnham, Somerville, and St. Hilda's Colleges ; Royal Holloway College, London.
Residential Accommodation : For 14.
Adult Activities : Men : Cricket, Football, Billiards, Darts, Carpentry. Women : Parents' Guild, Crafts, Dressmaking. Mixed : Drama, Speech-Training, Theatre Club, Tennis, Musical Appreciation, Singing and Recorder Classes, Socials and Dances, "Sunday Night in Southwark" (Programme of Educational Talks, Films, Concerts, etc.).
Children's Activities : Boys' Clubs : (15-20) Woodwork, P.T., Games ; (10-15) Stamp Collecting, Games. Girls' Clubs : (15-20) P.T., Cookery, Handicrafts, Singing ; (10-15) Drama, Games, Handicrafts. Mixed : (15-20) Dancing, Drama, Concert Rehearsals, etc. ; (10-15) Music. Play Centre (25 children). Nursery School (20 children).
Accommodation provided for other Social Agencies : I.C.A.A. and Moral Welfare Offices on the premises.
Special Activities : "Darby and Joan" Club once a week, Women's Meeting. Agent for Hospitals Savings Association.
Country or Seaside House : None.

B.—PROVINCIAL SETTLEMENTS

1. BIRMINGHAM SETTLEMENT, KINGSTANDING, BIRMINGHAM
Date of Foundation : 1931.
Founded by : Interested members of the Birmingham (Summer Lane) Settlement.
Denomination : Non-denominational.
Connected with : Birmingham Settlement (Summer Lane).
Adult Activities : Women : Handicrafts, Make Do and Mend, Keep Fit. Mixed : Orchestra, Drama.
Children's Activities : Boys : Schoolboys' Club, Scouts, Cubs, etc. Girls : School-girls' Club, Guides, Brownies, etc. Mixed : Youth Club.
Accommodation provided for other Social Agencies : Social Workers' Festival, Youth Advisory Committee, Christadelphian Sunday Services, Special M.D. School (Education Committee).
Country or Seaside House : Canvas camps for all ages for holidays and week-ends.

2. BIRMINGHAM SETTLEMENT, 318 SUMMER LANE, BIRMINGHAM
Date of Foundation : 1899.
Founded by : A Committee of Birmingham Citizens encouraged by the Birmingham Branch of the N.U.W.W.
Denomination : Non-denominational.
Connected with : Birmingham University and other Social Agencies.
Residential Accommodation : For 25.
Adult Activities : Women and Mixed : Dancing, Make Do and Mend, Talks, Social Evenings, Outings, Discussion Groups, Keep Fit, Music. Men's Group : Discontinued since war, premises now used as Day Nursery.
Children's Activities : Boys : Games, Woodwork, Camping, Scouts and Cubs. Girls : Talks, Keep Fit, Drama, Sewing, etc. Play Centre.

Accommodation provided for other Social Agencies : Interviewing Room for Poor Man's Lawyer and Citizens' Advice Bureau, Day Nursery, Folk Dance Society, Gymnasia lent to local Schools and in full use all day.

Special Activities : Visiting of children returned from Approved Schools, Visiting for J.E.B., Visiting for Old People's Committee, Camping and Summer Holidays, Training Students.

3. BRISTOL UNIVERSITY SETTLEMENT, BARTON HILL, BRISTOL, 5
Date of Foundation : 1911.
Founded by : Joint efforts of University, W.E.A., National Union of Teachers and East Bristol Residents.
Denomination : None.
Residential Accommodation : Twenty at Barton Hill, two at Twyford House, Shirehampton, three at Barrow Hill Farm. Accommodation at Speedwell still being looked for.
Adult Activities : Barton Hill, all ages ; Twyford House, 18 and over ; Barrow Hill, mainly under 18 ; Speedwell, over 18 only.
Accommodation provided for other Social Agencies : Various Groups meet at Barton Hill : Education Committee, Bristol Infant Welfare Centre, Barton Hill Branch U.N.A., Barton Hill Swimming Club, Ancient Order of Shepherds and Ancient Order of Druids, Carlton Park Old Boys' Football Club.
Special Activities : 1. Training of Social Science Students. All Bristol University Social Science Students have their first year's practical training at the Settlement and attend lectures by the Warden. Vacation students taken from other Universities for full-time training. Students from Diocesan Teachers' Training College for experience of Play Centres. 2. Social Research.
Country or Seaside House : Cottage for Mothers and Children near Wotton-under-Edge, Glos. Country Bungalow and Meadow at Cleeve, Somerset.

4. CHESTERFIELD SETTLEMENT, CHURCH LANE, CHESTERFIELD, DERBYSHIRE
Date of Foundation : 1902.
Founded by : Miss Violet Markham, C.H., LL.D., J.P.
Denomination : Undenominational.
Residential Accommodation : For four or five.
Adult Activities : Men : P.T. Women : Young Mothers' Club, Older Women's Club. Mixed : Married Club, Old Time Dance Club.
Children's Activities : Boys' P.T., Junior Girls' and School-Leavers' Club.
Accommodation provided for other Social Activities : Youth Hostels Association, Chess Club, National Council of Women, Townswomen's Guild, Crusaders, Rambling Club, Social Workers' Lunch Club, Women's Institute, Girls' Training Corps.
Special Activities : Guild Council organise money-raising efforts. Warden organises Brains Trusts, etc.
Country or Seaside House : Camping Hut, Darley Dale.

5. CORNER COTTAGE SETTLEMENT, LEINSTER AVENUE, KNOWLE WEST, BRISTOL
Date of Foundation : 1936.
Founded by : Miss M. Bolt.
Denomination : None.
Residential Accommodation : For seven Social Workers.
Adult Activities : Women's Meeting weekly. The members of this Settlement do neighbourhood work for various Social and Religious bodies, chiefly visiting.

6. EDINBURGH UNIVERSITY SETTLEMENT, CAMERON HOUSE, PRESTONFIELD ; HIGH SCHOOL YARDS, EDINBURGH ; AND KIRK O'FIELD COLLEGE, EDINBURGH
Date of Foundation : 1905.
Founded by : Group of University men and others interested in Social Work.
Denomination : Non-denominational. Works closely with the University but not directly connected with it.
Residential Accommodation : For 10 Students.
Adult Activities : Men : Men's Club, Bowling Club, Old Men's Meeting. Women : Craft Class, Sewing Class, Co-operative Women's Guild, British Legion, British Women's Temperance Association, Guild of Friendship, Nursery School Mothers' Club. Mixed : Old People's Meeting, Gala Day Meeting, Whist Drives.

Children's Activities : Boys : Clubs for all ages, Scouts, Sea Cadets. Girls : Clubs from ten upwards, Choir, Brownies. Nursery School Play Centre, two other Play Centres. Two Nursery Schools for 40 and 30 children respectively.

Accommodation provided for other Social Agencies : Distribution Centre for Protective Foods. Branch of Edinburgh Council of Social Service.

Special Activities : Children's Library. (Public Library, which has a Branch at Cameron House, does not cater for children). Gardening Club for Children. Work parties of ladies who make things for the Settlement and provide garments when asked for the Council of Social Service.

Country or Seaside House : Small cottage in the country used by Boys' and Girls' Clubs.

7. GLASGOW UNIVERSITY SETTLEMENT, 77 PORT STREET, GLASGOW
Date of Foundation : 1897.
Founded by : Group of Class Students at Queen Margaret College who wished to do Social Work.
Denomination : None.
Residential Accommodation : For eight Students of Glasgow School of Social Study.
Adult Activities : Men : Woodwork, P.T. Women : Country Dancing, Dressmaking, Talks. Mixed : Informal Talks, Badminton, Discussions, W.E.A. Class in Current Affairs, also Dramatic Art.
Children's Activities : Boys : Juniors and Youth Club. Girls : Juniors and Youth Club. Nursery School : (The Settlement provides premises, but School taken over by L.E.A. two years ago.)
Country or Seaside House : None.

8. GREY LODGE SETTLEMENT, WELLINGTON STREET, DUNDEE
Date of Foundation : Formerly Dundee Social Union and Grey Lodge Settlement, organised 1888.
Founded by : Mary Lily Walker.
Denomination : Interdenominational.
Residential Accommodation : For Warden, Staff of Four, Maid and three Residents.
Adult Activities : Women : Young Wives' Club, Mothers' Club, Dressmaking Class. Mixed : Discussion Group, Drama, Concert Party, Recreational Club. Old People's Club, Dance Club, Scottish Dancing Club.
Children's Activities : Boys' Clubs (three age groups). Girls' Clubs (three age groups), Guides, Brownies. Play Centre (two evenings per week). Kindergarten for Children of Mothers attending Club. Nursery School.
Accommodation provided for other Social Agencies: W.E.A. Class on Current Affairs, Scottish Association of Girls' Clubs Training Class, Dundee Boys' Clubs Leaders' Meeting, Parent Association, Mothers' Club, Conferences.
Special Activities : The Association factors certain properties and takes an interest in the tenants.
Country or Seaside House : Holiday Camp run near Kirriemuir, and other Groups go to Scottish National Camps.
In addition to the work of the Settlement itself there is the extension work at Mid Craigie and Linlathen Youth Centre where similar groups from Play Centre age are catered for, including Old People's Club and Mothers' Club.

9. LIVERPOOL UNIVERSITY SETTLEMENT, NILE STREET, LIVERPOOL
Date of Foundation : 1898.
Founded by : Sir Sidney Jones.
Connected with : The Department of Social Science, Liverpool University.
Children's Activities : Boys : York House Boys' Club. Girls : David Lewis Girls' Club. Mixed : Play Centre.
Country or Seaside House : None.
The Settlement is a Residential Centre of a group linked by tradition to the various organisations in the immediate vicinity.

10. MANCHESTER UNIVERSITY SETTLEMENT, EVERY STREET, ANCOATS, MANCHESTER
Date of Foundation : 1895.
Founded by : Staff and former Students of Owens College.

Denomination : Undenominational.
Connected with : Manchester University (formerly Owens College).
Residential Accommodation : For 12.
Adult Activities : Men : None. Women : Two Mothers' Clubs. Mixed : Parents'
  Social Club, "18 Plus" Social Clubs, Drama Group. Adult work has dwindled
  considerably since 1939. There are one or two groups which have kept going, and
  one or two small beginnings with Parents and Over-18s.
Children's Activities : Boys : Junior, Intermediate and Senior Clubs, Scouts, Cadets,
  cater for some 160. Girls: Cater for some 140. Mixed : Play Centre for under 8s.
Accommodation provided for other Social Agencies : Red Cross, Foot Clinic, Probation
  Service, Citizens' Advice Bureau.
Country or Seaside House : Children's Camp.
  The chief interests of the Settlement are in providing social and recreational
  facilities for Young People. Training of Social Science Students and the Promotion
  of Children's Holidays are other activities.

11. MIDDLESBROUGH SETTLEMENT, 133 NEWPORT ROAD, MIDDLESBROUGH
Date of Foundation : 1893.
Founded by : Yorkshire Congregational Group.
Denomination : Undenominational.
Residential Accommodation : For eight to ten Residents.
Adult Activities : Recreational Club, Veterans' Club (for people over 60), Womens'
  Guilds, Family Services Club, Handicraft Class.
Children's Activities : Boys : Woodwork, Physical Training, Plastics. Girls : Cookery,
  Country Dancing.
Accommodation provided for other Social Agencies : Unity Theatre, Trade Union
  Committees, M.D. Centre, Marriage Guidance Council, Cripples' Guild.
Special Activities : Dramatic Society, Film Shows, Debates.
Country or Seaside House : (1) Country Cottage, let to families only. (2) Holiday Home,
  with resident Matron, for Women and Children.

12. SPENNYMOOR SETTLEMENT, KING STREET, SPENNYMOOR, DURHAM
Date of Foundation : 1931.
Founded by : British Association of Residential Settlements with Pilgrim Trust Grant.
Denomination : None.
Residential Accommodation : Five staff only.
Adult Activities : Thirteen Groups or Classes are running this term :—Conditions in
  the Mining Industry, French and German, Political Theory, Current Affairs,
  Elementary Economics, Theatre School, Women's Craft Group, Girls' Mime and
  Dance Class, Theatre Company, Woodwork Class, Drawing and Painting Class,
  Sketching Class.
  All activities are mixed except Women's Crafts and Woodwork. Membership 90,
  about 40 men and 50 women.
Children's Activities : Wolf Cubs, Scout Troop, Girls' Mime and Dance Class.
  Play Centre not operating owing to war and lack of staff.
Accommodation provided for other Social Agencies : Citizens' Advice Bureau, Poor
  Man's Lawyer Service, County Library Branch.
Special Activities : Once a year the Settlement Sketching Club exhibits. Library
  serves about 400 people twice every week. Film Society gives specially chosen
  films once a month. Arts Council sends Plays, Concerts and Exhibitions, and
  Settlement's own Theatre Company produces plays in the theatre.
Country or Seaside House : None.

13. VICTORIA SETTLEMENT, NETHERFIELD ROAD, LIVERPOOL
Date of Foundation : 1897.
Denomination : Interdenominational.
Residential Accommodation : For Warden, Club Leader, two Students, Caretaker and
  family.
Adult Activities : Men : Club. Women : Young Wives' Club, Dressmaking. Mixed :
  Old People, Dramatics, Discussions, Whist Drives. Social Club for "18 plus" ages.
Children's Activities : Boys' Clubs : 11-14 and 14-18. Girls' Clubs : 11-15 and 15 and
  over. Play Centres : Boys and Girls.

Accommodation provided for other Social Agencies : Child Welfare Association, Maternity and Pre-Natal Clinic, Mothers' Welfare Clinic.
Special Activities : Monthly Luncheon Club for Teachers, Social Workers and Clergy of the district.

PRESENT-DAY NEEDS OF THE RESIDENTIAL SETTLEMENTS

The settlements were asked each to append to the other information supplied a brief note on their particular needs. Thirty-six did so, and their evidence is summarised below.

The picture is a clear one, but such as to cause no surprise. The most pressing needs are for money, and for accommodation. Twenty-two settlements referred in one way or another to the need for money : in several cases the need for an assured income to meet the costs of administration, particularly salaries and wages, was specified, and in others it was probably intended. Such remarks as "Increase of regular income" ; "Funds for staff salaries" ; "Money for salaries" ; leave little doubt that the lack of an assured income for general administration is a major problem. It may be remarked that one of the settlements desired "increased income for salaries (from voluntary sources)" : this is evidence in support of the statement in B.A.R.S.' memorandum that the "existence of the settlements depends on voluntary support—no case is known where a grant from the local authority is made towards the general work of the settlement."

Twenty settlements referred to the need for rebuilding or extended accommodation. Most of the settlements are, of course, in London, or in other large industrial areas which were heavily bombed, and this fact has worked to intensify the normal post-war difficulties of institutions.

The staffing problem emerged as the third major difficulty, being named by eight settlements out of the thirty-six. Two of these referred to the need for voluntary helpers ; no doubt in part a reflection of financial difficulties.

Six stated the need for more equipment, sports gear being specially mentioned. Three named playing fields, and it may be added that of those who required more accommodation, two stated that it was holiday accommodation which was particularly needed.

Nothing else had more than sporadic reference. It is clear that the needs of the settlements are an epitome of the needs of voluntary agencies generally : an assured income for general purposes ; more staff ; and the facilities to build and extend to meet a changing and expanding sphere of usefulness.

30th October, 1947

6. NATIONAL FEDERATION OF WOMEN'S INSTITUTES

1. *Aims and Work*

The main purpose of Women's Institutes is to "improve and develop conditions of rural life." The Women's Institute movement is based on the spiritual ideals of fellowship, truth, tolerance and justice. All countrywomen are eligible for membership, no matter what their views on religion or politics may be. The movement is non-sectarian and non-party political. It has a membership of 349,000 and there are 6,510 Institutes in 58 County Federations in England and Wales. It was started in 1915 and the National Federation has functioned since 1917.

The machinery of the movement from top to bottom is democratic, i.e., designed to give the individual member the fullest possible share in its government. Elections are by secret ballot; committees retire annually; fares of committee members and representatives are normally paid from funds; and a system of pooling of fares has been adopted for the Federation's large annual meeting, which decides on the policy of the movement.

The Federation does not advertise itself. The request for the formation of an Institute comes in the first instance from the village; that is one reason for the strong roots and steady growth of the movement.

The work carries out the aim. It may be sub-divided as follows :
  (a) Social Intercourse—the bringing together of the women of a village and the encouragement of friendliness and neighbourliness. The focus of social activities is the W.I. Monthly Meeting.
  (b) Education—the provision of informal education of all kinds, both practical and cultural. The latest development is the foundation of a residential W.I. College at Marcham Park, Abingdon.
  (c) Social Service—united action at village, county and national level to secure improved conditions throughout rural England and Wales, in such matters as housing, public services and public education.

2. *What changes are the N.F.W.I. finding have occurred as the result of new legislation and of the war, and what problems do they see ahead of them?*

(a) *Curtailment in members' spare time*

Practically all the activities of the Women's Institutes are carried out on a voluntary basis and the number of paid staff is extremely limited . . . The new conditions have greatly curtailed the amount of spare time of many members, since practically everyone is either occupied full time as a housewife or is in a paid job . . .

In spite of the above difficulties members are nevertheless continuing to give in full measure of their time and energy to the organisation of W.I. activities . . .

Though there is great hope that the scale of voluntary help will not greatly diminish even though members' spare time is curtailed, it will probably be necessary to increase the amount of out-of-pocket expenses paid to members in order to make it possible for them to leave home and to do the work . . .

(b) *Finance*

The majority of our members are probably better off than they were ten years ago; the reverse is true of the minority. In 1942 an increase in the annual subscription from 2s. to 2s. 6d. was accepted without great demur and had no adverse effect on membership. Members continue to raise a large part of the income of the Institute, the County Federation and the N.F.W.I., by co-operative efforts over and above the statutory subscriptions and affiliation fees. Latterly there has been a sharp increase in expenses due largely to the upward trend of salary rates. This must be met by a corresponding increase in income and we believe that it will be forthcoming. In other words, members have the money to give and are likely to wish to give it because their faith in and enthusiasm for the movement is great.

(c) *Representative character of Committees*

A possibly justifiable criticism of the N.F.W.I. is this :—

"The aim is democracy : but in actual practice the rank and file of the W.I. members are not often elected to the higher administrative positions either at county or at national level. In other words, the committees are not completely representative of the membership, but tend to be drawn mainly from the upper and middle classes."

Amongst the reasons for this weakness are :

1. The expense to the member of service at a distance from her home and village ;
2. The too-heavy claim which this would make on her time—many members cannot leave home for so long ;
3. Her inexperience and diffidence, which disincline her to accept nomination.

There is reason to believe that with the spread of secondary education and the general levelling of material conditions which is now occurring in this country, and with the training in self-government and leadership which the W.I. brings to every member, this weakness will disappear and the committees, both at county and at national levels, will as time goes on more truly reflect the membership as a whole.

(d) *Increase in Membership*

The membership, which dropped in the war, has jumped up again to an encouraging extent, and has now reached the highest level since the movement was started. Evidence shows that many of the new members are young women.

. . .

(e) *Effects of New Legislation*

Of the new legislation the Education Act is likely to have the most important repercussion on our work. It is too early to judge what the effect will be of the increased powers given both to the Ministry and to local education authorities. Wisely used they should enhance and not diminish the value of voluntary work and at present it is the declared policy of the Ministry of Education to encourage the full use of the voluntary organisations. There is, however, an alternative way of using the new powers which must be faced fairly and squarely. The local education authority is now responsible in a way hitherto unknown for almost every sphere of the life of the citizen, e.g., for his formal, for his informal education, for the control of the buildings in which he meets and for administration and control of many of his leisure-time pursuits. If the local education authority were to assume too direct control in making these provisions the effect might be to sap the freedom, vigour and independence of individual effort and of the work of voluntary societies. The complexity of local government administration tends to place more and more power in the hands of paid officials and sometimes what is described as the policy of the local education authority is really the policy of one man, the director of education. It would be a misfortune if the working of one man's mind (however intelligent his ideas and his policy) were to be too important a factor in the life of the citizen.

(f) *Representation on Committees*

Though the N.F.W.I. is not a feminist body it is anxious to ensure that countrywomen are appointed to committees dealing with matters of concern to them, both centrally and in local government. Too often committees have not been well balanced in this respect and the N.F.W.I. has then felt obliged to make representations. Sometimes it transpires that where women are appointed to committees (such as the County Council Education Committee) the woman who is socially important, or is the wife of a County Councillor, is put on instead of the woman with the real knowledge. To the plea that not enough suitable women are available the N.F.W.I. makes a practical answer in the training in citizenship which it gives to its members.

(g) *Government Grants*

The conditions under which grant aid has been given to the Women's Institutes have worked well. Their headquarters have received grants for certain activities from the Development Commission on the recommendation of the Ministry of Agriculture. The committee has been left a free hand in spending these grants, which have been on a percentage basis, i.e., conditional on a proportion of the expenditure being met from Institute funds. During the war additional grants for special purposes were received from the Ministries of Food and Supply. At the county level such financial assistance as low charges for the adult education residential courses, grants for lectures, provision of special tutors (as in Gloucestershire), are a great encouragement to the development of Further Educational work amongst countrywomen, a province in which we are especially fitted to help.

(h) *Government Recognition*

The help asked of the movement during both wars was considerable and by no means confined to food production and preservation. Almost every Department in turn has made requests of one kind or another to the N.F.W.I. The recognition has been continued in peacetime and now at this moment of national crisis at least six Government Departments have requested assistance and co-operation. They have made a direct approach in each case to the N.F.W.I., and though no compulsion can be laid upon the W.I.s to carry out the Government's requests, the help is likely to be given freely and willingly. This direct recognition of the national importance of the movement has been appreciated and it is hoped that it will continue to be the policy of the Government to recognise the value to the nation of free and democratically constituted organisations. It would be a misfortune in our view if the Government were to establish and finance on a permanent footing an intermediary women's service likely to overlap with and to undermine the strength of the long-established voluntary and independent women's organisations.

As regards recognition by local authorities, our evidence shows that whereas some local education authorities (e.g., Gloucestershire) recognise that the Women's Institutes are covering a substantial part of the educational field as mapped out by the Education Act, 1944, and encourage this partnership by various means, others look on the range of the Women's Institutes' work as limited to practical subjects and fail to see that it is providing adult education of a high standard and acceptable form for a large section of the community. 15th July, 1947

. . .

7. WOMEN'S VOLUNTARY SERVICES

. . .

. . . It is generally agreed that a new and valuable national service was established by W.V.S. during the war, and that a progressive modern technique was evolved for the handling of volunteers. Fundamental consideration must be given today first to the uses to which the organisation can be put during the next two years of difficult transition from conditions of war to peace, and secondly, on a longer term basis, to the part which the organisation can play in the new integration of voluntary services in statutory aid. W.V.S. has acted as a recruiting agency for women wishing to play a part in the national or community life, and directed many thousands of volunteers to other voluntary organisations and associations. Through the Advisory Council, which comprises representatives of all the main women's organisations, constant contact is maintained and programmes of work discussed and integrated and this achieves a twofold purpose of providing a forum where general discussion can take place, between all organisations taking part in any project or campaign, and of preventing overlapping in the carrying out of work throughout the country.

One of the most obvious advantages of W.V.S. is its availability in times of national emergency, and for this it is of infinite advantage that it forms a national network, organised on a local authority pattern. W.V.S. were ready on any airfield to welcome Prisoners of War; they are at hand to help with welfare in any Polish Resettlement Corps camp, however remote; they were on the spot with canteens and comforts within half an hour of the Bourne End railway disaster; they have visited and helped evacuees from Palestine who have scattered to all parts of the country; and they have recently done extensive relief work in evacuation, feeding, clothing, etc., in the flooded areas for the local authorities, the military and others working in the areas, and in helping with the distribution of the relief funds. It is true that there is no longer a centre and a clothing depot in *every* district, but there is everywhere a shadow organisation, and any small area which has now no representative is covered by the county organisation. It would obviously be impossible for the Government to maintain a paid organisation throughout the country to deal with emergencies such as the above, and it must not be overlooked that in the greatest emergency of all, that of future warfare, a nation-wide organisation equipped to deal with dispersal on a scale hitherto unknown, would be a primary need.

The keynote of all W.V.S. work has been the restoration of normal conditions. In all post-raid work the first objective was to help people to resume as quickly as possible their normal routine of eating, working and going to bed. In Services Welfare work at home and abroad the first aim is to introduce a homelike atmosphere and to keep the men in touch with their families. Conditions will not be normal in Britain till each family has its own home and reasonable living conditions, but much can be done to encourage people to "make do and mend" and to make the best of their existing circumstances. It seems unlikely that we can maintain even our present standards so far as material goods are concerned, but the effect of this can be counterbalanced by improving our standards of cooking and household management. The major need today is no longer to train the individual to care for people in bulk, but rather to create new and better standards on which to build home life. W.V.S. is working a scheme of Homecraft training with the Ministry of Education. As with all W.V.S. training, it will be on simple lines suited to local needs, and will consist of short talks and demonstrations rather than formal lectures. It will aim primarily at reaching those who would never go of their own volition to any kind of Education or Technical Institute, but those who show aptitude will be encouraged to go on to further courses. Much is also being done by W.V.S. to ensure that proper use is made of the equipment which is being put into prefabricated and other houses being built by the Government, and that fuel is used intelligently and economically. In some places gardens are being started around the new houses to prevent their becoming slummy because of their surroundings ; clothing exchanges for children's clothing are flourishing, and should be maintained as long as clothing continues to be rationed.

Another important task for the next few years is the settlement in this country of members of the Polish Resettlement Corps and their dependants, and of other displaced persons who may be brought over. Evacuees from Palestine have recently been escorted, met and helped, and the same work may shortly have to be undertaken on a much larger scale for British Nationals from India. It is obviously to the advantage both of this country and of the Poles and other displaced persons who have no country to which they are prepared to return, that they should be helped as much and as quickly as possible to become productive and contented British citizens, but so far they have been placed in isolated camps and somewhat grudgingly accepted as workers in the less-popular British industries, and no one Government Department has been appointed to consider their needs and welfare as a whole . . .

The reorientation of voluntary service to fit the needs of post-war society is a vital matter for the nation both from the point of view of morale and of economy. The State has greatly expanded its sphere of activity in the fields of Health and Insurance, and the public at the moment is inclined to resent the cost, and to wash its hands of the "giving" end of the services. The man in the street grumbles about taxation and his increased insurance contributions, and says flatly that if the State is going to take so much from him for the Health Services he is not going to contribute further to the local hospital, which is now the affair of the State.

The nation will be poorer spiritually if all voluntary giving of time, money and effort comes to an end; and, apart from this aspect, the State cannot afford today to give more than the bare necessities to the sick and suffering, and others in need of assistance : the extras and amenities should come from voluntary sources. What is needed is that the citizen should appreciate that he is the State—it is only from his pocket that funds can be found to pay for additional State services, and in view of the present state of the national purse it is very desirable that voluntary aid in gifts and even more in work should be invoked to supplement the effort of the State. The State, as an example, should provide the blind man with a sufficient pension for necessities, but a wireless set to enrich his life should come from voluntary sources.

One type of citizen who would appreciate this distinction is a W.V S. member who helped with a hostel for evacuated children during the war. She knows that the Government paid through the local authorities for the cost of the Evacuation Scheme, but she knows also that it was local voluntary effort which gave the children the extras which made their lives as happy and as normal as possible : the bag of apples for Hallowe'en, the materials to make a guy, the Christmas stocking and party, and above all the precious invitations to visit homes . . .

In the field of voluntary effort W.V.S. could be compared with the main body of infantry in an Army Corps, who are ready to undertake the attack and any general task arising in the field. The voluntary organisations of the country are generally more specialised and were founded to help one or other unfortunate section of the community—the sick, the deaf, etc. They are more comparable with the technicians and experts who accompany each Army Corps—the Medical Unit, the Signals Unit, the Transport Company. All voluntary work of a specialised nature should continue to be done by the specialist organisations, but there should be more co-ordination and less overlapping, and waste of effort, and this could be supplied through W.V.S. or by some co-ordinating Board of which W.V.S. was the spearhead. The officials of a local authority are often reluctant to use a number of societies, and for this reason work which would help the community sometimes goes undone, while in other areas no specialist organisation is available . . .

The right field for voluntary work under the new pattern has yet to be defined, but W.V.S. has already found a number of directions in which it can be used, in particular in work for children and for old people. The Curtis

Report has emphasised the importance of normal home life, and W.V.S. can help to give something of it to children without families. W.V.S. members have provided "godmothers" for many children in institutions, who ask them out, remember their birthdays and sometimes have them to stay in the holidays. The experience gained during evacuation has qualified many W.V.S. members to help the Official Visitors both of local authorities responsible for boarding out children and of the recognised Adoption Societies, and W.V.S. members also act as escorts taking children to and from Courts and institutions of all kinds. The new scheme outlined by the Government envisages that each local authority at County and County Borough level will have a Children's Officer to co-ordinate all work for the care of children, and W.V.S. should be able to afford these officers the same help in the field as they did to the Evacuation Officer during the war. W.V.S. has also assisted in the establishment of Mothercraft Hostels for unmarried mothers, and in many places provides "sitters-in" to relieve parents during the evening. Propaganda for diphtheria immunisation, and the distribution of welfare foods in rural areas is also undertaken.

The care of the aged is work which is made increasingly necessary by the housing and fuel shortages, the difficult conditions of everyday life and the larger numbers of old people in relation to the rest of the population. W.V.S. has started residential hostels for old age pensioners and those with small incomes who cannot maintain and look after themselves in their own homes. Darby and Joan Clubs have also been started where old people can go for part of the day to find warmth and company, and "meals on wheels" for delivering hot meals to old people. Visiting old people in institutions is another much appreciated piece of work, and it is noticeable that the humbler visitor is often the more popular. One W.V.S. member of the "old duck" type explained that the old folks in the institution liked her to come because they did not mind asking her to do a bit of washing or to buy a pennyworth of this and that. Without W.V.S. this member would never have found her way into the institution where she is bringing so much happiness.

There is, too, much scope for work in connection with hospitals, and this will extend as the Health Services develop. Voluntary work, properly supervised and organised can play a large part in alleviating worry on the part of patients and their families during incapacity caused by illness, and by so doing can help towards a more rapid recovery. W.V.S. has helped some of the local authorities with the difficult and delicate task of setting up an organisation of Home Helps, and has also provided volunteers for rotas of domestic work in hospitals, and more recently in mental hospitals. Broadly speaking, it is not easy to find volunteers to go out regularly to do domestic work, but there are many who are ready to help in time of epidemics, or to take patients home from hospital and visit and shop for them for the first few weeks. The Minister of Health has stated that there will be a great need for voluntary work under the Health Act, but if voluntary aid is to be successfully used it must be co-ordinated and available for the sick at all stages of illness and recovery. The active organisations should therefore be represented on the administrative boards and management committees, and work in close touch with the local authorities . . .

23rd April, 1947

8. THE BRITISH RED CROSS SOCIETY *

The British Red Cross Society is part of the International Red Cross Movement, which comprises :

(a) *The International Red Cross Committee*
This has as its main function to promote the adhesion of States to the Geneva Convention ; to afford recognition to new national societies ; to create international agencies in wartime for the relief of war sufferers ; and to maintain fundamental Red Cross principles.

(b) *The League of Red Cross Societies*
This has been described as a kind of Parliament of National Red Cross Societies. Its functions are mainly to establish co-operation between them.

(c) *The various National Red Cross Societies*
Of this, the British Red Cross Society is one.

(a) *Origin and Aims of the B.R.C.S.*

The B.R.C.S. began its activities in 1870 at the opening of the Franco-Prussian War ; in 1905 it was reconstructed on its present basis, and its Royal Charter of Incorporation was granted in 1908. The Charter stated that the primary object of the Society was to furnish aid to the sick and wounded in time of war.

In 1919 the Society was granted a Supplementary Charter, authorising the extension of its activities. In addition to the primary object, the objects and purposes of the Society were widened to include "the improvement of health, the prevention of disease and the mitigation of suffering throughout the world."

It is thus primarily an organisation for the relief of sick and wounded in time of war. In its secondary aims it may be described as *spontaneous* and *interstitial.* The slogan adopted by a kindred society might be paraphrased as "Where there is need, there is the B.R.C.S." In this the Society is helped by the fact that its organisation allows considerable initiative at the finger-tips —the smaller formations and units, such as Divisions and Detachments. For example, a certain London Division did valuable emergency work during the last war in staffing and providing nursing care at short notice for hostels for the bombed out, in starting a Rest Hostel for Civil Defence Workers, in organising a Mobile Canteen service, and in organising educational courses for Civil Defence workers. This was in addition to its more "normal" duties of providing staff for military and civil hospitals, first-aid posts, etc. All

---

* The statistics provided are based on the figures for 1947.

these emergency jobs could, no doubt, have been done by specialist services : but when the need first made itself felt, these specialist services were not there. The B.R.C.S. offered a flexible organisation of not too highly-trained personnel to fill the gap ; and when the more specialised organisations—the local authorities' services, and so on—were ready, the jobs were handed over to them. *Mutatis mutandis*, this experience is largely true today.

(b) Organisation

At the present day, the Society is governed by its Council, which appoints annually an Executive Committee. The National Headquarters is at Grosvenor Crescent, London. The work of the National Headquarters includes, besides the formulation of the Society's policy, other duties such as the administration of relief work overseas arising as a result of the war and carried out in co-operation with the military authorities. In addition, its functions may be summarised as follows :

Advice to branches on general and technical matters ; the maintenance of a Training College for Red Cross administrative workers ; direction in matters concerning personnel, education, welfare, etc., and the administration of certain special services. National headquarters is also directly responsible for the Civilian Relief Service in Europe, and for the Foreign Relations side of the Society's work. The Flood Relief Services by the Red Cross during the last winter and spring were also encouraged and financed by National Headquarters direct.

Apart from these activities, Red Cross work throughout the country is delegated very largely to the local County Branches.

Local Branches

There are County Branches in every county of England and Wales and in certain County Boroughs. There are also some Local Branches overseas. These branches are subject to the policy, regulations and directions of headquarters but retain administrative control over their funds and personnel and property : they are on the whole financially self-supporting and can administer monies raised and properties received within their areas. Each Local Branch possesses a County President and a Committee responsible to the Council and the Executive Committee of the Society. It has also a County Director as executive officer and staff. So far as work within Great Britain is concerned, the British Red Cross largely relies on the activities of its County Branches. The County Branch is responsible for Red Cross work in general within its geographical area : in particular :

Recruitment, and training and administration of Red Cross personnel ;

The maintenance of an active Red Cross organisation, capable of rapid extension and mobilisation when necessary ;

The aid and support of National Red Cross appeals ;

General instruction to the public on matters of health and hygiene, and co-operation with Government and Local Authorities in the area.

Most County Branches are sub-divided into Divisions, and under these comes the lowest unit of organisation, the Detachment.

Central Council Branches

These are autonomous except only as to general policy which is prescribed by National Headquarters. Their constitution is also approved by National Headquarters. Central Council Branches exist in Scotland, Northern Ireland and in certain British Colonies, and their organisation and functions in the smaller colonies correspond to those of a County Branch, while in larger colonies and in Scotland and Northern Ireland they possess their own Local Branches, their relationship to which corresponds to that between National Headquarters and County Branches in England.

(c) Membership

The basis of the Society is voluntary service; although a proportion of Headquarters and Branch Staffs, and a very small proportion of Divisional staffs, are paid, the large majority of workers give their services free. Membership was, at 31st October, 1945, 144,616; of them, 19,930 were men and 124,686 were women. This indicates clearly one of the salient features of the B.R.C.S., that it is predominantly an organisation of women. There were 131,796 fully-trained members and 12,820 probationers.

An individual may be enrolled as a full member of the B.R.C.S. if he or she is already in possession of the Society's First Aid and, in the case of women, Home Nursing Certificates. If the individual is not already in possession of these certificates, he or she is enrolled as a probationer, and undertakes a course of instruction and practical training followed by examinations.

In addition to the full members and probationers, the Society also makes a provision for subscribing members, honorary and life members, associate members for whom special Red Cross training is not required, and junior members. Junior members form the Junior Red Cross side of the British Red Cross and are an extremely important aspect of the Red Cross movement. There is a Junior Red Cross in most countries possessing a National Society and the international link between the Junior Red Cross of each country is very strong. Boys and girls of school age are admitted either in Cadet units, or, for the younger children, in "Links," formed in schools. The aim of the movement is to inculcate the spirit of voluntary service, the motto is "Serve one another," and to teach and encourage healthy habits of living. The Junior Red Cross is growing in this country rapidly.

A note may be added on the question of payment to personnel at Headquarters. The position, broadly speaking, is that personnel doing purely clerical and similar duties are remunerated on the ordinary commercial scale. At the other end, the highest executive positions are unremunerated, except for possible honoraria in one or two cases. In between, the position is that a member may be remunerated, but is willing to accept payment on a lower scale than his or her abilities would warrant in the ordinary commercial world, because he or she finds that the work offers scope for initiative and unusually interesting experience.

(d) Finance

The question of Red Cross finance is one of peculiar complexity, for the following reasons :

(a) Prior to the war the Society and the Order of St. John operated on their own, from their own funds, and their County Branches supported themselves by local appeals. During the war funds were raised centrally under the Duke of Gloucester's Red Cross and St. John Fund, Branches to a large extent giving up local collections to the Central Fund. Now the Society and the Order are again operating on their own, their finances being strengthened by grants from the Red Cross and St. John Fund to enable them to carry on certain work arising from the war and to develop their peacetime work. County Branches are resuming local appeals for local work. The balance of the Red Cross and St. John Fund, over 80 per cent. of which was spent during and immediately after the war, is administered by a joint St. John and Red Cross Committee for purposes almost entirely for the benefit of disabled ex-servicemen, carried out through the Red Cross channels, that is to say, in the main, personnel of the Order and the Society.

(b) Owing to the general tendency to autonomy in Branches, the accounts of the County Branches are kept entirely separate from those of Headquarters. Furthermore, at the moment, no particulars of County Branch accounts in a consolidated form are available at Headquarters, although each Branch sends in its Annual Report and Accounts. It is certain, however, that Branch funds are quite considerable in amount, and therefore any account of B.R.C.S. finance which omitted them would be entirely misleading. It is also to be noted that, not only are Branch Headquarters accounts separate from National Headquarters accounts, but that Divisional and Detachment accounts are generally separate from Branch accounts, although again proper accounts are rendered individually. The resulting complexity makes it, at the moment, impossible to say very much as to the full extent of Red Cross income and expenditure. It may be noticed that the expenditure of National Headquarters in 1946 was about £87,000 and its receipts, excluding legacies, about £70,000, and these figures are likely to be higher in 1947. The Society's capital funds are not in the form of a permanent endowment and may be drawn upon for expenditure or current relief work, training, etc. The Duke of Gloucester's Red Cross and St. John Fund ceased to appeal on 30th June, 1945, and its contributory sections, including the well-known Red Cross Penny-a-Week Fund, have also been wound up. The present state of affairs is :

(i) *National Headquarters*

is carrying on its work (including its international and foreign commitments) by means of the funds accumulated over the years, legacies, and

145

subscriptions and donations made spontaneously by the public, and the grants from the Red Cross and St. John Fund already mentioned. The Society is not making any public appeals for National Headquarters but believes that with its great goodwill it would always be able to call upon the generosity of the public for further support to enable it to carry out its services. It has not been the practice in the past for Branches to contribute to National Headquarters.

(ii) *The Branches*

As was said above, Branches are expected to support themselves by local appeals. During the war, as has been mentioned, they surrendered to a large extent their claims on local funds in favour of the Duke of Gloucester's Fund and in recognition of this have since the war received some financial assistance from National Headquarters out of grants received from that Fund.

In the County of London the Branch is organising a Flag Day to be held in alternate years. St. John Ambulance Brigade will have their flag days in the years when the Red Cross does not. This arrangement removes any difficulty about the precise allocation of the proceeds between the two organisations. Apart from this, the Branches will be expected to raise their funds by such sporadic efforts as fêtes, sales of work, etc., and to a small extent, by subscriptions and donations.

CURRENT ACTIVITIES OF THE BRITISH RED CROSS SOCIETY

This report is based on figures received from sixty County Branches in England and Wales.

Medical Services

The British Red Cross and its County Branches are running 10 Auxiliary Hospitals and 10 Homes, apart from certain Homes run jointly with the Order of St. John. There are also 150 B.R.C.S. Clinics run by Branches and Red Cross personnel assist in a further 615 Clinics organised by other authorities. Fifty-five County Branches recruit donors for the Blood Transfusion Service, on behalf of the Ministry of Health, and 40 on behalf of individual hospitals : 59 counties have members assisting at Bleeding Sessions.

The Nursing Aid Service is operating in 56 counties and there are a total of 1,040 Medical Loan Depots. Personnel assist with supplementary nursing and domestic duties in

> 586 Voluntary Hospitals
> 257 Local Authority Hospitals
> 181 Public Assistance Institutions.

Welfare Services

The Society has over 2,081 members doing welfare work a minimum of one day a week for ex-service and civilian cases, and has welfare officers in 169 "Service" Hospitals, Sick Bays, etc., and 265 Welfare Workers in Civilian

Hospitals. Personnel assist in 74 Almoners' Departments, mostly with clerical work, visiting and after-care. County Branches run 51 Out-patient Canteens and 41 Trolley Shops. The Hospital Library of the Order of St. John and the British Red Cross Society is operating in 685 hospitals and the B.R.C.S. Picture Library in over 35. A "Sitters-in" Scheme is working in 124 areas and Branches are running 7 Old People's Hostels and 83 Old People's Clubs. Supplementary staff is also provided for a further 33 Old People's Hostels run by other authorities. There are 67 Diversional Handicraft Depots and 343 Members and Associates teaching this to invalid or crippled persons in Hospitals and Sanatoria and a further 229 teaching in the patient's home.

Other welfare activities include, visiting old people in institutions and in their own homes, shopping for them, changing their library books and arranging outings, parties, etc. The Meals-on-Wheels Service, providing a hot meal for old folk in their homes once or twice a week at a small charge is also operating in some counties. Visits are paid to crippled and invalid children at their home and in Hospitals and Sanatoria, and escorts are provided to and from hospitals for service and civilian patients.

First Aid

County Branches have a total of 62 Road Posts at local danger spots : they also provide First Aid Services at 10 Lifeboat Stations and approximately 40 Beach Huts. Branches and Detachments also provide personnel for various sporting fixtures, places of entertainment and other public occasions or as required. Camp Dispensaries were staffed in a total of 120 camps for outside organisations last year and a total of 52 Hop-picking Dispensaries were manned by B.R.C.S. personnel.

General Services

Red Cross members assist with 474 Ambulances either as drivers or as attendants. They also provide instructors for courses of uncertificated First Aid and various other subjects to 70 outside organisations. The Hospital Car Service is organised and run in co-operation with S.J.A.B. and the W.V.S. to provide transport by private car for routine cases attending hospital, who are unable to afford taxis and for whom there is no other form of transport available. Orders for cars have to be sanctioned by, and made through, the Hospital Almoner. Drivers receive a mileage rate of 3d. per mile.

These activities are carried out by various sections of the Society's personnel, i.e., Men, Women, Juniors and Associates. In addition to those mentioned above, Juniors help with visiting crippled and invalid children and boarded-out children, organising various outings and treats for them. They also collect rose-hips, books for hospital libraries, silver paper, stamps, and help in Hospitals and Babies' Homes.

Associates help with most welfare activities and also do mending and sewing for Hospitals and Institutions.

9. THE ST. JOHN AMBULANCE BRIGADE

(i) *The Order of St. John, the St. John Ambulance Association and the St. John Ambulance Brigade*

The Venerable Order of the Hospital of St. John of Jerusalem, the origin of which can be traced back with certainty to the time of the Early Crusades and may even reach as far back as 120 B.C., is the oldest Order of Chivalry in existence today.

The original Members of the Order undertook the care of the sick at the Hospital of St. John in Jerusalem and it is known that at the time the conquering Crusaders entered Jerusalem, in 1099, they were tending over one thousand patients a day.

The Ophthalmic Hospital in Jerusalem still carries on its good work and during 1946 the attendances totalled 123,428—the patients coming from all parts of the Middle East.

In the twelfth century the Order of St. John became a Military Order, like that of the Templars, and its history in the succeeding years was dominated by incessant battles against the infidels.

In England, about the year 1130, ten acres of land were given to the Knights of St. John at Clerkenwell and here they built their Grand Priory. The Order suffered persecution under King Henry VIII and its estates were confiscated by Queen Elizabeth but it was re-established in 1831 and two years later secured possession of St. John's Gate (with the exception of the Church all that was left of their original property at Clerkenwell) and the Church was handed back again to the Order in 1930, but was later destroyed during the Blitz on London. The Headquarters of the Order are still at St. John's Gate.

The primary objects of the Order of St. John include "the encouragement and promotion of all works of humanity and charity for the relief of persons in sickness, distress, suffering and danger . . . the rendering of aid to the sick and wounded in war and the promotion of such permanent organisation during time of peace as may be at once available in time of emergency, including the provision of Technical Reserves for the Medical Services of the Forces of the Crown . . ."

His Majesty the King is the Sovereign Head of the Grand Priory in the British Realm of the Venerable Order of the Hospital of St. John of Jerusalem, of which there are subordinate establishments overseas. The Sovereign Military Order of Malta has its headquarters in Rome, with Associations in Austria, Poland, France, England, Germany and America, and there are also independent Protestant Orders in Sweden, Holland and Germany.

The various grades in the Order range from Bailiff Grand Cross to Serving Brother, or Serving Sister. The Badge is a white eight-pointed cross and takes precedence immediately before the Albert Medal.

The St. John Ambulance Association, instituted in 1877, is the foundation of the Order charged with teaching and examinations and is also responsible for Stores and Publications.

Since the formation of the Association over 5½ million certificates have been issued to successful candidates in First Aid, Home Nursing, Hygiene, Child Welfare and kindred subjects. The figures for 1946, although lower than for the preceding years, include nearly 28,000 First Aid Certificates at home and nearly 98,000 overseas.

It has been estimated that of the persons who qualify in First Aid under the Association, one in six becomes a member of the St. John Ambulance Brigade, but a much larger number are linked with the Association Centres and Branches in connection with the Railways, Post Offices, Mines, Factories and Police and Fire Services. Every candidate for a Certificate of Efficiency as Master or Mate in the Mercantile Marine, or Skipper or Second Hand of a fishing boat must hold a First Aid Certificate of the St. John Ambulance Association, as well as all members of the Metropolitan and City Police; furthermore, the Coal Mines Act lays down regulations regarding the provision of First Aid equipment and number of trained personnel in mines, and about one man in twenty employed underground holds a First Aid Certificate.

The textbooks of the Association have been published in many languages and dialects, those for First Aid in twenty-five, with German in the course of preparation for the purpose of instructing the German Police.

The Stores Department in London supplies a large amount of First Aid and Home Nursing equipment, not only in connection with Association Classes and Brigade activities but also to outside persons and, in large measure, to the mines and railways. The total value of orders in 1946-7 was £65,000; in the peak year, 1942-3, the figure was over £91,000.

At the present moment the Association is also engaged, in conjunction with the statutory authorities and professional bodies interested, in producing a textbook in Industrial First Aid which it is hoped may become the recognised Manual for this subject. At the request of several women's organisations two very elementary books on First Aid and Home Nursing, specially suited to the rural housewife, have recently been published.

The St. John Ambulance Brigade, formed in 1887, is a body of certificated, uniformed members whose efficiency is maintained by constant practice and annual re-examination and whose service is given, in a voluntary capacity, over a wide field of First Aid and Auxiliary Nursing. All members are holders of First Aid Certificates, and the women of Home Nursing also, which they are required to keep up to date by annual re-examination; many of them hold additional qualifications.

The strength of the Brigade at home at the end of 1946 was 61,000 men, 31,000 women, 20,000 boys, and 29,000 girls—a total of 141,000 : the Overseas membership was 68,000. The pre-war (end of 1938) figures were 56,000 men, 18,000 women, 9,000 boys, and 7,000 girls—a total of 90,000—with 26,000 members overseas.

. . .

(ii) *Brigade Organisation :*

The Headquarters of the Brigade is at 8 Grosvenor Crescent, London, S.W.1, where Departments for the Ambulance (men), Nursing (women) and Cadets (boys and girls) are administered under a Chief Commissioner (Lt.-General Sir Henry Pownall) with a Superintendent-in-Chief (The Countess Mountbatten of Burma) for the Nursing personnel.

While the organisation, administration and discipline of the 141,000 certificated and uniformed members is under the control of the Chief Commissioner, the Brigade is a part of the Ambulance Department and therefore all major matters have to be referred to, and receive the approval of, the Order, whose Grand Prior (H.R.H. the Duke of Gloucester) holds supreme authority.

The Senior Officers of the Brigade (several of whom give full-time service day by day in the Office) receive no remuneration beyond travelling expenses (and very often not even these are claimed). At Brigade Headquarters a paid staff of 21 is maintained with voluntary assistance from 10 others, five of whom give whole-time service.

In the Counties a County Headquarters is often maintained without any paid staff, although in some cases the County Secretary is paid a small salary and in others paid clerical assistance is secured on a part-time basis. The control of the County is under the County Commissioner—sometimes a business man, often a member of the medical profession—who undertakes his Brigade duties in addition to his own work. He is assisted by a woman as County Superintendent, who supervises the Nursing personnel, and various other County Officers, including a County Surgeon and a County Nursing Officer (S.R.N.) for the professional training and examination work. All these persons are unpaid, and are, of course, required to keep themselves efficient in First Aid—the women in Home Nursing also.

The personnel of the Brigade is enrolled into Divisions, numbering between 12 and 60 men, women, boys, or girls, each having its own Divisional Superintendent, Surgeon and Officers (Nursing personnel usually having a Nursing Officer—S.R.N.—also).

The higher executive Brigade appointments, including County Commissioners and Assistant Commissioners, must receive the sanction of the Grand Prior.

Channels of communication are strictly laid down, on the Army pattern, and democratic principles are safeguarded by Regional representation on Headquarter Committees. County Commissioners meet together regionally and one representative of each Region attends the Brigade Sub-Committee ; and similarly with the Women's Advisory and the Cadet Advisory Committees.

Members of the Brigade are required to remain efficient by passing an annual re-examination, attending an annual inspection, and a minimum of 12 Divisional practices, and to undertake various First Aid and Nursing duties to the satisfaction of their Superintendent. Two years' inefficient service entails discharge from the Brigade.

(iii) *Finance*

All Headquarters expenses are a charge on the funds of the Order. Counties make no contribution towards the central administration but are responsible for meeting their own day-to-day expenses.

In the past the Counties' chief source of income has been the annual St. John Flag Days but during the war years these were in abeyance, since such collections were then only undertaken under the auspices of the Joint War Organisation (of the British Red Cross Society and the Order of St. John). Now, with the end of the war, the general public has shown a tendency, in many instances, not to appreciate the need for financial support of the Brigade —particularly in view of the new Health Services—with the result that Flag Day proceeds have dropped considerably. In addition, many Police Authorities are unwilling to allow both St. John and the British Red Cross Society to hold Flag Days, so that the one permitted in the year has to be shared, or taken in alternate years. (For example the amount collected in the London district in the two years preceding the war totalled nearly £15,000 ; the 1947 collection, which must also cover 1948, only amounted to £11,870.) From this source County Headquarters expenses are met and each Division is given a small grant towards administrative expenses.

Apart from the allocation received from the Flag Day proceeds each Division is responsible for raising its own funds by annual contributions from its members, supplemented, if need be, by local money-raising efforts, such as dances and whist drives.

The cost of equipping the Brigade is not fully appreciated by the public, nor the saving to the State by the voluntary provision of uniform (a matter of £13 for the men and £10 for the women) and first aid material ; it has been reckoned that the value of this in Wales alone amounts to some £100,000.

In addition to his contribution towards Divisional administrative expenses each member meets the expenses, such as travelling, meals and laundry, incidental to the various duties which he undertakes, a not inconsiderable amount when it is remembered that some members do two or three duties each week. There is a tendency at the present time for local authorities, who apply for Brigade assistance in staffing Hospitals and Ambulance Services, to meet out-of-pocket expenses and make subsistence allowances, but in many cases members pay these into Divisional Funds so that the spirit of voluntary service may be unimpaired.

The Brigade has not heretofore received any money from public funds, but under the new Health Services local authorities will be grant-aiding the Ambulance Service where the Brigade is carrying out this service on their behalf. The Brigade Cadets, being a National Voluntary Youth Organisation, are eligible for assistance from the local authorities under the Education Act of 1944, and receive a grant from the Ministry of Education in respect of the salary of a Headquarters Training Officer.

(iv) *Contact with Statutory and Voluntary Organisations*

The Brigade maintains close contact with the Ministries of Health, Pensions,

Labour, Civil Aviation and Education and also the Admiralty, the War Office and the Air Ministry. It is often consulted by them in connection with various services, such as Service Hospitals Welfare, Civil Nursing Reserve and Part-time Nursing, V.A.D.s, Blood Transfusion, Hospital Car Service, etc.

To facilitate co-operation the Brigade has Regional Liaison Officers with the Ministries of Health, Labour and Pensions who can be contacted by the Ministry's own Regional Officers whenever assistance, or information, is required locally. It was contended, on behalf of the Ministries, that a method of approach to the British Red Cross Society and St. John jointly would be welcomed, but while the Ministries continue to consult both Organisations at Headquarters level there still remains no recognised machinery in the Counties whereby one representative (or Committee) can be approached on behalf of both organisations. The newly instituted St. John Councils may help to overcome this difficulty but, meanwhile, it has been noticeable that the statutory authorities have not made much contact with, or use of, our Liaison Officers who are in a position to co-ordinate, over a wide area, the Brigade work for the Ministry concerned.

Recently certain Government Departments have inaugurated St. John training for their personnel, notably the Treasury, the Home Office, the War Office and the Ministry of Civil Aviation.

Among the Professional and Voluntary Organisations with whom St. John works in close co-operation, being represented, in many cases, on their Councils or Committees, are the Royal College of Nursing, the Queen's Institute of District Nursing, the National Council of Social Service, the Central Council for Health Education, the Royal Society for the Prevention of Accidents, the National Association for the Prevention of Tuberculosis, the Girl Guide Association and the Women's Voluntary Services. Other bodies, such as the Association of Hospital Matrons, the Institute of Hospital Almoners and the British Overseas Airways Corporation, are consulted from time to time whenever Brigade work concerns their sphere of activity.

(v) *Brigade Duties*

... Each year Brigade members deal with more than half-a-million cases of First Aid—the majority being treated by members when on Public Duty, including Ceremonial Parades (on Jubilee Day 7,500 cases were dealt with and at the Victory Day Parade 5,016), sporting events (such as the Bolton Cup-Tie disaster) and at entertainments of various kinds. Many thousands of hours' voluntary attendance on duty is put in at theatres and cinemas by members —for instance a permanent First Aid Room is maintained at the Royal Albert Hall and members of the Brigade are on duty every day at whatever event is taking place (in 1946, 1,713 of these duties were performed). Hundreds of minor injuries are treated at the Beach Huts, maintained throughout the holiday season at many seaside resorts, and assistance is also given in staffing First Aid Huts and Tents in Holiday Camps. A new feature of Brigade work in First Aid is the training of Air Crash Crews and the provision of First Aid Parties at Civil Aerodromes.

The Brigade also maintains a Road Service, with roadside First Aid Posts, and during 1946 the 588 Ambulances (representing 70 per cent. of the voluntary Ambulance Services of the country) travelled nearly three million miles and moved more than 184,000 patients. St. John co-operates with the British Red Cross Society and the Women's Voluntary Services in organising the Hospital Car Service, which conveys an average of 19,000 patients a month between home and hospital or clinic.

In the field of Auxiliary Nursing help is given in hospitals ; the annual returns for 1946 show that 347,000 hours of voluntary part-time duty were undertaken, and 167 members gave full-time service. In addition, many members have enrolled for service under the Part-time Nursing Scheme : for example in East Suffolk, where the Brigade has for long taken a special interest in the nursing of the aged and infirm, the Brigade's County Nursing Officer, at the request of the local authority, has undertaken the entire organisation of this scheme and 44 Brigade members are giving an aggregate of 404 hours' service each week. The Brigade has also been called on by the Ministry of Health to help staff mental institutions and some members have found this a most interesting field of service. Nursing assistance is also given in the home and the Brigade has a Nursing Aid Scheme, worked out in conjunction with the Queen's Institute of District Nursing, whereby its members may be called on to work under the District Nurse. In this connection members are also available to assist with the administration of analgesia and facilities have been offered to the District Nursing Associations for the storage of nitrous-oxide cylinders in Ambulance Halls.

Among other duties undertaken by the Nursing personnel of the Brigade are those connected with Child Welfare Clinics, Day and Residential Nurseries, School Medical Services (including Care Committee visiting), Blood Transfusion Depots, Immunisation Centres, etc. Local Authorities also seek the co-operation of the Brigade when organising Health Exhibitions or Safety-First Campaigns.

Another form of service to the community is rendered through the Medical Comforts Depots, which are established throughout the country, for the loan of sick-room requisites for use in the home. Tens of thousands of articles are issued from these Depots each year. There are more than 600 Depots, the total value of whose stocks are estimated to be worth more than £18,000.

The Brigade provides an Escort Service for sick persons travelling by land, sea or air (an air-attendant duty was recently undertaken in connection with the transfer of an ex-Service T.B. patient from Switzerland to this country for treatment, and a five-week-old baby was flown from Northern Ireland to Great Ormond Street Hospital).

More than 100 St. John members are at present employed as Resident Welfare Officers—96 of these in Service Hospitals overseas—undertaking such duties as distribution of welfare stores, organisation of entertainments, supervision of diversional therapy and compiling progress reports for patients' relatives; other Brigade members are assisting in this work on a part-time voluntary basis.

Another form of welfare which is proving of great benefit to Hospital patients is Hospital Libraries, which St. John runs jointly with the British Red Cross Society—nearly 1,600 Libraries are maintained and 1,500 librarians work under the Joint Committee, in addition to many other persons who assist the service by the collection and repair of books.

Among other Brigade interests is work for old people; although many members are assisting at Darby and Joan Clubs, with old people's outings and parties, etc., the Brigade is chiefly concerned with the *infirm* aged and those who are bedridden. Two Officers of the Brigade (one a State Registered Nurse) have recently set up a home for old people at Tankerton, assisted by members of the local Nursing Division: the residents pay a small charge and receive adequate nursing attention if this is required.

It is hoped that Community Centres may ask St. John to co-operate in providing First Aid Rooms, but this idea, so far as is known, has not as yet been put into practice. Other contacts with Community Centres have been made—the Headquarters of the Brigade in Cornwall is housed in a Community Centre and at Heston the local authorities enlisted the help of the Brigade to run the Medical Comforts Depot which they established in their Centre—and there would appear to be scope for further co-operation in many fields between them and the Brigade.

(vi) *Recruitment*

The London District accounts for nearly one-eighth of the total membership of the Brigade at Home, the Divisions being fairly evenly distributed throughout the Greater London area. Members are drawn from all strata of the community but the vast majority are wage-earners rather than salaried persons. The Brigade asks from its members only the minimum financial support necessary for administration, but expects much in personal service . . .

Although there are many rural Divisions of the Brigade the bulk of the membership is to be found in the big industrial areas where accidents in works and factories bear witness to the necessity for first aid training. Birmingham and its outlying district, for instance, has a total membership (including Cadets) of 3,440; Lancashire's figure is 10,444, while, at the other end of the scale, Cambridgeshire has a total membership of 638 and Shropshire 734.

During the recent war the total membership reached a peak figure of over 178,000 and although there has, naturally, been a falling off with the end of hostilities (many members having only joined for war service purposes, and others who were overdue for retirement having resigned), it is of note that the 1946 figures are 51,000 higher than those for 1938. In the London District the year following the war saw a drop in personnel of 600 but numbers are now on the increase again and the present strength, nearly 17,000, is approximately 7,000 above the pre-war figure . . .

(vii) *The Future*

The new Health Services have put before the country a tremendous challenge—it would seem that under existing conditions they are impossible of achievement without the help of such voluntary organisations as the St. John Ambulance Brigade.

Already the Brigade is being called upon from all sides to help ease the serious situation caused by the shortage of nursing and domestic staffs in hospitals, and to provide assistance in connection with the various Welfare Services. If these are to be expanded, more, not less, voluntary assistance will be necessary.

No statutory authority has suggested making provision for First Aid Services in the home, or on the road ; nor where crowds collect for sport and pleasure—the Public Duties of the Brigade will remain.

Although local authorities are now responsible for providing an efficient Ambulance Service they have been urged to make use of existing voluntary organisations' schemes where these are satisfactory, and in most instances the Counties are asking the Brigade to continue their service for them on an agency basis (Oxfordshire has assumed complete responsibility ; out of a total of 49 Ambulances provided for Sussex, 39 are Brigade Ambulances and two of the other ten are staffed by St. John personnel).

With regard to Medical Comforts Depots—while local authorities are to arrange that sick-room equipment can be obtained on loan they are at liberty to avail themselves of existing facilities provided by other bodies and it is anticipated that in many cases they will gratefully look to St. John to continue this service.

It is at present uncertain how the necessary recruits to the nursing services of the future are to be obtained, but undoubtedly the Brigade, together with the British Red Cross Society, is in the unique position of being able to supply part-time volunteers who will have already received a basic training in Home Nursing and, in many cases, have had practical nursing experience. Whereas in the past the part-timer has been taken on only if she could fit into the routine of the hospital the present Ministry directive is that all offers of assistance should be accepted and the time-table built up accordingly.

(viii) *Some Problems and Suggestions*

Hitherto the Brigade has been fortunate in securing voluntary (unpaid) service from its executive officers and from all its members. Today the number of people who can afford (either financially or from a point of view of time) to give such service is steadily diminishing owing to increased home ties (shortage of domestic help, rationing and shopping difficulties) and travelling restrictions (abolition of the basic petrol ration is a very great deterrent to all Brigade activities). It is obvious that if the work is to be covered one of three things, or a combination of them, must happen : new members must be enrolled ; or those who are only doing a little must undertake more so that those overtaxed can ease off ; or some of the duties must become paid so that those who must earn wages can make Brigade work their livelihood.

The Brigade has always been proud of its record of voluntary service to the community and does not wish that this tradition should in any way be undermined, nevertheless there are certain avenues of service (such as the Ambulance Service and Part-time Nursing) where already the State is offering payment and anxious that it should be accepted. Brigade members would prefer to be in a position to give their services free but, undoubtedly, they could hardly refuse to help because payment is offered, moreover it is obvious that more members would be in a position to help if they could receive financial remuneration.

Recruiting to the Ambulance Divisions is likely to be retarded by the National Service Act (although steps are being taken to maintain contact with the Ambulance Cadets during their service so that they are not lost to the Adult Divisions). It has been suggested that some provision might be made whereby Brigade Service could count towards the five years' Territorial Service—at any rate for men in Medical Units, such as the Royal Naval Sick Berth Reserve.

Rationing of uniform is now a definite deterrent to those wishing to take up full-time work in connection with such activities as Hospital Libraries, Service Hospitals Welfare, etc. While some concessions are allowed, principally to those undertaking part-time Brigade duties, those in administrative appointments still have to find most of their outfit (shoes, shirts, gloves, ties, stockings and collars) from civilian coupons.

The general tendency on the part of the public to allow their independence to be whittled away, or at least to believe that this is inevitable, is resulting in a *laissez-aller* attitude and an impression that "the State will provide." With the end of the war came a period when the man-in-the-street considered the Brigade's work was over ; he is being proved wrong but he still considers that once the National Health Service is in operation there will certainly be nothing left for others to do. This attitude is not conducive to either further recruitment or continued financial support.

(ix) *Voluntary Social Service and the Future*

Admittedly the present moment is a difficult one in which to assess the future usefulness of the Brigade, but it is felt that there will be no lack of opportunity to render service to the community through the promotion of positive health and the alleviation of suffering.

With the nationalisation of the Hospital Service, and free medical and nursing facilities for everyone, the call for nursing aid of all kinds is tremendous, while more emphasis on preventive treatment by hospitals and clinics will result in an increased demand for Ambulance and Hospital Car Services. In both these fields the Brigade is pre-eminently suited to supply auxiliary personnel.

The care of old people is receiving special consideration and since much chronic sickness prevails amongst them the auxiliary nursing assistance offered by Brigade members will be of special value—more especially when the small flats, community homes, etc., are available for the aged in lieu of accommodation with their relations.

The Brigade is more than ready to co-operate with the statutory authorities in any way possible although naturally preferring to operate and control its own personnel in doing so ; but at the same time it is prepared to hand over any of its work to local authorities as soon as the latter are in a position to carry it out. Meanwhile it is felt that the best results of statutory and voluntary co-operation, and the maximum benefit to the community, will be achieved through full understanding, mutual trust and adequate representation and opportunity of contribution by the voluntary bodies on all statutory Committees, Advisory Boards and Commissions which may be set up.

The Brigade does not seek for any enabling legislation in order to carry out the Mottoes of the Order—"For the Faith : For the Service of Mankind"— but it holds that, however efficient the State Social Services are, there will always be a place for individual, personal service, between neighbour and neighbour, and many opportunities for voluntary bodies to adventure and pioneer in new spheres of service to the community.

October, 1947

10. NATIONAL OLD PEOPLE'S WELFARE COMMITTEE
(in association with the National Council of Social Service)

. . .

The Needs of Old People

There are three categories of old people :

(1) *Those who can lead an independent life*

NEED :

(*a*) Proper housing

(*b*) Many becoming frail need also Domestic Help, Home Nursing, Meals Services (Lunch Clubs or Mobile Canteens)

(*c*) Many living alone need help towards a full life in the community, i.e., clubs and visits

(*d*) Some want employment.

PRESENT POSITION :

(*a*) *Housing.* Although some housing authorities have included special dwellings for old people in their new scheme, it was stated in February of this year that only 7 per cent. of the housing authorities in England and Wales are including small-size dwellings in their housing plans.
We should like to see the Minister of Health make the provision of a proportion of small dwellings obligatory on housing authorities.

(*b*) *Domestic or Home Help* schemes are badly hampered by lack of personnel. Here a voluntary organisation has sometimes found it easier to recruit the right type of personnel, e.g., Plymouth Old People's Welfare

Committee, and the Women's Voluntary Services. Under the National Health Service Scheme the local authority continues to have the power to provide this service, but it is not compulsory.

Home Nursing, at present nobly performed by District Nursing Associations as far as personnel permits. British Red Cross personnel in some places are helping through the local Nursing Associations. This will be provided as a duty by the local authority probably through extending the existing services.

Meals Services. Apart from British Restaurants where special facilities are sometimes given to old people provided that voluntary help is available, e.g., Woolwich Old People's Welfare Committee and Weybridge British Red Cross Society, meals services are provided by voluntary bodies, e.g., B.R.C.S. and W.V.S. "Meals on Wheels" service and Mobile Canteens organised in some places through Old People's Welfare Committees.

(c) *Social Amenities*. Clubs are being provided practically entirely by voluntary organisations, e.g., Old People's Welfare Committees, W.V.S., B.R.C.S., Rotary, and various women's organisations and also Settlements. This is excellent as it provides variety. There is no doubt of their value and of their appreciation by elderly people, who come together in a normal fashion and make friends. A further important result is that from the club members the organiser can discover other lonely people who cannot get to the club, and visit them.

While the number of organisations providing clubs is excellent, it is very necessary that there should be a body to bring them together for consultation, i.e., an Old People's Welfare Committee, to avoid overlapping and also to avoid leaving large areas with no provision at all.

(ii) *Those who need some care, the frail and infirm, but not sick*

NEED :

Small hostels or homes providing service, and care and attention in times of illness (not requiring medical or surgical care). These homes must be small and avoid an institutional or hospital atmosphere. They must be run on friendly lines in such a way that the old people preserve their feeling of independence and dignity. They should be situated in their own district, i.e., close to their friends and relatives.

PRESENT POSITION :

Homes, hostels and residential clubs are being established by a number of voluntary bodies. Some are "old hands," e.g., religious organisations such as the Salvation Army, Church Army, Little Sisters of the Poor, etc. ; Old People's Welfare Committees, the Society of Friends, B.R.C.S., W.V.S., etc., have come into the field during and since the war. The N.O.P.W.C. and local O.P.W.C.s encourage small groups to join themselves into a Housing Society for this purpose, e.g., Hants Old People's Housing Society Ltd., which is running two hostels and plans to extend.

Great impetus has been given to this work by the Lord Mayor's National Air Raid Distress Fund, and it is hoped that the Nuffield Foundation will also help in this work.

In the Ministry of Health Circular 49/47 local authorities are encouraged to establish more small homes, but the need for this accommodation is really desperate as only about 7 per cent. of those urgently in need of places can find them. This is underlined by the Nuffield Survey Committee's Report who estimate the number needed as several thousand.

(iii) *The infirm and those who need medical and surgical care*

NEED :

Proper means of admittance to hospital, proper diagnosis, proper treatment, e.g., physiotherapy, etc., including occupational therapy, in short, every chance of rehabilitation. If they then have to be classed as chronic sick and remain in hospital the wards must be made as homely as possible with every opportunity for contact with the outside world, i.e., frequent visiting hours, etc.

PRESENT POSITION :

It is perhaps this category of old people who are most neglected today. First, it is extremely difficult to get an old person a bed in hospital and many old people urgently in need of medical care are unable to reach hospital at all.

Those who do reach hospital in the main are kept in bed and not encouraged to get up and in a short time become bedridden with no occupation and little or no attempt made at relieving pain, and practically none at rehabilitation. It is only fair to say that this is in large measure due to shortage of staff, but unless the status of those nursing the chronic sick is very materially raised, we shall not get the best nurses going in for this type of nursing. There is need for special training as part of the general nursing curriculum. There are a few notable exceptions, e.g., the work of Dr. Margery Warren at West Middlesex Hospital. From figures given, both by her and those with similar enlightened methods, it appears that a high proportion of the chronic sick can be rehabilitated and enabled, if not to lead an independent life, at least to be well enough to live in a residential home.

6th June, 1947

II. THE NUFFIELD FOUNDATION

THE NEEDS OF OLD PEOPLE

The Rowntree Committee's Conclusions

1. The views about the needs of old people contained in this memorandum will be based on the Report, entitled "Old People," which was prepared for the Nuffield Foundation by a Committee which, under the chairmanship of Mr. Seebohm Rowntree, C.H., LL.D., conducted a survey into the problems of ageing and the care of old people. Much of the report was appropriately addressed to central and local public authorities as the bearers of the major responsibility for the welfare of old people ; but nevertheless the report made

abundantly clear the opportunity still existing and likely to continue for voluntary enterprise.

2. The conclusions and recommendations of that Committee were set out in Chapter 7 (pages 95-105) of the Report. Stated very briefly the main ones were as follows :

(1) The vast majority of people of pensionable age—probably more than 95 per cent. of them—live in private dwellings, and a large proportion are on their own or living with their spouse, children, other relatives or strangers. Some of those attempting to live independent lives are really unfit on physical or mental grounds to do so.

(2) Largely as a result of the supplementary pensions scheme under the Old Age and Widows' Pension Act, 1940, acute poverty has been substantially abolished among the aged, although there is still a considerable measure of austerity. When retirement pensions under the National Health Insurance Act, 1946, are payable "many persons will be better off and none of the present old-age pensioners worse off" ; and the new rates will be adequate "unless there is a startling and general rise in the cost of goods necessary for subsistence."

(3) When the new retirement pensions come fully into force a proportion (put by the Committee at about 60 per cent.) will lose their supplementary pensions and, in so far as charitable grants to supplementary pensioners in excess of 7s. 6d. a week have led to a reduction of such pension (and in effect to a subsidy of the Exchequer), the net result of the new retirement pensions will be a widening of the field where charitable pensions can be granted without subsidising the Exchequer. (It should be noted in passing that, notwithstanding this fact, the more or less general view among benevolent funds that the need for out-pensions for aged people from charitable funds is declining with the development of the State pension schemes is not challenged. On the contrary it is believed to be the right view.)

(4) The needs of old people for medical appliances such as spectacles, dentures, hearing-aids, etc., should be met under the provisions of the National Health Service Act.

(5) There is an urgent need for more accommodation of all types (flats, flatlets, small houses and bungalows, rest homes and residential clubs) suitable for and within the financial means of old people, with domestic help and nursing care available when required. Although the present supply of homes of all kinds represents only a small fraction of the number required, there is one class of the community which at present is scarcely catered for at all, namely those who have some private means and could pay up to £4 or £5 a week, but who are unable to pay the normal fees of a nursing home.

(6) Better provision is required for old people who are seriously infirm and long-term sick not requiring active hospital treatment.

(7) The number of clubs, particularly for old men, should be greatly increased.

3. *The case of the infirm and chronic sick most urgent*

The problem of the infirm old people is specially pressing. There seems no doubt that a fair proportion of the old people bed-ridden in public institutions have become bed-ridden prematurely. For example, at one hospital in Middlesex, by sympathetic treatment and encouragement the physical and mental condition of 30 to 35 per cent. of the old people in the wards for chronic sick has been so improved that, though still infirm and often crippled, they need no longer be bed-ridden. Some of those so rehabilitated can go to live with relatives; but for others—probably the majority—it is most desirable that accommodation should be available with a homelier atmosphere than can be developed in an institution and where they can receive the daily attention and simple nursing supervision that they require. The converse of this problem is that with timely medical attention chronic sickness and infirmity causing an old person to become bed-fast could often be postponed or prevented.

4. *Variety of provision needed for old people*

The old people are a cross-section of the population who are having to cope, in differing degrees, with the difficulties occasioned by declining powers. No single type of accommodation is the answer to all needs. Before any area can be said to have made adequate provision for its old people it requires a comprehensive range of accommodation and facilities catering for all categories of old people in need and so arranged that transfer from one type of accommodation to another is simple, smooth, and uneventful, whether the transfer is due to improving health or growing infirmity. This range should include : (i) residential accommodation of different types for able-bodied old people ; (ii) communal home (or homes) where the infirm and long-term sick not requiring active hospital treatment can be given such care and attention as they need ; (iii) provision for the treatment of short-term sickness and for the convalescence of old people who have had treatment in hospital ; (iv) accommodation for short-stay residents normally living with relatives ; (v) clubs providing meals, recreational and occupational facilities, and perhaps also a simple health centre for old people living in the area. The list is not exhaustive but it comprises the essentials.

5. *The role of voluntary effort*

Although at the present moment probably as much is being done by voluntary organisations as by public authorities to meet the urgent needs of old people—even in respect of accommodation for the able-bodied—in time it seems clear that public authorities (through the operation of housing schemes, of the National Health Service, and under the powers likely to be conferred by the National Assistance Bill) will play an increasingly large part. On the distant view it is not possible to see the exact field for voluntary enterprise, but all the same there seem no reasons to expect the complete

161

L

exclusion of voluntary organisations from this side of social provision. For those who believe that voluntary enterprise is not a luxury but a vital necessity in a democratic society—a complement to State action, making for vigour and progress—the pressing problem is to find means whereby voluntary organisations, while adapting themselves to changing conditions, continue to have effective opportunities and power to make their contributions to the life and thought of society.

6. *Care of aged simpliciter not a "charitable" purpose*

The voluntary organisations at present concerning themselves with the welfare of old people are predominantly—perhaps entirely—of a charitable nature. There are the benevolent funds of professional and trade organisations, religious organisations such as the Salvation Army and the Church Army, charitable trusts both ancient and modern, and housing associations registered as charities under the Industrial and Provident Societies Act, 1893.

As the law stands at present most of the charitable trusts are working for the poor or infirm aged, and the housing associations for "persons of the working classes." The law has not defined poverty, infirmity, or working class ; and exactly who, at the present time, comes within those categories no one can say with complete confidence.

7. Public authorities have been guided for practical purposes by the following definition of destitution which was put before the Royal Commission on the Poor Law of 1909 : "Destitution, when used to describe the condition of a person as a subject for relief, implies that he is, for the time being, without material resources—(1) directly available, and (2) appropriate for satisfying his physical needs—(a) whether actually existing, or (b) likely to arise immediately. By physical needs in this definition are meant such needs as must be satisfied—(i) in order to maintain life, or (ii) in order to obviate, mitigate or remove causes endangering life, or likely to endanger life or impair health or bodily fitness for self support."

8. Obviously this gives a wider scope than is open to charitable bodies at the present time. If the law were amended to provide that the relief of old age was itself a charitable purpose, it would enable these voluntary organisations to meet any needs of all old people.

Mutual-aid insurance for the needs of old age

9. Some thought has been given to the question of whether it would be desirable and practicable to encourage mutual-aid insurance, not merely as a means of providing old people with a pension supplementary to their State pension, but also as a means whereby they could secure the guaranteed right to such accommodation and amenities as they may need if they reach advanced years. There is not likely to be much dispute on the issue of whether such an arrangement is desirable or not ; but is it practicable ? A final decision cannot be reached in the absence of detailed actuarial estimates and these have not been obtained ; but the following tentative conclusions have been reached :

(i) The novel feature would be the securing, through an insurance scheme, of the right to the use of certain accommodation and amenities. It seems unlikely that an insurance scheme that was for such benefits alone would be a success, since it is improbable that it would be sufficiently attractive to the young, to whom (as a rule) the prospect that they will be in need one day of special care and attention is (fortunately) very remote. The appeal would probably be strongest to those over 40 years of age, who are beginning to realise the problems with which eventually they may be faced. If the age-composition of the member-ship was, in fact, principally that of middle age, the result would be either financial instability of the scheme or the charging of an unattractively high premium.

(ii) If, however, the right to the use of accommodation and amenities was a supplementary or alternative benefit to a private insurance pension scheme, the doubts about the practicability of the scheme become much less, provided that the scheme is operated by an organisation with country-wide contacts and with ample capital funds for its inauguration. The kind of scheme contemplated is one which, based on weekly, monthly, or annual premiums, provides at (say) retiring age (*a*) a guaranteed weekly cash benefit, and/or (*b*) at the same age or later, first call on accommodation and amenities available under the scheme.

10. The accommodation and amenities available should cover as many as possible of those listed in paragraph 4 above. Whether the organisation should own and run the various premises in which beneficiaries would be accommodated or whether instead it should arrange to have a call on places in homes, etc., run by other bodies, is a question to be decided to a large extent by the nature of the organisation. Probably a combination of the two methods would be desirable.

June, 1947

12. NATIONAL INSTITUTE FOR THE BLIND

CO-OPERATION BETWEEN THE STATE AND THE INDIVIDUAL

1. *Growth of Blind Welfare*

The existing system of blind welfare in Great Britain is an elaboration of many local voluntary efforts which have been gradually extended into a national system. From 1791, when the first institution for the blind in Great Britain was established by Edward Rushton in Liverpool, to the passing of the Blind Persons Act in 1920, the system of welfare, though widely extended, was necessarily partial and incomplete. With the passing of the Blind Persons Act, 1920, the system became for the first time comprehensive, in the sense that a purposeful attempt was made to provide for all the needs of all the blind. To achieve that comprehensiveness it had to compensate the handicap of blindness at every age and to adapt existing social services to the

THE EVIDENCE FOR VOLUNTARY ACTION

specific requirements of the blind. It aimed, in fact, at complete ascertainment of blindness from birth, at giving the blind child equal educational opportunity with the sighted, at securing training for blind adolescents and young trainable adults, at providing sheltered employment and securing unsheltered employment, at opening the door to the community's industrial, social and cultural life and, as a minimum basis, at rescuing from destitution any blind persons incapable of earning their living . . .

2. *Organisation—Voluntary and Official*

The essential character of the *Blind Persons Act*, 1920, lay in its imposing a duty on the Councils of each County and County Borough to make arrangements, to the satisfaction of the Minister of Health, for promoting the welfare of blind persons ordinarily resident within their area and to submit to the Minister a Scheme for the exercise of their powers under the Act. Schemes varied in their scope but usually they provided for :

"(*a*) Registration ; (*b*) Children under School Age ; (*c*) Education and Training of (i) Children, and (ii) Young Persons and Adults ; (*d*) Employment (i) in Workshops, (ii) by means of Home Workers' Schemes ; (*e*) Augmentation of Wages ; (*f*) Hostels for Blind Workers ; (*g*) Homes ; (*h*) Home Teaching ; (*i*) Necessitous Blind."

The Scheme usually recorded that the Local Education Authority would deal with education and training, and might provide for the carrying out of any services, by one or more Voluntary Agencies working in the area of the Local Authority.

The *Local Government Act*, 1929, had three important effects on Blind Welfare.

(i) By transferring Poor Law administration to the Councils of Counties and County Boroughs it put Blind Welfare in the same hands as the Poor Law.

(ii) It empowered County Councils or County Borough Councils to declare that domiciliary assistance to blind persons should be rendered under the Blind Persons Act and not as poor relief.

(iii) It terminated direct grants from the Exchequer for the welfare of the blind.

All Schemes could and can be operated directly by the Authority or indirectly through Voluntary Societies and Associations. In the middle part of the 1920-39 period there was a tendency on the part of Local Authorities to take all services of the blind under their direct administration. Just prior to the war, there was a slackening of this tendency and even a reversal in a few areas. Since the last general election there has been a renewed tendency to direct control, to standardisation of earnings in workshops irrespective of production and to dependence on the public purse rather than on personal effort.

None the less, Voluntary Societies and Associations persist in great variety covering the greater part of the country in more or less complex inter-relationship with each other and with Local Government.

In the areas of most County Councils and County Borough Councils there are voluntary societies which in varying degree are subsidised by the appropriate Local Authorities in respect of work which is left in their hands or delegated to them. In addition to these local voluntary Societies there are a number of institutions, providing employment and education, which serve areas larger than local but smaller than national. These more-than-local areas are defined purely by practical convenience ; they may, and in fact do, frequently overlap. There are in addition several societies of national character and scope . . .

Schools for blind children have, for the most part, developed from sporadic local charities dating back to the beginning of the 19th century. They did not originate as a logical national scheme. One group of Local Authorities in East Anglia combined in 1912 to found a residential school for their blind children at Gorleston-on-Sea. The County Council of Glamorganshire in 1929 founded a boarding school which admits blind children from other areas. Elementary, now primary, education is provided by a number of institutions in different parts of the country which in the past have been unevenly distributed but are now under re-organisation, impelled by the Ministry of Education with a view to covering the country equitably and providing separately for blind and partially-sighted children. Secondary education is provided by the National Institute for the Blind with public schools for boys at Worcester and girls at Chorleywood, Herts., and an independent organisation, the Royal Normal College for the Blind, provides "technical" education in respect of music (teaching and tuning) and typewriting. The N.I.B. also provides a school for blind children with other defects and residential nursery schools (Sunshine Homes) for children under seven or, in some cases, nine years of age.

Sheltered workshops and training establishments grew up in much the same sporadic way from local initiative. Of 62 workshops for the blind in the country, 11 are now maintained and managed by Local Authorities. The others are maintained and managed by Voluntary Societies, some of which also maintain and manage schools for blind children. Sheltered employment is also provided by Home Industries Schemes, the largest of which, with 300 home workers, is managed by the National Institute for the Blind anomalously but at the request of the Ministry of Health. The others are managed by workshop agencies which regard them more or less as an annexe to their workshops, or by County Agencies.

3. *Statistics of Blindness*

The corner-stone of the blind welfare system is Registration, based on two definitions of blindness : (1) educational ; (2) industrial. The definition of educational blindness is of a practical nature ; blind pupils are pupils who have no sight or whose sight is or is likely to become so defective that they require education by methods not involving the use of sight. The industrial definition, much criticised, is that a blind person is one who is so blind that he is unable to do any work for which eyesight is essential.

The following tables give (i) the Age Distribution and (ii) the Industrial Status of registered blind persons in England and Wales at March 31st, 1946.

Table E.31
Blind Persons Age Groups—1946

Age	0-1	1-5	5-16	16-21	21-40	40-50	50-65	65-70	70 & over	Unknown	Total
Total	13	201	1,375	1,048	7,372	6,834	17,367	8,977	32,606	104	75,897*

*Ratio to Total Population, 1945-46 .. .. 193 per 100,000

Note.—As a guide to trends, a comparison with corresponding statistics for 1941 shows a total increase of 1,573 ; the increase in the 70-and-over Group is 5,256 ; the Age Groups 5-16 to 65-70 show a decline and there is a slight increase in the Age Groups 0-1 and 1-5.

Table E.32
Training and Employment—Age 16 and upwards

Employed :

By Blind organisation (a) Workshops ..	..	..	3,327
(b) Home Workers	..	..	1,527
All others not included in (a) or (b) ..	..	..	4,156
Total employed		—	9,010

Undergoing Training :

Industrial	..	..	..	..	614
Secondary	..	..	..	..	110
Professional or University	..	..	..	..	64
				—	788
Training, but unemployed	..	..	..	..	446
No training, but trainable	..	..	..	..	469
Unemployable ..	..	..	..	..	63,595
				—	64,510
TOTAL ..	..	..	..		74,308

4. *Expenditure on Blind Welfare*

A.—Non-Contributory sources of financial assistance for the blind and the total expenditure under each heading so far as it is known :

(a) From the Treasury : £

(i) For Blind Old Age Pensions, payable on a Means Test at the age of 40 : 10s. per week (increased in October, 1946, to 26s. for a single person, 42s. for a married couple). Total cost to the State, 1945-46, for 21,041 old age pensioners age 40-70 553,000

To this must be added pensions paid to blind persons over 70 years of age, the amount of which for, say, 25,000 persons may be estimated at 650,000

1,203,000

(ii) War Disability Pensions for 2,419 blinded ex-servicemen and civilians surviving from two world wars, estimated 1946-47 at approximately .. 442,000

Unknown proportion of Block Grant paid by the Ministry of Health to Local Authorities x

(b) From County Councils and County Borough Councils, i.e., Local Authorities responsible under the Blind Persons Act—as at 31st March, 1941 .. .. £ 2,461,846

This figure includes :

(i) Domiciliary Assistance given on varying scales to unemployable blind persons.

(ii) Contributions towards the Augmentation of Wages of blind persons employed in workshops for the blind, and in home workers' schemes, and to a small extent of blind persons otherwise employed.

(iii) Per capita grants for employees in workshops, home workers' schemes, etc.

(iv) Payment of fees for residents in Homes.

(v) Payments under Section 102 (I) of the Local Government Act, 1929, being contributions in respect of embossed literature for the Blind, etc.

(vi) Cost of local administration of blind welfare services where municipalised, and payment of home teachers.

(vii) Other incidental payments made to or on behalf of blind persons from rate funds.

B.—Payments from Local Education Authorities for the education of blind children aged 5-16, and the training of blind persons aged 16-21 for the year 1945-46 350,000

Total A and B, i.e., payments from public funds .. 4,456,846
plus £x

C.—Expenditure by Voluntary Organisations :

(a) By 44 Pensions Societies on providing 2,919 pensions in 1944-45 48,000

(b) By Voluntary Societies for the Blind (other than Pensions Societies and St. Dunstan's Organisation for Blinded Soldiers, Sailors and Airmen), a total estimated for the year 1945-46 for the 73,713 "Civilian blind" at .. 700,000

(c) By St. Dunstan's Organisation for Blinded Soldiers, Sailors and Airmen in respect of the care of approximately 2,184 blind ex-servicemen, 1945-46 430,000

Total Expenditure by Voluntary Organisations .. 1,178,000

Total A, B and C 5,634,846
plus £x

D.—Under the Workmen's Compensation Acts, a small and unknown amount is received by some blind persons by reason of compensation awards .. .. y

E.—Contributory sources of financial assistance. From $£$
Contributory Schemes of general application payments are
made to the blind for sickness benefit, contributory pensions
and unemployment benefit .. .. z

   Grand Total of Expenditure on Blind Welfare from all
sources 5,634,846
                          plus $£x$, $£y$ and $£z$

The greater part of the expenditure under A and the whole of the unstated
amounts under D and E are cash payments to blind persons. The expenditure
under B and the greater part of that under C in the same Section is not cash
payment, but the cost of services providing for education, training, employment and general welfare of the blind.

The total figure under A (*b*) above is for March, 1941. No up-to-date
figures under that heading are obtainable, and the amount has undoubtedly
increased.

5. *Local Agencies*

The term "Local Agency" may be used to describe the body carrying out
local services for the blind, whether it is a public body or a voluntary society.
The Local Agency's work is indispensable. It operates registration ; its prime
task is to ascertain the blind, and to meet their needs, in all their variety, either
by its own resources or by putting them under the care of more-than-local or
national agencies.

To create the network of Local Agencies requisite for putting the Blind
Persons Act into operation use was made of seven Counties' Associations for
the Blind, which had been created in 1906 to 1911, whose main task was to
bring County (or County Borough) Associations into being where they had
previously not existed. They were linked together by a Union of Counties'
Associations for the Blind but their objects were fulfilled when County
Associations generally were established wherever public policy permitted the
existence of Voluntary Societies. The *de facto* regional bodies were succeeded
in 1937 by Regional Bodies so named. In the meantime the Local Agencies,
whether official or voluntary or, to some degree, composite, established a
generally similar technique of operation. They deal with Domiciliary
Assistance, employ Home Teachers and, in varying degrees from place to
place, voluntary helpers. In general they carry out standard services for the
blind, i.e., those covered by the approved local Scheme. In some areas,
where the standard services are performed by the Public Authorities through
their own officials, Voluntary Societies continue a semi-recognised existence,
supplying extra comforts and special services of sundry kinds. The County
of London is a notable example of this kind of arrangement.

6. *Regional Bodies*

In 1937, as stated above, Regional Bodies were brought into existence as a
result of a Scheme for the co-ordination of blind welfare proposed in the first
instance by the Joint Blind Welfare Committee of the County Councils'

Association and the Association of Municipal Corporations. That Scheme was one of the products of the Local Government Act of 1929 which compelled the C.C.A. and A.M.C. to make arrangements for co-ordinating the policy of their constituent members to discharge the greater responsibilities of blind welfare thrown on them by the Act. One of the first matters it took into consideration was "the apparently excessive number of voluntary bodies undertaking functions in connection with the welfare of the blind." The result of its considerations was a request to the Minister of Health to "endeavour to secure a greater combination of efforts, preferably under the aegis of the National Institute for the Blind."

The final Scheme, arrived at after negotiation with the National Institute and some other organisations, was one of complete co-ordination, the National Institute for the Blind re-organising themselves as described below, and the local societies being grouped in regional bodies. It sets out in close detail the functions of the national body and the regional bodies ; and it indicates in very general terms the work of the local agencies.

7. *National Agencies*

The largest of the national societies, the National Institute for the Blind, has, as a result of an agreement made in 1926 between the Institute and the Ministry of Health, and later of an agreement between the Institute and the County Councils' Association and the Association of Municipal Corporations, been placed under the government of a representative Council, on which are represented :

(*a*) the Regional Bodies referred to in Section 6 above ;
(*b*) the County Councils' Association ànd the Association of Municipal Corporations ;
(*c*) certain national agencies for the blind ;
(*d*) organisations of blind persons ;
(*e*) "persons interested in national work for the blind," i.e., the original voluntary element.

Local Authorities are represented both through the Regional Bodies and through the Local Government Associations referred to under (*b*) above.

The function of the National Institute for the Blind is to provide those services which can most economically and effectively be provided on a national scale . . .

Other national bodies serve specific needs on a national scale. In this category fall the National Library for the Blind which (with a London head-quarters and a Northern branch at Manchester) produces a large number of hand-written books and operates a nation-wide lending library service ; St. Dunstan's, which makes total provision for blind ex-servicemen, and a small number of other societies . . .

8. *Central Government*

The Joint Blind Welfare Committee continues in being as an advisory body co-ordinating blind welfare in Local Government. The powers of the

Ministry of Health have become more remote as the Local Government Act transferred much of its detailed responsibility to the Local Government Authorities. The Blind Persons Act of 1938 relieved the Local Authorities of the duty of submitting their schemes of blind welfare for the Ministry's approval. The Ministry now retains a general advisory function with ultimate power of enforcement, which can be exercised by reducing the block grant, payable under the Local Government Act, in the case of any Local Authority deemed not to be fulfilling its responsibility to the blind. In addition the Ministry has the function of revising for each fixed-grant-period the payments to be made by Local Authorities to voluntary associations in virtue of the services recognised by the 1929 Act ; and, in the event of a dispute between any Local Authority and Voluntary Agency in this matter, it acts as a Court of Appeal.

An Advisory Committee on "matters relating to the care and supervision of the blind in England and Wales" was appointed in 1917 to advise the Minister of Health on questions of Blind Welfare . . .

9. *Workshops and Home Workers' Schemes*

The 62 workshops for the blind in this country employed 3,327 blind persons in 1940-41. The workshops vary in size from seven to 230 workers. It is obvious that most of them are too small to be economic units of production, for managerial and supervisory expenses are multiplied over and over again. Specialisation is virtually impossible, and the proportion of sighted help per blind worker is necessarily at its maximum in the smallest shops. Some degree of co-operation in buying and selling has been effected by the National Association of Workshops for the Blind and by the Workshops Committee of the Northern Counties Association for the Blind ; but there is still an undesirable amount of poaching and unfair competition in tendering and retail selling between neighbouring workshops for the blind.

Home Workers' Schemes, by the last return, employed 1,527 blind workers in England and Wales. They enable their blind workers to carry on their trades in their homes, buying their material, supervising their work, finishing their product and, to some extent, selling it. The uneven distribution of Home Workers may be illustrated by the fact that more than a third of the total of Home Workers in England and Wales are in the two schemes which serve the Home Counties south and north of the Thames. In many parts of the country the number of Home Workers is small and their earnings are low, although it has been proved that with effective management such schemes provide a practical alternative to workshop employment, of particular value to blind persons who want to continue their own home life in country places or their home towns . . .

11. *The Achievement of the Local Authorities*

The great achievement of the Local Authorities has been to bring into the scope of blind welfare every blind person who needs and desires assistance. That has been made possible by the registration. There is no similar register of any other class in the community. No system of blind welfare can now be regarded as satisfactory which is not based on it.

The register is the envy of blind welfare organisations in other countries. Great Britain is in fact the only country where the total number of blind persons is known with anything like full accuracy. Ascertainments by census prove always to be understatements.

It does not follow, however, that the same criteria are used in all areas to judge suitability for admission to the register. There are remarkable discrepancies in the registered incidence of blindness in the Counties and the County Boroughs of England and Wales. One of the remarkable facts illustrated is the apparent higher incidence of blindness towards the West of England and in Wales. The range of variation is too great to be explained by factors of age distribution or the local prevalence of certain diseases.

12. *The Service of the Old and Unemployable Blind*

The table of the age distribution of the blind in Section 3 above shows an overwhelming incidence of blindness in the higher age groups. To the 59,000 blind persons over the age of 50, domiciliary assistance and home visiting are services of outstanding importance.

For home visiting the majority of Local Agencies engage Home Teachers who have taken the Certificate of the College of Teachers of the Blind, which demands knowledge of Braille, Moon, and handicrafts. In practice the Home Teachers are seldom able to give much time to teaching. They are predominantly social workers, rather than teachers.

A recent return from a South of England county shows that 95 per cent. of the visits paid by Home Teachers in the course of the last two years were purely social, a percentage somewhat exaggerated by the evacuation problem but fairly representative of ordinary conditions in many places. Nearly everywhere the number of teachers is small in relation to the number of blind people who need visiting. The attention given in recent years to the peculiarly hard lot of the deaf-blind has emphasised that Home Teachers with, say, 120 blind people on their books, cannot possibly give all their charges anything like the attention they require. They do their best under considerable difficulties. Their salaries on the whole are low ; but their work is both skilful and devoted. They themselves are the first to lament the inadequacy of their numbers. The cost of their service is, practically always nowadays, met from public funds, for even those Voluntary Societies which direct the work of the local Home Teachers receive grants for the purpose from the Local Authorities. It is the Local Authorities which are responsible in the long run for the adequacy or inadequacy of the service.

13. *Workshop Management and Training*

As managers of workshops for the blind, popularly elected bodies have great difficulties to contend with. They are open to political influence, particularly when public opinion can be organised by "pressure groups" of blind persons. Even apart from that, there is a temptation to earn kudos by ostentatious kindness. When workshops for the blind have been taken over by municipalities their operations have often become less and less economic. Running costs have increased; economic wages have declined; increased augmentation and grants of various kinds have tended to become the main factor of the total remuneration; trading losses have increased.

In the matter of training for manual occupations there is also some ground for criticism. The figures in Section 3 above show that the total of unemployable blind persons, 63,595, exceeds the total of blind persons over the age of 50. There are in fact among them a considerable number of comparatively young people. Some of the younger blind have other defects, mental or physical, which make them beyond doubt unemployable; but there is a temptation for public bodies to take the easiest way out of the difficulty presented by the loss of sight, and to have regard only to the prevention of destitution. They pay the cash and let the training go.

14. *The Role of Voluntary Societies*

To voluntary societies are due not only the initiative of all work for the blind, but its extension to all parts of the field. The persistent energy of voluntaryism has been conspicuously demonstrated since 1920. New developments in that period include the establishment of Sunshine Homes for Blind Babies, which have developed into residential nursery schools of particular educational interest; the foundation and the development of the one secondary school for blind girls, Chorleywood College, and the development of Worcester College, the one public school for blind boys; the foundation of schools for retarded blind children and mentally defective blind children, and arrangements for the education of epileptic blind children. Important research work into education and technical problems in great variety has been undertaken and carried through by voluntary agencies and at the cost of voluntary funds. Voluntaryism has developed Talking Books for the Blind, and in conjunction with the B.B.C. has provided the blind with wireless sets on a vast scale. The problem of the deaf-blind has been investigated, their number ascertained and work on their particular behalf initiated. The number of Homes for the Blind has been substantially increased. The retraining and after-care of the war-blinded was a voluntary enterprise in the last war; it has been carried on in the interval between the wars on a purely voluntary basis and has been extended solely at the cost of voluntary funds in the present war to include civilian war-blinded as well as ex-Service men.

This enumeration of new services brings out the technical character of much work for the blind, and the need in blind welfare for some organisation with wide scope able to finance new undertakings from voluntary funds.

Voluntaryism, too, must be an element in effective personal service. Many blind people need friendship and personal care such as cannot be rendered by any official however competent and kind-hearted. In the nature of things a Local Authority Committee cannot be so successful in enrolling this kind of help for the blind as a society whose whole motive is voluntary. One of the irreplaceable values of voluntaryism is indeed its ability to select from the community at large the people who have time and are disposed to give themselves devotedly to helping people suffering from a handicap which engages their sympathy.

15. The Public-Voluntary Partnership

It is evident that blind welfare cannot revert to the partial effectiveness of voluntaryism ; and that under purely public administration it might too easily become stereotyped and static . . . The comprehensiveness which follows from Local Authority responsibility having once been established cannot be dispensed with. The Local Authorities have in fact accepted their responsibility generously and with great good will. They cannot, however, move far in advance of public opinion or incur expenditure on experiments. Experimentation, research, pioneer work and new enterprise generally must be undertaken by voluntary agencies . . .

There should be everywhere in the country a well-balanced and sympathetic partnership between the public and the voluntary element, a public authority responsible for ensuring that a scheme of blind welfare is carried out in all its parts and a wide public interest showing itself in personal service and voluntary organisation. It is highly desirable that the need for this balance should be everywhere recognised, that central government and central organisations of local government should have adequate powers to ensure that local authorities carry out their duties, giving full play to the personal initiative of the blind themselves and to the experimental initiative and direct human sympathy of volunteers and voluntary organisations ; and that voluntary effort should be co-ordinated and, to some extent, unified, so as to maintain everywhere its vigour and efficiency.

There is room for the development and regularising of certain services in logically defined regions, e.g., sheltered employment, schools and homes. There is certainly need for even closer co-operation between the local agencies and the national bodies, both voluntary and official. Personal service of the blind is essentially local in character, demanding neighbourhood and neighbourliness and depending for efficiency on human factors little accounted of in offices and places where they plan. On the other hand, the present impulse to planning the life of the community as a whole emphasises the importance of many services which can only be carried out on a national scale. The need for integrating the schools for the blind throughout the country into a national system is evident, for only so can every blind child wherever he lives be given equal opportunity and diversity of educational opportunities according to his abilities and aptitudes. The constant attention given in recent years to research for the prevention of blindness, for testing the intelligence of blind children, for vocational guidance and placement in open industry, for the application of scientific discoveries and mechanical inventions to the needs of the blind, and to many other aspects of what is one of the most complicated forms of social service, emphasise the necessity of focussing experience and ideas from all levels of blind welfare on a point where adequate resources are available.

16. *The Consumer Interest*

However greatly blind welfare is affected by legislation for social security, the participation of the blind themselves must be ensured. More than the beneficiaries of any other branch of social service, the blind have contributed to the building up of their own welfare system. The National Institute for the Blind, for instance, founded by a blind man, owes as much to the numerous blind men and women who have served it, either as members of its Council or as employees, as to the sighted men and women who have insisted on the right of the blind to play their full part in its work. Generally, voluntary societies for blind welfare have been most successful when they have welded together people who have public spirit and experience of public affairs, people who have a strong sense of social duty and capacity for personal service, and blind representatives of the blind community. Some Local Authority Committees have greatly benefited by including blind councillors ; but the number of blind persons who can take part in Local Government is small and, apart from other considerations advanced in this Memorandum, the desirability of the blind being given the largest possible measure of self-government might be advanced as a further reason for delegating the detailed work of blind welfare as far as possible to voluntary organisations.

27th May, 1947.

13. CENTRAL COUNCIL FOR THE CARE OF CRIPPLES

Introductory

The Central Council for the Care of Cripples is a central co-ordinating body for all organisations working for the welfare of cripples, and in this capacity is recognised by the Ministries of Health, Labour, and Education, and by other Government departments. Its membership includes orthopaedic hospitals, vocational training colleges and rehabilitation centres, associations for the welfare of cripples, individual members, and associated societies. Its objects are to promote and support measures for the early discovery, prompt and efficient treatment, education, training and general welfare of cripples of all ages. It maintains touch with international work for cripples and acts as a central bureau of information.

Its status is national, and its main functions are planning, organisation and development. One of its principal tasks has been to promote regional and county associations which are concerned with all aspects of the care and welfare of individual cripples within the area, co-operating wherever possible with Local Authorities, Regional Officers of the various Ministries, and with other voluntary societies. The constant aim is to ensure that there is in each county or region a complete *Orthopaedic Scheme*, which comprises treatment in an orthopaedic hospital and its associated after-care clinics, education, rehabilitation, vocational training, restoration to employment, and facilities for general welfare.

Part I. The Care and Welfare of the Crippled

It will be realised that the social legislation of the past five years has taken some part of the care of the physically handicapped out of the hands of the voluntary agencies, and it is desirable therefore to examine briefly the various measures in order to disclose the gaps which still exist, and to show why it is considered that the Central Council and its affiliated members still have an extensive field of work, quite apart from the fact that it has become increasingly evident that voluntary societies can do much to ensure the smooth working of Statutory measures.

The four Acts which to some extent cover the component parts of the Orthopaedic Scheme are :

 (*a*) The Education Act

 (*b*) The Disabled Persons (Employment) Act

 (*c*) The National Health Service Act

 (*d*) The National Insurance Act (including Industrial Injuries)

The Education Act, 1944

. . . In theory the Act covers the education of every handicapped child in the country, but it is only reasonable to suppose that, since so much additional accommodation and so many new facilities are required for the normal school population and for more mobile crippled children, many severely disabled children (for whom no further hospital or surgical treatment is recommended) will not have much chance of regular education unless the voluntary societies make further provision for them. The official regulation which permits grants or loans from the Ministry for capital expenditure eases the financial burden for the societies to some extent, but a considerable portion of the money required must still be raised from voluntary sources. Maintenance costs present little difficulty ; experience has proved that Local Education Authorities are only too willing to pay the fees at schools managed by Voluntary Societies. The pioneer work in the provision of such schools has been done by the Central Council for the Care of Cripples in co-operation with the Shaftesbury Society.

The combined treatment and education of children suffering from spastic paralysis and allied diseases, for which special facilities are necessary, is to a large extent being provided by voluntary agencies.

Disabled Persons (Employment) Act, 1944

. . .

It should be noted that the Act is a Disabled Persons *Employment* Act, and that persons who are considered in the opinion of the Ministry's Officers and the Disablement Advisory Committees to be incapable of employment are refused registration. It would be difficult at present to state the extent of this problem of non-registered disabled persons, but it is one which is still left to the voluntary societies to solve.

Up to the present little provision has been made by the Ministry for transport to and from the place of employment when work has been found, although it has been possible in a few instances to secure the provision of wheeled chairs. It is frequently found, however, that the applications for such chairs have been made at times which are not suitable from the Ministry's point of view. Either the persons concerned have just left training and have no employment in sight, or they have already entered employment and it is too late for the Ministry to do anything. The same applies to the provision of surgical appliances and boots. Here then is another problem which still absorbs much of the time and resources of voluntary societies.

National Health Service Act, 1946

. . .

The position with regard to Convalescent Homes is not very clear under the Act; voluntary societies will probably continue to find a big field of work here. Convalescent and Holiday Home accommodation for crippled people is practically non-existent, and is a most urgent need.

So far as clinic services are concerned, Local Authorities may find it difficult to carry on without the aid of voluntary organisations, particularly in rural areas. Great assistance has been given in the past in Orthopaedic Clinics by voluntary workers who have acted as secretaries to clinics; have assisted the trained nurses and physiotherapists; have provided transport for the patients, and have followed them up to ensure the regular attendance which is vitally necessary in the treatment of orthopaedic disabilities.

The National Health Service Act envisages that certain of the services to be provided by Local Authorities will in whole or in part be possible only by arrangements made between the Local Health Authority and voluntary organisations. The Minister of Health's Circular 22/47 calls the attention of Local Authorities to the need to serve copies of their proposals on the voluntary bodies, the latter being required to make such representations as appear to them desirable within two months after the service of such notices.

It appears to the Central Council that the County and Regional Associations for the welfare of the crippled alluded to in the second paragraph of this memorandum can very well be of the greatest assistance to Local Health Authorities. Many of them have already given such assistance and have had long experience in helping in orthopaedic clinics, in after-care, in home industries, and in the welfare of the crippled generally. They can be of great service in providing a buffer between the crippled person and the Local Authorities, and indeed between him and all statutory provisions for his welfare.

So far as "appliances" are concerned there is, as yet, no specific definition of the term, and it does not appear to include wheeled chairs.

National Insurance Acts (including Industrial Injuries)

. . .

The Acts do not in the Central Council's view make adequate provision for the severely disabled cripple who never has and never will work. Some solution must be found for his difficulties and for the relief of his relatives, upon whom the burdens of nursing and support lie very heavily.

The urgent need for residential homes for severely-disabled adult cripples is generally acknowledged, but, as far as can be seen at present, the provision of such homes will be largely left to voluntary societies for many years to come. They can, however, do little unless adequate maintenance payments become part of National Insurance legislation. A voluntary society may be willing to raise the capital sum required if there is assurance of adequate statutory payments for maintenance.

For the homebound cripple incapable of regular work, welfare services and diversionary occupations must be provided.

Part II. Co-ordinating Functions of the Council

The Central Council has taken a wide view of the services which it can render to its affiliated organisations, and has provided a central meeting-place for many sections of the community whose work is connected with Orthopaedic and Rehabilitation schemes. It has, for instance, provided such a meeting-place and the secretariat for the following :

Secretary-Superintendents of Orthopaedic Hospitals (the Orthopaedic Group of the Association of Special Hospitals)

Matrons of Orthopaedic Hospitals

The Association of Orthopaedic Physiotherapists (i.e., Members of the Chartered Society of Physiotherapy who also hold certificates in Orthopaedic Nursing)

Head Teachers in Hospital Schools

Secretaries of County and Regional Associations for the Welfare of Cripples

A further notable example of the exercise of its co-ordinating functions is the setting up of a National Certificate in Orthopaedic Nursing. Prior to 1937 each Orthopaedic Hospital issued its own certificate of proficiency, and it was obvious that standards differed considerably, providing no reliable criterion when applications for posts in other Orthopaedic Hospitals and Clinics were being considered. It was therefore decided to set up central examinations based on a uniform syllabus, and these have continued since 1937. Their increasing success led to the formation in 1943 of a Joint Examination Board of the British Orthopaedic Association (the professional body representing Orthopaedic Surgeons) and the Central Council for the Care of Cripples. Perhaps still greater evidence of success may be found in the wish of the General Nursing Council in 1944 to take over the examinations and to set up a special part of the State Register for Orthopaedic Nurses. At the time of writing this memorandum, the Minister of Health has not yet given his final approval to the proposals of the General Nursing Council, and the Joint Examination Board is still the national examining body, its certificate being specifically recognised in the Regulations made by the Minister under Section 6 (1) (B) of the Nurses Act, 1943.

M

In 1928 the Central Council, at the request of the Board of Education, instituted an annual Refresher Course for teachers working in hospital, special and open-air schools, and this was continued until 1938, being cancelled in 1939 owing to the outbreak of war. The Course was renewed in 1946, but the Ministry of Education has now decided to take over the whole responsibility, and the Council's work in this direction has ceased. It still maintains its Education Sub-Committee, however, and will keep in touch with the education of physically-handicapped children and with Special School teachers.

Many people who have been employed by voluntary organisations in Orthopaedic and Rehabilitation Schemes will shortly become a part of the National Health Service, but while it is still too early to make any definite statement, it appears to the Central Council that it can continue to provide a general meeting-place for all the various groups, even if the members of such groups must attend in their individual capacities.

. . .

Conclusion

It will be evident from this memorandum that the Central Council sees no reason why its work should not continue and develop, even though a certain amount of alteration may be necessary in its general policy.

The question of finance is a very serious one, since it will naturally not have the same opportunities of collecting funds from the general public, while its income from affiliation fees may be materially reduced when the Hospitals come under State control. The possibility of grants from the State and from Local Authorities will have to be considered. The administrative work already being done by the Council necessitates expenditure very far in excess of its present income, and it has no funds of any kind for further developments such as the setting up of schools and homes for the severely disabled.

16th June, 1947

CRIPPLES NEEDING RESIDENTIAL HOME CARE *

(Cases from the Surrey Voluntary Association for the Care of Cripples)

Name	Age	Disability	Income	Present Whereabouts	Reason for Needing Home
Mr. X. Y.	59	Paralysis	Some private means —can pay up to £5	In Home where with very old women	Is unhappy in present Home, which obviously most unsuitable
Miss X. Y.	41	Paralysis Agitans	Very small income, ? on P.A.C. as well	At home	Father has just died and she now has no one to care for her at home
Miss X. Y.	43	Cerebral Diplegia	On P.A.C.	At home	Two sisters are working; father is 80 and care of daughter getting too much for him. She does good handwork. Efforts being made to get into Putney or Streatham Homes, but long wait anticipated
Mr. X. Y.	51	Paralysis from stroke	No income. Relatives support him	In Home	Is very unhappy. Present Home is too expensive and is unsuitable as mostly full of old ladies
Miss X. Y.	34	A.P.M.	Small income. In P.A.C. Institution	In P.A.C. Institution in Essex	Only relatives two aunts. Mother recently died and left a little money. Girl is able to get about and help with household tasks or children, but needs some help herself on account of disability. Is very unhappy in P.A.C. Institution and aunt going to Australia so wants to get her placed soon. Is R.C.
Miss X. Y.	39	Arthritis	No income. Parents both on O.A.P.	At present East Surrey Hospital	Want to discharge to free bed in Hospital
Miss X. Y.	45	Disseminated Sclerosis	P.A.C. Relief	In Kingston County Hospital	Sister unable to have at home. Hospital referred to Surrey Voluntary Association, but they could not find a Home. May be in Institution now
Miss X. Y.	40	Deformed Hands Epileptic	P.A.C. Relief	At home	Father is too old to care for her properly

* The initials "X. Y." replace actual initials throughout.

CRIPPLES NEEDING RESIDENTIAL HOME CARE

Name	Age	Disability	Income	Present Whereabouts	Reason for Needing Home
Mr. X. Y...	40	Simmonds Disease, both feet; toes amputated	P.A.C.	In P.A.C. Institution	P.A.C. asked Surrey Voluntary Association to find Home. Some query as to mentality and may be M.D. in slight degree
Miss X. Y.	41	Rheumatoid Arthritis	Kept by aged parents. Mother goes to work and sisters and brothers contribute	At home	Extremely nice people, but home most unsuitable as parents both old and bungalow very damp. Hospital concerned about effect of this on disability. No suitable Home can be found
Miss X. Y.	58	Arthritis	P.A.C. Relief	In Redhill County Hospital	Anxious to discharge to free bed
Mr. X. Y...	31	Hydrocephalus	Working–class family. Father postman	At home	Getting beyond care. Mother has died and there is no one to care for him
Miss X. Y.	50	Arthritis	"Poor circumstances"	In lodgings	At present in hospital, but too helpless to return to former lodgings
Mr. X. Y...	44	Disseminated Sclerosis	No details	At home	P.A.C. asked Surrey Voluntary Association to find Home, but they could not do so. Very few details given
X. Y. (girl)	5	Spastic Paralysis	Working–class family	At home	Is on waiting list for St. Margaret's School, Croydon. May have to wait years for admission. Meanwhile is getting past mother's care and no Home or School can be found
Miss X. Y.	46	Paralysis. Deformed Hands. Deaf	P.A.C. Relief	At home	Referred by many agencies. Is a very difficult woman, not mental but highly neurotic. Will not stay in hospitals and quarrels violently at home. Both parents over 80, mother bedridden and father nearly blind

Annex to Memorandum 14—continued

CRIPPLES NEEDING RESIDENTIAL HOME CARE

Name	Age	Disability	Income	Present Whereabouts	Reason for Needing Home
Mr. X. Y...	44	Rheumatoid Arthritis	Working class	St. Peter's Hospital, Chertsey	Anxious to discharge to free bed. Is very depressed. British Legion tried for Home, but result of this unknown
Mr. X. Y...	46	Muscular Atrophy..	Working class	Dorking County Hospital	Anxious to discharge but no parents. Brother unsympathetic and will not have at his home
Miss X. Y.	26	Spastic Paralysis	Working class	Farnham County Hospital	Admitted to hospital as beyond mother's care. Query slightly M.D. Hospital want discharged to Home, but no suitable one available
Miss X. Y.	30	Fractured Spine	Working class	Farnham County Hospital	Very difficult temperamentally. Fell from window and was queried as suicide. Hospital think should be in Home, but none will accept this "history"
X. Y. (girl)	7	Hydrocephalitis	No details ..	? Stanmore Orthopaedic Hospital	S.C.C. asked for Home while mother had operation, to be permanent if possible. Suggested a convent, but unknown whether this was pursued. May have been sent to Hospital
Miss X. Y.	50	Disseminated Sclerosis	P.A.C.	? P.A.C. Institution	Put into Home but became too helpless and had to go into Institution where unhappy
Miss X. Y.	31	Paralysed Legs and one Arm	P.A.C.	In Mary Yolland Home	In Home at Farnham, but due to leave as she is over age limit
Miss X. Y.	45	Amphytrophic Lateral Sclerosis	About £1 per week..	Redhill County Hospital	Hospital want to discharge to Home to free bed
Mr. X. Y...	55	Disseminated Sclerosis	P.A.C. Relief	At home	Wife elderly. Cannot manage on P.A.C. so does part-time work to supplement. Man very helpless and beyond care of wife

Annex to Memorandum 14—continued

CRIPPLES NEEDING RESIDENTIAL HOME CARE

Name	Age	Disability	Income	Present Whereabouts	Reason for Needing Home
Miss X. Y.	27	Spastic Paralysis	P.A.C.	P.A.C. Institution	Not happy. Slightly M.D. and too young for P.A.C. Institution
Miss X. Y.	52	Rheumatoid Arthritis	Working class	? Farnham County Hospital	Hospital want to discharge to free bed. Very helpless and no Home will take her
X. Y. (boy)	18	Paralysed and Blind in one eye	Gypsy traders ? Father £3 per week	At home	Home unsuitable and dirty. Family unco-operative. Boy makes wooden pegs for sale. Could be taught handicrafts in suitable Home, but none available
Miss X. Y.	50	A.P.M.	£53 per annum from Pensions (F.W.A. and Putney Home)	Was in Red Cross Home	This Home closed. Unknown whereabouts now but Friends of Poor probably put into nursing home temporarily. Is accepted for Putney Home for Incurables but will have long wait. (If goes on relief loses vacancy at Putney Home)
Miss X. Y.	45	Hips immobilised	P.A.C.	Netherne—ready for discharge	In Institution. Was unhappy and got into Home. Difficult and did not settle. Now back in different Institution and says is happy
Miss X. Y.	49	Nerves of leg affected. Said to be progressive	P.A.C. Relief	? At home	Only has one sister. Needs Home where can be taught some useful occupation
Mr. X. Y.	25	Friedreich's Ataxia	Working-class family	At home	Parents find him a great strain at home. Is a temperamentally difficult man. Has been in two Homes and was discharged on account of tempers from both
Miss X. Y.	39	Spinal Tumour	About £1 per week from legacy. P.A.C. supplement this when in a Home	? in Mayday Hospital	Rather difficult woman. Not settled well in several Homes. Now back in Hospital

CRIPPLES NEEDING RESIDENTIAL HOME CARE

Name	Age	Disability	Income	Present Whereabouts	Reason for Needing Home
X. Y. (boy)	17	Anyotomia. Very badly deformed	Working class family	Red Cross Home, Cambridge	Is at home now, as Home is closing down, but needs residential care as has weak chest in addition to other disabilities
Mr. X. Y...	43	Spondylitis ..	Details unknown	? Sutton Hospital ..	Hospital wish to discharge to free bed
X. Y. (boy)	15	Spastic Paralysis ..	Working class	At home	Boy is very helpless and mother finds strain very great as he gets bigger
X. Y. (boy)	20	Spastic Paralysis ..	Working class	At home	Parents killed in road accident. Grandparents have brought up. Both are getting old. Is quite happy at home, but the future is worrying them
X. Y. (boy)	18	A.P.M. (severe) ..	Working class	At home	Home dirty and unsuitable. Hospital put off discharge for some time on this account. Now waiting vacancy at Searchlight Cripples' Workshops, but may have to wait years
Mr. X. Y...	30	Friedreich's Ataxia..	Working class	At home	Severely crippled, but intelligent. Parents getting old. Mother in hospital for cancer operation. Might do some handicrafts in a suitable Home.
Miss X. Y.	37	Muscular Atrophy..	Working class	? Surrey County Hospital	Mother moved Sussex. Another daughter at Home with similar crippling. Is in Surrey Hospital and wants to be in Home in Sussex. Rather difficult woman
Miss X. Y.	41	Paralysis	Sister has small business	? At home	Sister maintains by running small business, but finds this means she cannot give adequate care
X. Y. (boy)	9	Spastic Paralysis ..	Working class	At home	Is quite intelligent and needs education. Is getting beyond mother's care in every way. Awaiting vacancy St. Margaret's, Croydon, may be years before admitted

Annex to Memorandum 14—continued

CRIPPLES NEEDING RESIDENTIAL HOME CARE

Name	Age	Disability	Income	Present Whereabouts	Reason for Needing Home
X. Y. (Girl)	5	Spastic Paralysis	Working-class	Residential Nursery	As above re St. Margaret's. Has been in residential nursery since a few months old
X. Y. (boy)	11	Spastic Paraplegia	Working-class	At home	Needs education and occupation. Is very severely crippled and highly strung
X. Y. (boy)	16	Spastic Paraplegia	Working-class	At home	Having home education arranged by Surrey Voluntary Association. Reported to have improved in every way since this began. Should be having residential education and tuition in walking (?)
X. Y. (boy)	16	Spastic Diplegia	Working-class	At home	Waiting for vacancy at Searchlight Cripples' Workshops for over two years. Not very bright and needs occupation
Miss X. Y.	32	Disseminated Sclerosis	P.A.C. Relief	At home	Getting beyond mother's care. Is very difficult indeed and neurotic
X. Y. (boy)	8	Spastic Diplegia	Working-class	At home	Needs some form of residential school. Not suitable for St. Margaret's, Croydon, as is queried as M.D.
Mr. X. Y...	23	Paralysis from spinal injury	Working-class	? St. Luke's Hospital, Guildford	Hospital anxious to discharge, but home not good or co-operative. On waiting list for Searchlight Workshops for a long time
X. Y. (boy)	19	Muscular Atrophy	No details	P.A.C. Institution	Was at St. Loyes College and placed with firm in Somerset. Mother lives Weybridge. Broke down there and very unhappy and unsuitably placed in Institution, but is bedridden and difficult to find Home. Mother cannot have with her as in flat. Is illegitimate and resents this. Permanent Home with some nursing needed

Annex to *Memorandum* 14—*continued*

CRIPPLES NEEDING RESIDENTIAL HOME CARE

Name	Age	Disability	Income	Present Whereabouts	Reason for Needing Home
Mr. X. Y...	44	Creeping paralysis..	P.A.C. Relief ..	At home	Mother worked till last May when she had to give it up. She is now 68. Finds it very hard to manage. Man is quite helpless and can only feed himself, so difficulty of finding Home bound to be almost insuperable
Miss X. Y.	Elderly	Arthritis	Family comfortably off	Living with sister ..	Tried many Homes before approaching Surrey Voluntary Association. Tried many more suggested by Voluntary Association without result, although could afford to pay. On waiting list for Streatham Home for Incurables but may have two-year wait. Cannot live with sister for long
Mrs. X. Y.	65	Arthritis	On Relief	At home	Very helpless. Lives with married daughter who goes out to work. Cannot attend to herself at all.
Mrs. X. Y.	78	One leg amputated and wears peg leg..	O.A.P. supplemented by P.A.C.	At home	Needs a Home Could pay pensions towards keep. Lives with daughter-in-law suffering from heart trouble whose doctor says she should not have Mrs. X. Y. with her.
Mrs. X. Y.	75	Arthritis	14s. per week from £1,000 invested. Been refused pension on this account	At home	May have to go into Institution Living with relations but they are old and say they cannot keep her much longer. Daughter has had serious cancer operation and is working again. Suffers badly, is drawing on capital to live. Very superior type of family and quite unsuitable for Institution

185

Annex to Memorandum 14—continued

CRIPPLES NEEDING RESIDENTIAL HOME CARE

Name	Age	Disability	Income	Present Whereabouts	Reason for Needing Home
Mr. X. Y...	51	Myelomalecia	Not eligible for P.A.C. as own their own house. Wife earns about £1 per week doing sewing	At home	Left leg badly affected and right beginning to get bad. Superior family. Relieving Officer says the doctor wants X. Y. to go into a Home now as he is getting beyond care of his wife. Only vacancy obtainable was £6 6s. od. per week and this is too expensive
Mrs. X. Y.	Over 70	Fractured femur in accident, arthritis and Parkinson's Disease	No details ..	Epsom County Hospital	Was living with daughter-in-law, but doctor said beyond her care as she was not strong. Admitted to Hospital as a temporary measure as no Home could be found and presumably still there

14. THE NUFFIELD FOUNDATION:
PROVIDENT ASSOCIATIONS

Definition

In the Trust Deed which established the Nuffield Provident Guarantee Fund, Provident Associations are described as "mutual insurance associations formed to assist the members thereof to meet expenditure necessitated by illness involving medical or surgical treatment or maintenance in hospital pay-beds or nursing homes." Their main features are : (1) assistance towards meeting the cost of major illness, and (2) a mutual basis ; and it is convenient to include within the definition all Associations which provide benefits of this kind, whether or not they are organised on a strictly insurance or actuarial basis.

Present Position

At present "provident" benefits can be obtained from three sources :
(a) Provident Associations ;
(b) Extended Benefit Schemes of hospital contributory schemes ;
(c) Pay-bed Associations attached to voluntary hospitals.
The main characteristics of each are as follows :

(a) Provident Associations

These are formed on an insurance basis. Any profits which may accrue from favourable claims experience or economy of management are used to reduce contributions or increase benefits. The benefits are available throughout Great Britain, and in some cases even abroad. The first Association was formed about twenty-five years ago and others have gradually followed. The movement has never been very widespread and has been of slow growth. One of the existing bodies (the British Provident Association) offered its benefits throughout the country, but others (e.g., Oxford, Merseyside, Manchester, and Bristol) recruited members mainly from their own localities, although not refusing members from other districts. The success of these local schemes was sufficient to bring into being in 1941, through the generosity of Lord Nuffield, the Nuffield Provident Guarantee Fund, with the object of assisting the organisation of similar schemes throughout the provinces, and of providing a guarantee to meet any deficits in their early years . . .

(b) Extended Benefit Sections of Hospital Contributory Schemes

The Hospital Contributory Schemes were established after World War I to provide funds for Voluntary Hospitals by means of weekly contributions from the lower income groups. In order that their members should be admitted to the general wards of the hospital without further financial enquiry, they had to limit their membership to persons having incomes within the limits of the National Health Insurance. These Schemes proved immensely successful, and those whose incomes debarred them from membership, and treatment in public wards, demanded similar facilities for treatment in private wards or nursing homes. Many of the schemes, therefore, organised extended benefit sections whereby, for an increased weekly contribution, they could make grants to their members towards the cost of treatment in the private beds of hospitals. Some of these schemes are linked to individual hospitals, and others work throughout one area. In most cases the tables of contributions and benefits are not on an actuarial basis and often there is only one rate of contribution, which is the same for single or married members and covers all dependants.

(c) Pay-Bed Associations attached to Voluntary Hospitals

Some Voluntary Hospitals with blocks of pay-beds have organised their own Pay-Bed Associations. Some of them are run as an integral part of the Hospital, and any surplus is used to augment the income of the Hospital : others are a separate entity and the surplus is used for the benefit of the members of the scheme, either by reducing contributions, or increasing benefits . . .

Future Position

In the near future nearly every citizen will have to pay a National Insurance contribution, and everybody will be entitled to the health services, institutional or domiciliary, provided by the State and the Local Health Authorities. They will not, however, be compelled to use these services. Specialists will still be able to have private patients and to charge fees to such patients. Special accommodation in hospitals may be available on part payment of the cost, or for private patients on payment of the whole cost, and specialists on the staff will be allowed to admit patients to private beds and to charge prescribed fees. Nursing Homes (other than those (a) not carried on for profit and (b) owned by Local Authorities, both of which classes will, presumably, be transferred to the Minister) will still be available to the medical profession for the treatment of their private patients . . .

When specialist medical attention is easily available to everybody, and part at least of most specialists' time is given to the National Health Service, it can be assumed that all patients will receive the same grade of medical attention. The variation of the service obtained by a private and a general patient will arise principally from the difference in the residential amenities, and this is due mainly to the fact that a pay-bed in a hospital or nursing home ensures privacy. Moreover, it is medically important that a patient shall be treated in surroundings equivalent to his social background. It is most likely that this is a privilege for which a number of people will wish to pay even though it entails additional fees and charges. At the same time the high levels of taxation and cost of living will make it increasingly difficult to meet the cost of private treatment out of current income. It remains to attempt to estimate to what extent the population as a whole might demand a private service.

It is known that in 1938 the number of persons in Great Britain with a net income of over £1,000 was approximately 230,000 and with a net income of over £500 was approximately 680,000.

It is impossible to estimate the effect of war-time conditions and high taxation on the income groups and the distribution of income, but it is most likely that at least for some time to come a substantial proportion of this section of the population will be anxious to obtain their hospital treatment within the privacy of a private room.

The other governing factor is the extent of the provision for private patients. It is not yet possible to determine the effect of the introduction of the National Health Service on the number of hospital pay-beds, or whether it will lead to an increase in the number of nursing homes. The total beds available, however . . . are 29,115, and assuming that each bed can be used by 12 people in one year, there would be accommodation for 350,000 cases annually.

It is felt, therefore, that membership of a Provident Association will still give a valuable sense of security to that considerable section of the public which is likely to prefer the privacy of a private room to the general ward of a hospital. It may well be that in the course of time such privacy will be available as a part of the National Hospital Service, but not until extensive building can take place. Obviously, this will not be possible for some years.

It is unlikely that Provident Associations described in (a) above will be very much affected by the new Social Insurance and Health Acts. The position of schemes in class (b) will depend very largely on the size of the individual organisation. If, as seems likely, Hospital Contributory Schemes are no longer required, their extended benefit sections will not be able to continue unless their membership is sufficiently large to enable them to bear the full administrative cost (which, in the past, has been shared with the parent body) and their resources are sufficient to give a feeling of financial security to members. In the case of class (c) it seems probable that when the hospitals are transferred to State ownership, schemes of this nature must cease.

Thus, although the need for Provident benefits is expected to continue, it seems likely that many of the schemes which at present give these benefits will not be able to carry on. The Trustees of the Nuffield Provident Guarantee Fund have, in conjunction with several of the largest existing schemes, for some time been considering how best to meet this situation.

The fact that insurance companies seldom cater for this branch of insurance work is sufficient proof that it is not commercially attractive. It must be organised on lines which are financially sound and as in the case of any service connected with the health and comfort of the community, must give the greatest benefit at the lowest cost. It was felt that these conditions could only be satisfied by a mutual insurance scheme which was actuarially sound and organised on national lines. Moreover, the idea of a country-wide body with regional branches would be fully in keeping with modern trends and could follow the pattern of the National Health Service.

The schedules of contributions and benefits of existing Provident Associations or similar bodies, although approximately identical in scope are by no means uniform. If a new service is to be organised on a national basis it is essential that every member of the community shall be able to obtain equal benefits for equal contributions. It follows that the amalgamation of existing Provident or similar Associations should be effected. The advantages of amalgamation might be summarised as follows :

(1) in matters of medical health politics, a National Scheme could speak with a more effective voice ;

(2) it should offer its members, by reason of the wider spread of risks, greater financial stability than a small fund can expect to do ;

(3) it should accumulate, in course of time, a volume of homogeneous data large enough to enable its business to be placed upon a sounder statistical basis than anything hitherto available in this relatively young branch of insurance business ;

(4) it should, by reason of its size, operate with maximum efficiency in such important matters as :

    (a) a country-wide availability of the service,

    (b) attractive publicity,

    (c) local facilities, through a network of regional branches, to members all over the country.

Accordingly, the Trustees of the Nuffield Provident Guarantee Fund called a conference of all schemes and associations giving benefits in respect of treatment in a hospital pay-bed or nursing home, and as a result, a Provisional Committee was set up to consider the formation of a national scheme.

The Committee considered first the method of amalgamation of existing schemes. After the most careful consideration of the advantages and disadvantages of various possible alternatives, they decided that each existing association should transfer the whole of its assets and liabilities to a new and national body, thereby securing the full effect of an immediate and complete merger. The new body would have its own tables of benefits and contributions which would be available both to new members and to the existing members of the merging bodies. Alternatively, subject to proof of actuarial or other satisfactory standard, members of a merging association might, if preferred, renew their contracts under the existing tables of that body.

In order to preserve the local goodwill and prestige built up by the merging associations, and to encourage local interest in new areas, it was agreed to form branches of the Association which might perhaps conform as far as convenient to the Hospital Regions established under the National Health Act. It is the intention, wherever possible, to enlist the skill and experience of local committees or officers, and in all cases, to allow the greatest possible measure of local autonomy.

The Provisional Committee was representative of most of the larger Provident and similar Associations, and four of these bodies have decided to amalgamate, and a Company limited by guarantee has been incorporated under the title of the British United Provident Association Ltd. . . .

The new Association was not registered until 3rd April, 1947, so it is not yet possible to tell how successful it may be. The existing membership of the amalgamating bodies is over 30,000 and their reserves total at least £60,000.

In addition, Lord Nuffield, through the Nuffield Provident Guarantee Fund, has made available a guarantee of £50,000. There is, therefore, no doubt of its financial stability.

As is stated above, one of the objects in forming the national scheme was to afford continuous cover to members of those schemes which would cease to operate on the commencement of the National Health Service. The Association is willing to accept a transfer of such members without imposing the usual waiting period of three months before benefit is paid and is also waiving the age limit of sixty years for these members. Pay-bed schemes throughout the country are being advised of the offer, and already some of the larger ones have decided to co-operate in this way. In one case the administration of the scheme has already been transferred to the British United Provident Association, together with its assets and liabilities.

When the financial arrangements to be prescribed by the Minister for private patients are known, the tables of contributions and benefits will be adjusted to meet the requirements of the members, and it seems that while private treatment is available to the public, a mutual aid organisation of this nature will be necessary and welcome. The potential membership of such a body is necessarily limited and only by a unified national scheme will it be possible to secure complete financial security, and afford to members the maximum benefit at a minimum cost.

June, 1947

. . .

15. THE LIBERAL PARTY ORGANISATION
LIBERAL POLICY AND THE VOLUNTARY SOCIAL SERVICES

The Right of Free Association

It is a Liberal principle that individuals must have the right to associate freely with those of like mind in pursuit of cultural development, friendly interest, recreation and social intercourse. It follows that the Liberal Party demands with our changing social system that there shall be opportunity for such associations to carry on their chosen activities through the natural medium of voluntary organisations.

The voluntary organisations with which this memorandum is concerned are of six main types.

Six Main Types of Voluntary Organisations

These would seem to be :

(1) Those which perform some particular social service such as that provided by Family Welfare Associations, Invalid Children's Aid Associations and Societies for the care of children deprived of normal home life, etc. These Societies were generally started to meet an emergency. Under recent legislation their functions have been or will be undertaken by central or local State authorities. They will therefore probably continue as auxiliaries to the State authorities and, given that sufficient grant-aid is forthcoming to allow

for adequately-paid staffs, the Liberal view would be that such development would be a fitting extension of their pioneer work. In this connection, the position of the large numbers of "case workers" employed in important social work today needs a great deal of consideration. In order that members of this highly-skilled profession shall be adequately paid, Treasury or Local Authority grants to their organisations are imperative. Further, it must be remembered that the future may hold emergencies as great as those of the past and voluntary effort must be free to battle with them.

(2) Those which carry out services the essence of which is the goodwill of voluntary workers. There are situations in which the power to say "No one is paying me; I am here because I want to help" gives an influence and authority obtainable in no other way. This is particularly true in the case of those whom Society has condemned. Prison visiting and Rescue work afford examples of this type of service.

(3) Those which advocate ideas in the van of current opinion, such as the abolition of capital punishment, etc. Unless opinion is to become static, such societies must be welcomed but before the degree of appeal of new ideas can be measured they must be publicised. Of necessity, these "van" organisations find it difficult to pay the necessary staffs for such publicity. Because enough people have the wish to undertake new work, all voluntary associations are enabled to start unaided. Once the belief is established, the society for its propagation should expect to depend for financial support upon its supporters.

In the category of "van" organisations may also be placed those societies which exist to demonstrate a remedy not yet generally recognised. These fall into two main sections—those which are educational and those which are medical.

In the educational world, Froebel, cripple schools, school children's meals, nursery schools were first established by voluntary effort. It is not impossible that educationally independent bodies will continue to be vitally needed as pacemakers and in order to maintain ever higher standards. It may also fall to the lot of the voluntary society to keep before the public the necessity to prevent any risk of neglect of the introverted type of child who learns best in a small group.

In the medical world, voluntary service established open-air treatment of tuberculosis, psychological medicine, ambulance service, etc. Liberals are naturally anxious that if the State is to be the main body of medical care the importance of independent experiment shall not be lost sight of. A combination of departmental tradition and professional orthodoxy may not be the best nursery for new ideas.

(4) Those which pursue definite cultural, recreational and social aims. Amongst these are Scouts and Guides organisations, The National Federation of Women's Institutes, Townswomen's Guilds, The Workers' Educational Association and many other bodies. Liberals would wish valuable societies such as these to grow and to increase. Those which, like the Federation of Women's Institutes, work upon sound democratic lines and, although often

receiving some local support from education authorities, rely upon membership fees for the greater part of their income, exist to encourage the all-round development of the individual citizen upon independent lines and thus act as a brake upon present tendencies to over-standardisation.

(5) Those which exist to draw attention to errors and omissions on the part of the Government or local authorities. Such are societies as Housing Associations. Here is another public right which Liberals would have retained.

(6) Co-ordinating and consultative societies which seem to be increasing in number and in influence with the Government. In their dealings with Ministries these societies claim to speak for a variety of organisations and it is open to question whether they are in a position to do this. Obviously it is easier for a Government Department to consult with one organisation than with many, but it is a modern tendency which Liberals must deplore. It is impossible for a co-ordinating society to be aware of the up-to-the-minute views of all organisations which it may claim or be deemed to represent. Further, it can present only a majority view at best. And just as Liberals believe that every individual should have the right to a hearing, so they also believe that individual societies have the right to be heard by the appropriate Ministry. Some consultative societies have a considerable paid staff and receive Government grants. They are also the channel for Government grants to other organisations. There is among Liberals some anxiety with regard to the risk of their exercising considerable power without the obligation of publicly reporting their activities or of being challenged in Parliament.

The Present Challenge to Voluntary Organisations

With the growing dependence of formerly self-supporting societies upon State grants, Liberals fear that a valuable means for the expression of initiative and voluntary co-operative effort may be lost. Local Education Authorities are required to provide a comprehensive programme of educational activity from the nursery school to the adult community centre. The Youth Club Advisers and the Community Centre Wardens will presumably be trained to a national syllabus and thus their teaching may result in the standardised citizen.

At the same time, with the State supervising so many activities which were formerly the concern of voluntary societies there is a special risk that these societies may collapse through lack of subscriptions because members believe —often erroneously—that the need no longer exists. This is disastrous for bodies which have undertaken the support of children. A charitable body which is as rigid and unwieldy as a Government Department and which is obliged to spend much of its funds on raising more funds, without becoming secure, combines the disadvantages of both worlds. The special attribute of voluntary societies should be flexibility.

For the preservation of our national enterprise Liberals desire the continued existence of strong voluntary associations, but they urge that the associations must not accept a State-planned existence. Their vitality must spring from spontaneous desire.

N

Summary of Conclusions

The Liberal Party urges :

(*a*) That to counter the present trend towards the production of a standard-ised citizen, public opinion should encourage the existence of completely independent voluntary societies, particularly when these have educational aims.

(*b*) That established voluntary societies should retain their right of direct approach to Whitehall.

(*c*) That the specialised knowledge of certain voluntary workers is of great benefit in some circumstances and should be continued to be used.

Recommendations

(1) There should be no attempt on the part of the State to plan the future activities of voluntary societies.   These must exist by their own volition.

(2) Small central and local Government grants are advantageous, provided that they are not accompanied by absolute control.   At the same time in order that efficiency standards shall be maintained, a Government grant must naturally carry with it representation on the administering committee.

(3) Members of voluntary organisations should be stimulated in the belief that they should become increasingly responsible financially for the mainten-ance of efficient staffs in proportion as these organisations expand.

(4) Where organisations accept large grants of public money, they must submit to public control and be subject to challenge in Parliament.

(5) Legislation is required to introduce a cheaper method of altering charters to meet changing conditions.   Almshouses which have funds to give allow-ances to inmates—for instance—may have no money available for repairs or reconditioning.   As allowances are now supplied by the State, these resources could be more usefully applied to modernise the premises.

17*th September*, 1947

PART V

MEMORANDA BY INDIVIDUALS ON SPECIAL TOPICS

I. EARLY FRIENDLY SOCIETIES

by Lord Beveridge

The following Table E.33 sets out all the Friendly Societies without Branches established before 1800 and still on the Register in 1905.

The societies are arranged under counties. A date in brackets after the name of a county means that there is no society before 1800 and gives the date of the earliest society on the register in 1905.

The word "none" in brackets after a county means that in 1905 no unitary Friendly Societies appeared in the Registrar's return under that county.

Within each county the societies are arranged in the order of their establishment.

Before the name of a Society :

    i means address at an inn

    t   „   „   a coffee tavern, etc.

    s   „   „   a school

    c   „   a church or chapel connection

Societies marked ‡ are described in Section XI of the Registrar's Reports for 1906, pp. x-xix.

Societies marked § are Huguenot in origin

Societies marked ★★ are Specialised Societies not as a rule giving Sick Benefit.

In the Report for 1900 a list of "centenarian" societies was given. Presumably this means all societies established before 1800. These societies number 36 more than the corresponding number in 1905, which was 161 in England, 30 in Scotland, i.e., 191 altogether. The 18th century or earlier societies surviving at various dates are thus :

1899	..	..	227	1928	..	..	70
1905	..	..	191	1945	..	..	53

According to the 1900 Report (p. ix.) the only Orders (i.e., Societies with Branches) dating from the 18th century are Independent United Order of Mechanics established in 1756 or 1757, with 343 members and £3,975 of funds in 1928 (in process of dissolution in 1945) and the United Ancient Order of Druids, established in 1781, with 55,843 members and £576,300 of funds in 1928.

Table E.33

FRIENDLY SOCIETIES ESTABLISHED BEFORE 1800, AND ON REGISTER IN 1905

Name of Society and County	Date of Establishment	1905 Members	1905 Funds £	1928 Members	1928 Funds £	1945 Members	1945 Funds £
ENGLAND							
Bedfordshire :							
i Melchbourne Club ...	1781	14	93	—	—	—	—
Berkshire :							
i Blewbury Friendly Society ...	1756	116	1,639	—	—	—	—
Buckinghamshire :							
i Russell's Arms Benefit Society, Ellesborough..	1797	70	683	—	—	—	—
Cambridgeshire (1837)							
Cheshire :							
i Nantwich Friendly Knot ...	1777	19	207	—	—	—	—
Dukes Club Friendly Society, Runcorn	1790	284	1,838	431	5,693	448	11,988
Northwich Flatman's Friendly Society	1792	113	1,293	—	—	—	—
i Rainow Church and King Friendly Society	1796	45	961	—	—	—	—
Cornwall :							
Launceston Tradesmen's Friendly Society	1765	128	1,771	—	—	—	—
Antony Union Society, Torpoint	1781	57	1,407	—	—	—	—
Millbrook Permanent Annuitant Society Plymouth (*Widows' and Orphans' Society*)**	1787	48	11,366	50	10,665	13	11,275
i Launceston Fellowship Society	1794	29	638	—	—	—	—
i Kilkhampton Union and Friendly Society	1799	133	581	70	790	38	781
Cumberland :							
s Lamplugh Friendly Society ...	1788	219	2,071	109	1,235	50	767
Derbyshire :							
i Eckington Old Friendly Society ...	1751	37	187	—	—	—	—
i Wensley Jubilee Friendly Society ...	1763	101	259	—	—	—	—
i Humane Friendly Indefatigable Union Society, Tideswell	1764	160	2,565	—	—	—	—
i Ashford Men's Friendly Society ...	1769	104	1,563	104	2,705	82	3,329
i Norton Old Friendly Society ...	1773	60	1,465	—	—	—	—
i Friendly Society, Middleton, Wirksworth	1774	101	1,747	—	—	—	—

Table E.33—continued

	Name of Society and County	Date of Establishment	1905 Members	1905 Funds £	1928 Members	1928 Funds £	1945 Members	1945 Funds £
cs	Spondon Friendly Benefit Society	1777	97	2,402	—	—	—	—
i	Joseph and His Brethren Lodge 296, United Ancient Order of Druids	1786	41	517	—	—	—	—
i	Benign Friendly Society, Beeley, Rowsley	1787	125	896	—	—	—	—
s	Ashford Female Friendly Society	1788	39	458	43	546	34	957
	Longford Friendly Society	1789	215	3,813	—	—	—	—
i	Amicable Society, Mapperley	1790	64	412	33	665	18	898
i	Ticknall Friendly Society	1794	67	1,025	—	—	—	—
i	Black Swan Sick and Friendly Society, Crich	1794	43	855	—	—	—	—
s	Female Friendly Society, West Hallam	1795	54	434	—	—	—	—
s	Loyal Evans, Darley Abbey	1797	129	1,976	132	2,132	98	1,852
	Devonshire :							
s	Axminster Male Friendly Society	1762	74	1,223	dissolved 1906			
	Union Benefit Society, Hatherleigh	1763	172	1,890	143	2,178	112	2,301
s	Beer Male Friendly Society	1763	29	103	—	—	—	—
i	Okehampton Free General Society	1764	156	1,064	—	—	—	—
	Friendly Society for Benefit of Widows of Officers of the Royal Marine Forces	1766	96	69,247	52	61,847	30	87,536
i	Exeter Just Doing Society	1769	19	400	—	—	—	—
i	Original Friendly Society, Lifton	1778	209	1,801	—	—	—	—
t	Union Female Benefit, Torrington	1786	122	702	—	—	—	—
i	Lynton Society of Good Fellowship	1786	148	1,441	—	—	—	—
i	Loyal and Constitutional Society, Newton Abbot	1786	40	498	—	—	—	—
i	Friendly United Society of Women, Chudleigh	1786	60	593	—	—	—	—
s	Women's Friendly Society, Sampford Courtenay	1788	46	254	—	—	—	—
i	United and Friendly Society, Woolsery*	1788	111	365	36	439	18	549
i	Female Aiding Society, Newton Abbot	1789	244	1,319	209	2,248	142	2,325
i	Mariners' Union Society, Clovelly	1792	50	968	21	802	dissolved 1945	
i	Loyal Union Society of Females, Hatherleigh	1793	157	1,309	86	1,614	dissolved 1935	
i	Male Union Friendly Society, Dolton (*Dividing*)†	1797	63	203	14	140		

*At Bideford in 1928   †At Torrington, 1928.

199

Table E.33—continued

Name of Society and County	Date of Establishment	1905 Members	1905 Funds £	1928 Members	1928 Funds £	1945 Members	1945 Funds £
i Female Society, Dolton	1799	56	108	18	157	dissolved 1936	
Dorsetshire :							
t Sherborne Old Friendly Society (Dividing)	1761	139	319	105	371	56	324
Durham :							
i Middleton-in-Teesdale Miners' Friendly Society	1797	50	334	—	—	—	—
Essex :							
i Society of Brotherly Love	1761	53	644	—	—	—	—
Gloucestershire :							
t Friendly Society for Women, Dursley	1790	50	1,191	—	—	—	—
Hampshire :							
i Emsworth	1763	29	3,127	31	4,679	35	5,509
Herefordshire (1828)							
Hertfordshire (1802)							
Huntingdonshire :							
i Friendly Society, Great Staughton (Dividing)	1782	11	41	—	—	—	—
Kent :							
i Canterbury Friendly Society	1737	164	2,591	—	—	—	—
i Amicable, Minster	1762	127	182	—	—	—	—
Lancashire :							
Brotherly Knot Society, Manchester	1780	97	1,443	78	1,864	dissolved 1945	
i Downham Benevolent Society	1785	78	1,210	—	—	—	—
i Pool of Bethesda Society, Pilling	1786	136	544	—	—	—	—
Rivington Male Friendly Sick and Burial Society	1786	29	276	—	—	—	—
s Wrigley Head Burial Society**	1794	4,735	11,010	4,415	19,874	4,196	19,947
Female Union Society of Hawkshead	1798	37	225	—	—	—	—
Leicestershire :							
s Earl Shilton Friendly Society	1714	45	339	—	—	—	—
s Bottesford Friendly Society	1744	128	1,712	88	2,689	44	3,314
i Grove Lodge 868 Nottingham Oddfellows	1767	9	16	—	—	—	—

Table E.33—continued

Name of Society and County	Date of Establishment	1905 Members	1905 Funds £	1928 Members	1928 Funds £	1945 Members	1945 Funds £
Newtown Linford Female Society	1780	73	700	—	—	—	—
s Hathern Friendly Society	1789	151	546	—	—	—	—
s Prince of Wales Friendly Society, Sapcote	1791	23	305	—	—	—	—
i Old Friendly Society, Hinckley	1792	45	266	—	—	—	—
i Friendly Society of Tradesmen, Newtown Linford	1794	32	294	14	207	5	177
s Great Dalby Friendly Society	1794	64	372	—	—	—	—
i Queniborough Friendly Society	1795	28	567	—	—	—	—
i Newbold Verdon Imperial Friendly Society	1795	53	170	—	—	—	—
Lincolnshire :							
Friendly Society, Epworth	1773	27	502	—	—	—	—
London :							
i Friendly Benefit Society, Norfolk Arms, Bethnal Green§‡	1687	60	1,274	—	—	—	—
c Union Friendly Society, Newington	1690	21	573	—	—	—	—
i Norman Society§‡	1703	63	3,170	61	2,974	49	4,056
i Society of Linton§‡	1708	62	2,828	63	2,791	52	3,144
i Goldsmiths' Friendly Society	1712	107	2,809	104	3,997	74	4,435
i Friendly Society, Baxendale Arms	1720	33	564	—	—	—	—
Society for Benefit of Widows of Officers of Royal Regiment of Artillery**	1752	279	148,267	300	288,682	309	382,035
Protestant Refugees from High and Low Normandy Friendly Society§‡	1764	37	1,351	37	1,963	32	2,102
Royal Laboratory Burial Society**	1772	457	1,108	dissolved 1906			
i Amicable Benefit Society, Saddlers and Harness Makers, etc.	1779	—	—				
Beaconsfield Friendly Benefit Society (Bethnal Green)	1783	73	869	—	—	—	—
Laudable and United Society	1783	25	1,588	—	—	—	—
Christian Brotherly Society, Roehampton	1783	80	2,836	68	5,404	63	6,282
Social Union Friendly Society	1786	26	1,042	30	1,258	20	1,520

Table E.33—continued

Name of Society and County	Date of Establishment	1905 Members	1905 Funds £	1928 Members	1928 Funds £	1945 Members	1945 Funds £
Chesterfield Union Benefit Society ..	1792	153	2,784	—	—	—	—
i Amicable Society of United Britons ..	1796	82	1,985	—	—	—	—
Protestant Union (*Widows and Orphans*)§	1798	202	90,649	250	105,934	301	151,596
Middlesex (1817)							
Monmouthshire (1821)							
Norfolk :							
i Snettisham, King's Lynn	1783	38	1,564	—	—	—	—
Norfolk and Norwich Benefit Medical Society**	1786	20	8,952	42	16,258	67	22,726
i Friendly Society, Aylsham	1787	16	871	—	—	—	—
i Young Friendly Society, Snettisham	1794	31	2,736	—	—	—	—
Northamptonshire :							
s Welford Friendly and Humane Society	1771	98	392	26	320	dissolved 1930	
i Amicable Society of Several Trades and Callings, King's Cliffe, Wansford	1772	133	1,251	76	772	32	654
i Elder Amicable Provident Society, Finedon	1773	55	240	—	—	—	—
i Society of Good Fellowship, Peterborough	1777	39	721	—	—	—	—
i East Haddon Friendly Society	1783	155	941	49	308	dissolved 1932	
i Friendly and Humane Society, Rugby	1786	31	197	—	—	—	—
i Original Tradesmen's Friendly Society	1790	25	1,036	—	—	—	—
i Guilsborough and Hollowell Club	1791	30	122	—	—	—	—
Northumberland :							
i Prudhoe Friendly Society	1770	53	245	—	—	—	—
i Keelman's Benefit Society	1786	33	100	—	—	—	—
i Newcastle-on-Tyne Printers' Benefit Society	1797	245	2,297	318	3,094	282	3,273
Nottinghamshire :							
Chilwell Men's Old Sick Club	1772	109	1,619	97	2,063	105	2,408
i Amicable and Frugal Society or Club, Melton Mowbray	1785	61	830	—	—	—	—
i Heart and Hand Friendly Society, Ruddington	1794	32	376	—	—	—	—
Oxfordshire :							
i Friendly Society, Stonesfield, Woodstock	1765	69	186	—	—	—	—

Table E.33—continued

Name of Society and County	Date of Establishment	1905 Members	1905 Funds £	1928 Members	1928 Funds £	1945 Members	1945 Funds £
Rutland:							
i Morcott Friendly Society	1773	42	405	—	—	—	—
Shropshire:							
Union Society, Whitchurch ..	1788	114	2,744	—	—	—	—
Nesscliff Friendly Society, Great Ness ..	1794	176	3,152	—	—	—	—
Somersetshire:							
s Female Club, Cheddar ..	1790	5	1,464	91	1,334	109	2,039
s Shipham and Rowberrow Female Club ..	1792	52	1,073	43	827	50	863
s Wrington Female Friendly Society ..	1797	85	756	69	616	46	980
Staffordshire:							
i Cannock Friendly Society	1780	78	1,029	—	—	—	—
i Wolverhampton Benevolent Society ..	1786	32	743	—	—	—	—
i Wolverhampton Brotherly Society ..	1790	169	1,766	99	1,483	45	1,647
i Royal Oak Friendly Society, Stoke-on-Trent ..	1792	29	484	—	—	—	—
s Elford Friendly Society	1794	48	1,082	—	—	—	—
i Yoxall Old Friendly Society (Dividing)	1794	82	217	109	387	83	341
Suffolk (1807)							
Surrey:							
s Epsom and Leatherhead Friendly Society ..	1794	70	3,228	—	—	—	—
Sussex:							
i Society of Good Fellowship, Petworth ..	1794	28	3,133	—	—	—	—
Warwickshire:							
i Birmingham Musical Society	1742	109	2,890	204	9,936	203	13,077
Birmingham Roman Catholic Friendly Society	1795	262	6,134	539	31,308	360	39,558
Birmingham Unitarian Brotherly Benefit Society	1798	662	15,215	—	—	—	—
Westmorland (1840)							
Wiltshire:							
Hand-in-Hand Friendly Society, Salisbury ..	1778	101	296	—	—	—	—
Worcestershire:							
i Friendly Society, Wythall	1772	25	244	—	—	—	—
c Provident Society in connection with Presbyterian Chapel, Stourbridge	1784	54	3,391	—	—	—	—

Table E.33—continued

Name of Society and County	Date of Establishment	1905 Members	1905 Funds £	1928 Members	1928 Funds £	1945 Members	1945 Funds £
i Old Rose and Crown Friendly Society, Rubery	1795	95	1,701	33	1,230	dissolved 1936	
Yorkshire:							
i Skelton Friendly Society	1737	51	1,122	—	—	—	—
i Friendly and Brotherly Society, Pontefract	1744	301	3,657	—	—	—	—
i Barwick Brotherly Society	1760	37	239	—	—	—	—
i Armley Clothiers' Loyal and Friendly Society	1760	200	2,494	121	2,513	88	1,900
New Union Society, York	1767	141	4,738	196	2,891	217	4,428
Helmsley Orderly Society	1767	135	5,171	127	4,600	103	4,349
York Amicable Society	1767	125	4,454	—	—	—	—
i Young Amicable Society, Wadworth	1779	37	412	—	—	—	—
i Loyal Georgean, Halifax	1779	197	5,471	199	8,022	200	10,176
i Mutual Beneficence Society, Braithwell	1780	54	412	—	—	—	—
i Bolsterstone Sick Benefit and Funeral Society	1780	24	46	dissolved 1906		—	—
i Brotherly Society, Wetherby	1781	26	244	—	—	—	—
i Wombwell Club	1786	81	279	—	—	—	—
i Amicable Society in Bolton-by-Bowland	1788	124	1,667	55	861	dissolved 1943	
i Oulton and Woodlesford Friendly Society	1789	63	1,817	64	1,366	54	1,660
i Ecclesall New Friendly Society	1789	39	1,970	—	—	—	—
i Royal Victoria Female Benefit Friendly Society, Northallerton	1790	36	136	26	612	dissolved 1937	
i Aston Sick Club, Sheffield	1790	42	1,464	—	—	—	—
i Patrington Amicable	1792	265	2,828	—	—	—	—
Old Provident Society, Park Street, Leeds	1795	81	3,422	53	2,383	dissolved 1931	
i Thorpe Salvin Friendly Society, Sheffield	1795	32	174	dissolved 1906		—	—
Female Benefit Society, Meeting House Lane, Sheffield	1795	120	2,487	—	—	—	—
i Amicable Independent Oddfellows, Sheffield	1798	57	3,052	—	—	—	—

Table E.33—continued

Name of Society and County	Date of Establishment	1905 Members	1905 Funds £	1928 Members	1928 Funds £	1945 Members	1945 Funds £
WALES							
t Newtown First Benefit Society (*Montgomery*)	1762	119	1,823	dissolved	1906	—	—
i True Ancient Britons Society, Pyle (*Glamorgan*)	1766	60	645	—	—	—	—
i Ancient Britons Friendly Society, St. Dogmaels (*Pembroke*)	1777	106	561	—	—	—	—
i Kidwelly Benefit Friendly Society (*Carmarthen*)	1785	20	626	—	—	—	—
i Maesteg Faithful Friend Society (*Glamorgan*)	1794	201	2,162	158	3,626	128	4,027
i Welshpool Second Friendly Society (*Montgomery*)	1795	153	2,291	—	—	—	—
s Cwmystwyth Friendly Society (*Cardigan*)	1798	93	158	—	—	—	—
s Llanarmon-Dyffryn-Ceiriog Friendly Society (*Denbigh*)	1798	216	2,787	143	3,793	127	4,596
SCOTLAND*							
Aberdeenshire : St. Andrew's Society of Aberdeen**	1788	90	15,562	83	15,672	56	17,766
Argyllshire (1843)							
Ayrshire (1812)							
Banffshire (none)							
Berwickshire (none)							
Buteshire (none)							
Caithness-shire (one, 1884)							
Clackmannanshire :							
Devon Colliery Friendly Society	1741	196	345	—	—	—	—
Dumbartonshire :							
Old Kilpatrick Friendly Society	1756	56	1,378	37	1,374	dissolved	—
Dumfries-shire (1842)							
Edinburghshire :							
Incorporation of Carters in Leith†	1555	65	7,212	68	7,620	51	11,007
Friendly Society of Fishermen of Fishherrow..	1760	113	230	—	—	—	—
Corstorphine Friendly Society	1789	29	319	—	—	—	—
United Presbyterian Ministers' Friendly Society	1797	387	88,291	—	—	—	—

Table E.33—continued

Name of Society and County	Date of Establishment	Members 1905	Funds 1905 £	Members 1928	Funds 1928 £	Members 1945	Funds 1945 £
Elginshire (none)							
Fifeshire :							
Poor Sea Box of St. Andrews‡	1643	7	2,646	—	—	—	—
Burgesses and Trades Poor Box of Anstruther Easter	1701	—	6,649	40	6,979	38	7,583
Ancient Society of Gardeners, Dunfermline	1716	21	3,537	173	3,931	153	4,019
Halbeath Friendly Burying Society	1796	263	47	—	—	—	—
Forfarshire (1812)							
Haddingtonshire (1820)							
Inverness-shire (1842)							
Kincardineshire (1873)							
Kinross-shire (none)							
Kircudbrightshire (1874)							
Lanarkshire :							
Lesmahagow Masonic Friendly Society	1736	84	132	—	—	—	—
Journeymen Baker's Friendly Society of Glasgow	1765	109	2,068	—	—	—	—
Glasgow Journeymen Coopers' Society	1770	79	1,214	—	—	—	—
Glasgow Water of Endrick Friendly Society	1771	301	6,157	231	10,517	Registered but no members or funds	
Camlachie Old Friendly Society	1772	97	2,130	27	1,473	dissolved 1939	
Airdrie Weavers' Friendly Society	1781	100	1,372	91	2,019	116	3,177
Clydesdale Upper Ward Society, Glasgow	1785	203	1,558	43	1,980	—	—
Airdrie First of August Friendly Society	1789	37	87	—	—	—	—
Glasgow Galloway Brotherly Society	1791	192	5,658	273	11,578	dissolved 1937	
Glasgow Hibernian Funeral Society	1792	57	377	—	—	—	—
Friendly Society of Sons of Bakers in Glasgow	1793	80	6,331	—	—	—	—
Master Bakers Friendly Society of Glasgow	1795	89	3,513	77	7,597	dissolved 1937	
Parkhead Friendly Society	1798	93	838	47	792	28	1,827
Linlithgowshire :							
United General Sea Box of Borrowstounness Friendly Society‡	1634	45	8,310	36	10,002	45	11,328
Fraternity of Dyers, Linlithgow‡	1679	48	4,075	30	5,497	15	5,780

Table E.33—continued

Name of Society and County	Date of Establish-ment	Members 1905	Funds 1905 £	Members 1928	Funds 1928 £	Members 1945	Funds 1945 £
Beneficent Society in Borrowstounness .. :	1781	48	4,455	42	6,125	40	5,983
Nairnshire (none)							
Orkney (none)							
Peebles-shire (none)							
Perthshire (1881)							
Renfrewshire :							
Society of Weavers in Pollokshaws .. :	1749	110	2,567	109	5,028	97	7,276
Inverkip Society (Female) .. :	1798	8	1,183				
Ross and Cromarty (none)							
Roxburghshire (1875)							
Selkirkshire (1889)							
Shetland (none)							
Stirlingshire :							
Carron Friendly Society .. :	1762	192	1,015	—	—	—	—
Sutherlandshire (none)							
Wigtownshire (none)							

*The nomenclature used for Scottish counties in the Chief Registrar's Reports was revised in 1932 and the following alterations were made :—Midlothian for Edinburghshire ; Westlothian for Linlithgowshire ; East Lothian for Haddingtonshire ; Moray for Elginshire ; Angus for Forfarshire ; Zetland for Shetland.

2. UNITARY FRIENDLY SOCIETIES IN 1905 AND 1945

by LORD BEVERIDGE

Tables E.34 to E.40 are designed to show what has happened to the Unitary Friendly Societies of various kinds between 1905 and 1945. For this purpose the societies have been classified under five main heads : Accumulating and Deposit, Juvenile, Dividing, Death and Burial, and Other Specialised ; for this purpose Holloway Societies are reckoned as the Registrar reckons them, among the Deposit Societies. The first three heads are grouped together as General Societies ; the last two are grouped as Specialised, the "Other Specialised" including societies for widows and orphans, institutional treatment, accident, etc. Under each head the societies have been analysed by size : with less than 100 members, 100 to 199 members, 200 to 499 members, 500 to 999 members and 1,000 members and upwards. To save labour the analysis has been confined to 16 counties altogether with a total population of 19,102,000. The counties selected include London, Lancashire, Yorkshire and Warwickshire with large industrial populations, though in the last two there are also extensive rural areas, eight mainly rural counties in England, Glamorgan in Wales, and three mainly industrial counties of Scotland.

In Britain as a whole the number of Unitary Friendly Societies was 6,700 in 1905 and 2,500 in 1945, representing a fall to 37.3 per cent., little more than a third. In the selected counties the number of such societies was 3,774 in 1905 and 1,399 in 1945, representing almost exactly the same proportionate fall, to 37.1 per cent. The total of 3,774 unitary societies in selected counties in 1905 includes 112 which were dissolved almost immediately thereafter. These have been omitted in the analysis of societies by size as, being near dissolution, they had very few members in 1905 ; their inclusion would have swollen unduly the proportionate number of very small societies.

The change in the numbers of societies under the five main heads in the selected counties is shown summarily as follows :

Type of Society		Number of Societies 1905	1945	1945 as percentage of 1905
Accumulating and Deposit	..	2,028	490	24.2
Juvenile	..	390	198	50.1
Dividing	..	991	380	38.3
Death and Burial ..	..	202	165	81.7
Other Specialised ..	..	51	166	325.5

In the forty years from 1905 to 1945, three-quarters of the Accumulating and Deposit societies, half the Juvenile societies and nearly two-thirds of the Dividing societies have disappeared from the Register. The mortality among Death and Burial societies has been much less, not one in five. The small number of societies registered in 1905 for Other Specialised purposes has increased more than threefold.

A considerable proportion of the small Accumulating societies in 1905, particularly in Lancashire and Yorkshire, are shown by their names to represent secessions from Affiliated Orders. Presumably some of these rejoined the parent body. Others no doubt contributed to the high mortality of such societies.

Analysis by size shows that in 1905 four out of five (80.9 per cent.) of the general societies (Accumulating and Deposit, Juvenile and Dividing) had less than 200 members each, and only 3.2 per cent. had 1,000 members or more. By 1945 the proportion of General Societies with more than 1,000 members had risen to 10.5 per cent. and the proportion of small societies had fallen, but more than three out of five (63.2 per cent.) were still composed of less than 200 members each.

The Specialised societies tend in general to be larger. Only three in place of six or eight out of every 10 have less than 200 members ; one out of every three or four has 1,000 members or more.

While the general movement in the counties examined, taken as a whole, is probably typical of the country as a whole, the examination shows striking local differences.

Thus, in Lancashire, Dividing societies in 1905 outnumber the Accumulating and Deposit societies ; in Yorkshire there are hardly any Dividing societies. Suffolk has a substantial number of such societies, while Norfolk has only one. In Warwickshire, Dividing societies are even stronger than in Lancashire, totalling 277 against 119 of the Accumulating, Deposit and Juvenile societies. London also shows a relatively large number of Dividing societies. Apart from Suffolk they are very rare in the rural counties of England and are all but unknown in Wales and Scotland.

For each of the four counties with the largest numbers of societies the 1905 figures are shown in two sections, divided roughly into registrations before and after 1889 in London, 1872 in Lancashire, 1873 in Yorkshire, 1899 in Warwickshire. This brings out the extent to which in the later period a growing proportion of all registrations was that of Dividing societies. In Warwickshire hardly any others were registered in the second period.

o

Table E.34

SAMPLE COUNTIES FOR UNITARY FRIENDLY SOCIETIES

County	1945 Popu-lation	1905			1945		
	(000)	General	Special-ised	All Societies	General	Special-ised	All Societies
London	2,882	466	27	493	258	101	359
Lancashire	4,659	948	159	1,107	182	113	295
Yorkshire	4,189	592	22	614	197	41	238
Warwickshire	1,682	396	8	404	118	14	132
Bedfordshire and Hert-fordshire	811	101	1	102	49	2	51
Lincolnshire	620	154	2	156	41	7	48
Norfolk	471	129	2	131	53	6	59
Suffolk	381	104	—	104	33	10	43
Cornwall, Devonshire, Somersetshire ..	1,724	190	2	192	47	11	58
Glamorganshire ..	1,119	216	4	220	45	10	55
Lanarkshire*	291	61	18	79	25	6	31
Midlothian*	84	34	2	36	14	5	19
Fifeshire	189	18	6	24	6	5	11
Totals	19,102	3,409	253	3,662	1,068	331	1,399

*As at 30th June, 1945, excluding large burghs. Population : Edinburgh B., 421,006 ; Glasgow B., 993,124.

Table E.35

ACCUMULATING, DEPOSIT, JUVENILE AND DIVIDING SOCIETIES

Summary, 1905

Numbers grouped by class and by size of membership ; percentages according to size of membership

	Under 100		100—199		200—499		500—999		1,000 and over		Total	
	No.	%age	No.	%age	No.	%age	No.	%age	No.	%age	No.	%age
Accumulating and Deposit ..	938	46.3	634	31.3	295	14.5	77	3.8	84	4.1	2,028	100.0
Juvenile	272	69.8	67	17.2	31	7.9	11	2.8	9	2.3	390	100.0
Dividing ..	649	65.5	199	20.1	104	10.5	23	2.3	16	1.6	991	100.0
Total	1,859	54.5	900	26.4	430	12.6	111	3.3	109	3.2	3,409	100.0

Summary, 1945

Numbers grouped by class and by size of membership ; percentages according to size of membership

	Under 100		100—199		200—499		500—999		1,000 and over		Total	
	No.	%age	No.	%age	No.	%age	No.	%age	No.	%age	No.	%age
Accumulating and Deposit ..	183	37.3	120	24.5	90	18.4	30	6.1	67	13.7	490	100.0
Juvenile	104	52.5	44	22.2	25	12.6	12	6.1	13	6.6	198	100.0
Dividing	148	38.9	77	20.2	93	24.6	30	7.9	32	8.4	380	100.0
Total	435	40.7	241	22.5	208	19.5	72	6.8	112	10.5	1,068	100.0

Table E.36

SPECIALISED SOCIETIES

Summary, 1905

Numbers grouped by class and by size of membership; percentages according to size of membership

	Under 100		100—199		200—499		500—999		1,000 and over		Total	
	No.	%age	No.	%age	No.	%age	No.	%age	No.	%age	No.	%age
Death and Burial	27	13.4	28	13.9	35	17.3	38	18.8	74	36.6	202	100.0
Other Specialised	12	23.5	8	15.7	15	29.4	6	11.8	10	19.6	51	100.0
Total	39	15.4	36	14.2	50	19.8	44	17.4	84	33.2	253	100.0

Summary, 1945

Numbers grouped by class and by size of membership; percentages according to size of membership

	Under 100		100—199		200—499		500—999		1,000 and over		Total	
	No.	%age	No.	%age	No.	%age	No.	%age	No.	%age	No.	%age
Death and Burial	26	15.8	23	13.9	49	29.7	31	18.8	36	21.8	165	100.0
Other Specialised	35	21.1	18	10.8	33	19.9	26	15.7	54	32.5	166	100.0
Total	61	18.4	41	12.4	82	24.8	57	17.2	90	27.2	331	100.0

Table E.37

"OTHER" i.e., ACCUMULATING AND DEPOSIT, JUVENILE AND DIVIDING SOCIETIES, 1905

Numbers grouped according to size and County of Registration

Total	County	Under 100			100—199			200—499			500—999			1,000 plus			All sizes		
		Oth.	J.	D.	Oth.	J.	D.	Oth.	J.	D.	Oth.	J.	D.	Oth.	J.	D.	Oth.	J.	D.
244	London I	60	17	24	43	4	15	30	1	6	12	—	3	26	1	2	171	23	50
222	London II	50	16	43	29	2	27	9	4	22	2	1	3	6	1	7	96	24	102
358	Lancashire I	87	2	64	78	—	9	71	3	8	16	—	5	12	1	2	264	6	88
590	Lancashire II	75	27	263	58	6	78	28	4	35	5	2	2	5	1	1	171	40	379
287	Yorkshire I	139	2	4	97	—	1	38	—	1	1	—	2	2	—	—	277	2	8
305	Yorkshire II	105	30	7	78	12	8	36	3	5	10	3	2	4	2	—	233	50	22
223	Warwickshire I	34	31	66	21	5	29	8	2	10	6	1	2	4	1	3	73	40	110
173	Warwickshire II	5	—	127	1	—	28	—	—	10	—	—	2	—	—	—	6	—	167
101	Bedfordshire & Hertfordshire	40	17	—	22	5	—	13	1	—	3	—	—	—	—	—	78	23	—
154	Lincolnshire	57	30	4	34	4	—	18	2	—	4	—	—	—	1	—	113	37	4
129	Norfolk	39	45	1	18	13	—	6	6	—	1	—	—	—	—	—	64	64	1
104	Suffolk	20	25	20	18	9	—	2	3	2	3	—	—	2	—	—	45	37	22
37	Cornwall	19	2	—	10	2	—	4	—	—	—	—	—	—	—	—	33	4	—
70	Devonshire	34	—	1	25	—	1	4	—	2	2	—	—	1	—	—	66	—	4
83	Somersetshire	23	14	24	6	4	1	6	1	2	1	—	—	1	—	—	37	19	27
216	Glamorgan	113	11	1	57	—	1	9	—	—	7	1	—	16	—	—	202	12	2
61	Lanarkshire	20	—	—	18	1	1	6	1	1	1	3	2	5	1	1	50	6	5
34	Midlothian	12	1	—	16	—	—	5	—	—	—	—	—	—	—	—	33	1	—
18	Fifeshire	6	2	—	5	—	—	2	—	—	3	—	—	—	—	—	16	2	—
3,499	Totals	938	272	649	634	67	199	295	31	104	77	11	23	84	9	16	2,028	390	991

Table E.38

"OTHER" i.e., ACCUMULATING AND DEPOSIT, JUVENILE AND DIVIDING SOCIETIES, 1945

Numbers grouped according to size and County of Registration

Total	County	Under 100			100—199			200—499			500—999			1,000 plus			All sizes		
		Oth.	J.	D.	Oth.	J.	D.	Oth.	J.	D.	Oth.	J.	D.	Oth.	J.	D.	Oth.	J.	D.
258	London	14	4	—	11	2	36	14	2	49	7	1	16	32	—	28	78	9	171
182	Lancashire	20	11	42	19	6	20	18	5	13	3	3	1	6	2	—	66	27	89
197	Yorkshire	47	13	55	50	8	4	29	7	6	11	3	3	8	3	1	145	34	18
118	Warwickshire	4	11	4	3	4	11	4	2	23	1	—	7	6	1	2	18	18	82
49	Bedfordshire & Hertfordshire	18	10	39	6	3	1	4	2	1	2	—	1	—	1	—	30	16	3
41	Lincolnshire	17	6	—	6	—	1	5	—	—	1	1	—	1	—	—	30	7	4
53	Norfolk	9	25	3	3	13	1	—	2	—	—	1	—	—	—	—	12	40	1
33	Suffolk	5	12	—	2	3	—	3	3	1	2	—	—	1	—	—	13	19	1
47	Cornwall, Devonshire & Somersetshire	17	7	4	6	1	2	3	1	—	—	—	—	—	—	—	31	9	7
45	Glamorgan	19	4	—	10	1	1	6	—	—	1	—	—	5	1	—	38	6	1
25	Lanarkshire	7	—	1	3	2	—	3	—	—	1	1	2	2	3	—	16	6	3
14	Midlothian	5	1	—	—	—	—	1	—	—	1	2	—	5	2	—	10	4	—
6	Fifeshire	1	1	—	1	1	—	—	1	—	—	—	—	1	—	—	3	3	1
1,068	Totals	183	104	148	120	44	77	90	25	93	30	12	30	67	13	32	490	198	380

Table E.39

SPECIALISED SOCIETIES, 1905*

Numbers grouped according to size and County of Registration

Total	County	Under 100		100—199		200—499		500—999		1,000 plus		All sizes	
		D.B.	Other	D.B.	Other	D.B.	Other	D.B.	Other	D.B.	Other	D.B.	Other
20	London I	6	1	1	1	3	2			1	5	11	9
7	London II		1			2	1	3				5	2
100	Lancashire I	6	2	10	2	21	2	13		42	2	92	8
59	Lancashire II	8	1	11		5	1	16	1	16		56	3
14	Yorkshire I		2		2		2			6	2	6	8
8	Yorkshire II		2				1	1	1	2	1	3	5
8	Warwickshire I		2		2		1		1	2		2	6
Nil	Warwickshire II												
1	Bedfordshire and Hertfordshire								1				1
2	Lincolnshire				1				1				2
2	Norfolk						2						2
Nil	Suffolk												
Nil	Cornwall												
Nil	Devonshire												
2	Somersetshire						2						2
4	Glamorgan	1	1				1		1			1	3
18	Lanarkshire	5		2		3		5		3		18	
2	Midlothian	1		1								2	
6	Fifeshire			3		1				2		6	
253	Totals	27	12	28	8	35	15	38	6	74	10	202	51

*DB in column-headings = Death and Burial

215

Table E.40

SPECIALISED SOCIETIES, 1945*

Numbers grouped according to size and County of Registration

Total	County	Under 100		100—199		200—499		500—999		1,000 plus		All sizes	
		D.B.	Other	D.B.	Other	D.B.	Other	D.B.	Other	D.B.	Other	D.B.	Other
101	London	1	13	4	6	9	17	3	14	6	28	23	78
113	Lancashire	15	3	16	4	26	5	15	5	19	5	91	22
41	Yorkshire	5	4		1	3	5	8	2	5	8	21	20
14	Warwickshire ..	1	2		1	1	3		2	2	2	4	10
2	Bedfordshire and Hertfordshire					1					1	1	1
7	Lincolnshire	1	1		1			1		1	2	3	4
6	Norfolk		2	1	2						1	1	5
10	Suffolk		2	1		3				2	2	6	4
11	Cornwall, Devonshire, Somersetshire	2	2			4	1				2	6	5
10	Glamorgan		2			1	2	1	2		2	2	8
6	Lanarkshire			1		1		3			1	5	1
5	Midlothian		2		2					1		1	4
5	Fifeshire	1	2		1				1			1	4
331	Totals ..	26	35	23	18	49	33	31	26	36	54	165	166

* D.B. in column headings = Death and Burial

216

3. NOTE ON CINEMA ATTENDANCES

by Lord Beveridge

Attendance at the cinema has been the subject of two recent inquiries, one by the Government Social Survey relating to March-October, 1946, one by Research Services commissioned by Hulton Publications Ltd., relating to January-May, 1947. Each was made by similar methods—of questioning individuals chosen, so far as possible, as a random sample of the population. The Research Services Survey does not cover children under 16 at all and the age groupings of the others are different, e.g., the Research Services Survey has a group of ages 16 to 24 inclusive, while the Government Social Survey divides into 16-19 inclusive and 20-29 inclusive.

The Research Services Survey yields in general higher figures of attendance than the Government Survey, e.g., for all persons 16 and upwards 44 per cent. regulars (going once a week or more) as against 32 per cent. in the Government Survey. This difference may be due in part to the later date of the Research Service Survey, after greater return to normal life. It may mean also that it is nearer the truth ; there are some grounds for thinking that the Government Survey understates the extent of cinema-going. The total expenditure on cinema seats in a year as derived from the Government Survey is put at about £100 million. This is materially less than the £121 million in 1946 shown in the White Paper on National Income and Expenditure. The difference appears to be more than can be accounted for by the fact that the Survey excludes, while the White Paper includes, Northern Ireland and expenditure by H.M. Forces and visitors from abroad.

There is a difference in the results of the two surveys in relation to the habits of different economic classes. The Government Survey classifies families in three groups according to the wage-rate or salary of the chief earner or if there was no earner the pension or other income of the head of the family :

Lower, up to £4 per week.

Middle, over £4 up to £5 10s. od. per week.

Higher, over £5 10s. od. per week.

The proportions of regular attendants (once a week or more) are highest in the middle group (36 per cent.) and lowest in the poorest group (26 per cent.) with the richer group intermediate (30 per cent.). This suggests that cinema-going is restricted in the lower group by lack of means and in the higher by other interests. This, however, relates only to adults. The children of the two less-prosperous groups go with much the same regularity and those of the higher group much less frequently ; they find their amusements more at home.

The Research Services Survey shows also three main social classes, lower, middle and higher, but the classification is different and the results are different. The poorest are the most regular (47 per cent.), then the middle group (41 per cent.), with the higher group coming last (32 per cent.). The cinema appears as essentially the poor man's delight.

In most other respects the results of the two inquiries are similar, particularly in the emphasis on adolescence as the peak period of cinema-going. Nearly half of the young people (46 per cent. 16-24, 45 per cent. 16-19) go twice a week or oftener. Three-quarters (77 per cent. 16-24, 69 per cent. 16-19) go once a week or oftener ; 2 per cent. only do not go at all. The cinema-going habit of adolescence is acquired at the school age. According to the Government Survey, two-thirds of the boys and girls 10-16 (65 per cent.) go once a week or oftener.

There is no marked difference between the sexes. More women than men, slightly more boys than girls, go regularly.

The average number of visits each week per head of the population is for all adults put at .83 by Research Services Survey, .56 by the Government Survey. The averages for adolescents in the two inquiries are similar, 1.53 at 16-24, 1.43 at 16-19, that is to say 1½ in a week. The average for children 10-15 is given in the Government Survey as .75.

Using the Research Services results, Mr. Mark Abrams estimates that the 4,800 cinemas in the United Kingdom sell each week 30,000,000 tickets (27,000,000 to adults and 3,000,000 to children under 16) at an average price of 1s. 6d. Of the £121 million spent on cinema tickets in 1946, roughly £40 million came from people aged 16-24, and another £30 million from those aged 25-34.

4. WIRELESS APPEALS FOR THE WEEK'S GOOD CAUSE

by Lord Beveridge

The Week's Good Cause became a regular feature of the B.B.C. in January, 1926, although appeals had been made sporadically before that time. In the past 21 years well over three million pounds has been contributed by listeners. In 1927 the Central Appeals Advisory Committee, composed of social service experts, was formed, the present chairman being the Countess of Limerick. In 1934, Regional Appeals Advisory Committees were set up, and, after being in abeyance during the war, have been revived on the basis of one Sunday in the month devoted to regional appeals, the remainder being national. These committees consider and sift requests from organisations for wireless time in the Week's Good Cause. In wartime appeals from certain organisations were permitted yearly ; but the B.B.C. has now reverted to its pre-war practice of requiring as a rule at least a two-year gap between appeals by the same organisation, though exceptions are made for one or two funds.

Need is the criterion of selection. Five minutes is allowed for each appeal. The terms of reference are "that in general appeals should be restricted to causes which concern themselves with the relief of distress, the preservation of life and health, and the amelioration of social conditions," which means that not only work of a purely humanitarian nature but social amenity schemes, and those of research, appear quite frequently.

It is not possible to draw hard and fast deductions from the figures of receipts of appeals. The result varies greatly according to the personality of the speaker, and may be affected by the season, and the weather ; there are normally more listeners on a winter evening than on a summer evening, and more listeners in the summer when it is wet than when it is fine, but the figures as set out in the two tables attached yield some interesting points. In general terms the most successful appeals are those directed to purely humanitarian causes, primarily the relief of distress at home and abroad. On the other hand, schemes for general social amenity and those of an educational nature meet with less response.

Table E.41 attached deals with the period from November, 1939, to November, 1944, during which there were altogether 268 appeals ; 31 of these each produced more than £10,000. A slightly greater number, 37, each produced less than £1,000. The Table gives a list of these two sets of appeals. Naturally, during the war, appeals for the Services, for sailors and for sufferers by war, found marked response.

One of the interesting points in the Table is the extent to which appeals for help to countries other than Britain were successful. There were altogether some 36 appeals for money to go to other countries ; these produced between them nearly £420,000, or an average of nearly £11,700 each. Only one of these foreign appeals produced less than £1,000, that for British Medical Missions Overseas made in 1940. Only one other appeal resulted in less than £2,000 ; this was for Women's Work in Ethiopia in 1942, for which £1,600 was subscribed.

In contrast to the strong humanitarian interest in foreign causes may be put the small results achieved by appeals for prevention of tuberculosis at home, for residential and educational settlements, for Citizens' Advice Bureaux, for the Social Hygiene Council and for dental aids. Moreover, though relief of physical needs of men and women in the Services found ready response, two appeals by the Churches' Committee for Promoting Religious Work in H.M. Forces, in 1941 and in 1944, on each occasion yielded less than £1,000.

Wartime appeals were naturally affected in their results by war conditions. The record of nearly £102,000 obtained for King George's Fund for Sailors at the end of 1939 or £100,000 for the Finland Fund through two appeals made in January and March, 1940, are easy to understand, as is the £50,000 raised in 1941 by an appeal for the R.A.F. Benevolent Fund.

The second of the two Tables attached (E.42) deals with the time from the beginning of 1946 and shows for each quarter the two appeals which led to the two largest results, and the appeals with the smallest results. The Table is limited to appeals made over all Home Services. Appeals limited to particular regions would naturally yield, as a rule, smaller results.

The Table shows the continuance of British interest in other countries, with the large collections made for Aid to Austria, for Medical Missions in China and for the "Save Europe Now" Relief Fund. By contrast with these the Citizens' Advice Bureaux and the Settlements continue to draw small sums only.

An interesting new feature of the Table is the interest shown by listeners in the professional classes. Three successive appeals in the list of best results in the early part of 1947 are for the help of "professional classes" or "gentlefolks."

Table E.42 includes the result of the Christmas Appeal for Wireless for the Blind in 1946. This whilst not strictly a "Week's Good Cause" (being treated as such only when Christmas falls on a Sunday) is one of the most widely known and one which has had the greatest sustained success, reaching a record of £77,142 in 1943. In all over £300,000 has been subscribed by listeners to this Fund from 1930 to 1946.

The figures for individual years from Wireless for the Blind, 1930 to 1946, are as follows :

	£			£
1930	5,096	1939		13,642
1931	5,600	1940		11,436
1932	5,575	1941		28,276
1933	6,600	1942		15,880
1934	11,385	1943		77,142
1935	10,509	1944		no appeal
1936	19,851	1945		11,685
1937	23,171	1946		40,749
1938	42,103			

The popularity of the Week's Good Cause as an outlet for charitable instincts is shown by the fact that some people regularly send lump sums to be divided up among the various Week's Good Causes. In fact, some people send money to the cause without having heard the wireless appeal merely from having seen it advertised. Organisations can often themselves help to ensure the success of their wireless appeal by securing notices in the Press at the same time and in other ways.

In general it may be said that the wireless appeal is a good way to get money for a familiar purpose. It is not a good introduction to begin, as I did in getting a very small result for the Brentwood Recuperation Centre in July, 1947, to say that one is going to talk about a new idea. Helping women generally seems to be a new idea to listeners, and, as Table E.42 shows, they tend to come off badly.

Table E.41
RESULTS OF "WEEK'S GOOD CAUSE" APPEALS, 1939–1944 (ALL HOME SERVICES)

Over £10,000

R.A.F. Benevolent (1941)	£50,120
Seriously Disabled Ex-Service Men (1943)	12,332
Church of Scotland Huts (1940)	13,025
King George's Fund for Sailors (1939)	101,756
Ditto (1942)	16,956
Ditto (1943)	61,638
Ditto (1944)	12,437
Ditto (1944)	33,850
British Sailors' Society (1940)	11,100
Merchant Navy Comforts (1941)	11,030
Ditto (1943)	30,133
Voluntary Hospitals (1939)	19,443
Prince of Wales Hospital, Plymouth (1942)	10,249
British Empire Cancer Campaign (1942)	10,186
St. Martin's Christmas Fund (1942)	10,302
Ditto (1943)	10,640
Ditto (1940)	15,381
Lord Mayor's National Air Raid Distress Fund (1940)	21,572
British Medical Missions in India (1944)	13,763
Bengal Cyclone Disaster Relief Fund (1943)	23,607
Polish Relief Fund (1939)	27,400
British Fund for Warsaw (1944)	13,700
British Fund for Relief of Distress in China (1942)	13,007
Aid to China Fund (1944)	15,634
Finland Fund (1940, January)	80,000
Ditto (1940, March)	20,000
King Haakon's Fund for Relief in Norway (1940)	10,000
Anglo-Turkish Relief Fund (1940)	42,000
Lord Mayor's Greek Relief Fund (1940)	25,242
Red Cross Work in Greece (1941)	28,715

Under £1,000

Churches Committee for Religious Work in H.M. Forces (1941)	£572
Ditto (1944)	900
Free Churches' Homes and Canteens for Forces (1941)	606
Belfast Hospitals (1942)	818
Hertford British Hospital, Paris (1940)	835
West End Hospital for Nervous Diseases (1943)	815
Sussex Maternity Hospital (1943)	928
Royal Waterloo Hospital for Women and Children (1944)	974
National Association for Prevention of Tuberculosis (1940)	413
Ditto (1941)	404
British Social Hygiene Council (1940)	536
Ditto (1944)	153
Tavistock Clinic (1941)	895
Queen's Institute of District Nursing (1941)	485
Ditto (1942)	337
Ivory Cross National Dental Aid Fund (1942)	241
Ditto (1944)	287
Reedham Orphanage (1942)	985
N.S.P.C.C. (1944)	975
Musicians' Benevolent Fund (1940)	470
Ditto (1942)	912
Friends of the Poor Ivory Cross C.O.S. (1943)	953
Artists' General Benevolent Fund (1940)	650
Alliance of Honour (1942)	462
Care and Protection of Young People (1942)	593
Moral Welfare Councils (1944)	951
Safety and Friendship for Girls Away from Home (1940)	966
Youth Hostels (1941)	633
Y.M.C.A. and Y.W.C.A. (for Youth Work) (1943)	881
Church Lads' Brigade and Girls' Friendly (1943)	464
Girl Guides and Girls' Life Brigade (1943)	146
Residential and Educational Settlements (1940)	733
Ditto (1942)	201
British Medical Missions Overseas (1940)	660
Citizens' Advice Bureaux (1940)	800
Ditto (1943)	950
French Benevolent Society (1943)	909

Table E.42

RESULTS OF "WEEK'S GOOD CAUSE" APPEAL, 1946-47 (ALL HOME SERVICES)

Period	Two Largest Results		Smallest Results	
1946, January-March	Aid to Austria Fund ..	£13,002	Catholic Women's League for Huts and Canteens for H.M. Forces ..	£485
	British Medical Missions in China ..	7,585	Diabetic Association ..	1,238
1946, April-June	Army Benevolent Fund ..	9,032	Citizens' Advice Bureaux ..	144
	Victoria and Belgrave Hospital for Children	7,245	Glasgow Royal Infirmary ..	374
1946, July-September	Friends' Relief Service ..	5,663		
	King George's Fund for Sailors ..	3,951		
1946, October-December	Wireless for the Blind ..	40,749	Lidice Shall Live Fund ..	534
	St. Martin's Christmas Fund ..	17,337	Home for Invalid Children, Margate ..	733
1947, January-March	Professional Classes Aid Council ..	5,819	Birmingham Accident Hospital ..	545
	Home of Rest for Gentlewomen and Friendly Almshouses ..	3,843		
1947, April-June	Gentlefolks' Help Department of the Friends of the Poor ..	2,535	Soldiers', Sailors' and Airmen's Families Association ..	809
	Royal Cancer Hospital ..	2,175	College of the Sea ..	244
1947, July-September	"Save Europe Now" European Relief Fund ..	8,660	Women's Land Army Benevolent Fund ..	640
	Ex-Services Welfare Society ..	8,555	Combined Theatrical Charities ..	337
			Brentwood Recuperation Centre ..	398

5. YOUTH

by Joan S. Clarke

Society as a whole has still not found within itself a place for adolescents. With one hand they are urged to continue education in secondary schools, county colleges and evening institutes, while with the other they are forced into long hours of often monotonous work. Their holidays are too brief for true recreation,* too long for their scanty resources to fill adequately with any pursuits yielding long-term satisfaction. In wartime they are urged to join pre-service units, but, when the war is over, society's need for their help and interest is much less clear. It is not, therefore, surprising that adolescents themselves, particularly those who do or might join clubs, are confused and unruly. Physiologically they are in difficulty. They have outgrown childhood without yet fully developing their potentialities of mind or body. Awkwardly placed at home, they alternate between lapses into childhood dependency and grandiose parades of adult behaviour which they are unable to sustain. Their new biological urges are neither fully understood by them nor yet ripe for normal expression. Old interests are left behind, new ones not yet apprehended. Particularly the young person who has just left an elementary school is in difficulty. He finds within himself a vacuum which childhood, receding, has left, and which maturity has not yet filled. The public or secondary schoolboy has this vacuum more or less filled by athletics, cultural development and intellectual growth. The elementary schoolboy, proceeding into the adult work world, finds himself involved in a type of living which he can neither enjoy nor comprehend but to which, for his own social survival, he must conform. It is primarily these awkward adolescents whom the youth movement seeks to serve and must serve until or unless society evolves a better instrument.

The Service of Youth, actively promoted by the Ministry of Education since 1939, is not a new development in British society. Various forms of clubs and of young people's meetings centred round churches have been run successfully for many years ; the central organised movements, Scouts and Guides, the Y.M.C.A. and Y.W.C.A., have steadily increased their membership, irrespective of the more formal blessings of a Ministry. What is new since 1939 is the public realisation that young people have a place in the community, a right to its attention and even something which they can contribute. This awareness has been emphasised by the war years and by young people's keenness to come into the pre-service organisations. So enthusiastically have boys joined these that it is estimated that the total

---

*"We are convinced . . . that the hours which some young people are required to work are too long . . . Even if continued long hours did in fact increase production . . . we should still feel that the damage to our young people is a price which the community cannot, on any long view, afford to pay." *The Youth Service after the War*. Ministry of Education, Report of Youth Advisory Council, H.M.S.O., 1943, p. 8.

membership of the three pre-service boys' organisations is as large as that of all the other recognised boys' groups.

The war, too, showed that Society has a vested interest in raising good-quality citizens; we discovered a disastrous lack of health, hygiene and education among Service recruits, both men and women; illiteracy and vermin appeared with startling frequency. Evacuation, itself a by-product of the war, demonstrated the type of next generation parents who will emerge if their morals and habits are not radically altered before they become irrevocably set into maturity.

Home and Club

There is a resultant tendency among enthusiasts to disparage any young person who is not on the roll of some youth group or evening institute. However, the boy or girl who does not appear at youth meetings is not necessarily hanging about the street corner or wandering in asocial or possibly amoral gangs. He may be lucky enough to have satisfactory family relationships, sufficient space at home to be either quiet or active as he feels inclined; he may have parents wise enough to let him pursue even messy hobbies, and to bring into the ever-open door of his home both his developing outside interests and also his friends. It is arguable that the better the home the less need there is of a youth group, although the training inherent in membership of "a voluntary society of contemporaries"* will still be valuable. It is also true that youth organisations should be constantly aware of their relationship, through the adolescents, to the homes from which their members come. It is not enough to draw young people out of their homes. If we really believe that society as a whole is founded now and in the future upon a fully developed harmonious and rich home life, created, each for itself, by the families of the country, then the Youth Service cannot consider its work fulfilled until, through its members, it has done something to replenish and refurbish the content of home life.

"The extension of facilities for youth should therefore be so designed as to strengthen home life and parental responsibility."†

Both the Guides and the Scouts, for example, emphasise service to others and they give young people the tools with which to serve, by training them in many useful and relevant activities.‡ Both organisations make a great point of cleanliness, personal appearance and basic hygiene. It is not for nothing that routine inspections frequently include a scrutiny of the back of the badge as well as its highly-polished front. This type of training, as also the religious aspirations of youthful members of the Y.M.C.A., Y.W.C.A., Young Christian Workers and the Salvation Army must, in a good percentage

---

*The Purpose and Content of the Youth Service, Ministry of Education, Report of Youth Advisory Committee, H.M.S.O., 1945, p. 16.

†Partnership in the Service of Youth. Standing Conference of National Voluntary Youth Organisations, N.C.S.S., 1945, p. 3.

‡Girl Guides, for example, are required for their first-class test to keep a child happily amused for one hour.

of cases, be reflected in a gradual raising of home standards. This will be more marked where organisations reach out to the parents and through various types of open days or parents' evenings make the parents feel that they, too, are an integral part of the organisation.*

Clubs

However, the adolescent from a basically filthy, vicious or feckless home is not likely to appear in one of the organisations which exacts from its members relatively high standards of behaviour, morals and hygiene. Those youngsters who do not fit readily into uniformed or disciplined or ethically regimented organisations come under the purview of that vast amorphous collection of youth organisations known generally as "clubs," which must fill out almost the entire content of young people's lives and which often cannot even count on the backing of a stable and purposeful home life. It is these clubs which have been stimulated and increased by recent public interest in youth work of all types. Their many and varied units, varying in membership from some 15 to over 100 young people, can only thrive and multiply in a favourable social climate.

The clubs suck in those adolescents who are neither the most intellectual nor the most prosperous of their generation and for whom leisure would otherwise be boredom or temptation. This negative view of the clubs as something to keep young people off the streets was one of the original principles of youth work.

"Even in 1939 one of the objects of the Government's Service of Youth campaign was frankly and openly a 'first-aid' policy, with the aim of keeping young people off the streets and out of trouble. This was an early stage, both chronologically and theoretically."†

Only latterly has there been general recognition of the need for a positive approach which will give young people constructive alternatives to wasted time and which will set them on the road to fruitful and mature citizenship.

Youth organisations cannot remedy those major defects of our society which find only one of their reflections in the problems of young people. Two things, however, the youth movement can be expected to do. In the short-term period it should ameliorate the results of those graver influences which are morally, physically, intellectually and emotionally injuring young people today. Secondly, when social conditions have improved—when housing, health, knowledge and education have made measurable advances—they

---

*The Leader "must remember that if he is to make the Club an 'extra' contribution to the boy's growth, it must retain its identity as something quite separate from the boy's family life, something of the boy's very own, his first venture as a ship without convoy into the uncharted seas of the society of his fellow-men." *Voluntary Work with Boys*, D. H. Barber, Vawser & Wiles, 1946, p. 30.

† *The Purpose and Content of the Youth Service, op. cit.,* p. 7.

P

should provide for young people that opportunity for comradeship and that primary practice in juvenile citizenship which the best of the youth organisations now supply.

Needs of Youth

The youth service has to fulfil both the needs of the young people themselves and the relevant needs of society. Young people, especially the least privileged, have many needs which the satisfactory youth club can fulfil. Their homes so often provide neither a comfortable chair nor space on a table and young people, if present, are expected to help with dull household chores which merely transfer to another field the monotony of their day's work. They need, therefore, a place of their own where there is room to move about freely, to dance, to play games and to sit quietly round a fire relaxing after the tension and exhaustion of a working day. Secondly, they look to the youth club for something that is different, something that is bright, vivacious, alert and slightly unpredictable. They may need gymnastics, dancing or games in which the coiled spring of their cramped muscles and energy can be released. They may need the opportunities of self-expression normally denied in their work and which the club member finds in music, dramatic work and various forms of action.* They may just need a chance to talk both with their contemporaries and with older people, with whom, indirectly at first, but later frankly, they can unravel the social and perhaps sexual problems which are bothering them. They look to the club for a place in which the atmosphere suits them and will continue to suit them for a number of years as they develop. They want to grow without pressure in the companionship of those of roughly the same age and type. It may be that adolescents, for whom work has been just a monotonous disillusionment leading only to the satisfaction of the pay packet, may find through youth organisations that sense of function in society, the lack of which so frequently leads young people to the Courts.

Some young people want to learn and this zest counts, in part, for the popularity of such bodies as the Young Farmers' Clubs and the pre-service organisations (the Scouts and Guides are, of course, basically educational, but they draw their membership predominantly from school-age people and their appeal to adolescents is far less clearly demonstrated.) However, the thirst for learning is not the hall-mark of the average member of a youth club. He or she is likely to learn only incidentally and as a by-product of some more spectacular activity.

Needs of Society

If youth clubs, therefore, were to fulfil only these relatively simple needs of adolescents they would have little more to do than to provide themselves with satisfactory premises and facilities for diverse recreation. But society's

---

*"For many girls, clothes are the only medium through which they can create anything." *Clubs for Girls*, Pearl Jephcott, Faber & Faber, 1943, p. 40.

concern about the morals and activities of young people is increasingly reflected in rising standards of expectation about the content of the youth movement as a whole. Society assumes that the clubs, once they have recruited the young people, will inculcate both moral values and new levels of personal hygiene. The youth movement is expected to give young people an awareness of their functions as citizens so that, through resultant knowledge of the social and political structure of their locality and country, they eventually will pass on to active co-operation as mature citizens. Adolescents are likely to respond to these standards and to absorb this knowledge only if, as a prerequisite, the clubs inculcate in them habits of seriousness and self-discipline, emotional and intellectual, which the majority certainly do not bring with them on their first attendance. To the extent to which there is a superficial conflict between the demands of youth and the demands of society, the clubs are in a quandary ; a full educational programme drives away young people—but a totally recreational content earns the disapproval of society as a whole and of a club's sponsors in particular.

The major nation-wide youth organisations have attempted to solve these problems in a variety of ways, and according to their diverse methods can be roughly classified in five major groups.

Types of Movement

(I) Free Entry and Association

In this group come those organisations of which membership is open to any person within a certain age range. Members are not required to make any affirmation, nor to maintain a minimum number of attendances, nor to engage in particular forms of service, activity or training*; they are, generally speaking, consumers. They find themselves in an environment in which they have the opportunity of developing their personalities and abilities but in which nothing specific is demanded of them. Clubs should be listed here, particularly all those affiliated to the National Association of Boys' Clubs and to the National Association of Girls' Clubs and Mixed Clubs. In this group, too, one may roughly classify both the clubs affiliated to the Association of Jewish Youth and the Welsh League of Youth. Both are selective, nationally and racially, but are otherwise generally open ; both mix into their extensive recreational and cultural programmes education in the history, traditions and cultural heritage of their respective peoples. About the numerous unaffiliated small clubs, usually attached to churches and chapels of various denominations, it is less easy to generalise, because these do sometimes ask their members for specific forms of service or religious observance.

(II) Service to Others

There is a second group where membership implies service to others. This is expressed in its simplest form in the daily good turn expected of Guides and

---

*e.g., "The qualification of a member . . . shall be the payment of an annual subscription of not less than one shilling."—Welsh League of Youth.

Scouts. It is more overt and elaborate in the juvenile units run by St. John Ambulance Brigade and the British Red Cross. It is true that these organisations, particularly the Scouts and Guides, include in their programme a great deal of education which is useful to the members themselves and which may, unwisely directed, lead to "badge-hunting," a form of self-aggrandisement in which the service motive is submerged. However, these organisations differ from those in Group I in that their members face outwards towards society and are constantly reminded that the things they are learning are ultimately for use in service.

(III) *Missionary or Evangelistic*

Much more emphasised is the outgoing function of members both of the Young Christian Workers and of the youth sections of the Salvation Army. Both organisations, particularly the Young Christian Workers, are highly disciplined and exceedingly militant, regarding their members as crusaders whose task is to Christianise their environment. They raise to a much higher power the conviction of the Scouts and Guides that enrolment in the movement should permeate the whole life of each member.

(IV) *Self-dedication*

The spiritual dynamic of Group III organisations is present also in other religious youth organisations which, however, apart from this basic Christian (and sometimes denominational) emphasis are more akin to organisations in Group I in that they have neither service nor missionary emphasis. These bodies include the Y.M.C.A. and the Y.W.C.A., both of which require an affirmation of Christian faith from potential members, the Boys' Brigade with its insistence on a Sunday Bible Class and the Church Lads' Brigade which runs under the auspices of the Church of England.

(V) *Pre-Service Units*

These organisations developed rapidly during the war but have not yet found a satisfactory substitute for the *pro patria* motive which caused young people to flock into them during the war years. Their emphasis on drill, discipline and what are generally known as "school subjects" shows how susceptible young people are to relatively regimented youth clubs, provided that the psychological conditions are attractive. In the British pre-service units these conditions include uniforms which are replicas of those worn by adults in the fighting forces, and a sense of being part of the service organisations which is emphasised by the rank, titles and uniforms of its officers. Those who criticise the activities of the Group I type of organisation for being incoherent, undisciplined and non-educational compared with the pre-service units, may do well to consider the values inherent in such elastic bodies which are less reminiscent of the undoubted attractions of the Hitler Youth.

Young Farmers' Clubs

There are two other bodies of interest which do not fit into any of the above groups : *The Young Farmers' Clubs* and the *Outward Bound School*. The former enrol young people in rural areas who are interested in various forms of farming. Programmes are planned by members themselves and the main content is agricultural, although this definition is wide enough to include such modern aspects of farm life as engineering and fitting. Stock-keeping is also an important feature, and means that club activities provide a continuing interest for members and is not restricted to the weekly meeting.

"From nearly twenty-five years' experience I know that the best, most alive, and financially soundest clubs have been founded on livestock rearing. It teaches so many things of great value better than by any other means, and is a daily interest and source of pride to the younger members"*

Members are stimulated by exhibitions and competitions organised by the County Federations. Work throughout is on a high technical level; the Young Farmers are sometimes more modern in outlook than the local farmers themselves, so that a really active Club has a long-term effect in stimulating local interest in new methods and new knowledge.

Outward Bound

The Outward Bound School is a residential Sea School, founded in 1941 and taking boys from 15 to 18 for one month at a time. Since August, 1943, 2,246 boys have passed through the school, of whom 1,530 came from school, and 1,116 from work. The majority were between 16 and 17. Training falls into two parts, sea and land, the former culminating in an overnight cruise in a ketch, the latter in a 36-mile hike. The aim of the school is to arouse in boys a sense of self-reliance and adventure, and to enable them to carry this back to their ordinary lives so that they can find for themselves active and constructive outlets. To make this easier, bicycles have been added to the School's equipment and boys are taught to use these not for endurance tests but to extend their range of exploration. All boys at the school are asked to write their daily impressions in Log Books which they may illustrate, and some of them learn for the first time the joys of self-expression as well as those of physical development. Failures are very rare, for the School cleverly sets its standards at a level which is adaptable for each boy's ability; he who can jump three feet is encouraged to jump 3 feet 2 inches, and so forth. The result is that boys discover within themselves latent powers, the use of which really revolutionises the content of their lives; such powers include leadership, for those who lead must do so not by virtue of official appointment or seniority but of inherent quality. Nor are the boys dominated by the staff, for these, apart from three residents, are recruited for only three to six months and many of them come as part of their own training as ship's officers. They therefore stand to learn as much, though with different emphasis, as the boys. The success of the School is such that other similar ones are planned which will be based on forestry, mountaineering and mining respectively, for the

---

The Young Farmer, September-October, 1947, p. 134.

sponsors believe that these mediums can promote the same qualities as training through the sea.

Statistics

No comprehensive statistics of membership of youth groups are available for two reasons :

(i) There are some small clubs attached to churches and chapels which are not affiliated to any central body and no census of which has been taken ;

(ii) The centralised organisations tend to affiliate to each other so that the total figures provided by each body involve some double counting. The statistics which follow (excluding pre-service units) are therefore indicative rather than global, especially as the various organisations split their membership into non-comparable age groups :

Table E.43

YOUTH WORK

Numbers in Principal Organisations, 1946-47

(England, E. ; Wales, W. ; Scotland, S. ; Northern Ireland, N.I. ; Southern Ireland, I.)

Girls :	Girl Guides (11-21)	247,000
	Y.W.C.A. (over 15) ..	51,000
	National Association of Girls' Clubs ..	122,000
	Girls' Guildry (over 11)	8,000
	Girls' Friendly Society (11-25) ..	9,507 (E.,S. and N.I.)
Boys :	Boy Scouts (11-20)	177,000
	Y.M.C.A. (over 14) ..	57,000
	Church Lads' Brigade (10-18) ..	30,000 (E.,W. and N.I.)
	National Association of Boys' Clubs (14-18)	191,900 (E.,W. and S.)
	Catholic Young Men's Society ..	30,000
	Boys' Brigade (9-18)	136,000 (E.,W.,S.,I. and N.I.)
Mixed :	Young Farmers' Clubs (10-25) ..	65,500
	Association of Jewish Youth (over 14)	7,000
	Co-operative Youth (11-20)	54,000
	Welsh League of Youth (over 14) ..	60,500
	St. John Ambulance Cadets (11-17) ..	42,830

Many of these organisations run junior branches, usually from age seven, as recruiting grounds for adolescent recruitment.

The Standing Conference of Voluntary National Youth Organisations affiliates bodies in which are enrolled 4,000,000 young people over 21. However this body recognises unavoidable double-counting, as does Mr. Barnes,* who, however, provides some valuable negative figures, showing that in the City of Nottingham in 1944, of 861 16-year-old boys and 817 girls who registered, 38 per cent. of the boys and 54 per cent. of the girls were *not* attached to any youth group.

Youth Service in an English County, L. J. Barnes, King George's Jubilee Trust, 1945, p. 39.

Special Problems

I. *Leaders*

There is no standard pattern prevailing throughout the Youth Movement for the appointment of leaders. Most organisations rely considerably on voluntary workers ; some, e.g., the Scouts and Guides, rely entirely on voluntary workers for contact with young people and have a relatively small percentage of paid administrative staff. Salaried staff in the Boys' Brigade is less than ½ per cent. of all its officers. The Guides have recently appointed five full-time and three part-time salaried trainers as an experiment because they have increasing difficulty in finding sufficient volunteers from the movement who can give time enough to travelling and training. Also the supply of Guiders for company work is dwindling ; the organisation writes :

"The supply of Guiders has at no time been equal to the demand for companies, and at the present time there is no doubt that every County Commissioner would say that a considerable expansion of the Movement is only prevented by the lack of Guiders."

This problem is shared by other bodies, notably the Y.W.C.A., whose recruitment was swollen during the war and has now shrunk again. Field workers' salaries, where paid, range from £200 in the Girls' Guildry to £400 for those employed under the auspices of the National Federation of Girls' Clubs and Mixed Clubs. The Co-operative Youth Movement is just introducing a new scale from £330 to £455 plus war bonus and, in some cases, an increment for responsibility.

Training of salaried staff is required throughout the movement (again with variations, the Y.W.C.A. even requiring already trained youth leaders and social science certificate people to take one year's special Y.W.C.A. training). The Ministry of Education makes grants to enable selected students to take a one-year full-time University course provided in collaboration with the national voluntary youth organisations.* Local Education Authorities and also voluntary youth bodies may claim grants in respect of short courses for voluntary and part-time leaders ; such courses may be either based on evening and/or week-end meetings, or may be short residential courses. Some voluntary organisations have their own training establishments, the Guides at Foxlease, the Scouts at Gilwell Park, the National Association of Boys' Clubs at Chepstow, the Girls' Guildry at Brighton.

An inherent problem in Youth Leadership is its impermanence.

"Few men or women are fitted to give full-time active leadership to a youth club throughout the whole of their professional lives ; and the full-time leader has a great advantage if he is also equipped to move about and take up other employment within the social and educational field."†

Their training should, therefore, "furnish the basis not only for this work

---

*Ministry of Education Circular No. 53, June 22nd, 1945. See also *Teachers and Youth Leaders*, Report of the Board of Education Committee, H.M.S.O., 1944.

†*Further Education*, Ministry of Education Pamphlet No. 8, p. 69.

but also for other work including organising and administration, both in the Youth Service and in related fields of social and educational work among adolescents and adults."* This proposal raises indirectly the problem inherent in other fields of social work—the need for unified salary and pension rates, and for pension rights to be transferable as in the Federated Universities scheme.

It is today recognised that Youth Leaders should be advisory rather than authoritarian. There is an increasing tendency to give the young people themselves responsibility. The Young Christian Workers' organisation is run entirely, apart from its spiritual side, by the members themselves. It is the only organisation where the visitor to the central headquarters is received not by an adult, ripe in years, but by a group of young people who know clearly that they will be out of office as soon as they become 25 or marry. The Young Farmers' Clubs, also, are primarily self-governing, although they have a voluntary adult leader and an adult advisory committee; until 1947 all local officers had to be under 21, but clubs may now elect members between 21 and 25 if they wish. The Scouts, Guides and the Boys' Brigade practice devolution of authority to patrol leaders, and to corporals and sergeants respectively, although the Brigade maintains the officer-status of its adults more formally than the other bodies. Youth Councils, representative of members of youth organisations in a specific area, are also developing. It is the Luton Youth Council which has just produced an admirable "Report on Leisure-Time Facilities for Young People in Luton." However, young people are still being insufficiently trained both in leadership and in independence. Last year young men lounging in an ineffective old boys' section of a flourishing youth club East of London complained to a visitor that they had "nobody to organise" them. A lecturer† recently met 20 young members of a cycling club who had, that Saturday, ridden 64 miles; only three knew where they had been. This passivity is both the problem and the challenge of the voluntary bodies.

II. *Premises*

Youth work is seriously handicapped by shortage of premises. "Nothing can or should take the place of a 'room of one's own,' especially if it has been equipped, decorated and furnished by the personal labours of those who use it."‡ This, the considered opinion of the Youth Advisory Council, is fortified by proposals that future legislation should contain provisions requiring planning and housing authorities at all levels to consult the appropriate education authorities before confirming plans, so that these shall provide adequate recreational facilities for youth. However, conditions are still exceedingly unsatisfactory. Not only do many organisations have no place of their own in which to leave their property, quite apart from decorating

---

*Circular No. 53, para. 12.

†Mr. Bedwell, Honorary Director of the Outward Bound School.

‡ *The Youth Service after the War, op. cit.,* p. 15.

their club room, but many meet in unsuitable school-premises, some even having to use infant desks and chairs, and a few having to use buildings devoid of sanitation. An Enquiry into the community life of small towns undertaken by the National Council of Social Service in 1939 shows that activities are curtailed in almost every case by lack of premises ; the report from Kidderminster, specifically referring to youth organisations, says "the question of premises is acute"; from Stamford, "there is no regular meeting place or possibility of fixed equipment"; from Wisbech, "available premises allow of no expansion." Similarly, an N.C.S.S. questionnaire sent to Community Associations in 1946, though not referring especially to youth, elicited depressing comments on bad premises :

   i. "Not good. No field."
   ii. "Underground. Damp."
   iii. "Totally inadequate."
   iv. "Needs gym. plus four rooms."
   v. "Temporary. No good."
   vi. "Inadequate for all purposes."
   vii. "To small. No sanitation."
  viii. "Noisy huts."
   ix. "Too small. No room for youth activities."
   x. "Most unsatisfactory. Derelict farmhouse."
   xi. "Very seriously handicapped through lack of accommodation."

Mr. L. J. Barnes* found that in the County of Nottingham, 40 per cent. of youth clubs and units met in school buildings, 34 per cent. in church halls and institutes. The remainder met in premises ranging from such "magnificent and entirely appropriate buildings" as the Central Y.M.C.A. to "drill halls, hutments, river bases of Sea Scouts, and even odd rooms in pubs and private houses." He also found a marked correlation between low average attendance and unsatisfactory accommodation.

III. *Leisure*

"When young people are living under unsatisfactory conditions and are employed for unduly long hours, often on work of a dull and arduous character, they cannot be expected to take full advantage of any facilities offered for the use of such leisure as is left to them."† This theme also runs through the reports of the Youth Advisory Council.‡ One of the tasks of the youth movement is certainly to show young people how to use their leisure fruitfully§ (the Report of Luton Youth Council suggests by implication that there is room for more of this teaching) but a parallel, and more basic, need facing the whole community is to increase the amount of leisure available for

---

*Op. cit., p. 61.
†Board of Education Circular 1486, November 27th, 1939.
‡Youth Service after the War, op. cit.
§ v. Sociology of Film, J. P. Mayer, Faber & Faber, 1946.

young people, to spread it more evenly throughout the week, and to reduce the fatigue with which so many of them reach these leisure hours.

IV. *Finance and Control*

Youth organisations are helped by the Ministry of Education, Local Education Authorities, the Carnegie (U.K.) Trust and King George's Jubilee Trust.

(i) *The Ministry of Education** makes grants to the headquarters of the principal national voluntary youth organisations in aid of their central and regional expenditure on training, organisation and administration. Direct grants both to local units of these organisations, and to independent local bodies were, before 1945, made both for maintenance and for use as capital. The maintenance grants are now discontinued, and the capital grants are so scarce that, in the Nottingham area, Mr. Barnes† "found only six examples of such grants for premises between 1939 and 1945."

(ii) *Local Education Authorities* must, under Section 53 of the 1944 Act, "secure that the facilities for primary, secondary and further education . . . include facilities for recreation and social and physical training" ; they "shall, in particular, have regard to the expediency of co-operating with any voluntary societies or bodies whose objects include the provision of facilities or the organisation of activities of a similar character." Local Authorities vary widely in their interpretation of this section ; much depends on the attitude of the Director of Education ; voluntary bodies in some areas get an instantaneous response to their requests; others wait many months in a discouraging atmosphere before they receive any answer. On balance, however, the devolution resulting from Circular 51 has had good results in stimulating local interest, and, of many complaints received from voluntary organisations, the Standing Conference of National Voluntary Youth Organisations has found only very few justified. Facilities include free use of school premises for voluntary youth organisations, free admission to evening classes for enrolled members of youth groups, grants towards leaders' salaries, free provision of instructors. Local Authority interest in youth activities has been enhanced since, in 1939, they were requested to set up Youth Committees representative of relevant statutory and voluntary bodies.

(iii) *The Carnegie (U.K.) Trust* makes grants for equipping such non-local institutions as youth hostels, which tend to fall outside the purview of the local authorities.

(iv) *King George's Jubilee Trust*, by providing funds through the war years, helped to keep many organisations financially afloat. Detailed plans were not demanded. This policy has now changed. The Trust makes development grants for three-year periods, preferably towards schemes which would not be possible without the help of the Trust ; such grants are not meant to cover day-to-day expenditure. Special projects are also financed

---

*Ministry of Education, Circular No. 51, June 15th, 1945.
†*Op. cit.*, p. 61.

by the Trust; these have included a grant to the National Association of Boys' Clubs for (i) bursaries for paid leaders, (ii) senior boys' training, (iii) the salaries of two resident tutors at Chepstow; the Girl Guides' Association received £1,500 yearly for three years for an experiment in training girls in homecraft, and £3,000 towards reconditioning Foxlease; the Girls' Friendly Society was helped to buy a caravan for work in rural areas, and was granted £500 yearly for three years towards the salary and expenses of the Captain of this caravan. Voluntary youth organisations particularly appreciated the work of the Trust because it acts promptly as well as generously, and its grants are predictable, so that these bodies can budget ahead for specified periods—something which many of them are nervous of doing in the expectation of continued Ministerial aid.

Diversity

Although it is usual to talk about "the Youth Service," the distinguishing feature of this service is its diversity. The Ministry of Education Circular 1486 lists the following as the principal voluntary organisations:

Boys' Brigade, Boy Scouts' Association, Church Lads' Brigade, Girl Guides' Association, Girls' Friendly Society, Girls' Guildry, National Association of Boys' Clubs (including the Association of Jewish Youth), Girls' Life Brigade, National Council of Girls' Clubs, Welsh League of Youth, Y.M.C.A., Y.W.C.A., National Federation of Young Farmers' Clubs.

Not all of these are present in every town. The fourteen distinct youth organisations found in Blyth, Northumberland, in 1939-40 represented a different selection and did not include the Youth Fellowships and Young Men's Societies attached to the religious bodies in the town; 30-35 per cent. of the total youth of the town were then enrolled in these various organisations. Basingstoke, a larger town, listed in the same period only nine types of youth group, plus youth sections or guilds attached to the churches, a Boys' Gymnastic Evening, a Junior and Lads' Football League covering about 14 clubs and a Model Aeroplane Club. The pre-service units always, and the youth sections of the British Red Cross Society and the St. John Ambulance Society usually, are found in addition to the Ministry's list, with Salvation Army youth groups in most large towns. In addition, many young people who regularly attend classes at Evening Institutes also find their recreation there in dancing and gymnastics, and have neither time nor inclination to attend clubs or other activities as well.

Age Range

Until this year the various bodies reviewed in paragraph 34 were almost the sole form of organised activity for the majority of young people over 14. Now adolescents will be 15 before they are stranded without the companionship of school, and soon they will find a similar companionship in the County Colleges until they are 18. Later the school-leaving age will be 16, thus further closing the gap before, for most boys, the period of conscription from 18-19½.* Young people who were formerly abandoned by the State at 14 will now be in touch, compulsorily, with statutory provisions until they are 19½ (boys) or 18 (girls). The effect of this change on voluntary youth organisations is unpredictable, except in so far as young people are unlikely to tolerate the various forms of inadequacy which they now sometimes accept *faute de mieux*. Rising standards of accommodation, leadership and programme may be only one of the repercussions felt in the voluntary movement as a result of statutory expansion.

ANNEX TO MEMORANDUM 5

By A. F. Wells

Note on the Tynemouth Youth Survey

The organisations of opinion and expression among Youth—the Youth Associations and Youth Councils—have, of course, given a good deal of thought to the specific problems of their generation. Mrs. Clarke's paper has mentioned the "Report on Leisure-Time Facilities for Young People in Luton," published by the Luton Youth Council recently. This brief report undertaken entirely by Young People is evidently the result of careful study of some of the problems of Youth within its area, and makes a number of practical suggestions thereon.

Another Youth Council, that of the County Borough of Tynemouth, published in October, 1947, a document which is of particular interest as being an attempt at an accurate study of young people's opinions and preferences by means of the normal opinion survey technique, using a representative sample of the population in the borough between the ages of 14 and 21.

The document, published by the Youth Council, is well worth study by those interested. This survey, again, was carried out entirely by young people. An Appendix to the Report discusses its technique. The representativeness of the sample was determined by consideration of four points : sex, age, occupation and income-level; their distribution in the whole population being obtained from official sources. The size of the sample is not, however, stated in the report, which gives its results only in percentages. The interviewing field work was carried out also by young people, in the early part of 1947. The appendix includes a discussion of the reliability of the results.

Fifty-four questions were asked, covering the informant's experience and opinions relating to occupation, education, recreation and social relationships, and his or her knowledge and opinions on some aspects of current affairs. Here there is no space to refer to more than a few. Some results of the

---

*The Church Lads' Brigade is already being affected by conscription, which is taking away its senior boys.

Survey, however, afford interesting comparisons with the results of other studies. Thus, as regards cinema-going, it was found that of the whole sample (boys and girls combined) 42 per cent. went twice a week or oftener and 69 per cent. once a week or oftener. As is noticed in Memorandum 3 of this Part, a survey by Research Services Ltd. in January-May, 1947, found that 77 per cent. of the 16-24 age group attended once at least a week, and 46 per cent. twice a week or more. A government survey at the end of 1946 found, for the 16-19 age-group, corresponding percentages of 45 per cent. and 69 per cent.

The survey provides interesting facts on other uses of leisure. For example, it was found that out of the combined sample (boys and girls) 27 per cent. were, and 73 per cent. were not attending evening schools at the time of the survey. Among the girls the proportion of attenders was 17 per cent.; among the boys 37 per cent. Most evening scholars of both sexes were among the under 18's. The only age-group in which more than half went to evening schools was the 17-year-old boys. In no age-group did more than a quarter of the girls attend. It is not known how far Tynemouth is representative in these respects.

In view of the slight information available on the frequency of Church attendance, it is interesting to find that 39 per cent. of the combined sample said that they attended Church regularly. Among girls 43 per cent. did so and 57 per cent. did not; among boys, the proportions were 35 per cent. and 65 per cent. respectively. The peak ages for church attendances were, for both sexes, 14, 17, 19 and 20 years. Between these ages attendances appeared to drop distinctly, the 18's being poorest attenders. It would be interesting to have a comparison of these data both with findings from other areas and with those relating to other age-groups.

6. URBAN AND RURAL AMENITIES

by A. F. Wells

I. *The Growth of Leisure during the Nineteenth Century*

The shortening of hours of work during the nineteenth century has been dealt with in many works on English Social History; and here only the main stages need be recalled.

The movement appears to have begun during the 1840's. In 1844 the merchants of Manchester decided to make Saturday a half-holiday for all their employees: a decision which was followed by the publication of a number of special guides to the surrounding country, such as *The Half-Holiday Handbook*. In 1847 came the Ten Hours Act, which J. L. Hammond considers to be "in a sense the most important event of the first half of the century," since it was the first official recognition of the need for leisure of the common man.

The Factory Act of 1850 ordered the stoppage of work by women and young persons in textile factories at 2 p.m. on Saturdays. This, the first legislation for a Saturday half-holiday, was later extended to other trades, and the Saturday half-holiday became the rule.

The Bank Holidays Act was passed in 1871.

Professor Clapham shows (*Economic History of Modern Britain*, Vol. II, pp. 449 ff.) that the hours of labour were reduced in the 1870's to an average of approximately 54 a week. At this they stayed until the 1914-18 war. After that war, principally in 1919-1920, they fell, according to an estimate made by the Director of Statistics of the Ministry of Labour, to about 47 in the normal working week. They remained at this point until after the second world war; during the course of 1946-1947 they fell again to approximately 44 hours in a normal working week.*

(II) *The Disappearance of Amenities during the Nineteenth Century*

"We . . . take this opportunity to express our surprise that so little is known by English men and women of the beauties of English architecture. The ruins of the Colosseum, the Campanile at Florence, St. Mark's, Cologne, the Bourse and Notre Dame, are with our tourists as familiar as household words; but they know nothing of the glories of Wiltshire, Dorsetshire and Somersetshire. Nay, we much question whether many noted travellers, men who have pitched their tents perhaps under Mount Sinai, are not still ignorant that there are glories in Wiltshire, Dorsetshire and Somersetshire." So wrote Trollope in 1857, chiding the ignorance of the influential classes of his day, the classes upon whose activity the preservation of countryside beauty had then to depend.

The obstacles to its preservation may be seen in the case of common land.

In England the Lords of Manors had had, at least since the Statute of Merton in 1235, the right to enclose commons on certain conditions. Since Tudor times, the progress of enclosures grew more rapid, particularly in the sixteenth and seventeenth and in the early nineteenth centuries, and it has been estimated that by the 1860's the total extent of common land still unenclosed was only between one and a half million and two million acres. Resistance to the enclosing by Lords of Manors of common land could only, since Gateward's case (1603) be based on property rights. In that case the claim of the inhabitants of a village or manor, as distinguished from the tenants therein, to the legal recognition of rights of common which they had in fact always enjoyed by custom, was negatived by the justices on the grounds that the inhabitants of a district were too vague a body to enjoy a right of a profitable nature and that such right could only attach to property. Thus in cases where a Lord of a Manor desired to enclose part of his common, any action taken to restrain him from doing so, could only, up till the end of the

---

*For changes in hours of labour in 1946-47 see *Ministry of Labour Gazette*, January, 1947, p. 5, and August, 1947, p. 273.

nineteenth century, be taken on the ground that it infringed the right of a commoner, and not on any such ground as the public interest.

Between 1845 and 1869, 614,800 acres of common land were enclosed in England and Wales. Of these only 4,000 were set aside for public enjoyment. There appears to have been little public objection to these enclosures. Indeed in 1851 Parliament passed without any special ado a bill to disafforest and enclose Hainault Forest, on the eastern edge of London, an invaluable open space.

However, in the 1860's a change of attitude made itself felt. In part this was due to the lessening importance of agriculture in this country, consequent upon the free-trade policy. At the same time, while owners of common land saw less need to enclose it for corn or cattle, the quickly increasing population made an obviously greater need for lungs. But unfortunately this increase of population led Lords of Manors, especially near London, to recognise the potential value of their open spaces for building sites.

The degradation of the town during most of the century need scarcely be commented upon any further. As J. L. Hammond pointed out in his Hobhouse Lecture on the "Growth of Common Enjoyment," England in the eighteenth and early nineteenth centuries was outside the Graeco-Roman tradition of common enjoyment; leisure and the enjoyment of leisure were the prerogative of the few. This state of affairs had led Berkeley in 1721 to exclaim: "Such is the corruption and folly of the present age that a public spirit is treated like ignorance of the world and want of sense; and all the respect is paid to cunning men who bend and wrest the public interest to their own private ends, that in other times hath been thought due to those who were generous enough to sacrifice their private interest to that of their country." (Essay towards Preventing the Ruin of Great Britain: Works, 1871 ed., III, 208.)

Two things were mainly responsible for this; firstly, the Puritan outlook which had led Whitefield to exclaim that scarcely any recreation could be called innocent; secondly, the fact that in general the English territorial aristocracy, as Hammond points out, were not interested in town life. The city state scarcely existed in England, and during the industrial revolution the territorial aristocracy, both new and old, resided upon their country seats and took little interest in the towns which some of them were responsible for creating. In these circumstances it became increasingly difficult in the early nineteenth century to connect the idea of beauty with the idea of the town.

(III) *Voluntary Associations for the Protection of Amenities*

Reaction against the circumstances referred to briefly above led, from the middle of the nineteenth century onwards, to the rise of a number of associations to protect and preserve the beauties of town and country. There are at the present day a large number of them: the following list cites a few leading examples:

(a) *Those mainly concerned with rural amenities :*
The Commons, Open Spaces and Footpaths Preservation Society
The Council for the Preservation of Rural England
The Scapa Society
The Rural Reconstruction Association

(b) *Those interested both in country and town :*
The Society for the Protection of Ancient Buildings
The National Trust

(c) *Those interested mainly in the town :*
The Central Council of Civic Societies
The Georgian Group

(d) As a cross classification, a considerable number of local societies, both town and country, whose main function is the care of their own locality. Of such, examples are :

The Oxford Preservation Trust
The Cambridge Preservation Society
The Coventry City Guild
The Hastings and St. Leonards Civic Society
The Peak District and Northern Counties Footpaths Preservation Society
The Metropolitan Public Gardens Association

(e) A large number of bodies with special interests which however involve the common one of interest in the preservation of countryside and urban beauty. These include holiday organisations such as the Ramblers' Association, the Camping Club and others ; natural history Societies such as the Royal Society for the Protection of Birds ; architects' and artists' associations, and so on. Some idea of the variety of these can be obtained from the list of bodies affiliated to the Council for the Preservation of Rural England.

Some notes on the more important of these organisations follow :

The Commons, Open Spaces and Footpaths Preservation Society

The history of this society during its first fifty years is amply told in the book, *Commons, Forests and Footpaths*, written in 1910 by its first chairman, C. J. Shaw Lefèvre, first Lord Eversley.

In 1864, Earl Spencer, Lord of the Manor of Wimbledon, wished to exercise his assumed right to enclose Wimbledon Common and to make of it a public park. He asserted that the rights of the commoners of Wimbledon had fallen into disuse and that he therefore had full legal right to do what he wished with the common. This aroused considerable opposition amongst the commoners and as a result a Parliamentary Committee was set up in 1865 to survey the position. The Committee recommended that the common should not be enclosed, on the grounds, it is interesting to note, that it would be less expensive to avoid doing so, and that if it were not enclosed there would be no reason for recompensing the commoners. In addition, the Committee pointed out that there was at that time no general right of exercising on London commons. It recommended that commoners' rights, having in London fallen into disuse, should be transferred to the public at large.

Earl Spencer did not proceed with his intention of enclosing ; but it became clear that othe: Lords of the Manor around London had become alarmed, and were proposing to enclose their commons as quickly as they could.

To meet this threat the Commons Society, as it was originally called, was set up in 1865. Shaw Lefèvre was its first chairman ; other members included John Stuart Mill, T. H. Huxley, Sir T. Fowell Buxton, James Bryce, Leslie Stephen, Miss Octavia Hill and Sir Robert Hunter.

Its early work consisted mainly in the resisting of enclosure movements in and around London. Proceedings in the earliest days were cumbersome, since litigation had to be by an action taken by one of the commoners affected. By these means the energy of the Society's members was instrumental in saving, among other open spaces, Hampstead Heath, Berkhamsted, Plumstead Common, Wandsworth Common and Epping Forest. It is clear that to this Society Londoners owe an immeasurable debt which is far from being adequately realised.

Some of its work in the early days was carried out by direct action. Eversley gives an account of how on one occasion a large area of Berkhamsted Common was enclosed by an agent of the owner, Lord Brownlow, with an iron railing many feet high. The Society decided to contest his right to do so and took the step of sending down an army of navvies, armed with crowbars, in the dead of night by special train. At the last moment the contractor in charge of the navvies got himself drunk and incapable ; but the army was led to victory by the Society's confidential clerk. They completely uprooted the fencing by the morning, laying it neatly in piles, and the Society won a subsequent action for trespass. (Eversley, op. cit., Ch. V.)

Among the Acts which the Society has been instrumental in having passed are the Metropolitan Commons Acts of 1866 and 1869 and the Commons Acts of 1876 and 1899, all of which provide regulations to reduce the power of the Lords of the Manor over their commons in favour of the public ; and an important provision in the Law of Property Act, 1925, whereby the enclosure of any common land without the sanction of the Ministry of Agriculture was made illegal, and the public gained statutory right of access for air and exercise to every common any part of which is situated within the Metropolitan area or within any Municipal or Urban district.* In 1932 the Society secured the passage of the Rights of Way Act, the object of which is to protect the existing facilities for public rights of way. Again in 1939 it secured the passage of Access to Mountains Act which provides that members of the public shall have, under certain restrictions, free access to mountains, hills, etc. It may be added that this last Act has not given full satisfaction. Certain other bodies, Ramblers' Associations for instance, have felt that the restrictions under which access is permitted are unduly hampering to the

*See *Commons, Village Greens and Other Open Spaces,* by Commons Society (revised edition, 1939).

Q

pedestrian. Also the Act can only come into operation when it has been applied by an order to any specified extent of country, and so far no order has been made.

The Society amalgamated in 1899 with the Footpaths Society and its present view is thus wider than its original one. Its objects, as stated in one of its current pamphlets, are now :

"To preserve for the public use all commons and village greens, to assist local authorities and others in securing recreation grounds and other open spaces ; to promote the formation of national parks and nature reserves ; to preserve public rights of way over footpaths, bridle paths, carriage roads and tow paths ; to protect road-side wastes ; to preserve access to cliffs and seashore, and the fullest enjoyment of the countryside generally ; and to advise local authorities and the public on all questions relating to any of the above matters."

The question of footpaths referred to in the above extract has long exercised the Society. It is typical of many such problems, in that while it requires in the last resort legislation on a national scale, it is also one in which local vigilance is equally essential. The Special Committee on Footpaths and Access to the Countryside, in their report (Cmd. 7207, Section 21) pointed out the lack of and the need for a complete survey of footpaths and rights of way. In the past such surveys have been carried out sporadically, that made by Essex County Council being noteworthy, but over a large part of the country the preservation of footpaths from the depredations of farmers and others has had to depend upon the vigilance of local members of such societies as the Commons Society and upon legal action in individual cases.

The Society points out that the danger to footpaths has been increased as a result of the war, when in order to increase agricultural output, farmers were permitted in many cases to plough up rights of way. If these are not now speedily returned to public use there is great danger that they will completely disappear.

There is no doubt of the value of the Commons Society's work in drawing public attention to the value of the footpaths and of the future need of it in this respect if and when the survey comes to be undertaken.

The Society is at present incorporated and works mainly through its head office, although it has a small number of regional associations such as the Peak District and Northern Counties Footpaths Preservation Society. Its work is largely done by unpaid enthusiasts.

The Society depends for its income almost entirely on subscriptions and donations and as a consequence of the notorious public indifference to all work of this class, its financial position is causing its officers concern. The Society has in the past obtained grants from one or the other of the charitable funds, but feels that it is unreasonable to expect anything like a continued subsidy from such bodies. It could perhaps be said indeed that the main problem is now that of finance, including the difficulty of convincing the people that even with the greatly increased public control over the use of land there is still an important place for the voluntary society which exercises vigilance over encroachments of one sort or another upon scenic beauty and the access thereto.

The Council for the Preservation of Rural England

"There are many societies," wrote Patrick Abercrombie in 1926, "dealing each with a special aspect of the subject, and more individuals whose strength of power to influence the application of rural planning would be enormously enhanced if their efforts were combined and if they could call on expert information from headquarters when necessary."*

There had been a previous effort to form such a joint body. The Scapa Society formed a combine of amenities organisations and a "House of Commons Amenities Committee," in 1898 ; the formation was contemplated of a network of local associations all over the country which were to form the base of a great Amenities Party having its apex at St. Stephens.† What ultimately came of this plan is not clear, but the first co-ordinating body of this kind which came to birth was the C.P.R.E., founded in 1926 with Abercrombie as its chairman.‡

The Council is composed of representatives of 44 constituent bodies and in this respect can fairly claim to be very widely representative. There are also affiliated to it some 160 societies. It is unincorporated. It consists of a headquarters and of some 37 district or county branches which are microcosms of the headquarters organisation. In the same way as the headquarters comprises representatives of national bodies so does the district branch comprise representatives of interested organisations within its own area. Again, the function of the district branch is to carry on in its area the same propagandist, educational and vigilance work as the headquarters does on a national scale.

The objects of the C.P.R.E. are :

   (a) To organise concerted action to secure the protection of rural scenery and country and town amenities from disfigurement or injury ;
   (b) To act directly, or through its members, as a centre for furnishing advice and information upon any matters affecting the protection of amenities ;
   (c) To arouse, form and educate public opinion in order to ensure the promotion of these objects.

Its annual reports and other publications show the wide range of matters upon which the C.P.R.E. is engaged.

It is for example represented on various advisory planning committees, including those of the New Forest and Shropshire ; it is quick to supply evidence in support of its objects before official committees of enquiry, as for instance the public enquiry conducted by the Ministry of Town and Country

---

*Abercrombie : *The Preservation of Rural England* (1926), p. 44.
†Richardson Evans : *Scapa* (1926), pp. 74 f.
‡There are also Councils for Wales and Scotland.

Planning relating to surveys of mineral working, the New Towns Committee, and others.

Again, during 1946, it made representations in appropriate quarters in relation to such matters as the location of industries, rural housing, advertising control, and numerous other matters.

The Council has for many years been interested in the subject of National Parks and Nature Reserves. In 1921 it memorialised the Prime Minister suggesting that the problem of establishing National Parks in this country should be studied. Although a committee was set up under Dr. Addison (now Viscount Addison) the crisis of the following years prevented the project from going very far. However, the C.P.R.E. and the similar council for Wales established in 1935 a Standing Committee on National Parks, which has since been active. A member of that committee, Mr. John Dower, produced in 1945 a report on National Parks (Cmd. 6628) which has formed the basis of the Hobhouse Committee's enquiries. The Hobhouse Committee in their report say that : "It would be no exaggeration to say that the popular movement in support of National Parks has been sustained and vitalised by the enthusiasm of the Council for the Preservation of Rural England and Rural Wales and their constituent organisations both national and local. If our enquiry is crowned, as we hope and believe it will be, by the statutory establishment of National Parks, it will be the consummation of over half a century of pioneer activity by these voluntary societies." (Report [Cmd. 7271] Section 23.)

The Council has a somewhat interesting quasi-official function in respect of the land requirements of the Services.* When, towards the end of 1946 the Ministry of Town and Country Planning became involved in the question of Service claims to land for training purposes it requested the Council to collect and represent in evidence the views of voluntary societies concerned with amenities and natural history.

At the end of 1946 the Service departments between them had outstanding claims to some three-quarters of a million acres of the countryside, including such beauty spots as about 70,000 acres of Dartmoor ; Ashdown Forest ; an extent of coast at Fylingdale, Yorkshire ; and Braunton Burrows in Devonshire. These were obviously cases in which the fullest expression should be given to public opinion, and the Ministry of Town and Country Planning took the step of giving the Council the fullest information on these and other claims of which it was itself in possession.

The method of deciding upon these Service claims involves local investigation by the regional officer of the Ministry of Town and Country Planning ; later, if necessary, consultation with the County Councils and finally, if no agreement has been reached, a public enquiry. At all these stages the opinions of interested people can make themselves known separately, but

---

*For further remarks on this question, see *The Journal of the Commons Society*, September, 1947, pp. 189 ff.

such procedures by themselves might well be inadequate. The views of local individuals and local bodies might not be considered to carry sufficient weight, and the benefits of the public enquiry, of which only two have been held (that on the Dartmoor areas giving great dissatisfaction) may not be great. It can well be claimed, therefore, that the additional protection to the public afforded by a widely representative national body with local links and in possession of as much information as is available is of definite advantage.

*The Scapa Society**

Founded in 1893, the Society for Checking the Abuses of Public Advertising was largely instrumental in getting upon the Statute Book various acts to regulate advertisement and in encouraging action by local authorities under these acts. Its efforts to combine the actions of amenities societies were noted above. It has, however, done little work since the beginning of the last war and feels that now that powers have been given to the Ministry under Section 31 of the Town and Country Planning Act, 1947, its future scope is rather uncertain.

The Society for the Protection of Ancient Buildings

"The Anti-Scrape" was founded in 1877 by William Morris to fight the vandal restoration, then so popular, of old and beautiful buildings. Incensed finally by a proposal for the "restoration" of Tewkesbury Abbey by Sir Gilbert Scott, Morris wrote a letter to *The Athenaeum* protesting and suggesting the formation of such a society. Morris was its first chairman, and other early members were Ruskin, Burne Jones, Holman Hunt, Carlyle (who needed considerable persuasion to join) and Charles Keene.

The history of the S.P.A.B. reflects interestingly the change in the English taste since its beginning. Founded as a militant organisation and apparently earning its share of kicks at first, it has gradually become a body whose main task is to give technical advice and assistance. The change is not one of object but of method. The original objects of the Society, as Morris drafted them, appear in every annual report, and govern the Society, but they are now accepted by the many rather than the few, and the problem is more of the technique of giving effect to them.

The change of course was gradual; but if any point of abrupt change could be found it would probably, in the Society's opinion, be in the early war years, perhaps about 1941 : the reasons are obvious. An example of their propagandist work in the inter-war years is shown in their booklet *An Old Cottage Saved*, describing the repair by the Society of two old rural cottages.

The annual report for 1943 (the latest issue) gives some idea of its more recent activities, and three reports prepared by it for the corporations of Bath, York and King's Lynn, give a good idea of the consultative side of the Society's work at the end of the war and after, particularly in relation to preservation and reconditioning of old and beautiful buildings. These three reports have been accepted by the corporations concerned.

---

*Richardson Evans, *Scapa* (1926).

The Society works closely with the Ancient Monuments Department of the Ministry of Works and with the Maclagan Committee which is preparing a classification of historic buildings under Section 30 of the Town and Country Planning Act, 1947. Nevertheless the Society is still wholly voluntary. It is unincorporated and works through a committee, whose chairman is Lord Esher ; the meetings of which, it is interesting to know, may be attended by any member of the Society. The Society has a technical adviser, consultants and an administrative staff. It is entirely dependent for income upon subscriptions and donations. It has recently been fortunate in the receipt of some substantial bequests but nevertheless its income is insufficient to develop its work to the extent the Society would desire.

Among other problems, the Society sees at the present time a danger that there will be insufficient opportunities for younger architects to acquire special training in the technique of preserving ancient buildings which it has been its function to amass. The Society would like to subsidise the special training of students, but its resources do not allow it to do much in this direction.

The Society points out that its vigilance functions are still necessary, as well as its technical ones. Although under the Town and Country Planning Act, Sections 29 and 30, preservation orders may be made in respect of buildings of special architectural or historical interest, and a list of buildings of such a character is being compiled, there will be a particular need for vigilance until these sections are in full operation and no doubt even after-wards. An example was given in the case of Bowland Hall, Norfolk, referred to recently in *The Times*. The fact that this ancient monument was about to be pulled down was unknown to the Ministry until they were apprised of it by the S.P.A.B. In this case, unfortunately, the warning came too late.

The National Trust

In Chapter XVIII of Miss Moberly Bell's *Life of Octavia Hill* it is stated that as early as 1884 Miss Hill and Sir Robert Hunter (mentioned above in connection with the Commons Society) had been convinced of the desirability of founding some corporation which could hold land and buildings in trust for the people. Among Octavia Hill's varied activities, crusading on behalf of open spaces took a large place. Her first action in this regard was an unsuccessful effort in 1875 to preserve the Swiss Cottage fields in North-West London. This was the first of many such actions. She later founded the Kyrle Society, which had a committee for open spaces.*

The importance of such a corporation was brought home to Hunter and Miss Hill in 1885 when a Mr. Evelyn, a Deptford landlord, wished to hand over to the people Sayes Court with its large garden, and was unable to carry out his scheme in its entirety because there was no public body able to hold both building and land.

"The National Trust" (Miss Hill was responsible for the name) came into

---

*E. Moberly Bell, *Life of Octavia Hill* (1938), Ch. XIII and XVIII.

being in the 1880's, the third leading member being Canon Rawnsley, who had been active in preserving open spaces in the Lake District. It was incorporated as a public company in 1895 and reincorporated in 1907 under the National Trust Act. Further Acts have been passed subsequently (in 1937 and 1939) with the objects of widening its powers in respect of the acquisition and preservation of lands and buildings.

At the present day the objects of the National Trust are to acquire and preserve for the benefit of the nation,

(a) "Land of outstanding natural beauty and interest";

(b) "Buildings of exceptional historic, architectural and national significance."

Under its various Acts it possesses important privileges which include the following :

(a) Properties held by it can be declared inalienable ;

(b) Properties left to it and held for permanent preservation are exempt from death duties ;

(c) It has special powers to accept covenants for the protection of privately-owned land ;

(d) It can make byelaws to regulate its properties ;

(e) The National Trust is exempt from Income Tax and in some cases from rates ;

(f) Local authorities are empowered to contribute funds to the work of the Trust or the maintenance of special properties.

The Trust is a wholly voluntary organisation. Under its constitution it is governed by a Council of whom 25 are elected annually by the members and the remainder are appointed by various bodies, including the trustees of the National Gallery, the President of the Royal Academy of Arts, the Vice-Chancellor or Senate of certain Universities, and the governing bodies of certain learned societies (see National Trust Act, 1907, Section 18).

There is a headquarters staff and a number of local groups. These groups are financially self-supporting and their functions may range from that of simple propaganda for the Trust to the actual management of estates. There is also a devolution of functions through full-time area agents who are usually professional land agents or surveyors and more recently through regional representatives who are mainly concerned with aesthetic matters.

The Trust receives no grant from the Government. It is, with an exception to be noted later, entirely dependent on subscriptions and on voluntary gifts in money or in kind. Anyone can become a member upon payment of ten shillings, a minimum which is fixed by statute. The exception referred to above is that in the course of the Jubilee appeal for the Trust in 1946 the Chancellor of the Exchequer promised to ask Parliament to make a grant on a pound for pound basis with a view to doubling the proceeds of the appeal. The appeal brought in £62,000 and Parliament granted an additional £60,000. This is the only cash benefit that the Trust has derived from public funds.

A good deal of confusion appears to have arisen from a reference once made by the Chancellor to the use of the Land Fund to assist the Trust. All that this means is that land handed over to the Inland Revenue in payment of death duties may be handed on to the National Trust for management, if it is of a suitable character. The Trust derives no monetary benefit from this'; indeed it is saddled with the additional responsibility of managing such estates and has in consequence been unable to accept some for which no income was available to maintain them.

The Trust has never regarded its function of preservation as involving the maintenance of properties without any change as though they were museum specimens. Indeed this would be wholly impossible. Accordingly, much of its work lies in the maintenance and development of its properties, both of countryside and of country houses, in such a way that the balance of nature and of society is maintained to the optimum degree for the purpose. There is an interesting discussion of this in the Trust's Jubilee book.* It can be conceived as an experiment in natural and social ecology, the ecology of country estates and that of areas of natural land where the balance has been upset by the incursion of human visitors. The Trust is accumulating much special experience in the management and upkeep of this unique type of property, and like those of the S.P.A.B. its technical resources will be necessary even when the State has taken on much wider functions of land preservation and administration than it has today.

The Georgian Group

Among the societies mainly concerned with the preservation of civic beauty the Georgian Group is prominent. It was founded in 1937 and in its early stages was closely allied with the S.P.A.B. But the older society was interested in all beautiful buildings and it was felt by the founders of the Georgian Group that a body whose object should be to care especially for examples of classical architecture was sorely needed.

The functions of the Group are similar to those of the S.P.A.B., but of course in a narrower field. It has done considerable technical and advisory work, including the giving of evidence before public committees. It is probable that its evidence to the committee investigating the Regent's Park Terrace houses was influential in bringing about their preservation. The Group has also published a number of technical papers and propaganda material.

The Group is unincorporated and is governed by an elected council and an executive committee.

Ir depends for its income wholly on subscriptions and donations. These are increasing with the increasing membership but the last accounts showed a deficit stated to be due to the "present town planning activity with the

---

*The National Trust : A Record of Fifty Years' Achievement (London : Batsford, 1945), pp. 123, 124.

consequence that the Group cannot let increased expenditure wait on increased income."

Local Societies

Leaving aside local branches of such national bodies as the C.P.R.E., the National Trust, etc., and societies existing chiefly for purposes other than the preservation of amenities, like archaeological or natural history clubs, there are a large number of local civic and rural societies. Many of the former are loosely affiliated to the Central Council of Civic Societies which exists for the purpose of circularising information and giving other assistance to its affiliated bodies. They are of various scope, some confining themselves to educational and propaganda work within their areas while others, such as the Cambridge Preservation Society, can also acquire and preserve property. There is no space for any discussion of these valuable bodies; information on some of them is contained in the publications of the Central Council.

General Remarks

In this field of the preservation of amenities of town and country it is clear that the far-sighted individual and the voluntary group have led the general public and the State.

"When I first began to work," Octavia Hill remarked to her sister, "people would say, 'I'll give you money for necessaries for the poor but I do not see what they want with recreation'; then after a few years they said, 'I can understand poor people wanting amusement but what good will open spaces do them?' and now everybody recognises the importance of open spaces."*

Whether or not the last clause is true, even today, it is a fact that the far-seeing individual has been continually advancing into new fields where public opinion, at any rate, influential opinion, was not for some time ready to follow him. The preservation of commons from the landlord without public spirit; the preservation of buildings from destructive restoration; the preservation of scenery in trust for the nation; the control of unsightly advertisements; the preservation of special and at the same time unfashionable classes of building; the ideas of regional planning and of National Parks—all these germinated in the minds of individuals, were fought for by voluntary groups, and at length were accepted by the public and the State. But the need for ceaseless vigilance, local as well as national, remains.

Secondly, as a consequence of their original purpose, such bodies acquire special skills of which the State and the public can make use when they have accepted the ideas for which the societies stand.

Thirdly, their weakness is that of finance. None of these societies has a public grant; and all of them are hampered in their development through lack of funds. This situation is not going to improve in the near future. The Georgian Society, for instance, "views with great disquiet the provision of the recent finance bill which prevents charitable subscriptions under

---

*See Moberley Bell, *op. cit.*, Ch. XVIII.

covenant from being deductable for surtax purposes. If alienation of income for a period of seven years to another individual is to be deductable from taxable income for surtax purposes (as it rightly is) it is not clear why charities should be treated less favourably," in their view.

It may be noted that in their early crusading work for the preservation of London open spaces, the Commons Society were greatly aided by a number of wealthy public-spirited people. Without doubt there is as much public spirit now, but certainly fewer private fortunes.

These bodies face also the difficulty that many of them cannot compete for public interest with bodies which offer a more obvious charitable appeal—the public, rightly or wrongly, prefers blind men and sailors—and those of them which are national lack the advantage of a local tie.

The question may be put whether it is not time to consider a means of subvention for such bodies which will be free from detailed State control with its attendant disadvantages and which will allow them still to use that initiative which has been their making in the past.

7. THE NATIONAL COUNCIL OF SOCIAL SERVICE

by Joan S. Clarke

1. "If we are to avoid confusion, chaos, overlapping and indiscriminate begging, it will be absolutely necessary that there should be some form of centralisation." Thus crystallised the thinking of the Conference on War Relief and Personal Service which, sponsored by the C.O.S. and the Guilds of Help in 1915, fructified in the National Council of Social Service in 1919. The early years of the First World War had severely strained both statutory and voluntary machinery, although the Government had tried to forestall the muddles that developed. As early as August, 1914, a Government Committee, chaired by the President of the Local Government Board, had sent a circular letter (P.R.D. 1) to all Mayors and Chairmen of Local Authorities. This asked them to set up local committees in all places exceeding 20,000 population "to consider the needs of the localities and co-ordinate the distribution of such relief as may be required." The Committees were to include representatives of Local Authorities, Boards of Guardians, Distress Committees, Trade Unions, the S. and S.F.A. (as it then was) and philanthropic organisations. Some members were to be women.

2. However this letter did not, and could not, produce the nationally unified voluntary social service front which the organisations themselves considered necessary. A speaker at the 1915 Conference said, "There now exists in the country a wide-felt desire for co-ordinating social work on a voluntary basis on a scale sufficiently wide to render it worthwhile for the Government to recognise it and to make arrangements to meet it." This was the more necessary as voluntary bodies were having to substitute for properly directed Central Government activity. For example, the scandalous time-lag in paying

dependants' allowances to the families of servicemen was ameliorated only by the Soldiers' and Sailors' Families Association filling the gap with advances.

3. As a result of the Conference a Joint Committee of Representatives of the National Association of Guilds of Help, of Councils of Social Service, of the S. and S.F.A., of the C.O.S. and of Committees for the Prevention and Relief of Distress was formed ; it was "to consider and promote schemes for securing some measure of uniformity in local organisations and also to strengthen the existing bonds between the voluntary workers and the various Government departments making use of their services." Regular sessions of this Committee between 1915 and 1918 led to the formation of the National Council of Social Service.

4. Aims of the National Council of Social Service

In 1920 the N.C.S.S. issued a Report of the first Conference held under its auspices, that on Reconstruction and Social Services. This Report defined the aims of the new Council :

1. To promote the voluntary organisation of social work, national and local.
2. To provide information, especially re legislation, etc., to voluntary social workers.
3. To co-operate with Government Departments and Local Authorities making use of voluntary effort.
4. To assist the formation for each Local Government area of organisations of a uniform character representative of the voluntary effort.

In 1924 the Council was incorporated, and its Memorandum and Articles of Association redefined its objects :

"To promote all or any purposes for the benefit of the community which now are or hereafter may be deemed to be charitable and in particular the advancement of education, the furtherance of health and the relief of poverty, distress and sickness.

"To promote and organise co-operation in the achievement of the above purposes and to that end to bring together in Council nationally and locally representatives of voluntary agencies and statutory authorities engaged in the furtherance of the above purposes or any of them."

Since then the Council has continuously thought about its function as new needs arise and as the social pattern changed. It is not a static organisation. In a memorandum of 1944 the Council asked how it could "be made a more effective instrument for the social life of tomorrow ?" Discussing this question the memorandum continues : "The task of the Council is to help forward the advance along the whole front of social life."

5. Past Achievement

Preoccupation with its functions and philosophy is probably a condition for the continued vitality of a voluntary body. But the N.C.S.S. knows that talk is not enough. It has a long line of practical activity to its credit. Its methods of operation were detailed in its Annual Report, 1937:

> "The Council seeks to achieve its objects in three main ways—by calling conferences for the interchange of experience and ideas and by setting up groups for inquiry and co-ordination; by promoting new voluntary movements and fostering them until they are able to achieve independence; and by organising, and by administering funds in aid of, social services which call for the union of those forces which it is the aim of the Council to bring together."

Evidence of its successful spadework lies in the following list of organisations which the Council helped to start:

1. *The National Association of Boys' Clubs*, 1925.
   The Secretary of the N.C.S.S. acted as Honorary Secretary of the Association, which was housed in the Council's offices.
2. *The Council for the Preservation of Rural England*, 1926
   The N.C.S.S. provided intitial free accommodation for this Council which it helped to found.
3. *The National Federation of Young Farmers' Clubs*, 1928
   The Ministry of Agriculture asked the N.C.S.S. to co-operate with it and with the Carnegie Trustees in organising Clubs which the Rural Community Councils had already been developing. The N.C.S.S. provided accommodation and staff until the Federation was founded as an independent body in 1932.
4. *The Youth Hostels Association*, 1929
   The Y.H.A. was founded in 1930 as the result of conferences called in 1929 by the N.C.S.S. and attended by 40 relevant national and regional bodies.
5. *Council of British Societies for Relief Abroad*, 1943
   The N.C.S.S. was active in helping to form this Council, the first secretary of which was formerly Secretary of the London Council of Social Service.

Initiation of all these organisations required familiarity with a wide variety of voluntary organisations. The N.C.S.S. is so broadly based that it can move into any sphere of voluntary activity in good harmony with those already in or near the field; they know and trust it and do not fear that it will set up rival bodies. Further, voluntary organisations are willing to attend conferences and committees called by the N.C.S.S. because its past record proves that something is likely to happen as a result.

6. *Government Contacts*

Not only are fruitful new ideas planted in the voluntary field—for example Citizens' Advice Bureaux—but Government Departments and Committees, and even the laws, have been influenced. In fact the Council's enemies say that its permeation of relevant Government machinery is too complete.

Government Departments are represented on the Council itself, and Civil Servants attend meetings of some of the Council's Associated Groups as observers or advisers. Conversely, members of the Council's staff have been members of the Scott, Rushcliffe, Curtis and Austin Jones Committees ; the Council has been mentioned in two recent Ministry of Education publications ("Community Centres" and "Further Education") and in the House of Commons by the Minister of Food when he introduced the Civic Restaurants Bill. The Rushcliffe, Scott and Cohen (Industrial Assurance) Committees also referred specifically to the work of the Council, and the Resettlement Advice Service was modelled on C.A.B.s. Beyond these official relations, much of the contact between the Council and statutory bodies lies in un-spectacular friendliness between members of its staff and public servants, and in the resultant frequent but informal interchange of opinions, knowledge and informed prophecy.

7. Structure of the Council

The National Council of Social Service is really a Council. It is large, representative, and meets once a year. It is constituted as follows :

65	representatives of	National Voluntary Organisations
8	„	Area Councils of Social Service
10	„	Councils of Social Service in towns
12	„	Community Associations
21	„	Rural Community Councils
6	„	Community Service Clubs
9	„	Associations of Local Government Authorities and officers
10	„	Government Departments
27	individual members	
8	Honorary Officers	

176

This large Council provides the general mandate under which the varied activities are organised. It normally meets once a year to consider the general report on policy and activities, but is obviously too large and amorphous to exercise close control over details. It is represented by an Executive Committee of 43 persons which meets quarterly, but even this body is too large and meets too rarely for effective control at all levels. Decisions involving expenditure are, therefore, taken by the Finance and General Purposes Sub-Committee at its monthly meetings. There is, however, a great deal of residual authority vested in the Honorary Officers and the Secretary, whose views and decisions can have far-reaching effect. The close association of the constituent members of the Council is secured in a variety of ways and the application of one broad principle safeguards the fundamental co-operative character of all its operations. In undertaking a piece of work the various bodies, whether voluntary or governmental, are brought together to consider a particular problem and to decide what line of action, if any, shall be taken and what committee or group shall be responsible for it. Thus, a Standing Conference of National Voluntary Organisations representing in fact more national voluntary bodies than the Council itself is convened from time to time when there is some very wide issue to be considered which affects them all and the main lines of the Council's wartime work were considered by this Conference. This leads to the formation of a variety of committees or groups, some of which continue only for a time, while others of a permanent or semi-permanent nature become an integral part of the Council's structure. The most important of these are the autonomous Associated Groups of the Council which, although their secretaries are on the payroll of the N.C.S.S. and they all require subventions from the Council's budget, draw their authority from their constituent members. There are seven of these groups :

1. The Standing Conference of National Voluntary Youth Organisations
2. The Women's Group on Public Welfare
3. The National Old People's Welfare Committee
4. The National Federation of Community Associations
5. The National Association of Parish Councils
6. The Standing Conference of Councils of Social Service
7. The Standing Conference of Citizens' Advice Bureaux

8. At least seven pivotal members of the Council's staff must therefore continuously face outward to the constituent members of their respective organisations. Even where these organisations were, directly or indirectly, the creation of the N.C.S.S.—Citizens' Advice Bureaux, Community Associations, Councils of Social Service—they are now pursuing an independent and vigorous life of their own and are deeply rooted in their local soil. The considerable extent to which they still look to the N.C.S.S. for guidance and information derives less from a sense of dependency (although in some cases money is involved, see paragraph 26) than from practical experience of the continuing usefulness of the Council's services ; the Council has to keep in step with provincial needs and developments and cannot afford to have a didactic metropolitan outlook. Even less could it survive if it tried to dominate the many old and reputable organisations which it has succeeded in fusing into the Standing Conference of National Voluntary Youth Organisations and the Women's Group respectively.

The National Council works very closely with the Scottish Council of Social Service and the Council of Social Service for Wales and Monmouthshire. The Scottish Council was established in 1944 on the basis of an advisory committee which the National Council had set up in Scotland at the beginning of the war. The Council of Social Service for Wales was established more recently, combining the work of the South Wales C.S.S. and the National Council's own regional office in North Wales. Both these Councils maintain close contact with the national body, which still continues to accept a measure of financial responsibility for their work without infringing on their autonomy.

The Northern Ireland Council of Social Service is also represented on the main committees of the Council. In certain counties and areas in England there are area Councils of Social Service ; Service through which it works and it maintains its own regional offices at Leeds, Birmingham, Cambridge, Bristol and Reading.

9. Diverse Activities

However, these Groups and their secretariats do not comprise the whole of the Council's staff or activities. Some 1,400 Social Service Clubs, a legacy from the days of unemployment, are nurtured by the Council ; there is an excellent Library which also issues lists of recent books and articles ; a journal, *The Social Service Quarterly Review*, has been recently revived ; there is a Churches' Group (including representatives of the British Council of Churches, the Roman Catholic Church, and the Jewish Community) which confers under the auspices of the N.C.S.S. and which receives clerical help from the Council.

One very important development is in the matter of international relations. The Council is responsible for the re-establishment of the British National Committee of the International Conference of Social Work ; this Committee comprises representatives from approximately 70 national organisations. It established the British Committee for the Interchange of Social Workers and Administrators to encourage exchanges of personnel in the social work field between different countries. In the field of youth work the Council is developing important associations with consultative bodies in many other countries. It provides information on social work and social services for organisations overseas, particularly in the Dominions and the U.S.A. It arranges visits for social workers from other countries and works in close association with the British Council and other agencies which seek to interpret British life and institutions for students from other countries.

10. Apart from these continuing activities, other branches of work arise and fade as the need for them occasions, and the Council finds the staff to service each. The New Estates Community Committee,* for example, founded about 1930, discoursed on and ameliorated the plight of those who, although rehoused, were simultaneously deprived of all sense of neighbourhood grouping and community life ; an *ad hoc* representative committee recently sponsored two short courses for people who, released from war service, wanted either to sample social work or to use the waiting time until they could get into one of the Social Science Departments ; a Post-War Holidays Group studied the Holidays With Pay Act and published their findings in "Holidays—A Study." These so diverse activities have aroused criticism that the N.C.S.S. spreads its energy too widely and therefore too thinly, and that some of its work is of low quality. It is true that its work varies in effect

---

*This developed in 1937 into the Community Centres and Associations Committee, superseded in 1945 by the National Federation of Community Associations. See paras. 11-15.

and in standard, but it is also true that the Council owes much of its resilience to its willingness to range widely and to tackle new problems as they arise; as it said itself in its 1938 Report, "A National Council of Social Service can have little value or meaning if it does not collect and make available the knowledge, and deepen the thought, of the Movement of which it aspires to be the common centre." Some of the more solid and enduring achievements of the Council are described below. As social contributions they far outweigh those relatively minor projects to which the Council has devoted transitory, but sometimes fruitful, speculation.

11. Community Centres and Associations

A Community Association is "a voluntary association of organisations and residents in a given neighbourhood in a common effort to provide facilities for physical and mental training and recreation, and social and intellectual development, and to foster a community spirit for the achievement of these and other such purposes as may by law be deemed to be charitable, and to establish, maintain and manage a Community Centre for activities promoted by the Association and its constituent members."* The N.C.S.S., through the National Federation of Community Associations, supplies much of the dynamic in a movement which, were the Council to become extinct, might develop in a slightly different form. The initiative would then lie increasingly with Local Authorities which may, under various Acts,† finance both provision and maintenance of Community Centres, and which would probably take the easy way of concentrating on the Community Centre as an institution rather than laboriously stimulating the slow growth of a Community Association, rooted in the voluntary local life of the area; only later would such an Association, acting on the N.C.S.S. pattern, seek Local Authority co-operation and finance to build or acquire a Community Centre. But such a Centre would, at least theoretically, have deeper values for the community than one provided, after relatively remote Committee discussions, by the Local Authority among its routine erection of public buildings.‡

12. A Community Association can pool local information and experience, minimise overlapping, reduce hostility between rival organisations, and initiate new activities where needs exist. It is more securely rooted when it is linked with a Community Centre, as this is a tangible proof of the shared interest of the constituent members of the Association; a Centre is also a place where the Association can be certain of accommodation for any new experimental venture which its members wish to start. Local groups meeting

---

*Constitution of the National Federation of Community Associations.

†Housing Act, 1936 (Sections 80 and 94); The Physical Training and Recreation Act, 1937 (Sections 3 and 4); The Education Act, 1944 (Sections 41 and 53), also Circular 51 of the Ministry of Education, June 15th, 1945.

‡Although the pride of the people of Watford in their Town Hall, of Manchester in their Library, of Sheffield in their several civic buildings, suggests that voluntary bodies underestimate the volume of local pride which may be evoked by good municipal provisions coupled with up-to-date publicity.

in a pleasant Centre tend to multiply. Their internal self-government is frequently expanded to include a share in managing the Centre as a whole, and a spreading comradeship develops. These Centres, based on members' self-government, are a modern manifestation of that focussed neighbourhood sense which has contributed to the persistent vitality of the Settlements.

13. Without a Centre, or with a badly housed one, much potential initiative evaporates before the impossibility of finding a proper room or hall for proposed activity. In mid-1946 the N.C.S.S. sent a questionnaire to members of the Federation of Community Associations ; 68 of these replied, catering for populations ranging from 1,400 to 80,000 ; 42 of the 68 had Community Centres, but only four of them were satisfied with their Centres' premises. The deplorable lack of accommodation for group activities not only discourages potential participants ; it also prevents the full fruition of that neighbourhood sense which both voluntary and statutory bodies are at pains to foster, and which can find one among many suitable forms of expression in a thriving Community Association.*

14. The N.C.S.S. has welded some 120 Community Associations into the National Federation of Community Associations. Its elected Executive Committee meets quarterly, and is responsible to a Council consisting of one representative from each member organisation. There is thus a full interchange of opinion and advice between Associations ; their members become aware that similar bodies, geographically separated and working in differing conditions, are equally engaged in enriching social life and may even be evolving methods applicable to other areas. Community Associations may be members of the Federation only if they are :

1. Self-governing.
2. Contributing to the social, educational, recreational and general welfare of the neighbourhood.
3. Open both to individual local residents without discrimination, and to societies and groups.

The Council's travelling officers visit and advise prospective and established Associations as needed, with the result that cross-fertilisation is constantly proceeding ; it is furthered by such infectiously imaginative publications as the Council's *Living Communities,* and by the mobile exhibition with the same title.

15. There are, of course, disappointments in this work ; it depends heavily on the willing collaboration of many persons ; there is a wastage of collapsed Community Associations ; the Council has too few staff to spend sufficient time on local problems which look ominous. However, the Council has ensured that the best experiences are shared, the worst practices eliminated, and that local roots are strengthened all the time. The achievements far outweigh the failures in a complicated field.

Community Centres, Ministry of Education, H.M.S.O., 1946.

R

16. Councils of Social Service

Local Councils of Social Service are an older conception than the N.C.S.S. The earliest Council of Social Welfare was formed in Hampstead early in the present century; the Halifax Citizens' Guild of Help began work in 1905. The idea that voluntary organisations devoted to casework and personal service could be integrated as a whole into the municipal and social life of their towns was crystallised by the Webbs* in the Minority Report of the Poor Law Commission when they wrote of

"The opportunity for initiating a really systematic use of voluntary agencies and personal service, to give to the public assistance that touch of friendly sympathy which may be more helpful than mere maintenance at the public expense, and to deal with cases in which voluntary administration may result in more effective treatment than can be given by public authorities exclusively."

The operative words here are "*a really systematic use.*" Local Councils of Social Service, on which are usually represented all relevant statutory and voluntary social service organisations, seek to systematise local voluntary effort, to strengthen collaboration with Local Authorities (since, through the medium of the local C.S.S. the constituent bodies can speak with one voice instead of many) and to initiate gap-filling work in their locality.

17. The N.C.S.S. is concerned with the activities of some Councils of Social Service out of a total of about 120. These 40 do more than casework, although some of them include casework. They are combined into the Standing Conference of Councils of Social Service, formed in 1945; the other Councils are those which are exclusively engaged in casework and which look for information and advice to the Family Welfare Association. The N.C.S.S. acts as a focus of knowledge for the Councils in the Standing Conference through its headquarters and regional officers. It provides a meeting ground where representatives of Councils from all over the country can discuss their similar, and often related, problems. As the N.C.S.S. itself remarks:

"Every Council has both something to contribute to the common pool of experience, and something to gain from it."

The N.C.S.S. conceives its task as that of facilitating this give and take of accumulated wisdom.

18. The Rural Department

The rural parallel of these urban organisations are the Rural Community Councils. Contact with these is only one of the several activities of the National Council's Rural Department, which comprises the largest and most varied section of its work. In 1919, when this Department was started, the rural areas had few social service organisations, and little had been done to replace the weakened influence of the Church and the landed gentry. The

---

*Chapter XIII, Section E. Beatrice Webb was the member of the Commission, but Sidney Webb wrote most of the Minority Report. The Fabian Society published it.

N.C.S.S. therefore evolved a long-term rural plan, based on the common characteristics of village life—the traditional sense of community, the close connection between the countryman's work and his domestic life, the existence of native skills, and the comparative absence of modern social services. This plan, aimed at enriching village life, had four main parts : first to provide *village halls* ; secondly to assist *rural craftsmen* ; thirdly to revive *parish government* ; and fourthly to establish *county organisations* to carry out the plan. Also informal adult education was to strengthen intellectual life (and, incidentally, to stimulate a demand for those higher standards of community provision which the N.C.S.S. had decided to purvey). The success of this audacious plan is briefly sketched below.

19. *Village Halls* are essential if communal activities are to be pursued to the full. Such halls need to be available to all groups in the village, and they should have a hall, a stage, small meeting-rooms, cloakrooms and cooking facilities. The N.C.S.S. has between 1928 and 1945 been in touch with 1,400 village halls and has administered grant-aid from the Carnegie United Kingdom Trustees totalling £81,697, and loans made available through the Development Commissioners totalling £96,053. The Council has published a book* explaining both the administrative procedure for establishing and running a communally-owned village hall and also the technical questions governing its construction or adaptation. Applications for grants and loans and for assistance under the Physical Training and Recreation Act have to be made, first, to the National Council,† which refers all plans to a committee representative of the Ministries of Agriculture and Education, the Carnegie United Kingdom Trust, the National Federation of Women's Institutes, the National Playing Fields Association and the Rural Community Councils. A Panel of Architects appointed by the R.I.B.A. examines all such plans in detail, and the N.C.S.S. provides legal advice. The Hall may be insured under a special insurance policy negotiated by the National Council, and village communities may benefit from a national agreement between the Council and the Performing Right Society. This practical and relevant activity is perhaps the best answer to those who say that the N.C.S.S. talks too much and does too little. Only the Women's Institutes can claim as much credit for improving village life.

20. *Rural Industries* are less directly indebted to the Council which administers, through the Rural Community Councils, loans made through the Development Commissioners ; it also works closely with the Rural Industries Bureau, which is a Government-financed body equipped to provide technical advice to rural craftsmen. The wartime Equipment Loan Fund, a small capital interest-free loan fund, was furnished by the Treasury : this was increased from £2,000 in the first year to a total of £17,000 in the sixth

---

Village Halls and Social Centres in the Countryside, fifth edition, 1945. (It is interesting to see that this contains among many commercial advertisements, an equally business-like one from Papworth Industries Building Department.)

†Circular 51, Ministry of Education.

year, and out of this revolving fund £118,000 worth of equipment was bought for village craftsmen to enable them to undertake repairs to agricultural machinery. Incidentally the bad debts incurred in the administration of this fund have proved negligible. This work proved so successful that an independent society has now been launched by the Council to undertake the administration of larger loans for the repair and building of new workshops for local craftsmen.

21. *Parish Councils* were, about 1930, threatened with extinction. The N.C.S.S., a voluntary body, moved in to save these smallest units of statutory democratic government. As a result, after 17 years' work, there is the National Parish Councils Association, and 70 to 80 per cent. of all Parish Councils belong to it through County groupings. There are already signs of the revitalising effect of this campaign ; requests for polls, instead of election by show of hands, increase ; the National Association has given evidence before the Committees on Electoral Law Reform and on Expenses of Members of Local Authorities, and it is in touch with the Boundary Commission. The N.C.S.S. has itself published an excellent series of Parish Councils Advisory Handbooks, the subjects of which range from *Constitution and Powers* to *Public Lighting in Rural Parishes*; its Parish Council Leaflets give technical information on Allotments, Refuse and Litter, Town and Country Planning and other relevant topics. The N.C.S.S. has consistently aimed at showing country people that the village need not be an area from which vitality has ebbed ; it can instead be a focus of abundant life.

22. *Rural Community Councils* were first formed in Oxfordshire in 1920 and in Kent in 1921. They now exist in 33 counties, and are based on close co-operation between voluntary and statutory bodies in the area ; in fact establishment grants from the Development Fund are conditional on financial help from the County Council being already secured, thus ensuring a firm foundation. Generous development grants are also now available through the Development Commissioners. Rural Community Councils, strengthened by the approval both of this body and of the Minister of Agriculture, greatly enhance the interest of country life. Most Councils employ County Music and County Dance Organisers, to whose salaries the Carnegie United Kingdom Trust contributes, and some also employ Rural Industries Organisers and Rural Tutors. Several enterprising Councils produce handsomely illustrated magazines as well as their annual reports, and one, Oxfordshire, advertises its activities in a magnificently produced booklet in which descriptive paragraphs are coupled with artistic photographs.

23. One of the interesting facets of the N.C.S.S.'s rural work is the close co-operation between its Rural Department and the *Development Commission*. The latter, since its creation by a Liberal Government in 1909, has made a steady and imaginative contribution to rural life. An unobtrusive background body, the Commissioners are accessible for consultation, and can, through their contact with the many relevant Government Departments, facilitate

rural developments which might otherwise lose their way in the mazes of Whitehall. Holding a balance between voluntary and statutory bodies, on good terms with all sections of both, the Development Commissioners contribute much more than money to rural life. They provide a constant fund of wisdom and benevolence. As a Government institution their position is unique.

24. *The Women's Group on Public Welfare*

At the outbreak of war the diverse women's organisations became increasingly concerned about the problems of evacuation ; to voice their concern more effectively the N.C.S.S. founded the Women's Group on Public Welfare in 1940. Unlike the Rural Department, it is neither an executive nor an activating body ; it forms, mobilises and expresses opinion, and is thus an excellent example of another side of the manifold activities of the N.C.S.S. The headquarters of 47 women's organisations are now represented in this Group, which is much used by Government Departments as a convenient spokesman and focus of women's views. Its publication in 1943 of *Our Towns*, a study of the more sordid aspects of city life, had, and is still having, a far-reaching constructive effect.

25. *Information and Survey*

The Council has a continuous function in making available to organisations and individuals information on the social services. In addition to the work in this field undertaken by particular departments, there is a special Information Department which keeps a close watch on social changes and impending and new legislation. It publishes *Citizens' Advice Notes*, which is kept up to date as an accurate summary of new government legislation. It is extensively used by government departments, business houses and voluntary organisations. Information surveys have been undertaken from time to time, notably on Dispersal, British Restaurants, and Holidays With Pay.

26. *Benevolent Fund*

One of the most striking examples of the Council's service to voluntary agencies is afforded by the Benevolent Fund. During the past few years an average of £500,000 per annum has been collected under deed from individual subscribers, the income tax rebates on these gifts recovered from the Inland Revenue, and the donations paid out to many hundreds of hospitals and other charitable organisations. The Council undertakes this work as a trust for the individual donors and the recipient charities.

27. *Finance*

The National Council of Social Service handles sums of money much larger than its own income. Loan and grant funds which it is currently administering include :

Village Halls :

Development Commissioners .. £20,000 (loan)

£10,000 (grant ; further £40,000 on call)

Carnegie Trustees .. .. £4,000 (loan)

£100,000 (grant)

Rural Community Councils :

Development Commissioners .. £20,000 (grant)

Social Service Clubs :

Ministry of Education .. £30,000 (grant)

The work of the N.C.S.S. is itself grant-aided by the Government, which met 36 per cent. of its expenditure in the year 1946-47. The Council gathers this money by applying *seriatim* to separate Departments interested in particular aspects of its work. There is therefore a tendency to plan the work in directions which will attract grant and to employ staff on these lines ; this involves a certain rigidity. Also, since the grants are for one year only, it is difficult either to look far ahead or to give staff adequate security. It would be much easier, not only for the N.C.S.S., but for other voluntary bodies, if these could, on financial matters, deal with one Government Department instead of several, in the same way that organisations concerned with rural development communicate with the Development Commissioners.

28. The extent and outlay of the National Council's finance is shown in the following table :

Table E.44

FINANCE OF THE NATIONAL COUNCIL OF SOCIAL SERVICE, 1946-7

Activity	Expenditure			Income			
	Head-quarters	Field-work	Total	Govern-ment Grants	%age of Total	Voluntary Funds	%age of Total
	£	£	£	£		£	
Social Service Clubs	4,322	2,069	6,391	2,900	45%	3,491	55%
Art and Handicraft Advisers ..	—	700	700	700	100%	—	—
Community Centres and Associations	4,564	2,900	7,464	4,500	66%	2,964	34%
C.A.B.s	5,340	6,004	11,344	8,000	71%	3,344	29%
Rural Work ..	8,808	8,547	17,355	10,413	60%	6,942	40%
Youth Work ..	3,637	208	3,845	—	—	3,845	100%
Urban Work ..	3,334	1,423	4,757	—	—	4,757	100%
Old People ..	2,588	1,377	3,965	—	—	3,965	100%
International ..	3,581	2,117	5,698	—	—	5,698	100%
Women's Work ..	4,156	184	4,340	—	—	4,340	100%
Churches Group	354	7	361	—	—	361	100%
General Expenses	3,692	3,723	7,415	—	—	7,415	100%
Special Expenses a/c other bodies	—	351	351	—	—	351	100%
Total ..	£44,376	29,610	73,986	26,513	36%	47,473	64%

29. Résumé

For nearly thirty years the N.C.S.S. has been at work. It has shown an ability to initiate and to experiment and a willingness to release its grown-up protegés ; it has developed channels of communication between London and the provinces, between statutory and voluntary bodies, and between voluntary bodies and each other. By raising standards it has tended to produce a basic uniformity among those organisations closely connected with it, but has done this without eliminating social enterprise and diversity. Its passion for conferences has enabled it to generalise on the basis of exact local knowledge, to disseminate advice and to publicise good ideas. Finally, it has become a trusted partner both by government departments and by voluntary organisations ; its genius for tapping, and its readiness to disburse, both public and private funds, has emphasised its interest in practical achievements.

8. NOTES ON THE FUTURE OF VOLUNTARY SOCIAL WORK

by Roger Wilson

(University College, Hull)

THE traditional justification of voluntary social work has lain in its capacity to pioneer and in its flexibility ; but it is doubtful whether either social pioneering or flexible social administration will be as dependent on voluntary organisations in the future. Major changes in the philosophy of government are already well established and are in process of being translated into administrative forms. Experience during and since the war has shown that in certain conditions Government Departments can act with creative imagination on a vast scale. As more of the first-class ability of the country is recruited into national and local government service and into the service of public corporations, and as the conception of positive social responsibility takes a firmer place in our units of administration, whether public or private, the role of the voluntary social service organisation as the conceiver and executant of new developments, will diminish, though probably not disappear.

There is a second factor which is likely to affect voluntary social service—the drying-up of traditional sources of money. The large subscriber is probably disappearing, and the changes in the system of subscription by covenant have presumably hit many societies hard. Actually, there is probably a growing number of individuals who could make small contributions if they chose. If they were to contribute, the total might well exceed that produced by contributions formerly made by the well-to-do ; but few voluntary organisations except the hospitals have given any signs of being able to acquire the steady support of the small contributor, and few seem to be anticipating that they will be able to capture any of this support for their own rather different social purposes.

Neither of these social changes, however, affects the real basic contribution of voluntary social work to the life of the community. On the one hand it has given an opportunity for neighbourliness on the part of citizens who wanted to do something to help their fellows on a rather larger scale than was possible without organisation. That some voluntary social workers have wanted to obtain power for unsatisfactory reasons does not invalidate a system which allowed a vast amount of unpretentious and unselfish service. On the other hand, without going so far as to pioneer, the amateur who had creative social ideas and the ability to work them out in a small way in the first instance was able to make things happen. The value of these contributions has surely been that they have provided a link between the private citizen and social responsibility, which has meant that responsibility for preserving and developing the social structure has been distributed over a much wider constituency than if it had been the field of officials and elected representatives only. Even more important, it has been a profoundly educative process so far as participants have been concerned. The weakness of social responsibility placed entirely in the hands of trained administrators is that there is no independent body of citizens who understand the issues involved as a result of their own experience in carrying responsibility.

Put more concretely, unpretentious neighbourliness is good in itself and there is real danger that a society which thinks in terms of social planning may strike at the roots of spontaneous organised neighbourliness. Much of this may be incomplete and incoherent from the national point of view, but it *is* spontaneous. The well-equipped municipal Neighbourhood Centre may be less civically creative and educative than three half-baked and struggling community associations, of which two die and only one lives. In this country there is a tradition of wanting to help your neighbour and of wanting to join with him for some spontaneously conceived end of service, education, self-protection, or amusement. On the impersonal scale this want is expressed in a growing measure of socialisation. It is of the greatest importance that, along with its large development on the impersonal scale, its translation into personal terms should continue to be possible. The fact that surveys show that a very large portion of our population belongs to no voluntary association does not in any way invalidate the importance of the voluntary association for those who do want to join their fellows in some social enterprise.

The educative value of voluntary organisations has another aspect. Training in social responsibility begins in a small way. The trade union leaders of the 19th century often had their first experience of social responsibility in the chapel organisation. It is through the Women's Co-operative Guilds and Women's Institutes and the local Red Cross and Councils of Social Service and the like that many able leaders in the field of national social work come to maturity. It was through the Settlements that many of the ablest of our Government and near-Government social architects and builders obtained experience which enabled them to work with confidence in wider fields. The local trade union lodge, trade association, and ward organisation will cater for those who rise to responsibility in the economic and political fields. It is important that there should be growing points for those whose service to the community does not lie in economic and political groupings.

The form of these social service associations may, and certainly should, change from generation to generation. The Adult School and the University Settlement may give way to the Townswomen's Guild and the Community Association. An organisation for fighting the brewers may be succeeded by one for fighting the football pools. Flexibility of this type seems to me to be more dependent on the existence of voluntary social work than flexibility on the administrative side, which is a problem that will ultimately be solved by public social welfare institutions.

The growth of public institutions and the changing financial status of voluntary organisations do not therefore in any way weaken the *need* for voluntary social responsibility in this country if the gap between "they" and the community as a whole is to be bridged, if it cannot be closed. The question of how this shall be done seems to me to resolve itself into three questions : Does the official machine give scope within itself for amateur help ? Where is the money to come from for voluntary organisations ? And how is time to be found by volunteers ?

(1) *Amateur participation within official administration :* It seems to me that there is undoubtedly scope for large developments in the use made by official bodies of amateur advice and experience. Advisory bodies are made up in all sorts of ways. The membership and functions of the Assistance Board are different from the membership and functions of the Advisory Committee of the Ministry of Education, but are similar to the extent that use is made of part-timers who are not amateurs within the field with which they deal. Governors of the B.B.C., on the other hand, are basically amateurs, but the B.B.C.'s advisory committees and panels are in many respects much less amateur than the Governors themselves. The members of the local advisory committees of the Assistance Board or of the Ministry of Labour are also not amateurs in relevant fields, though public administration as such may be strange to them until they learn something about it from member-ship of the committees. Membership of local government authorities falls into this same general category, as does membership of a Bench of Magistrates. Co-opted membership of Local Authority committees has developed very little, and seems to me unlikely to develop unless and until something less cumber-some than mere party discipline is evolved as the basis of co-ordination and direction in Local Government administration. But the failure to use the power to co-opt more widely is in my view regrettable, and I should like to see Local Government developing in such a way that co-option on its committees could safely increase. With intelligent development of this kind of link between the independent part-timer and the official administration, I do not think that the community has anything to fear from the development of public social administration. The basic question seems to me to be one of finding the part-timers free to do their work properly, and this is referred to below.

(2) *With regard to money*, future help seems to me to depend on two developments. The first is the discovery by voluntary organisations of the techniques whereby they can obtain income in the way in which hospitals have obtained income from the small subscriber. I do not look for an increase in the number of flag days, but should like to see experiments with community chests and other methods of obtaining regular donations on an organised basis. The second approach should spring from more thought as to how public funds can be made available for operations of doubtful practical success. The community association which is a failure may be at least as valuable in the long run as the association which is an apparent success. Much adult education would be hard-pressed to justify itself by any outward standards. It is difficult to see how public money can be made available to the outwardly unpromising organisation, particularly if its financial arrangements are puzzling to orthodox accountants. This question of good account-keeping is a major bug-bear. Many public social enterprises lack real vitality precisely because we have not yet evolved any method of evaluating public work except by the inadequate standards of arithmetic. Somehow or other we must as a community try to solve the problem of how to finance from public funds the valuable failure and the entirely unconventional success whose value resides in its quality and not in its statistical appearance.

(3) But all this business of part-time voluntary work depends on people having the time available, and this is becoming increasingly difficult, partly because of the diminution of a leisured class and partly as the concerns in which we earn our living become less and less personal and more and more large-scale. In the past a great deal of heavy social responsibility has been taken by citizens who were their own masters in industry and commerce. With the growth in the number of large employers, including public corporations of one sort and another, there are fewer people who can please themselves how much time they give to earning their living and how much they give to their gardens or their public work. The general point needs no stressing. The question is how a remedy may be found. In this respect many trade unions and many large firms have given a lead by being prepared to allow their servants time off for public duties. Many local authorities owe their vitality to members who come from trade unions and from the senior ranks of local industry and commerce. I believe that, quite apart from civic-minded firms like the chocolate manufacturers, such a combine as I.C.I. recognises that it has a duty to the community to allow its servants both time off and secretarial assistance, to perform not merely public duties but voluntary social responsibilities that are of value to the community. On the other hand, I know of one man who had taken valuable part in the voluntary work of his provincial town and who was invited to serve on the local Bench of Magistrates. His employers, a national firm with a number of branches, flatly declined to allow him any time off to sit on the Bench. Although he was in no financial position to run risks, the man resigned from the firm rather than accept their restriction.

I have, however, never heard of any firm which declined to allow a man the necessary time off to serve in the Territorials and to go to camp in the summer. It seems therefore that employers are prepared to make the necessary organisational adjustments where, in fact, there is a recognised social obligation. If this is recognised when a man wishes to serve in the Territorials, why should it not be recognised for men and women who wish to serve the community in other ways? Admittedly, the scale would be enormous and the difficulties consequently great, but I cannot see that there is anything inherently impossible in allowing men and women time off in which to perform their service to the community. There are, of course, administrative difficulties in deciding where the line should be drawn. Membership of city councils and magistrates' benches is easily defined. What about the man who wishes to attend the annual or other representative meetings of his church which cannot or do not take place at week-ends? I do not see any clear answer to this question of defining the types of service for which employees should be released, but I believe that if the principle were conceded and if legislation were passed making it compulsory on an employer to release, not necessarily with pay, any employee with, say, more than three years' service for a limited maximum number of days in the year, the details of what absences were qualified could be worked out.

The point of view expressed in this memorandum may be summed up by saying that, just as in other fields, such as that of Parliamentary Government, considerable administrative changes have been made with a view to safeguarding the absolute values, so in the field of voluntary social work we should look to considerable administrative changes, with a view, however, to preserving the absolute value derived from the responsible participation in social organisation and social thought of the amateur and professional who are prepared to give part of their time to organised social responsibility without personal reward. Of the three problems—the use of the part-time volunteer in official administration, the finding of money, and the finding of time—the finding of time is the most important. Given that men and women who have a wish to serve can be freed to do so, they should be able to solve the other two problems. So far as I can see, both of these problems need for their adequate solution some social discovery whose nature is not yet plain. I do not think they will be solved by the process of pure thought. The discoveries will be made by a society which frees men and women to work practically in the appropriate fields. For any particular employer or administrator, the freeing of staff will usually be difficult. But the technical alternative is an inordinate increase in professional and full-time social administrators, whose economic maintenance will be the full responsibility of the community. And although this might be a technical solution, it would, over a period, be a social disaster, as a major contribution to the separation between administrative social responsibility and ordinary citizenship.

Appendix

Two simple comparisons of the structure of social service over three genera-
tions stimulate thought.

(i) H.J. (died 1914) was a Northern manufacturer.   He was a radical M.P.,
a magistrate, chairman of the local School Board, an active fellow-worker of
Josephine Butler, and a vigorous campaigner and social administrator in many
other directions.   Of his five children, two were industrialists, two followed
professional careers, and one married a minister of religion.   All gave much
time to public service on the Bench, or on City Councils, or in Parliament and
in many voluntary organizations.   Of H.J.'s ten grandchildren, three are
senior civil servants engaged in forms of social administration scarcely on the
horizon in 1914, one is the head and another is married to the head of social
science departments in universities, one is a doctor, one administers an
important voluntary social experiment, two are teachers and one is the wife of
a minister of religion.   Not one of the ten is in industry or commerce, and few
of them have the time for voluntary social service that was found by their
parents and grandfather.   Their instincts for public service find an outlet in
full-time government and professional employment, mostly paid for from
public funds.

(ii) During the recent war, the Quaker relief organization had great difficulty in acquiring an effective committee structure at all.   Its committee
members consisted largely of Quakers on the staffs of other voluntary
organizations, of elderly Friends, and of the organization's own full-time
administrators.   Only a handful of the committee were engaged in industry
and commerce.   The first Quaker war relief committee, appointed in 1870,
included in its membership eight Quaker M.P.'s and many other Friends
whose names were familiar in industry and commerce.   They met weekly.
The recent committee could not be summoned more often than once a month.
Administration was certainly much more complex and full-time administrators
had to carry much more weight in 1940-47 than in 1870-71.   But to the
extent that, though amateurs in relief work, they were completely absorbed in
administration—they were much less representative of the Quaker constituency as such than were their predecessors of the 'seventies.

June, 1947

9. PROBLEMS OF FRIENDLY SOCIETIES

by John A. Lincoln

INTRODUCTION

Friendly Societies are, first and foremost, Mutual Aid organisations and
have responsibilities and privileges as such.   Equally their problems, in part,
arise from these responsibilities and privileges on the Mutual Aid side.

Consideration of the problems of Friendly Societies is twofold : first there
is the consideration of their problems as Mutual Aid bodies and then as
Friendly Societies.   The problems of Mutual Aid organisations as such, in

this country, apply with only slight variations generally to all Mutual Aid bodies and are largely due to the circumstances under which Mutual Aid has evolved.

Mutual Aid as expressed in the early City State and in the Guilds soon became a dangerous occupation.   Later, in the Revolutionary period of the mid-seventeenth century the Mutual Aid tradition fared hardly at the hands of Cromwell whose treatment of the Levellers and the Diggers set the precedent for the harsh treatment meted out later to the Mutual Aid pioneers. There has certainly been a continuing apprehension by Authority of the potentialities of Mutual Aid.

This attitude persisted well into the nineteenth century and explains the limitations and compartmentalisation enforced by our legislation for the Mutual Aid organisations, by which Mutual Aid was limited to associations of the working classes for economic purposes.   These limitations, with their attached penalties and prosecutions, were all directed to the exclusion of community or social needs from Mutual Aid activities.   Paradoxically, as the motive and political pressure which applied these limitations lessened the Mutual Aid movements themselves paid less and less attention to the Mutual Aid mainspring and exploited instead the compartmentalism imposed by the Friendly Societies' Acts.

History shows that Mutual Aid could establish itself in a class, a city, in a religious belief, in the pursuit of knowledge, the provision of amenities and pleasure and in the furtherance of the crafts and industry.   History also shows that, to succeed, Mutual Aid requires a wide area of territory and full coverage of the social needs in that territory.   In short, it needs to be a free association for social purposes for the whole community—that community itself having to possess the pride and the privileges of citizenship.

The fate of the mediaeval Mutual Aid bodies was due to the fact that communications and transport, multiplicity of regions, and conflicts of social and religious bodies did not at that time allow a sufficient area for the existence of Mutual Aid.

Today the position is reversed.   The geographical, social and cultural areas which could support and maintain Mutual Aid exist, but the Mutual Aid movements themselves are cribbed and confined.

Now the task is not so much to make the world fit for Mutual Aid as to make the Mutual Aid bodies into efficient instruments.   The decline in the public's understanding of the Mutual Aid ideals which motivated the Friendly Societies and Co-operative movement, as revealed in the Reports of Mass-Observation and Research Services, all point to the fact that the Friendly Societies and other Mutual Aid organisations must be concerned with the establishment of vital standards and not with increased production of business in competition with lowering standards.

The problems of Mutual Aid are essentially direct and simple.   They are the problems of the removal of limitations.   First there is a problem of eliminating the limitations in the present Mutual Aid bodies by extending their range of vision and service from the provision of monies and goods, to the provision of amenities and services, and secondly, there is the problem of removing the legislative limitations which at present, if they do not constrain the Mutual Aid bodies, encourage them to remain unresponsive to the needs of the modern community.

The record of Mutual Aid in this country for the last 100 years in meeting the needs of the working classes by providing a security against misfortune and sickness through the Friendly Society, by protecting wage standards and securing improved working conditions through the Trade Unions, and by securing trading benefits through the Co-ops. leaves no doubt as to the potentialities of Mutual Aid. Mutual Aid, in fact, lifted the working classes of this country out of the morass of the Industrial Revolution by their own boot straps.

Today, despite the large membership and equally large capital assets of these Mutual Aid bodies, there can be no doubt that their impetus has not only been checked but that the first signs of decay can already be seen. On every hand there is a growth of centralisation and a lack of interest both in the member and by the member. With the lack of interest has come minority control and a façade of self-government. Meetings are not attended, members and representatives are not known to each other and have very little opportunity of knowing each other and the choice of who represents whom is very largely in the hands of local officials.

There is no longer the broad conception that these bodies represent the principle of Mutual Aid in action and there is, therefore, no appreciation by them of the fact that such action must and will change as the needs of society and the community change and vary. In fact for a century there has been a marked resistance by them to the fact that Mutual Aid, being a direct community reaction to present needs and conditions is subject to all the conditions that affect the community.

The paramount change that affects Mutual Aid bodies today is the fact that the pressure behind the working-class needs which they met in the past has been steadily declining and that they are already feeling the first effects of this reduced pressure.

The present difficulties of the Mutual Aid bodies are, therefore, due to the limitation imposed by the legislation affecting them; to the existence of administrations which grew up under those limitations and to the fact that both these factors constitute a barrier to transition and account for the lack of initiative necessary to make the changes of mind and habit now demanded.

The removal of the legislative limitations to Mutual Aid will not in itself be sufficient to meet the problems of Mutual Aid. The Mutual Aid bodies can resolve their problems by creating a positive urge to change and expansion. The rising standard of living and the emergence of new social needs in every class of the community makes an expansion of their ideals and activities inevitable.

If the existing Mutual Aid bodies do not meet these needs they will decline and be replaced by new Mutual Aid bodies which will. Whilst the belief is held that the things common to all men are as important as the things men hold separately and can be entrusted to no man, Mutual Aid *can exist*. If the things common to all men are made the concern of Mutual Aid bodies they *will grow*.

PROBLEMS OF FRIENDLY SOCIETIES

The problems of Friendly Societies fall into two categories :

(*a*) Those which are definitely due to the separation of the State Insurance from the Societies and (*b*) those problems which were hitherto concealed by the Approved Society system. By the latter I mean the problems which the Societies would have had to meet at the time by new methods and ideas, had they been dependent entirely upon their own efforts and policies for securing new members.

The problems which arise purely from the operation of the Act are :

1. A restricted field due to increased State contributions and benefits.
2. An increased actuarial loading on existing funds due to the operation of the New National Health Insurance Act.
3. A reduced investment income from Funds owing to decreased interest rates.

In general terms we may say that to meet the first set of problems the Friendly Societies will have to rationalise their administration and reduce administrative charges due to redundancy and repetition of work and effort ; expand their business by wider and better insurance tables ; and effectively inform the public of their purposes and of the advantages they offer.

The following general inferences can, I think, usefully be drawn in relation to the first set of problems :—

Firstly, that the problem of a restricted field will exist and can be met by propaganda amongst the present membership and by the extension of membership to the middle classes by the provision of new tables and by a wider range of activity ; and

Secondly, that the increased actuarial loading and the reduced investment income call for either putting the existing administrative machinery to the work of providing amenity services which will produce an additional income —or raising the present contributions of members.

New business could obviously be found if the Societies could provide an outlet to take up Family Allowance monies. They could devise many new tables with an appeal to middle-class membership, such as a "Social Liabilities" policy which would be a yearly life insurance policy sufficient to meet the sum required for the payment of income tax, to meet the needs of professional groups and business men. There is also the possibility of making loans to members through what might be called a Family Emergency Credit Table. Then, through the operation of a "No Claim Bonus" schemes could be made to coincide with the age groups showing the peak rate for lapses and would be used as a deterrent to a member lapsing, as in the event of a discontinuance of membership he would forfeit his right to these bonuses.

But these measures for new business are nothing more than an effective consolidation and rationalisation of present practices with a view to making sufficient savings to balance a loss of administrative revenue. They do not allow for an expansion by the Societies in the future, which would in any way compare with their rate of expansion in the past. Further expansion would demand a policy devised to meet the new needs of the community and to utilise the administration of the Friendly Societies to meet any of the foreseeable and major needs of their members on a cost (contributory) basis.

This now brings us to the consideration of the second set of problems unearthed by the removal of the Approved Society system. In the second category problems we come to matters not so concrete or so tangible.

First and foremost we have the decreasing interest of members in the Societies and the consequent representation and government of the Societies by the interest and votes of 3 per cent. of the membership.

Secondly, we have a lack of information, statistical information, of the structure of membership of the Societies with a consequent inability to gauge the full needs of the existing members. This lack of knowledge by the governing bodies of the Societies of the member and of his needs, hamstrings them when they come to consider new benefits and any extension of services.

Thirdly, we have to consider the lack of development on the Mutual Aid side of their activities. It was inevitable, with the establishment of the Approved Societies, that a strong emphasis would thereby be placed on the insurance aspects of Friendly Societies. What was not so obvious at the time was that the Friendly Societies themselves would allow the Mutual Aid side to lapse so quickly and so thoroughly. Much of the present trouble is the delayed price they are paying for doing just this.

Fourthly, having relied on the continual influx of new State members as providing the contacts and interest necessary for recruiting new members, the Societies were encouraged to ignore the need and value of propaganda and publicity. With the divorce from the State they are brought face to face with the problem of how to make themselves known.

To meet this second set of problems the Societies will have to decide how to expand their aims and policies. This must of course include the removal of the present legislative limitations and handicaps.

Consideration of these problems must, however, be prefaced by the following question, which is, I believe, the bedrock of any programme of reorganisation —namely : "Will consolidation of the present position through rationalisation, greater efficiency in administration, new insurance tables and increased membership, solve the Friendly Societies' problems ? Or does modern society demand a complete reorientation of the Friendly Societies ?"

The existence of these problems supplies, I believe, a conclusive answer to this question and also points to the necessity of drastic action by the Societies.

These problems may be summarised as follows :

(1) That the majority of the Friendly Society problems, both as regards material needs and membership incentive, arise out of the past emphasis on securing working-class membership and in specialising purely in insurance.

(2) That the raising of the standard of living of the working classes and the emergence of imperative needs amongst the middle classes makes the extension of Friendly Society policies and activities inevitable. In short, the standard of service to the community of the Friendly Societies must rise with the standard of living.

(3) That in the present critical times and era of austerity and shortages that lies before us, the public must turn more and more to the provision of amenities to make good its deficiencies in commodities.

(4) That an effective way of doing this is through the practical agency of the Friendly Societies.

(5) That with this wider appeal to a larger public comes the need for a greater incentive in the existing membership and an efficient medium—i.e., propaganda—to reach the public.

To be effective, a full Mutual Aid policy must not be primarily centred on a National Executive but should create a local focal point of interest. To do this the functions of the Friendly Society Lodge, Branch or District Committee, should be enlarged and they should be the active mediums and be serviced by the National Organisations.

The activities and amenities Friendly Societies could provide for their membership are : Clubs for the Aged, Housewives' Centres, Discussion Groups, Adult Education Groups, Arts, Theatre, Film and Music Guilds, Hobby and Handicraft Clubs, Members' Exchange and Mart, Parents' and Teachers' Associations, and Neighbourhood and Street Groups.

At the national level, Friendly Societies should do all in their power to bring their local Lodges, Branches, or District Committees into contact with their Local Authority and with Community Social Service Councils. They should certainly make a point of seeing that Friendly Societies are represented on the latter. Regional Councils of Friendly Societies would greatly assist this type of development.

The problems of the Aged, whilst presenting the Friendly Societies with perhaps their most difficult task, really present to them their own most vital problem in a very straightforward way. With the aged it is not a case of the provision of funds, but of the provision of help, amenities and sympathy. This in turn is the basic problem of the Friendly Societies. Can they evolve from Mutual Aid societies providing accumulated savings, into societies providing amenities secured through co-operative effort and common funds ? The Societies might very well consider inviting prominent men and women in many walks of life to form an Advisory Council to assist in exploring some of these major problems.

An amenity that could readily be provided by the Societies would be the meeting of the holiday requirements of members by a holiday service which

S

would allow for (a) interchange of visits between members of the Societies (b) interchange of accommodation, and (c) interchange holidays abroad through arrangements with European Friendly Societies. A referendum of their membership by the Societies on the question of additional services and activities would enable them to gauge the demand for these services and to establish a list of priorities.

In view of the percentage of members in the age group 16-45, every effort should be made by the Societies to reduce the age of executive members on their governing bodies from the present average of 60-65. In addition, the Societies who increase their field of service could justifiably impose sanctions and fines on members and branches persistently defaulting in attendances at meetings. Voting lists with the names and addresses of all members in the voting area should be supplied to members. A quorum should also be agreed for all meetings.

In view of the membership and capital funds involved in the administration of many of the large societies, payment should be made for services by elected members on National Executives, and they should be required to give the time necessary to the good government of the Society.

In the field of propaganda the Societies should devise the means to secure this for Friendly Societies as a whole or co-operate with some national body undertaking the task of propaganda for citizen services generally. They should also conduct their own propaganda through a national body. At present no particular society is desirous of conducting Friendly Society propaganda and publicity for the simple reason that the charge would be borne by one Society whilst the reward would be reaped by many.

It is now the duty, as well as the need, of Friendly Societies, to convince the public that the Societies are still Mutual Aid bodies and still possessed of the power to move aside the many obstacles in the path of social amenities and a fuller personal life. With such an end in view, with an awakened membership, and effective propaganda, there is no reason why the Friendly Societies should not once again boldly assist in creating the social order in which they can exist and serve the needs of the community.

November, 1947

PART VI

SOCIAL SERVICE AGENCIES

1. DIRECTORY OF SOME LEADING VOLUNTARY SOCIAL SERVICE AGENCIES

2. NAMES OF ORGANISATIONS WHICH GAVE INFORMATION FOR THE INQUIRY

1. DIRECTORY OF SOME LEADING VOLUNTARY SOCIAL SERVICE AGENCIES

AGENCIES FOR THE SICK AND INJURED

THE ST. JOHN AMBULANCE BRIGADE

The St. John Ambulance Brigade, a part of the Ambulance Department of the Order of St. John of Jerusalem, is a body of trained members giving voluntary service over a wide field of first aid and auxiliary nursing. This includes first aid duty at public events (more than half a million first aid cases are dealt with annually), ambulance transport and a first aid and ambulance service on the roads, auxiliary nursing, help to local authorities in connection with public health services, and general welfare of the sick and injured, including old people's welfare and child care. It maintains close contact and co-operation with statutory and with other voluntary bodies.

The Brigade, whose headquarters is in London, is administered under a chief commissioner, with a superintendent-in-chief for the nursing personnel. Under the national headquarters there are also headquarters in the counties, each under a county commissioner, with a woman county superintendent in charge of nursing members. The personnel of the Brigade is enrolled into divisions, each with its divisional superintendent, surgeon and officers.

The membership of the Brigade at the end of 1946 was 141,000, including 61,000 men, 31,000 women, 20,000 boys and 29,000 girls. In 1938 the figure was 90,000 ; its peak figure was 178,000 during the war. The bulk of the membership is to be found in the great industrial areas.

Members are required to be trained in first aid (women in home nursing also) and to remain efficient by passing an annual re-examination, inspection and practices. With the exception of a very small number, mostly paid clerical staff, members give voluntary service.

No money has so far been received from public funds, though in future some grants-in-aid will be received in respect of ambulance services. While headquarters expenses are a charge on the funds of the Order of St. John, the main source of income of the counties has been an annual Flag Day (during the war, this went into abeyance in favour of a national appeal for the Duke of Gloucester's Red Cross and St. John Fund). Each member is expected to contribute to the funds, as well as paying his or her own expenses incurred on duty.

8 Grosvenor Crescent,
London, S.W.1

Chief Commissioner :
Lt.-General Sir Henry Pownall,
K.C.B., K.B.E., D.S.O., M.C
Superintendent-in-Chief :
The Countess Mountbatten of
Burma, C.I., D.C.V.O., C.B.E.

AGENCIES FOR CHILDREN

CATHOLIC CHILD WELFARE COUNCIL

The Catholic Child Welfare Council is a consultative and not an executive body, founded on December 5th, 1929, by the late Monsignor Hudson, of Coleshill, and it now incorporates the Catholic Child Rescue Societies of the eighteen dioceses of England and Wales.

The object of the Council is to act as a medium of distribution and discussion between Catholic child rescue societies in all matters affecting child welfare work. It is entirely voluntary and no income is received from statutory bodies.

The seventeen constituent societies are at present accommodating 14,728 children in 250 Homes, as follows :

Type of Home	No. of Homes	No. of Children
For Boys	36	3,550
For Girls	73	4,944
For Babies	59	1,950
Maternity and Mother and Baby Homes	21	240
For Mentally Deficient Boys	6	594
For Mentally Deficient Girls	5	407
For Physically Defective Children	15	890
Probation Hostels	5	60
Approved Schools for Boys	15	1,450
Approved Schools for Girls	6	413
Working Boys' Homes	5	150
Training Farms	4	80

Coleshill,
Birmingham

Secretary :
Rev. Denis G. Murphy

CHURCH OF ENGLAND CHILDREN'S SOCIETY

The Church of England Children's Society, formerly known as the Waifs and Strays, was founded in 1881. It exists to rescue and care for children who are orphaned, homeless, cruelly treated, or in moral danger. At present some 5,181 children are in the care of the Society, most of them in small Homes, but some boarded out. The Society is also an Adoption Society. The major part of its income is derived equally from voluntary contributions and from payments for services. It is managed by a nominated governing body.

Old Town Hall, Kennington,
London, S.E.11

Secretary :
W. R. Vaughan, Esq., O.B.E.

DR. BARNARDO'S HOMES

Dr. Barnardo's Homes, founded in 1866, never refuses admission to any destitute child. There are 109 Homes in many parts of the United Kingdom. Children of all ages are accepted and so far as possible accommodated in family home types of unit, trained and placed in employment and where necessary their income is supplemented until they are self-supporting. Dr. Barnardo's Homes run two children's hospitals, three convalescent homes and twelve young people's hostels. There are twelve regional reception centres at which lost or destitute children can be admitted at any time. Dr. Barnardo's staff find that their work increasingly involves dealing with family and matrimonial problems and that they are often instrumental in mending homes which would otherwise be broken. They also frequently restore children to homes which, after a number of years, have become satisfactory and in which the parents are able to receive their children again. Thus, children accepted as apparently permanent charges sometimes leave the Homes ; others taken only for a short stay sometimes stay permanently. Dr. Barnardo's runs its own staff training school and is developing its training for child-care workers. The organisation is governed by a self-nominated Council and receives its income largely from subscriptions, donations, legacies and, to a much smaller extent, from payment for services rendered.

Stepney Causeway,
London, E.1

General Secretary :
F. J. Potter, Esq., A.C.A.

THE NATIONAL CHILDREN'S HOMES AND ORPHANAGE

Children applying to the National Children's Homes and Orphanage for admission are selected by a committee of the organisation which, founded in 1869, gives a home to orphan, afflicted and destitute children of both sexes, irrespective of payment. The organisation emphasises the importance of the family system which it adopts at all its 37 Homes, in which some 2,800 children are now cared for ; another 100 are boarded out in private homes. The organisation also runs five Approved Schools. The children are trained for a career before they leave their Home. The organisation is governed by general and local committees of nominated persons. The main part of its income is derived from voluntary contributions and interest, the balance coming chiefly from payments for services rendered.

Highbury Park,
London, N.5

Principal :
The Rev. John H. Litten

THE NATIONAL SOCIETY FOR THE PREVENTION OF CRUELTY TO CHILDREN

The National Society for the Prevention of Cruelty to Children was founded in 1884 to prevent all forms of cruelty and ill-treatment, intentional or unintentional, to children. It also takes an active part in promoting legislation designed to improve the lot of children. Latterly it has frequently been asked to advise parents and others who turn to the Society for guidance in problems involving children even where there is no question of cruelty or neglect. In this way, the Society acts increasingly in the preventive field, the number of prosecutions undertaken by it diminishing as the general standard of child-care rises.   The Society's officers are selected and trained by the Society, which tries to appoint persons not too far removed in outlook from those among whom they will mainly be working but who can exercise authority when necessary.   It is governed by a self-nominated Council and depends entirely on voluntary subscriptions and donations and on interest and dividends.

Victory House, Leicester Square,   *Director :*
London, W.1   The Rev. Wilton McCann, M.A.

THE NURSERY SCHOOL ASSOCIATION OF GREAT BRITAIN AND NORTHERN IRELAND

The Nursery School Association of Great Britain and Northern Ireland was founded in 1923, with Margaret McMillan as first President.

In 1945 the Association became an Incorporated Body recognised as a charity.

The object of the Association is to encourage the study in all its aspects of the needs of young children and the forms of care and education appropriate to their development.   Its main concern is to help in the establishment of nursery schools, to ensure that a high standard is maintained in nursery and infant schools, and to offer specialist help to local authorities and to others who are concerned with the education and care of young children.

The Nursery School Association is a voluntary organisation whose member-ship includes teachers, parents, doctors, psychologists, architects, admini-strators and all who are interested in early childhood education.

The governing body of the Nursery School Association is the Delegate Council which meets twice a year.   This Council is elected from N.S.A. members and includes representatives from every branch.   The N.S.A. Teachers' Council works in close collaboration with the Association and is represented on the Delegate Council and Executive Committee.

There are 10,000 members of the Association and 90 branches in different parts of the country.   The branches work in the closest co-operation with the local authorities, by whom they are constantly consulted.   The educational work done by the branches is far-reaching.   The minimum annual subscrip-tion is 5s., 2s. 6d. being kept by the local branches to enable them to develop their own work.

The Association has its headquarters in a pleasant house overlooking Regents Park.   Here the Carnegie Reference Library is available for the quiet reading of books on education, child psychology, health and current literature.   There is a permanent Exhibition Room, where toys and educa-tional equipment are on show.

Many conferences are held during the year up and down the country arranged by Headquarters, the Teachers' Council and the branches.   In addition, the 90 branches usually hold a monthly meeting in their own locality, addressed by national or local speakers.

Two Summer Schools of a fortnight's duration are usually held each year, in this country or abroad, for teachers, parents, lecturers, H.M.I.s and representatives from local authorities.

Different types of courses are held at headquarters for supervisors and tutors, head teachers of infant schools and parents.

Pamphlets are issued from time to time dealing with the many aspects of education of children from two to seven years.

A News Letter is circulated to members, free of charge, on alternate months.

The Nursery School Association was the initiating body responsible for founding the World Council of Early Childhood Education, and takes an active part in its development.

1 Park Crescent,   *Chairman :*
Portland Place, London, W.1   Lady Allen of Hurtwood, J.P.

THE SAVE THE CHILDREN FUND

The Save the Children Fund, founded in 1919 by the late Miss Eglantyne Jebb, has as its aim to relieve child suffering and to promote child welfare throughout the world, without regard to race, nationality, or creed. This work is based on the Declaration of the Rights of the Child, drafted by Miss Jebb, adopted by the League of Nations Assembly as its "Charter of Child Welfare" (1924) and commended by the Social Commission of the United Nations (1946). Relief work and pioneer activities in the child welfare sphere—the Fund's two major tasks—are represented in its present-day work by the educational, medical and social welfare work of its relief workers in Austria, Germany, Greece, Hungary, Italy, Malaya and Poland ; and by its junior clubs for urban schoolchildren in Great Britain. Another important aspect of the Fund's work is the education of public opinion to the general and particular needs of children and to arouse consciousness of responsibility for the world's children. The Fund's income is from voluntary contributions.

20 Gordon Square,   *Chairman and Hon. Treasurer :*
London, W.C.1   Captain L. H. Green, M.A.
                               General Secretary :
                               Brig. T. W. Boyce, O.B.E., M.C., M.M.

AGENCIES FOR YOUTH

ASSOCIATION FOR JEWISH YOUTH

In 1927 the Association for Jewish Youth was founded, developing out of the Jewish Athletic Association, which was established in 1899. It is "a central organisation created for the purpose of co-ordinating and assisting the work of clubs and centres created for the benefit of Jewish youth," and its aim is to instil the ideals of Judaism and British citizenship into the youth of the Anglo-Jewish community. It is governed by a council representative of its 70 affiliated organisations, in which are enrolled 8,600 members ; much responsibility falls on to the elected Executive Committee. The Association exists both to serve clubs and to represent them in appropriate general and Jewish spheres. It promotes inter-club activities, and its headquarters is designed as a central meeting-place. It also owns a permanent camping site and playing fields in Essex. The Association plans, and advises on, training courses for Jewish youth leaders. It fosters Judaism among the members of its affiliated organisations. The Association is assisted by grants from the King George's Jubilee Trust. The clubs themselves depend considerably on voluntary help.

A.J.Y. House, Leman Street,
London, E.1

General Secretary :
David Mellows, Esq.

THE BOY SCOUTS' ASSOCIATION

Lord Baden Powell founded the Boy Scouts' Association in 1908, and it has spread from Britain to 41 other countries inside and outside the Empire. "The aim of the Association is to develop good citizenship among boys by forming their character—training them in habits of observation, obedience and self-reliance—inculcating loyalty, and thoughtfulness for others—teaching them services useful to the public, and handicraft useful to themselves—promoting their physical, mental and spiritual development." The Association stresses its international aspect ; in 1947, 6,000 Scouts from Britain went to a World Jamboree in France, and the Chief Scout visited Canada and West Africa. In 1946 there were 164,000 Wolf Cubs (8-11), 173,000 Scouts (11-15), 38,000 Senior Scouts (15-18) and 11,000 Rovers (18 and over). The Scouters, who lead the boys, are voluntary personnel from whom an appreciation of the aims of scouting, satisfactory personal character and willingness to train are demanded before they receive a Warrant. The movement is governed, under Royal Charter of 1912, by a Council of 70 members, acting normally through the Committee of the Council. About one-eighth of its total income in 1946 came from the Ministry of Education, the balance being earned by miscellaneous activities, including sale of equipment and publications, from interest, rent and subscriptions. In addition, there was a deficit of £12,000 on the year.

25 Buckingham Palace Road,
London, S.W.1

Secretary :
A. W. Hurll, Esq.

THE BOYS' BRIGADE

The Boys' Brigade, founded in 1883, is a Christian Protestant organisation with a British Isles membership of 137,000 boys, aged 9-18, in 2,687 companies. It exists for "the advancement of Christ's kingdom among boys, and the promotion of habits of obedience, reverence, discipline, self-respect, and all that tends towards a true Christian manliness." Local units all meet weekly for Bible class and drill and there is a wide range of other activities. Apart from administrative staff, amounting to less than 1 per cent., the officers are voluntary and unsalaried. Provision is made for the training of all officers. The Brigade is governed by a Council of officers meeting annually, immediate decisions being taken by an executive body appointed on a representative basis. The organisation is financed mainly by a collection which its members make in "Boys' Brigade Week," together with company contributions, subscriptions and interest. King George's Jubilee Fund makes a grant which meets about one-fifteenth of the Brigade's expenditure.

Abbey House,   *Secretaries :*
2 Victoria Street,   G. Stanley Smith, Esq., O.B.E., M.C.
London, S.W.1   W. H. McVicker, Esq., M.SC.

THE CHURCH LADS' BRIGADE

The Church Lads' Brigade is solely a Church of England organisation which, through "religious, educational, physical and recreative agencies" and "the symbolic use" of military organisation, seeks to "extend the Kingdom of Christ among lads and to make them faithful members of the Church of England." All leaders are voluntary. The Brigade, founded in 1891, is controlled by a Governing Body, consisting of three honorary officers, and of one delegate elected by the chaplains and company officers of the Brigade from each of the 13 areas with limited power of co-option. About one quarter of the Brigade's income is derived from subscriptions and donations, and nearly half from interest and dividends arising from invested legacies ; in 1946 the Ministry of Education grant was £1,050, and that from King George's Jubilee Trust, £250 ; the balance of revenue comes mainly from annual fees and sale of equipment.

58 Gloucester Place,   *General Secretary :*
London, W.1   The Rev. Harold F. Peerless, A.K.C.

THE GIRL GUIDES' ASSOCIATION

The Girl Guides' Association was founded in Great Britain in 1909. It is now a member of a world movement, with a world total of 2,132,000 Girl Guides (or Girl Scouts as some countries call them). In Great Britain there are 306,000 members of the movement between the ages of 11 and 21. These include Guides (11-16) and, between 16 and 21, Rangers (Land, Sea and Air) and Cadets (who are training to be Guiders). There are also 167,000 Brownies under 11. The movement is led by 35,000 adults, guiders and commissioners, all working in their spare time. These are assisted by District and Division Local Associations of interested persons who, in 1946, sent 1,300 delegates to a Local Association Conference in London. There is also a small administrative and training salaried staff of approximately 178. Operating under a Royal Charter of 1922, the movement is governed by a Council, although most policy decisions are taken by an Executive Committee elected by the Council. These bodies keep contact with the whole membership through Company, District, Division and County Committees. The greater part of the Association's income is from sale of equipment and literature (£93,000 in 1946), but grants representing about one-twelfth and one-sixtieth of this sum were additionally received from the Ministry of Education and the Jubilee Trust respectively. The Guide training policy emphasises service, self-reliance and loyalty to a religious faith; it specialises in outdoor activities—57,000 camped in 1946—and aims at promoting good citizenship in all its branches through individual and communal achievements in which health, recreation, perseverance and applied intelligence and skill are dominant. Members of the Girl Guides' Association have undertaken relief work in many parts of Europe through the Guide International Service, which was financed from a fund of £100,000 raised within the movement itself.

17-19 Buckingham Palace Road,   *Chairman of Executive Committee :*
London, S.W.1   The Hon. Mrs. Sydney Marsham,
    D.B.E.

THE GIRLS' GUILDRY

The Girls' Guildry, founded in 1900, exists "to help girls to be followers of the Lord Jesus Christ, and to promote in girls discipline, self-respect, helpfulness and reverence." The Guildry is interdenominational. There were, in 1947, 22,815 girls enrolled in Britain, of whom 13,449 were under 11; there were a further 1,655 enrolled in Jamaica and in African Mission Fields. All Leaders, called Guardians, are voluntary; the Guildry insists that they take a specified training within a year of their appointment. The control of the movement is entrusted by the General Council to a Headquarters Committee on which sit representatives of the English, Scottish and Welsh Councils. These, in turn, are built up from the units, *via* Centre Committees. The main sources of revenue are collections, subscriptions and interest on investments; the Guildry receives Grants from the Ministry of Education and from King George's Jubilee Trust for certain specific purposes.

212 Bath Street,   *General Secretary :*
Glasgow, C.2   Miss May J. McKinlay

NATIONAL ASSOCIATION OF BOYS' CLUBS

The objects of the Association are the promotion of the spiritual, mental and physical fitness of the 14-18-year-old working boy, by linking together the various existing bodies concerned with Boys' Clubs.

The National Association is concerned primarily with the 14-18 age-group, but also affiliates Old Boys' Clubs which cater for the 18-25 years. The affiliated clubs endeavour to create a community of boys wherein each boy learns in practice the art of human relationships, being given a share of responsibility and helped to grow from the imposed discipline necessary in childhood to the self-discipline of manhood. Before a club can achieve affiliation to the National Association it must be evident that no one side of the threefold aim of physical, mental and spiritual development is being stressed at the expense of the others. There is an affiliation fee of 5s. per annum.

Approximately 2,000 clubs are affiliated either directly or through local federations.

17 Bedford Square,
London, W.C.1

Assistant General Secretary :
G. B. Bradney, Esq.

THE NATIONAL ASSOCIATION OF GIRLS' CLUBS AND MIXED CLUBS

The National Association of Girls' Clubs and Mixed Clubs works through Divisions in Scotland, Wales and Northern Ireland, and Associations in England. There are also two affiliated and seven associated National Societies at home and overseas. The Association is governed by a representative Council, which elects an active Executive Committee. There are 2,181 clubs covering a membership of 139,618, which includes 45,791 girls in girls' clubs, 47,307 girls in mixed clubs and 46,520 boys in mixed clubs. Founded for girls' clubs in 1880, the Association in 1944 included mixed clubs in response to current trends in club work.

The Association provides educational material, including international exhibitions, hire of film strips, educational broadsheets and books. It maintains a London club house for members, leaders and organisers of the club movement, and facilitates the use of the affiliated Associations' holiday houses. It has a holiday house and training centre—Avon Tyrrell—in the New Forest. The Association has concentrated on raising the standard of club leadership, voluntary and paid, and advocates a University course for full-time leaders and part-time or short training courses for voluntary leaders and senior members. In 1946-47, 40 per cent. of the Association's income came from the Ministry of Education, 40 per cent. from voluntary sources and 20 per cent. (this is a fluctuating sum dependent on the special applications made from year to year) from King George's Jubilee Trust, the Carnegie United Kingdom Trust and other Trusts. Approximately 40 per cent. of the income of the Divisions and Local Associations comes from statutory sources and at least 50 per cent. from voluntary sources with approximately 10 per cent. from public bodies. The Association makes considerable efforts to raise money through its Appeal Fund.

Hamilton House,
Bidborough Street, London, W.C.1

Organising Secretary :
Miss Honoria Harford

NATIONAL FEDERATION OF YOUNG FARMERS' CLUBS

The National Federation of Young Farmers' Clubs, founded in 1932, is a body of young people, mainly from agricultural areas, who govern themselves by a Council, of which, in 1946, 69 of the 87 members were nominated by the Clubs. The Federation covers some 1,200 Clubs with 65,000 members.

These Clubs are helped, but not run, by honorary adult leaders. They are grouped in 54 County Federations which actively stimulate interest in and knowledge of livestock, agriculture and horticulture, including modern mechanised methods of farming. The Federations also arouse a keen competitive sense of County pride; most of them employ County organising secretaries. The Federation publishes a bi-monthly illustrated journal, *The Young Farmer*, and a series of booklets, of which 170,000 were sold in 1946. It is assisted by grants from the Ministries of Agriculture and Education, from the Carnegie United Kingdom Trust and King George's Jubilee Trust. This assistance totals 95 per cent. of the headquarters income.

55 Gower Street,   *Secretary:*
London, W.C.1   Major H. Hiles, O.B.E.

THE WELSH LEAGUE OF YOUTH

Founded in 1922, the Welsh League of Youth is a non-sectarian and non-political youth organisation. "Its object is to promote Christian Welsh citizenship amongst the youth of Wales and to strengthen the bond of friendship between Welsh youth and youth of other nations." There are 80,000 members of the League under 25, those under 15 gathering in Junior Clubs; they "concentrate mainly upon interpreting Wales to the members." Older children are either in Welsh-speaking Youth Clubs or in Young Wales Clubs speaking English. Clubs meet at least twice a week. Their programmes include music and athletics and emphasise Welsh history and culture. The League also runs residential and club centres for various large groups and it has a holiday and training centre for workers of all ages, who are members of the League. The League is governed by a Council of whom the majority are elected by members of the League at the annual general meeting. This Council normally delegates its powers to a Committee, some of whose members are appointed by the League's General Meeting and some co-opted. The annual subscription of members is one shilling minimum.

U.R.D.D. Headquarters,   *Secretary:*
Aberystwyth   R. E. Griffith, Esq., B.A.

YOUNG CHRISTIAN WORKERS

The objects of the Y.C.W. are "to win all young workers and all the world of labour to a realisation of their Divine origins and destiny." With this end in view the Y.C.W. sets out to be: *a school of training* for young workers, enabling them to achieve the demands of their Christian vocation in the whole of their life; *a network of services* for their material, moral and spiritual needs; *a representative body*, asserting the demands of Christian working youth before the nation and public authorities.

One of the essentials of the Y.C.W. is that it is a self-governing organisation of wage-earning youth. Its entire leadership and direction is in the hands of young workers. The basic unit of the movement is the local section. The section, which is directed by a committee of leaders, consists of a group of "militants" who are in charge of teams of members, organised on a local or workshop basis. The sections are grouped according to industrial regions, which in turn link up with the national organisation. At each level, chaplains, appointed by ecclesiastical authority, assist the movement by giving counsel and guidance, and ensure the spiritual training of the "militants" and members.

The method of the Y.C.W. is essentially *active*. Each year an enquiry into one of the main problems or needs of working youth is launched by the movement. The enquiry proceeds in three stages : SEE—JUDGE—ACT : *seeing* the reality of the young worker's life, *judgment* in the light of the dignity of the young worker as a child of God, *action*, either individual or collective, in order to bring about a greater conformity with the Divine Plan. The constant aim of the enquiry-method is the transformation of the environment of the young worker, so that he may be able to achieve his vocation as a worker and a Christian. The Y.C.W. organises Study-days and Study-weekends for all the problems that concern young workers, and it promotes their spiritual training by retreats and days of recollection. It encourages sections to organise clubs, camps, hikes and sports to serve the young workers in their leisure time. It pays special attention to the needs of young workers in hospitals and sanatoria.

Members in the Forces are a special concern of the Y.C.W.'s activity. The organisation is financed by its members' subscriptions, 6d. per month under 18 years, and 1s. per month over 18 years, and also by the sale of the movement's own publications and other contributions ; it is not grant-aided.

Y.C.W. Headquarters,
106 Clapham Road, London, S.W.9

Secretary :
Thomas Bryan, Esq.

THE YOUNG MEN'S CHRISTIAN ASSOCIATION

The Young Men's Christian Association is one of the oldest of the voluntary youth organisations : it was formed in 1844 by twelve young men. In 1947 it had a membership in England, Ireland and Wales of 5,000 boys under 14, 29,000 youngsters between 14 and 20, and 37,000 men over 20. It is part of a world-wide inter-denominational fellowship, the World's Alliance of Y.M.C.As., with its headquarters at Geneva, and a total membership of some two and a half millions. It aims at developing in its members a Christian character and a Christian understanding of life. Full members are responsible for the government of autonomous local Associations : these are grouped in 19 Divisions through which they are represented on the National Council. The latter has direct responsibility for the very considerable work among H.M. Forces at home and overseas, for training several hundred boys each year in agriculture and seamanship, for the national camps and holiday centres, for an extensive scheme of voluntary leadership training, and for the welfare of thousands of European Voluntary Workers and others engaged in industry and agriculture. The Y.M.C.A. is financed by public contributions and membership subscriptions : it also received grants from certain Trusts and from the Ministry of Education.   Such trading surpluses as arise in Forces centres are spent exclusively upon work among the Forces.   In all Y.M.C.A. centres a wide variety of religious, cultural, athletic and social activities is promoted.

112 Great Russell Street,
London, W.C.1

General Secretary :
Sir Frank Willis, C.B.E., M.A.

YOUNG WOMEN'S CHRISTIAN ASSOCIATION

The Young Women's Christian Association of Great Britain is part of the world-wide Y.W.C.A. movement of which the headquarters are in Geneva. The international aspect of the organisation is stressed in all its publications. The British Association was founded in 1855 and incorporated in 1913.   The responsible bodies of the Y.W.C.A. are its National Council and its Finance Committee of the Board of Governors.   Constitutional changes can be made only by the Biennial Conference of democratically-elected representatives from each local centre : other decisions are normally made by the National Council and its Executive Committee, on both of which representatives from the Divisions (themselves representative of the Centres) outnumber those from the National Headquarters Committees.

The Association's work is done partly by volunteer, partly by salaried workers.   Both are required to train, but the latter must do up to two years' special Y.W.C.A. training, irrespective of their previous qualifications, in respect of which, however, the training may be modified or shortened.   The Association runs hostels, which once equipped are self-supporting, and club centres.   The latter are financed as self-contained units by its members' subscriptions, of which 1s. per head goes to the national and international association, by canteen profits, donations and Local Education Authority grants.   Headquarters funds are raised by public subscription and are aided by the Ministry of Education, King George's Jubilee Trust, and the Pilgrim Trust.   There are some 52,000 members of the Association ; in addition at least twice as many are served by the Association but have not yet become members.   The Association promotes recreational, cultural and educational pursuits, provides a background of companionship and seeks to enrich the religious content of its members' lives.

Y.W.C.A. National Offices,
Central Building (4th Floor),
Great Russell Street, London, W.C.1

National General Secretary :
Miss May Curwen, O.B.E., M.A.

AGENCIES FOR OLD PEOPLE

NATIONAL OLD PEOPLE'S WELFARE COMMITTEE

The Committee was originally established in the winter of 1940-41 as a committee of the National Council of Social Service.   In September, 1944, it became an autonomous body working in association with the National Council of Social Service who provide the secretariat.

The main Committee consists of representatives of a large number of national bodies with wholly or partly similar aims, and of representatives of regional O.P.W. Committees. There are various sub-committees, by whom the executive work is carried out.

Its aims are to study the needs of old people and promote measures for their well-being.

In particular it pools the experience of its constituent bodies ; serves as a bureau of information for the service of interested persons ; promotes the establishment of O.P.W. Committees ; and draws attention to the needs of the old through conferences, publications and exhibitions.

The Committee is financed almost entirely by the National Council of Social Service, although substantial contributions have been received from other sources for particular purposes.

26 Bedford Square,   *Chairman :*
London, W.C.1   Fred Messer, Esq., J.P., M.P.
                                            Secretary :
                                            Miss D. Ramsey, M.B.E.

OLD PEOPLE'S HOMES COMMITTEE

The aim of the Committee is to act as a clearing house for old people needing accommodation with varying amounts of care.

Applications are received from such sources as the Assistance Board, Hospital Almoners, the Family Welfare Association, Citizens' Advice Bureaux, besides old people themselves and their relatives. Over 2,400 cases were handled in 1947.

Set up in 1943, the Committee is now a department of the Family Welfare Association, and has no separate constitution or accounts.

296 Vauxhall Bridge Road,   *Secretary :*
London, S.W.1   Miss M. Murray

AGENCIES FOR THE BLIND

THE NATIONAL ASSOCIATION OF WORKSHOPS FOR THE BLIND

The Association was formed in 1929 as a result of a resolution adopted at a conference of workshop representatives, who agreed that the problems affecting this phase of blind welfare work could best be solved by pooling the experience of experts from all parts of the country. It became an incorporated body in 1936.

Its objects include the following : fostering co-operation among workshops for the Blind ; the promotion of research into all problems connected with the training and employment of the Blind ; to raise the standard of efficiency in workshops for the Blind, by the dissemination of information and the encouragement of new methods and ideas ; and to enter into contracts for the

T

supply of raw materials used in the various industries practised in Blind Workshops, or for the sale of commodities made in those Workshops.

257 Tottenham Court Road,   *Secretary :*
London, W.1   S. W. Starling, Esq.

NATIONAL INSTITUTE FOR THE BLIND

The National Institute for the Blind, a voluntary organisation originally known as the British and Foreign Blind Association for Promoting the Education and Employment of the Blind, was founded in 1868 and incorporated in 1902. It is governed by a Council which represents local authorities, voluntary local organisations (through four regional bodies), other national organisations, the Blind themselves and individuals elected by reason of their interest in the national aspect of work for the Blind. Ninety per cent. of its income is derived from voluntary sources, the remainder being contributed by statutory bodies.

The N.I.B. exists to provide services which can best be rendered by national, rather than local or regional effort. Its activities include the production of Braille and Moon books and special apparatus ; the provision of nursery and other special schools and of homes for the blind and deaf-blind ; rehabilitation of the newly-blind ; placement in open industry ; supply of apparatus and appliances including talking books ; training in telephony and physiotherapy ; technical and educational research ; prevention of blindness ; case work assistance, and development of blind welfare in Great Britain and the Colonies.

226 Great Portland Street,   *Secretary :*
London, W.1   W. McG. Eagear, Esq., C.B.E., M.A.

AGENCIES FOR THE CRIPPLED AND OTHER PHYSICALLY HANDICAPPED PERSONS

THE AFTER-CARE ASSOCIATION (Physically Handicapped Youth)

The After-Care Association for Physically Handicapped Youth tries to find suitable employment for physically handicapped young people within the County of London in order that as large a proportion as possible may become self-supporting. Founded in 1902, the Association works closely with the London County Council and by arrangement gives advice on vocation to all children leaving L.C.C. Schools for the physically handicapped, the deaf and the more serious cases from Schools for the Partially Sighted. Employment Executive Officers of the Association are responsible for the placing and industrial supervision of these children ; regular home visiting is also undertaken partly by paid and partly by voluntary workers. The Association also does a great deal of incidental welfare work among physically handicapped juveniles as need arises. It is governed by a self-nominating Executive Committee and is financed partly by subscription and donations, but depends mainly on a grant from the Ministry of Labour and a smaller sum from the Social Welfare Department of the L.C.C.

2 Old Queen Street,   *Secretary :*
London, W.1   Miss Winder

BRITISH COUNCIL FOR REHABILITATION

The British Council for Rehabilitation, founded as lately as 1944, actively promotes information, research and study in the field of rehabilitation. It also co-ordinates organisations working in this field. It looks upon rehabilitation as a unified service, starting with treatment and ending with economic resettlement. Foreign enquiries about rehabilitation are now referred to this organisation both by the British Council and the Foreign Office. In 1946 it undertook a survey of rehabilitation needs in Poland at the request of UNRRA. The Council is governed by an Executive Committee elected by member organisations. It is financed by affiliation fees and subscriptions.

32 Shaftesbury Avenue,   *Secretary :*
London, W.1   Mrs. Marion E. Williams

CENTRAL COUNCIL FOR THE CARE OF CRIPPLES

The Central Council for the Care of Cripples exists : "to investigate the causes of crippling and to promote measures for their elimination and to organise schemes for the treatment, education, employment and general welfare of cripples." Founded in 1919, the Council has 89 organisations affiliated to it and forming, with individual members, the Council by which it is governed. Policy decisions are normally taken by the Executive Committee, a body nominated by the Council, but electing its own chairman. Major decisions emanate from the annual general meeting. The Council is financed by affiliation fees, subscriptions, the results of appeals and by grants from the Lord Nuffield Fund for Cripples.

34 Eccleston Square,   *Secretary :*
London, S.W.1   Miss M. Drury

THE INVALID CHILDREN'S AID ASSOCIATION

The Invalid Children's Aid Association was founded in 1888 and works for sick, invalid and crippled children in the London and Greater London area. It provides convalescence either in one of its nine homes, of which five are recognised by the Ministry of Education, or in another home on its approved list; it acts as a clearing house for children all over the country needing special accommodation and treatment; it visits, mainly through its voluntary workers, the homes of children referred to it by hospital almoners and others as being in need of convalescence or special residential treatment. The Association also assists in providing surgical appliances where patients cannot afford these. Through home visits it acts as friend and adviser both to patients and to their ill or handicapped children. The income of the Association is mainly derived from voluntary subsciptions together with a grant from the L.C.C. for services rendered under the Council's contact scheme. It is managed by an Executive Committee and has a representative Advisory Council.

4 Palace Gate, London, W.8   *Secretary :*
                                           Miss N. R. Manson

THE MENTAL AFTER-CARE ASSOCIATION

The Mental After-Care Association has existed since 1879 to afford assistance to persons leaving mental hospitals and therapeutic care for potential patients. In 1946 it supervised the convalescence of some 850 patients and boarded out a further 450. It also paid a thousand first visits in addition to further visits to persons already known to it. The main body of its income is derived from contributions for services rendered. It is also helped by voluntary gifts and by King Edward's Hospital Fund. The Association is governed by a self-nominating committee.

110 Jermyn Street,
London, S.W.1

Secretary :
Miss H. S. Russell

THE NATIONAL ASSOCIATION FOR MENTAL HEALTH

The National Association for Mental Health was formed in 1946. It amalgamates and continues the work of the former Central Association for Mental Health, the Child Guidance Council and the National Council for Mental Hygiene. The Association runs training courses for professional workers dealing with mental health problems ; it publishes books and pamphlets aimed both at explaining and preventing mental illness ; it runs homes and hostels for mental defectives ; it has a residential nursery for difficult children ; it maintains a national service of qualified workers to advise on facilities for the care of those suffering from mental disorder, and also provides help and supervision for such people living in the community ; it also employs centrally a staff of consultants on the various aspects of mental illness and behaviour problems. The Association runs courses of lectures for the general public who, although they have no professional concern with mental illness, need to have some awareness of its nature and implications.

It is governed by a nominated representative Council. Half its expenditure is met from payments for services rendered, subscriptions and donations and half from Government Grant, the largest part of which is for specific work undertaken for the Ministry of Health.

39 Queen Anne Street,
Wimpole Street, London, W.1

General Secretary :
Miss Mary C. Owen, M.B.E., M.A.

THE NATIONAL ASSOCIATION FOR THE PREVENTION OF TUBERCULOSIS

The National Association for the Prevention of Tuberculosis carries out research, education and propaganda. It has a large membership both in this country and overseas, especially in the British Colonies, to which field a large part of the Association's energy is now directed. Over 120 Tuberculosis Care Committees throughout this country are affiliated to the N.A.P.T., as well as a number of Tuberculosis Associations in the Commonwealth and Empire. *The N.A.P.T. Bulletin,* published six times yearly, is widely read by doctors, nurses, social workers engaged in tuberculosis work, and the quarterly *Health Horizon* is a health magazine for the layman. The N.A.P.T. also publishes many propaganda and technical leaflets, and a professional quarterly for doctors and research workers.

Tavistock House North,
Tavistock Square,
London, W.C.1

Secretary-General :
J. H. Harle Williams, Esq., M.D., D.P.H.,
Barrister-at- Law
Social Welfare Secretary :
Miss Nancy Overend,
Barrister-at-Law

NATIONAL INSTITUTE FOR THE DEAF

The National Institute for the Deaf exists for "the furtherance by propaganda or research into any matter affecting the interests of the deaf and dumb or the deafened throughout life." It subsists entirely on voluntary funds, but works in close co-ordination with educational authorities who, together with voluntary bodies, including schools, are represented on its Council. Its executive committee consists of members elected annually by this Council, together with representatives of major organisations and including also co-opted members. The Institute is particularly active in promoting lip-reading, suitable education for deaf children, and improved hearing aid appliances of a reliable character. Its journal, *The Silent World*, widens the outlook of the deaf as well as informing others about the condition of deaf and deafened persons. The Institute also publishes informative and educational books and pamphlets concerning the problems related to deafness.

105 Gower Street,
London, W.C.1

Secretary :
G. W. Lelburn, Esq., F.I.A.C.

PAPWORTH VILLAGE SETTLEMENT

Papworth is the original village settlement for the tuberculous. Founded in 1918, it includes a modern sanatorium and, during treatment, and as part of treatment, training in the village industries with the possibility of permanent settlement for those who need sheltered occupation and who desire to stay. The latter may bring their families, the members of which live normal community lives, the only difference being that the affected member of the family has the opportunity of sheltered employment and medical supervision. Papworth has facilities for treatment for 515 patients, factories for 1,000 workers, 200 houses for settlers, and hostels for trainees and the unmarried. In 1946 wages paid to patients totalled £71,000. The Settlement receives no Government grant but depends on profit from industries, payments from patients (the latter normally from statutory bodies) and the result of appeals. Residence and treatment charges normally diminish after the patient is able to work consistently for six hours daily. The Settlement is administered by a Committee of Management, advised by the Medical Director and assisted by a medical consultative committee.

Papworth Hall,
Cambridge

Medical Director :
R. R. Trail, Esq., M.D., F.R.C.P.

AGENCIES FOR THE HOMELESS

CECIL HOUSES, INC.

This is a voluntary non-sectarian organisation managing women's public lodging houses and a girls' residential club. It was founded in 1927 by Mrs. Cecil Chesterton, O.B.E. It is incorporated under the Board of Trade as a charity and is governed by a Committee of Management. It manages three lodging houses with accommodation for 164 women and ten babies, and one residential club with accommodation for 72 girls. It is intended to open a home for old ladies as soon as circumstances permit. These enterprises are self-supporting except that the initial funds required to start them are raised by public subscription. The Association employs paid staff.

193 Gower Street,   *Hon. Secretary :*
London, N.W.1   Mrs. Cecil Chesterton, O.B.E.

THE EMBANKMENT FELLOWSHIP CENTRE

Founded in 1932 by Mrs. G. I. Huggins, the Embankment Fellowship Centre has as its object to assist ex-Service men and ex-Merchant Seamen of all classes over the age of 45 and who are in distress by providing food, accommodation and clothing. The Centre also helps in finding employment. The Centre comprises a country home, "Downgate," near Tunbridge Wells, a rehabilitation centre accommodating 40 men, and "Hollenden House," at Bexhill-on-Sea, a permanent home for aged men, as well as a London hostel at 59 Belvedere Road, S.E.1. Interviews are held daily at Headquarters for admission to all branches of the Centre. The Council is the governing body, through a Committee of Management elected from their number. The Administrator is responsible for the general management to the Committee. Each house is controlled by a Resident Warden. The Centre is entirely supported by voluntary subscription. The income for 1946-47 was £8,400. A General Meeting is held annually to which all subscribers are invited to attend.

59 Belvedere Road,   *Chairman of the Council :*
London, S.E.1   Lord Hollenden

THE FELLOWSHIP OF ST. CHRISTOPHER

The Fellowship began in 1928. Its first work was the provision of temporary housing and assistance for destitute boys. It later perceived the need of residential houses as a means of caring for boys who have no homes of their own, and now directs itself mainly to this form of work. It has four houses in or near London, and hopes soon to open a fifth. The average number of boys in residence at any time in 1947 was 120. The Fellowship is a wholly voluntary body, whose affairs are carried on by a Board of Managers and an Advisory Council. It receives no money from public funds, beyond some help towards maintenance for a few of the boys. Apart from interest on some investments, the great bulk of its income is from subscriptions and donations.

53 Warwick Road,   *Organising Secretary :*
London, S.W.5   Brigadier N. MacLeod, O.B.E.

HOMES FOR WORKING BOYS IN LONDON (Inc.)

Founded in 1870 to provide a home for destitute and homeless boys in London, it had in 1946 four hostels open, two others being temporarily closed as a result of the war but one of them will reopen shortly. One hostel is a Probation Hostel. The average number of boys resident at a time is now some 150.

Boys are taken from all parts of the country, mainly through Children's Homes and Welfare and Probation Officers. They stay for a year on the average, and the aim is to give them what they have lost or never had— "home life" on the foundation of Christianity. Good jobs in industry are found for the boys, and recreational and social activities are provided for the evenings.

The Society receives small grants-in-aid from public funds, and a considerable part of its income is derived from contributions from the boys towards their upkeep. There is, however, a wide gap, to close which appeals are made for subscriptions and donations.

6 Buckingham Street,   *Secretary :*
London, W.C.2   Major G. B. Lee

"MORNING POST" EMBANKMENT HOME

This Home was established in 1898 after an article in *The Morning Post* had drawn attention to the numbers of destitute then to be found wandering on the Embankment. A home was founded in Millbank where destitute persons were given occupation until they were able to find a job. Later it was moved to the New Kent Road. In 1945, in consequence of changing conditions, it was decided to make a radical alteration in the objects of the Home. It was now to be directed, not to short-term relief, but to longer-term rehabilitation of "men whose cases were abnormal—men who for some reason were outside the scope of the Unemployment Assistance Act or who for some psychological reason were temporarily unable to fit into the normal conditions of working life." New premises were acquired at Elstree, Herts. This Home is managed by a Council. The major part of its income is derived from profits on invested funds.

Elstree, Herts.   *Secretary :*
            T. S. Cooper, Esq.

ROWTON HOUSES

This Company was formed in 1894. The aim of the Company was private hotels for working men, where they would be free of religious or political persuasion of any sort, and be able to mould their lives as working men in

London. It is a public Company, and has limited its dividend in accordance with Lord Rowton's wish, to five per cent. The average dividend is considerably below this figure.

It receives no income from voluntary sources, or from statutory bodies. The vast majority of the men are working men, who pay their own way, and use the Houses as clubs. None of the services are given voluntarily. Television rooms and billiard rooms are provided, and draughts, chess and darts tournaments held. Each of the six Houses is provided with a free library.

Ablution rooms and footbaths are provided free. The policy of the Company has been to improve each year, and to utilise its surplus profits (if any) for the improvement of the fabric, cooking, and lighting, and similar facilities in the buildings.

To date, the Company has housed approximately sixty million men. The majority of the men who stay in the Houses do so as there is no institutional or compulsory attendance at services, or irksome regulations. Each House has its own Residents' Committee, to run the sports and welfare section, and is in constant communication with the Directorate.

17 Buckingham Palace Gardens,   *Managing Director :*
London, S.W.1   K. Dulake, Esq.

SOCIETY FOR THE RELIEF OF THE HOUSELESS POOR

This charity dates back to 1820, when it was founded for the purpose of "affording nightly shelter and sustenance" to the "absolutely destitute wandering about the Metropolis." Its present objects are to maintain a Home (Western Lodge, Clapham Common, S.W.) for the accommodation of destitute persons of the blackcoated or professional class in the County of London ; to help them find employment, and generally to promote their well-being. Under a Scheme made by the Charity Commissioners, the Society is administered by a Board of Trustees, 14 of whom are appointed by various bodies, as laid down in the Scheme, and three co-opted. Its income is derived mainly from the proceeds of invested funds. The Society co-operates in the arrangements of the L.C.C. for dealing with the homeless poor in the County of London. Since the end of the war, the Trustees have enlarged their scope to include provision for persons who are homeless and in need of employment, but not otherwise destitute.

Western Lodge, 84 West Side,   *Secretary and Warden :*
Clapham Common, London, S.W.4   C. S. Dutton, Esq.

THE S.O.S. SOCIETY

The S.O.S. Society was founded in 1929. Prior to the last war its principal aim was the maintenance of hostels for the "rebuilding" of destitute men and youths. Since the beginning of the war it has taken on additional work ; in addition to five hostels for men in London and three for boys on probation (two in London and one in the provinces) it now maintains five homes for the old, three in London and two in Kent, and an Old People's Club in St. Pancras in conjunction with a local body. During the war the Society ran three Service Men's Clubs, all of which have now closed down. The Society is an entirely voluntary organisation, managed by a General Council. It receives no grants from public funds, the bulk of its income being derived from voluntary subscriptions and donations.

24 Ashburn Place,   *General Secretary :*
Gloucester Road, London, S.W.7   P. N. Shone, Esq., O.B.E.

THE WAYFARERS' BENEVOLENT ASSOCIATION

This was founded in 1926 by the late J. T. Gibbons, as a centre for the rehabilitation of young vagrants up to the age of 25 (the age limit is now 30). Originally housed at Windlestone Hall, Durham, and now at Chilton Hall in the same county, the Association has accommodation for some 20 youths and young men who are trained and cared for until suitable jobs are found for them. Since its foundation, over 1,300 young men have passed through its training centre. It is said to be the only organisation of its kind in the United Kingdom outside London.

The Association receives maintenance grants and fees from vagrancy authorities, but depends largely also upon voluntary subscriptions and donations.

Chilton Hall, Ferryhill,   *Secretary :*
Co. Durham   G. F. Bennett, Esq., M.B.E.

AGENCIES FOR SOCIALLY HANDICAPPED PERSONS

THE NATIONAL ASSOCIATION OF DISCHARGED PRISONERS' AID SOCIETIES

The National Association, a body corporate, regulated by its own Articles of Association, was set up in 1936 and is the central administrative body for Discharged Prisoners' Aid work in England and Wales. All local Discharged Prisoners' Aid Societies, of which there are now 38, are affiliated to it, and each society has one or more representatives on its Committee. Local Discharged Prisoners' Aid Societies, holding certificates from the Secretary of State, are entitled to work within prisons, and have the duty of maintaining contact with prisoners during their sentence, and of seeking to find them employment and generally looking after their welfare, after their discharge. These societies are voluntary bodies and the greater part of their income is derived from voluntary donations, though they receive also certain grants from public funds. The work of the National Association is mainly to co-ordinate the work of these local societies. It is the channel through which the Government grant is distributed to them, and through which representations are normally, though not necessarily, made by the societies to the Prison Commissioners. The Secretary of State's certificate of efficiency is granted to or withheld from local societies on the recommendation of the National Association. The responsibility for the welfare work at Special or Regional Prisons is the concern of the National Association, which has its own sub-committees at Wakefield, Maidstone and Askham Grange.

66 Eccleston Square,   *General Secretary :*
London, S.W.1   The Rev. Martin Pinker

THE NATIONAL COUNCIL FOR THE UNMARRIED MOTHER AND HER CHILD

The National Council for the Unmarried Mother and her Child was formed in 1918 "in order to help the illegitimate child and its mother." It works for legislative reform, and meanwhile urges Local Authorities to make the fullest use of their powers under existing Statutes. It does not itself run Homes and Hostels, but it tries to promote the provision of these. A Consultative Committee composed of representatives of the affiliated homes and of members of the Committee of Management meets when necessary to discuss problems affecting the homes. The Council also has a Case Department which deals with individual girls and families. New cases rose from a monthly average of 90 before the war to 450 at the beginning of 1946. Many of these cases involve difficult negotiations with representatives of the Dominions and of other countries. The Council receives a grant from the Ministry of Health, donations from many Local Authorities, and assistance from the London Parochial Charities ; these sums make up some three-quarters of the Council's income, the balance coming mainly from subscriptions and affiliation fees. The Council consists of individual members and of representatives of Local Authorities, of voluntary organisations, and of affiliated Homes. Immediate decisions are taken by elected Committees of the Council.

87 Tottenham Court Road,   *General Secretary :*
London, W.1   Miss Isabelle H. Granger

AGENCIES FOR FAMILY WELFARE

THE FAMILY WELFARE ASSOCIATION

Formerly the Charity Organisation Society, the Family Welfare Association was founded in 1869 to alleviate distress. The Association works mainly in the London area ; its District Offices not only deal directly with cases of need but act as a clearing house to refer these to other suitable statutory and voluntary organizations. The Association's staff are skilled in making wise use of the funds of charities and other organisations which will help cases recommended by the Association. The headquarters of the Association also administers the residue of various war relief funds. Its Old People's Homes Committee has its own secretary. In 1946 the Family Welfare Association trained some 350 students in the district offices. It runs free legal aid centres and six experimental marriage guidance centres. The information department is extensively used by voluntary and statutory bodies. There are also 54 affiliated agencies in the United Kingdom. These are required to have a representative committee, to have trained social workers in charge, to undertake general family casework and to publish annual reports and accounts. Each sends two representatives to serve on the Provisional National Council of the Association. Immediate decisions, however, are taken by the Administrative Committee, which is elected by the Council. District Committees consist of ministers of religion, local administrators and representatives of "principal local authorities." The Association receives no grants from Government departments and exists entirely on voluntary contributions, except for those grants for Citizens' Advice Bureau work which are made from Local Authorities. Its average annual expenditure on relief is £60,000, much of which is obtained for individual cases from various endowed and collecting charities. Expenditure on administration is rather more than half the total spent on relief, as the Family Welfare Association emphasises increasingly the need to work through trained and suitable personnel. Only a few carefully selected voluntary workers are now occupied in case work. Much interviewing is, however, done by meticulously supervised students during their training.

296 Vauxhall Bridge Road,   *Secretary :*
London, S.E.1   B. E. Astbury, Esq., O.B.E.

THE NATIONAL MARRIAGE GUIDANCE COUNCIL

Although the Marriage Guidance Council was founded in 1938, its effective organization dates from 1942. It aims at promoting marital harmony by giving advice through centres, correspondence and interviews with all those who seek its help. It is financed by voluntary funds which are at present inadequate. Most of its work in every department is done by voluntary workers; those actually interviewing clients are Marriage Counsellors who are carefully selected and trained, and Consultants who must be professionally qualified. The Council also uses Lecturers who, like all other field workers, are voluntary and are required to expound the aims and principles of the movement. The Council encourages the formation of local marriage guidance councils of which there are now about 60. These send representatives to the six-monthly meetings of the Council, the Executive of which meets monthly. The Council is not in receipt of any financial help from statutory bodies, and finds difficulty in raising sufficient voluntary funds.

78 Duke Street,   *General Secretary :*
London, W.1   David R. Mace, Esq., M.A., B.SC., PH.D.

AGENCIES FOR ADULT EDUCATION

THE NATIONAL COUNCIL OF LABOUR COLLEGES

The National Council of Labour Colleges was founded in 1921 to "provide independent working-class education" primarily among Trade Unionists. At present there are 58 Trade Unions affiliated to the Council with a membership of over five million. It is financed chiefly by unions paying affiliation fees, usually of 3d. per member; it also receives small grants, between one and two guineas, from the majority of Co-operative Societies, and larger grants from the T.U.C., the C.W.S., the S.T.U.C., and the S.C.W.S. The Council's students include 16,000 postal students; these, out of a wide choice, concentrate mainly on English, Economics and Local Government; there are also some 12,000 class students, while 53,000 students attend individual lectures to branches. A total of 634 attended the Council's nine Summer Schools in 1947, and 11,000 went to Day and Week-end Schools. Tutors are normally drawn from ex-students who are themselves active in the Labour Movement. The Council is ultimately controlled by the representative Annual Conference. Immediate policy decisions are taken by an Executive Committee of persons elected as representatives of affiliated organizations of Divisional Councils of the Organization, and of the N.C.L.C. Organisers' Association. The Council does not receive grants from any statutory authority. Its journal is *The Plebs*. It publishes its own text books.

Tillicoultry,   *General Secretary :*
Scotland   J. P. M. Millar, Esq.

THE WORKERS' EDUCATIONAL ASSOCIATION

The Workers' Educational Association was founded by Trade Unionists and Co-operators in 1903 to provide education for adults who wish to continue, or to resume, learning and who have not had the opportunity of attending a University. There were, in 1946-47, over 100,000 students enrolled in 5,435 classes and paying 2s. 6d. to 5s. per course. Courses are of three types : (1) Terminal Courses of ten or more meetings ; (2) Sessional Courses of not less than 20 meetings ; (3) Tutorial Classes lasting three years of 24 classes per year. The last two types are normally taken by University graduates of good standing, books are provided on loan, and students are expected both to read and write during the course. The Workers' Educational Association also organises informal courses designed to lead into serious study, and it promotes One-Day and Week-end Schools as well as running fifteen annual Summer Schools in Great Britain and six abroad. The Association is composed of individual members (now totalling over 45,000) and of some 2,600 affiliated working-class and educational bodies. The basic units are the Branches, the 932 of which are grouped into Districts ; Branches, affiliated organizations and individual members are represented on the District Councils, and these are represented on the Central Council of the Association. The Association is recognized by the Ministry of Education as a responsible body for administering adult classes. The Association and its branches are financed chiefly by grants from the Ministry of Education and from Local Education Authorities in respect of teaching services ; administrative costs are mainly met from subscriptions, affiliation fees, and the results of appeals. The Workers' Educational Association journal is *The Highway*, published monthly, 3d.

38A St. George's Drive,   *General Secretary :*
London, S.W.1   Ernest Green, Esq., M.A., J.P.

THE WORKING MEN'S COLLEGE

The Working Men's College was founded in 1854 by Frederick Denison Maurice, with the help of Charles Kingsley, Tom Hughes, J. M. Ludlow and others. Their aim was to "give the working man the opportunity of acquiring wisdom through education" ; by making him "wise" to make him "fit to be free."

Maurice's intentions were that the College should really be for Working Men (unlike the earlier "Mechanics' Institutes," which had often become places for the middle class) ; that it should be a College—a place of intimate fellowship between the teachers and the taught ; and that it should be a place for the teaching of liberal studies rather than of technical subjects. These views still inform the spirit and are exemplified in the activities of the College.

It is a Corporation registered as a Company limited by guarantee ; its government is vested in a Council, consisting of ex-officio, nominated, elected and co-opted members. The College is principally supported by subscriptions, donations, endowments and fees. A wide range of subjects is taught, and much attention is paid to the standard of teaching. The teachers are volunteers ; and it has long been a tradition that they are recruited largely from young civil servants and other professional men who have lately begun their career. In the 1946-47 session some 500 students enrolled, each at a fee of 10s. per class.

The first home of the College was in Red Lion Square ; after other changes, it moved to its present site, in Crowndale Road, N.W., in 1905.

Crowndale Road,   *Secretary :*
London, N.W.1   Dudley M. C. Gill, Esq., B.SC.

AGENCIES FOR PROMOTION OF THE ARTS

THE BRITISH DRAMA LEAGUE

The British Drama League is a voluntary society established for the purpose of fostering the development of the art of the stage, both professional and amateur, but particularly among the amateur. It was founded in 1919 by Geoffrey Whitworth and has made steady progress since. Membership is open to organisations, professional and amateur, to individuals, and (at a reduced fee) to recognised Youth Clubs. The membership in 1947 included some 6,000 dramatic organisations, 1,500 individuals and 700 Youth Clubs— the highest membership in the League's history.

The League has a large library, chiefly of plays and acting parts, which may be borrowed by members. In addition, the League has a number of travelling drama instructors, holds annual theatrical festivals at which amateur societies may compete for a prize, and gives instruction in acting, production and play-writing.

Apart from a grant given by the British Council for the special purpose of organising interchanges of plays and companies with the Continent, the B.D.L. is financed almost wholly by the subscriptions and donations of members.

9 Fitzroy Square,   *Secretary :*
London, W.1   Miss Francis Briggs

THE RURAL MUSIC SCHOOLS ASSOCIATION

The R.M.S.A. is a voluntarily-organised body, which aims at encouraging amateur music-making of the highest possible standard among people in all walks of life. Founded in 1934 (as the "Federation of Rural Music Schools"), it is now responsible for eight music schools in as many English counties, having a total of over 4,000 pupils. These Rural Music Schools "were started to meet the needs of persons of every age—particularly those living in country places—who want to play and sing and listen to good music." There is also a London Centre and a Teachers' Training Department. The Association, which is a non-profit-making company limited by guarantee, is governed by a Council on which the Schools are represented.

The Schools are grant-aided by Education authorities and receive income from students' fees, but are dependent to a considerable extent on voluntary subscriptions. The Association receives a grant from the Arts Council, and one from the Ministry of Education, the latter dependent on at least 25 per cent. of its income being raised from voluntary sources.

109 Bancroft,   *Secretary :*
Hitchin, Herts.   Miss Helen Wright

AGENCIES FOR PHYSICAL RECREATION AND HOLIDAYS

THE CAMPING CLUB OF GREAT BRITAIN AND IRELAND

This Club exists for the purpose of encouraging camping, to establish standards of camping, to protect the interests of campers and to arrange for the supply of camping appliances for its members.

The Club originated at the beginning of the present century out of the invention of lightweight camping kit. It grew by amalgamation with other Clubs. It is governed by a Council elected by a postal vote of members, and by officers.

Members undertake to camp in accordance with the Code for Campers, as laid down by the Council from time to time. Membership reached 11,500 for the year 1947.

There are a number of ancillary sections, including the Canoe Camping Club, Mountaineering Section, Association of Cycle Campers ; there are District Associations throughout Great Britain, and a Scottish National Council. There is also a Youth Camping Association.

The Club runs some 18 permanent camp sites in Britain, including National Fitness Camps, and publishes a Year Book of other sites where camping is permitted. The Club acts in an advisory capacity to various statutory bodies in the matter of camp-siting, and manages the Middlesex County Council National Fitness camp sites.

Except for a small paid staff at headquarters, service is given voluntarily and without pay. The income of the Club is derived almost wholly from members' subscriptions.

38 Grosvenor Gardens,   *General Secretary :*
London, S.W.1   H. W. Pegler, Esq.

THE CENTRAL COUNCIL FOR PHYSICAL RECREATION

The Council, set up in 1935, is a national voluntary organisation which aims at the improvement of the physical and mental health of the community through physical recreation. Over 160 national bodies are members of the Council, including the governing bodies of games, sports and outdoor activities, the national voluntary youth organisations, and many organisations interested in education. From its beginning the Council was recognised by the Board of Education, and it now receives substantial grants from the Ministry of Education and the Scottish Education Department, which constitute the bulk of its income.

The Council works with its constituent bodies, and with local authorities, to provide a wide range of services, including the following : training courses for coaches and leaders in all branches of physical recreation ; advice and assistance in various aspects of the organisation of games and sports, both indoor and outdoor, through a number of technical representatives in various parts of the country ; and the publication of training and advisory pamphlets.

The National Headquarters is in London. There are also Scottish and Welsh Headquarters, and Regional Offices in various parts of the country. These have paid staffs, but much voluntary work is also done.

6 Bedford Square,　　　　　　　　　*General Secretary :*
London, W.C.1　　　　　　　　　Miss P. C. Colson, O.B.E.

CO-OPERATIVE HOLIDAYS ASSOCIATION

The Co-operative Holidays Association was founded in the 1890's as a means of making known to the youth of towns the pleasures of country holiday-making. It owns or rents a number of guest houses throughout Great Britain. Its object is to furnish, at below normal present-day costs, holidays which provide not only for the recreational but also for the cultural and spiritual requirements of the guests. An essential part of its policy is that its guests shall spend their holidays not as isolated individuals but as a social group, participating in the excursions and other activities organised for them.

The Association has some ancillary activities such as the publication of a journal. It also arranges holiday parties abroad as a means of furthering its work for international goodwill.

The Co-operative Holidays Association is not a part of the co-operative movement. It is a company, limited by guarantee and governed by a president and committee elected by the members. Membership is open to anyone who has spent a week in the current holiday season at one of the Association's guest houses.

Its income is derived mainly from the charges made for holidays.

Birch Heys, Cromwell Range,　　　　*General Secretary :*
Fallowfield, Manchester　　　　　　D. W. Shilton, Esq., O.B.E., M.A.

THE HOLIDAY FELLOWSHIP

This exists to organise holiday-making, i.e., to provide for the healthy enjoyment of leisure, to encourage love of the open air and to promote social and international friendship.

It came into being in 1913 and by 1939 was the owner of over thirty properties and through these and by walking tours and other forms of "community holiday" in various parts of this country and the continent of Europe was providing for nearly 50,000 guest weeks per year.

Like the Co-operative Holidays Association, it seeks to provide a form of holiday in which its guests participate not as individuals but as a social group.

Its objects and ideals are carried out during the non-holiday periods by nearly 100 local groups in various towns and cities. By its Goodwill Fund it provides holidays for people of slender means at reduced charges, which, in certain circumstances, are waived altogether.

It is registered under the Industrial and Provident Societies Act and is controlled by a General Committee elected by members. Shareholding members have some privileges in priority booking and in centre charges.

142 Great North Way, *General Secretary :*
London, N.W.4 J. B. Henderson, Esq., O.B.E.

THE NATIONAL PLAYING FIELDS ASSOCIATION

This is a voluntary body incorporated by Royal Charter. Its principal aims are to secure adequate public playing fields and play grounds ; to co-operate in the preservation of threatened playing fields and playgrounds ; and to act as a centre of advice on all questions connected with them.

The Association provides Grant-Aid, mainly for (a) Children's Playgrounds, which are not eligible for assistance from the Ministry of Education under the Physical Training and Recreation Act ; (b) schemes in Northern Ireland ; (c) schemes in respect of lands vested in the Association.

The Association is governed, under its Charter, by a Council and Executive Committee. There are Affiliated County Playing Fields Associations in most counties in England and Wales, an Association for Northern Ireland and one for Scotland. There is a paid staff at headquarters, but otherwise a great deal of work is done voluntarily. The Association's income is received either from interest or investments, from membership subscriptions and donations and contributions from other voluntary bodies.

71 Eccleston Square, *General Secretary :*
London, S.W.1 Sir Lawrence Chubb

THE RAMBLERS' ASSOCIATION

The Ramblers' Association was founded in 1934. Its aims include the protection of the interests and maintenance of the rights of ramblers, the increase of knowledge and love of the countryside, and the preservation of its amenities.

It is governed under its constitution by a National Council which appoints an Executive Committee.   Membership is open to individuals and to national and local organisations.   Members are normally organised into District Federations, which in their turn largely determine the organisation of the National Council.

The work of the Association is almost entirely undertaken by voluntary unpaid workers.

The Association's income is mainly derived from membership fees and donations.

20 Buckingham Street,   *Hon. Secretary :*
London, S.W.1   L. E. Morris, Esq.

WORKERS' TRAVEL ASSOCIATION

Now one of the largest travel and holiday agencies in the country, the Workers' Travel Association Ltd. was formed in October, 1921.   It was registered as an Industrial and Provident Society in 1924 and is managed by a Committee elected by and from its shareholding members.

The Association, before the war, made an important feature of facilities of Continental and Overseas travel of an educational as well as of a purely holiday character.   It gives a complete travel service and is free from donations, subsidy or subscriptions.

To those holidaying in Britain it offers the choice of a large number of country and seaside houses, furnished as Guest Houses.   It runs several Holiday Camps and provides motoring, walking and climbing holiday centres.

Head Office :   *Secretary and General Manager :*
17-21 Trebovir Road,   J. J. Taylor, Esq., O.B.E.
Earls Court, London, S.W.10

YOUTH HOSTELS ASSOCIATION

Aims : "To help all, especially young people of limited means, to a greater knowledge, love and care of the countryside, particularly by providing hostels and other simple accommodation for them in their travels."

The structure of the Association is federal with 19 semi-autonomous Regional Groups, governed by councils and committees elected directly by the members at annual meetings or by annual ballots.   Each Regional Group receives a proportion of its membership fees and is entirely responsible financially for the running of the hostels in its area.   Each year there is a delegate conference called the National Council which elects an Executive Committee composed of representatives of the regional groups together with a limited number of representatives of bodies of kindred interests.

There is a paid staff at National Headquarters, and some paid workers in the larger regions, but work is mainly voluntary.

There were 265 hostels open in England and Wales in 1947.   Membership in 1947 was 186,930.

Welwyn Garden City,   *Secretary :*
Herts.   E. St. John Catchpool, Esq.

U

AGENCIES FOR URBAN AND RURAL AMENITIES

THE CENTRAL COUNCIL OF CIVIC SOCIETIES

The Council was formed in 1939 for the following purposes : (i) to enable Civic Societies to confer on matters of common interest ; (ii) to encourage the formation of new Civic Societies ; (iii) to enable Civic Societies to take concerted action as a representative national body ; (iv) to stimulate public interest in the improvement of urban amenities. Its activities include public meetings, assistance in the formation of new Civic Societies, provision of assistance to existing societies in connection with publicity, contacts with national bodies and a variety of other ways. The Council is governed by an executive committee, elected by the members at the annual meeting and by the usual officers. Membership is open to affiliated Civic Societies, to other bodies desiring to keep in touch with the work of the Council and individuals.

82 Pall Mall,   *Hon. Secretary :*
London, S.W.1   Miss E. Bright Ashford, B.A.

COMMONS, OPEN SPACES AND FOOTPATHS PRESERVATION SOCIETY

Founded in 1865. Its objects include the preservation and extension of public rights and privileges of access to commons and other open spaces and the coast and countryside generally, and the protection of all public rights of way. It was primarily responsible for preserving the chief Metropolitan Commons, including Epping Forest, Wimbledon Common, Banstead Downs, etc., and many others throughout the country, and it continues to watch for and prevent enclosures and encroachments. It has been responsible for much legislation, and takes action to secure amendments in Parliamentary Bills, public and private, in furtherance of its objects. It advises local authorities and the public, and publishes numerous pamphlets and a quarterly *Journal*.

It is unincorporated and is governed by a council and officers. Membership is open to private members (individuals and societies) and to local authorities. It works mainly through its London office, though there are a certain number of regional Footpaths Societies.

The Society depends for its funds almost wholly on voluntary contributions.

71 Eccleston Square,   *Secretary :*
London, S.W.1   Sir Lawrence Chubb
                                          Deputy Secretary :
                                          Humphrey Baker, Esq., M.A.

COUNCIL FOR THE PRESERVATION OF RURAL ENGLAND

The Council for the Preservation of Rural England is a co-ordinating body for organisations interested in the preservation of rural amenities. It was set up with this object in 1926. Its objects are (i) to organise concerted action, to secure the protection of rural scenery and country and town amenities from disfigurement or injury ; (ii) to act directly, or through its members, as a centre for furnishing advice and information upon any matters affecting the protection of amenities ; (iii) to arouse, form and educate public opinion in order to ensure the promotion of these objects. It consists of a headquarters and district or county branches. The Headquarters Council consists of representatives of fourty-four constituent bodies in their area. At headquarters there is a full-time paid staff, but the branches are almost entirely run by unpaid workers.

The Council for the Preservation of Rural England is dependent wholly on voluntary contributions. The branches are required to be self-supporting, and are expected to make some contribution to the upkeep of headquarters.

4 Hobart Place,   *Secretary :*
London, S.W.1   H. G. Griffin, Esq., C.B.E.

WOMEN'S ORGANISATIONS

THE NATIONAL COUNCIL OF WOMEN OF GREAT BRITAIN

In 1895 the National Union of Women Workers developed from a committee which for several years had organised conferences for the study and betterment of social and industrial conditions. It provided a platform for a large number of women's societies, social, political, educational. This Union subsequently evolved into the National Council of Women (federated to the International Council of Women) which has now some 12,000 individual members, 130 societies nationally affiliated, and 800 societies locally affiliated. Primarily a co-ordinating and educational body, non-party and non-denominational, the Council aims at promoting "sympathy of thought and purpose" among women by furthering the welfare of the community and by "working for the removal of all disabilities among women, whether legal, economic or social." The Council is financed by voluntary subscriptions : Branch membership fees vary, but the Branches pay a capitation fee of 5s. to central funds. The minimum subscription for headquarters members is 10s.

Drayton House,   *General Secretary :*
Gordon Street, London, W.C.1   Mrs. K. M. Cowan

THE NATIONAL FEDERATION OF WOMEN'S INSTITUTES

The Women's Institute movement originated in 1897 in Ontario. The National Federation of Women's Institutes was founded in Great Britain in 1915 "to improve and develop conditions of rural life." There are at present 6,700 local village Institutes with 350,000 members. These pay an annual subscription of 2s. 6d. per head which, together with the sale of the Institutes' journal (*Home and Country*) and grants from the Ministry of Agriculture and direct from the Treasury (on the recommendation of the Development Commission) finances the work, both of the National Federation and of the County Federations. The village Institutes elect their own officers and committee and the majority of members of the Executive Committee of the National Federation. Policy for the whole movement is laid down at the annual general meeting to which go one delegate from each two Institutes. Decisions so made are binding on all Institutes which are otherwise autonomous. Activities include lectures and demonstrations covering almost every branch of rural and domestic enterprise and handicrafts, as well as discussions, entertainments and competitions. Programmes, which are usually planned a year ahead, are enlarged by various educational facilities provided by the County Federations. The rigorously non-sectarian and non-party political attitude of the Institutes makes them a common meeting-ground for persons of all opinions even in times of national ferment. However, the Institutes keep abreast of current happenings by banning from discussion only those topics which are immediately before Parliament and have become a clear party issue.

39 Eccleston Street,　　　　　　　　　　　　*Secretary :*
London, S.W.1　　　　　　　　　　　　　　The Hon. Frances Farrer

THE NATIONAL UNION OF TOWNSWOMEN'S GUILDS

Founded in 1929, the Townswomen's Guilds, centred in urban areas, aim to encourage the education of women as effective citizens and to serve as a common meeting ground for their members. There are some 87,000 members grouped in about 850 Guilds. Members pay an annual subscription of 2s. per head, 6d. of which is forwarded by the Branch to the Headquarters of the Union. The latter is also assisted by the Ministry of Education and the Scottish Education Department. The Union is governed by a Central Council, formed primarily *via* Groups and Federation Executive Committees from the Guilds themselves. This Central Council elects the majority of the Executive Committee. Members have the chance at Guild meetings to take part in such activities as drama, music, "civics" and are discouraged from concentrating exclusively on recreational interests. They are given, through Guild meetings, opportunities to learn the technique of conducting public affairs.

2 Cromwell Place,　　　　　　　　　　　　*Secretary :*
London, S.W.7　　　　　　　　　　　　　　Mrs. Horton

WOMEN'S CO-OPERATIVE GUILD

Founded in 1882, the Women's Co-operative Guild is a body of women members of co-operative societies. There are now over 61,000 members, in 1,700 branches which are grouped in districts and sections. The educational work of this organization is not confined to the subject of co-operation, but is designed to give the members a wide knowledge of citizenship, and to fit them for public service. The educational programme of the Guild movement is reinforced by conferences, week-end and summer schools ; much attention is paid to current political trends. The Guild is governed by an elected Central Committee. Branches pay to headquarters a capitation fee of 1s. 6d. per member, and the Guild is mainly financed by these subscriptions, together with donations from the Co-operative Wholesale Society and from the Co-operative Union.

135 Leman Street,　　　　　　　　　　　　*General Secretary :*
London, E.1　　　　　　　　　　　　　　　Mrs. Cecily Cook

WOMEN'S GROUP ON PUBLIC WELFARE

The Women's Group on Public Welfare was sponsored by the National Council of Social Service in 1940. Now autonomous in policy, the Group is still mainly financed by the National Council, although there is an increasing attempt to obtain subscriptions from its 47 associated organizations and from the local Standing Conferences on Women's Organizations ; the latter covering approximately 2,000 local societies. The Group consists of one representative from each of the 47 national organizations, as well as persons with specialised knowledge appointed in an advisory capacity. These latter include representatives from Government departments. Originally it came into existence to ameliorate conditions arising out of children's evacuation. It now initiates, stimulates and undertakes pressure and publicity on any matter especially concerned with the welfare of women and children on which action, national or local, appears necessary. Such action, e.g., deputations and representations, is normally undertaken through the headquarters of the constituent bodies. If the Women's Group acts publicly itself, it can only do so with the approval of all its constituent organizations.

26 Bedford Square,
London, W.C.1

Secretary :
Miss D. W. Homer

WOMEN'S VOLUNTARY SERVICES

Women's Voluntary Services was founded in 1938 to help Local Authorities and the Central Government, first in recruiting women for A.R.P. work and later in carrying out post-raid welfare work and assisting with local and national schemes in connection with the war effort. The members of the Service, both full-time and part-time, are voluntary, except for a small number of salaried staff at Headquarters and in certain offices throughout the country (200 in November, 1947). Volunteers are allotted to work according to their qualifications and interests. They are required to give regular and punctual service and no differentiation is made between paid or unpaid workers. In March, 1945, there were 970,000 enrolled members ; these, if they fulfil certain conditions of service, are entitled to wear the green uniform and the W.V.S. badge. The Chairman of Women's Voluntary Services, the Dowager Marchioness of Reading, was appointed by the Home Secretary and the policy is decided by her in consultation with senior headquarters staff in accordance with the need for certain forms of service at various times. The Women's Voluntary Services are advised by a Council of representatives of women's organizations. All the administrative expenses of the Service are borne by the Government. Founded primarily for war service, the Service is remaining in existence for peace-time work.

41 Tothill Street,
London, S.W.1

General Secretary :
Mrs. L. M. Patterson

SERVICE ORGANISATIONS

THE BRITISH LEGION

The British Legion was founded in 1921 to help men and women who have served in H.M. Forces, also their dependants. It incorporates various previously existing ex-Service organisations. The Legion undertakes a wide field of social service, operating through Service Committees attached to Branches. Complicated cases needing financial help, as distinct from grants in kind, are referred to the Legion Area Offices and, if necessary, to Head-quarters. Service in respect of pensions includes legal representation where necessary, as well as advice and investigation. Grants in kind in cases of temporary need; help to those seeking employment; provision of financial aid in cases of sickness, towards the cost of surgical appliances and dentures; removal grants and contributions towards placing service orphans in homes, and training disabled men, are all undertaken by the Welfare Services of the Legion. It has four Homes and others planned for those in need of a period of convalescence, or a permanent Home for those who are aged and incapaci-tated. Expert advice as well as a loan is available to ex-Service people wishing to set up their own business. The Legion is controlled entirely by the votes of its members, and in each of the 5,000 Branches they appoint Committees and Officers and other officials who manage Legion affairs in the district.

It is financed mainly by funds raised on Poppy Day, aided by subscriptions, donations and legacies, and its Benevolent Department also administers the special funds of several army formations.

Pall Mall,   *General Secretary :*
London, S.W.1.   J. R. Griffin, Esq.

THE INCORPORATED SOLDIERS', SAILORS' AND AIRMEN'S HELP SOCIETY

Since 1899 the Soldiers', Sailors' and Airmen's Help Society has been helping Service and ex-Service men and women, both at home and overseas, in all their problems. The Society's versatile work includes administration of Convalescent Homes and the Lord Roberts' Memorial Workshops which, sponsored by the Society in 1904, were expanded and renamed after Lord Roberts' death in 1914. These workshops are open to all ex-Service men and women who have over 50 per cent. disability; both training and permanent employment is provided. Its casework is done by voluntary staff, usually clergy or retired professional people, who are initiated into the work (but not trained) by the Honorary County Secretaries and District Heads. The two latter officers can authorise assistance up to £5 and £3 respectively; cases needing greater sums must be referred to headquarters. No Government grants are received, the Society being financed by subscriptions, contributions and legacies, and by grants from such bodies as King George's Fund for Sailors and the Army Benevolent Fund. The Society is governed by an Executive Committee whose President is Brigadier-General the Earl of Gowrie, V.C.

122 Brompton Road,   *Comptroller :*
London, S.W.3   Miss E. M. Acton, C.B.E.

ST. DUNSTAN'S ORGANISATION FOR MEN AND WOMEN BLINDED ON WAR
SERVICE

St. Dunstan's, founded in 1914, trains war-blinded men and women, both
those blinded suddenly, and those who gradually lose their sight as the result
of war injuries. Training is divided into two phases, of which the first helps
the individual to approximate as nearly as possible to normal through personal
adjustment to his blindness; the second phase is occupational training for
almost any career chosen by the trainee and for which he is considered
suitable. St. Dunstan's training includes special provisions for those who
have additional handicaps beyond blindness. When the training is completed,
a St. Dunstaner is placed in work and is entitled to all necessary equipment,
tools, etc., and a furniture grant of £150; he is helped to find and to equip a
home when necessary, is lent a typewriter for life and is given a Braille watch,
and a wireless set if he wants one, the licence being obtained free. He is
visited regularly by St. Dunstan's officers. The organization is financed by
subscriptions, donations and collections, including, by arrangement with the
British Legion, a percentage of the Poppy Day Collection. St. Dunstan's
is a company limited by guarantee and is governed by an executive council
appointed by the members who are subscribers or voluntary helpers. The
Principal officers are : President, Sir Neville Pearson, Bt.; Chairman, Sir Ian
Fraser, C.B.E., M.P.; Hon. Treasurer, A. W. Tuke, Esq.

9-11 Park Crescent,   *Secretary :*
Regent's Park, London, W.1   W. G. Askew, Esq.

THE SOLDIERS', SAILORS' AND AIRMEN'S FAMILIES ASSOCIATION (S.S.A.F.A.)

The Soldiers', Sailors' and Airmen's Families Association was founded in
1885 as the Soldiers' and Sailors' Families Association. It aimed at caring
financially for the families of soldiers and sailors for whom the State then
made inadequate provision. S.S.A.F.A. still gives financial help to the
dependants of serving personnel, but its work includes a widening range of
welfare and advisory services where cash is not required; only about two
cases in eight now involve the issue of a grant. S.S.A.F.A. has an Overseas
Service effecting liaison between serving personnel and their families at home;
its Nursing Service supplies trained district nurses for the families of men
garrisoned at home and abroad. S.S.A.F.A.'s Clothing Branch distributed
over one million garments in 1946, and, in the same year, 1,000 children and
90 mothers passed through S.S.A.F.A.'s emergency and rest homes. The
Married Families' Club, opened in 1944, is a London hostel in which families
can stay for short visits, the children being cared for competently as required.
There is also a separate Officers' Branch which provides rent free accommodation for the necessitous widows and children of deceased officers. All
S.S.A.F.A.'s case-work is done by its 25,000 voluntary workers; a few of
these are given paid clerical help. At Headquarters the top staff and the
majority of executives are salaried, but of the aggregate of administrative staff

at Headquarters, in the Central Clothing and in the Children and Homes Departments, 48 per cent. are voluntary. The Association's policy is decided by its Council, and is transmitted through County Branches to some 1,500 divisions. The majority of its revenue comes from voluntary donations and interest; about one-sixth came, in the last financial year, from the Exchequer on behalf of the Service Departments and the India Office to finance administrative services. S.S.A.F.A.'s relief work is supplemented by some £300,000 annually which the Association administers on behalf of other Funds and Societies for specific cases.

23 Queen Anne's Gate, London, S.W.1

Controller :
Captain A. A. Andrews, O.B.E.

RESIDENTIAL SETTLEMENTS*

MARY WARD SETTLEMENT

The Mary Ward Settlement was opened in 1897 to continue and expand the educational, religious and social welfare work begun in 1891. At first named after its benefactor, Passmore Edwards, it was given its present title in 1921 to commemorate the founder, Mrs. Humphry Ward. Accommodation was provided for residents (now 30) who, while engaged in normal occupations or study during the day, contribute to the corporate life of the Settlement in the evening.

The Settlement is governed by a Council, whose chief officer is the Warden, and a Finance and General Purposes Committee. Income is derived from voluntary subscriptions, lettings, interest on capital, and grants (amounting to one-quarter to one-third of total expenditure) from statutory authorities.

Adult Education is provided for, in conjunction with the London County Council, in some twenty-five evening classes, in music, art, drama, crafts, languages, current affairs, psychology, elocution, etc. The theatre is in continual use by keep fit and dancing classes, drama, the Tavistock Repertory Theatre Company and outside amateur Dramatic Societies. An Eighteen Plus and a scientific film society meet at the Settlement. There is a canteen, common room and library for students.

For Youth there is a Girls' Club and a Boys' Club with their Old Members' Association. There are Play Centres for girls and boys up to 14 provided through the L.C.C. A day-time school, founded by Mrs. Humphry Ward and under the L.C.C. provides for physically defective children and is held in an adjoining Settlement building.

Welfare organisations which have offices or meet at the Settlement include the National Association of Maternity and Child Welfare Centres, National Council for Under Fourteens, the S.S.A.F.A., the S.O.S., and the Youth Hostels Association (International Travel Department). A Free Legal

---

*Particulars as to a number of other Settlements are given in an Annex to Section 5 of Part IV.

Advice Centre provided by the Settlement is open daily with a full-time staff of four lawyers.   About 5,000 cases a year are assisted.

Tavistock Place,   *Hon. Warden :*

London, W.C.1   C. C. Walkinshaw, Esq.

TOYNBEE HALL (THE UNIVERSITIES' SETTLEMENT IN EAST LONDON)

Toynbee Hall was founded at an informal meeting on 3rd December, 1883, at Balliol College by Canon Barnett, Rector of St. Jude's Church, Whitechapel, as a memorial to Arnold Toynbee who had died a martyr to the cause of social progress.

In the summer of that year he had also been approached by a young Cambridge man, G. C. Moore Smith, who told him that some men at St. John's College, Cambridge, also wished to serve the poor but were not prepared to start an ordinary College Mission.   In this way the two older British Universities became associated in an undertaking, The Universities' Settlement in East London, which was to blaze a pioneer trail in social service throughout the world.

At the outset there was no claim to provide a solution to the social problems of the day.   There was simply the quiet and earnest appeal to University men to come and see, to learn the needs "by sharing the life of that, to us, dim and outer world of East London."   These are Barnett's own words.

Barnett rejected the conception of another College Mission as too narrow. Nonconformists would be excluded from such a venture ; it was necessary to bring the life of the Universities to bear on the life of the poor irrespective of church or creed.   These reasons for adopting a non-denominational basis of course carried special weight in Whitechapel with its Jewish and Irish inhabitants.

The settlers themselves would help the clergy and visit and teach, the younger might help with work among boys, the elder would perhaps participate in local government.   As director or head there was to be a man "qualified by character to guide men, and by education to teach."   This was the pattern in the 1880's and, with modification to meet the altered social conditions and betterment, and with short breaks during the war periods, it remains the same now.

Toynbee Hall's main function in 1948 is that of education and experiment. There are upwards of twelve hundred students attending evening classes, which are non-vocational and concerned with the better use of leisure.   More than thirty local organisations make it their headquarters in East London. The Children's Theatre had its renaissance at Toynbee Hall in 1945 and inquiry concerning taste and inclination among children attending cinema clubs is providing material for discussion and action by interested authorities.

There is no doubt that material conditions at the present time cannot be compared with those when Toynbee Hall was founded ; but there is every-

313

where a lack of spiritual guidance by example, and, in this, Toynbee Hall's settlers hope to play their part in the future.

28 Commercial Street,   *Warden :*
London, E.1   Dr. J. J. Mallon, C.H., LL.D., J.P.

GENERAL AGENCIES

THE BOARD OF GUARDIANS AND TRUSTEES FOR THE RELIEF OF THE JEWISH POOR

The Jewish Board of Guardians was founded in 1859 to undertake social work among Jewish persons. The Board does not confine itself to a limited range of activity ; it fits its work to the problems presented to it. Its financial help includes fixed allowances, mostly to aged persons, as well as loans, grants and interim relief in cases of unexpected need. It distributes clothing and furniture, and will help people to equip themselves with tools and machines. All this work is carefully undertaken on a modern casework basis and mostly by trained social workers. The Board also runs a number of convalescent homes and hostels for young people and old people in London and the Home Counties ; it administers several blocks of almshouses. It administers a large number of charitable funds. Apprenticeship, equipment and placement of boys and girls is a specialised branch of the Board's work ; the responsible department keeps contact with the young people concerned and extends to them a wide range of welfare, cultural and recreational services. These activities are carried on through a number of committees appointed by the Board. It is financed by voluntary contributions and legacies from the Jewish community and by grants from public bodies.

127 Middlesex Street,   *Secretary:*
Bishopsgate, London, E.1   T. J. Phillips, Esq.

THE BRITISH RED CROSS SOCIETY

The British Red Cross Society is one of the National Red Cross Societies comprising the International Red Cross. It began its activities in 1870, was re-constituted on its present basis in 1905 and received its Royal Charter in 1908. It is primarily an organization for the relief of the sick and wounded in war. It is laid down in its Supplementary Charter of 1919 that the Society should extend its work to include the improvement of health, prevention of disease and the mitigation of suffering throughout the world. The Society is now running auxiliary hospitals and clinics, and over 1,000 Medical Loan Depots have been established. In the field of welfare services, it provides welfare officers and workers, canteens in out-patients' departments, assistance in visiting the old, and organises sitters-in schemes. First aid and ambulance services are an important part of its work. An individual may be enrolled as a full member if in possession of recognised first aid and nursing certificates. He or she, if not already trained, may be enrolled as a probationer for training. The Junior Red Cross is an important aspect of the Red Cross Movement. There were at the end of 1946 105,980 members, including 15,269 men and

90,621 women. Junior members, excluded from the above, totalled 98,000. Except for some salaried administrative officers at Headquarters and in the County Branch offices, personnel give their services voluntarily. The body of members have as such no direct control in the administration of the Society. This is governed, under its Charters, by a Council and appropriate committees. There is a National Headquarters in London, and Central Council Branches have been formed in Scotland, Northern Ireland, Isle of Man and overseas. There are also local Branch Headquarters in every county ; the Red Cross relies greatly on the activities of its county branches for the prosecution of its work, in particular for recruitment and training, and for the maintenance of efficiently running organisations. Apart from interest from investments and minor sources, the income of the Red Cross is mainly derived from public appeals.

14 Grosvenor Crescent,
London, S.W.1

Secretary :
W. J. Phillips, Esq., M.B.E.

THE CHURCH ARMY

The Church Army is a Church of England organization, founded in 1882, which, besides evangelical work, undertakes a very wide range of social work of a type which most usefully fills in the gaps between the more specialised bodies ; the Church Army can usually help distressed persons whose problems do not fit into the standard categories. Such miscellaneous work includes Holiday Homes for Mothers and Children, Girls' Training Homes, Medical Missions, a Private Aid and Distressed Gentlewomen's Department and Clergy Rest Houses. The Church Army also runs Homes and Hostels for lads and men, including delinquents and discharged prisoners as well as ordinary workers. It has Babies' and Children's Homes and Approved Schools. Its moral welfare work includes maternity provision and Homes for unmarried mothers and their babies as well as diocesan rescue work. Old people are cared for in Homes or in the Church Army's Churchill Houses in which individual bed-sitting rooms and kitchenettes are linked under the welfare supervision of an Army Sister. This latter work is the latest project of Church Army Housing Ltd., which, formed in 1924, had built by 1939 868 houses and flats for lower paid wage-earners, the rents being subsidised by donations and by the issue of Loan Stock at 2½ per cent. interest. During the war the Church Army was particularly active in running mobile canteens for persons on national service. It is financed by donations, trading profits and payments for services. It has no Government grants except for normal Home Office payments in respect of its Approved Schools.

Bryanston Street,
Marble Arch, London, W.1

General Secretary :
The Rev. Prebendary
Hubert H. Treacher

NATIONAL COUNCIL OF SOCIAL SERVICE

The N.C.S.S. (which is more fully described in Part V above) was set up at the end of the first world war, in pursuance of a desire to give some improvements and direction to social effort. It was incorporated in 1924. Its objects are:

"To promote all or any purposes for the benefit of the community which now are or hereafter may be deemed to be charitable, and in particular the advancement of education, the furtherance of health and the relief of poverty, distress and sickness.

"To promote and organise co-operation in the achievement of the above purposes and to that end to bring together in Council nationally and locally, representatives of voluntary agencies and statutory authorities engaged in the furtherance of the above purposes or any of them."

Since its foundation, the N.C.S.S. has helped to form numerous other organisations concerned in one field or another of social effort. For the Council's work in connection with Community Centres, local Councils of Social Service, Problems of Rural Life, etc., reference may be made to the Memorandum in Part V above.

The Council is composed of some 180 representatives of voluntary and statutory bodies; ordinarily it works through an Executive Committee and sub-committees. Connected with the N.C.S.S. are seven autonomous associated groups for special purposes: an example is the National Old People's Welfare Committee.

The N.C.S.S. is grant-aided to the extent of about one-third of its income, receiving the remainder from voluntary sources. (1946-7 figures: Government grants, £26,513; receipts from voluntary sources, £47,473.)

26 Bedford Square,   *Secretary* :
London, W.C.1   G. E. Haynes, Esq., C.B.E.

THE SALVATION ARMY

Founded in 1865, the Salvation Army has spread to 87 countries. It is a militant evangelical organisation, seeking to convert people to Christ but believing that bodily needs must be satisfied as well as those of the soul. The Army, therefore, engages in extensive social work, and will always help those who are too rough and outcast for easy acceptance elsewhere. Out of the Army's many activities in Great Britain, the following are currently of major significance: (i) the 36 Eventide Homes in which about 1,350 old people live in a warm home atmosphere; (ii) the 16 Homes for Unmarried Mothers and Babies, each taking 20 to 30 girls; the Army maintains contact with them for three years afterwards; (iii) the Maternity Hospitals, in the biggest of which, Clapton and its associated District Posts, there are 3,000 births annually; (iv) the many Shelters, where a bed in a dormitory costs 8d., in cubicles 1s. to 1s. 3d.; (v) the 50 Slum Centres from which 150 trained workers undertake miscellaneous work among the very poor; (vi) the six Children's Homes, admitting children from distressed and/or morally dangerous conditions;

(vii) the Agricultural Training Centres at Hadleigh taking about 200 men. The Army trains its own staff, adding Social Service training for those intending to do this work. The Army is controlled by its General who is elected by a Council of high-ranking Officers drawn from all parts of the world. Except for payment for services, including Home Office grants in respect of Approved Schools, the Army finances itself entirely by voluntary donations and by receipts from its various activities.

William Booth Training College,
Denmark Hill, London, S.E.5

THE SHAFTESBURY SOCIETY

Operating in Greater London except for the admission of children from all parts of the country to the residential schools for cripples, the Shaftesbury Society undertakes various social work according to need. It emphasises its Protestant and Christian background. Lord Shaftesbury was the first President of this Society, which was founded in 1844 and which has shown considerable adaptability to social trends; it has not been rigidly bound to any narrow terms of reference. The Society is today running Holiday and Convalescent Homes and Residential Schools for crippled children. It has an experimental Holiday Home for old people and 60 Missions; the latter are social service centres in the poorer parts of London. Its Sunday Schools were attended by 15,000 children in 1946; 13,000 attended the Society's youth clubs, 900 persons were members of its old people's clubs, 6,000 women went to its women's meetings, and 250 children were resident in its cripples' schools. The Society is a Company, limited by guarantee; more than half its income is derived from payments by local authorities and parents, the rest coming from donations and subscriptions.

32 John Street,   *Secretary :*
London, W.C.1   Clifford Carter, Esq.

2. NAMES OF ORGANISATIONS WHICH GAVE INFORMATION FOR THE INQUIRY

Aberdeen Association of Social Service
Actors' Benevolent Fund
A.F.D. Clergy Aid Society
After-Care Association
Aged Pilgrim Friend Society
Ancient Order of Foresters Friendly Society
Apostleship of the Sea
Architects' Benevolent Society
Army Benevolent Fund
Arts Council of Great Britain

Ashton House
Association of Certified and Corporate Accountants
Association for Jewish Youth
Association of Jewish Friendly Societies
Auctioneers' and Estate Agents' Institute Benevolent Fund
Auxiliary R.A.M.C. Fund
Ayr Society for Social Service

Baptist Union of Great Britain and Ireland Young People's Department
Barristers' Benevolent Association
Batesholme Holiday Home for Little Children
Bath Preventive Mission and Ladies' Association for the Care of
    Friendless Girls
Birmingham Adult Deaf and Dumb Association
Birmingham Citizens' Society
Birmingham Hospital Saturday Fund
Birmingham Royal Institution for the Blind
Board of Guardians and Trustees for the Relief of the Jewish Poor
Booksellers' Provident Institution
Border Counties' Home for Incurables
Boys' Brigade
Boys' and Girls' Refuges Inc.
Boys' Hostels Association
Boy Scouts' Association
Brentwood Recuperative Centre
Brigade of Guards Employment Society
Brighton Social Centre
British Association of Residential Settlements
British Broadcasting Corporation
British Council of Churches
British Council for Rehabilitation
British Council for the Welfare of Spastics
British Drama League
British Deaf and Dumb Association
British Dental Association Benevolent Fund
British Federation of Music Festivals
British Federation of Social Workers
British Home and Hospital for Incurables
British Hospitals' Association
The British Institute of Adult Education
British Legion
British Medical Association
British Red Cross Society
British Sailors' Society
British Seamen's Orphan Boys' Home

British Tourist and Holiday Board
British United Provident Association Ltd.
Broadway Congregational Friendly Society
Brotherhood Movement
Building Societies' Association
Butchers' Charitable Institution
Butlin's Ltd.

Cadbury Brothers Ltd.
Cambridge Central Aid Society
Cambridge Preservation Society
Camping Club of Great Britain and Ireland
Caravan Club of Great Britain and Ireland
Catering Trades' Benevolent Association
Carnegie United Kingdom Trust
Catholic Social Service Bureau
Catholic Young Men's Society of Great Britain
Cecil Houses Inc.
Central Council for the Care of Cripples
Central Council of Civic Societies
Central Council of Physical Recreation
Central Council for the Social Welfare of Girls and Women in London
Charity Commission
Chartered Accountants' Benevolent Association
Chesterfield Borough Council
Children's Convalescent Home, Beaconsfield
Chiswick Products Ltd.
Chloride Electrical Storage Co. Ltd.
Christian Service Union
"Christian Witness" Fund
Church Army
Church of England Children's Society
Church of England Moral Welfare Council
Church of England Pensions Board
Church of England Soldiers', Sailors' and Airmen's Institute
    Association
Church of England Youth Council
Church Lads' Brigade
Cinematograph Trade Benevolent Fund
City of Glasgow Society of Social Service
City of Edinburgh Education Department
City Parochial Foundation
Clergy Ladies' Home
Commercial Travellers' Benevolent Institution
Commons, Open Spaces and Footpaths Preservation Society

Commonwealth Fund
Community of the Epiphany, Truro
Congregational Union of England and Wales
Council for the Preservation of Rural England
Council for the Preservation of Rural Scotland
Co-operative Holidays Association
Co-operative Youth Movement
Council for Visual Education
County Badge
County Borough of Ipswich Education Department
County Borough of Tynemouth Youth Council
Coventry City Guild
Cripplecraft Limited
Croydon Guild of Social Service
Curates' Augmentation Fund

Dagenham and Becontree Personal Service Council
David Lewis Manchester Epileptic Colony
Deaf Children's Society
Derwen Cripples' Training College
Destitute Sailors' Fund
Distressed Gentlefolks' Aid Association
Dr. Barnardo's Homes

East Lancashire Tuberculosis Colony (Barrowmore Hall)
Edinburgh Council of Social Service
Edinburgh Deaf and Dumb Benevolent Society
Electrical Industries' Benevolent Association
Embankment Fellowship Centre
English Folk Dance and Song Society
Enham-Alamein Village Settlement
Epsom College
Ex-Services' Welfare Society

Family Welfare Association
Federation of University Women's Camps for Schoolgirls
Fellowship Houses
Fellowship of St. Christopher
Field Lane Institution
Fishmongers' and Poulterers' Institution
Friend of the Clergy Corporation
Friends of the Poor
Furnishing Trades' Benevolent Association

Gardeners' Royal Benevolent Institution
Gentlewomen's Employment Association and Ladies' Work Society
Georgian Group
Georgian Society for East Yorkshire
Girls' Friendly Society
Girl Guides' Association
Girls' Guildry
Given-Wilson Institute
Glasgow Sailors' Home
Goldsmiths' and Jewellers' Annuity Institution
Governesses' Benevolent Institution
Grand United Order of Oddfellows Friendly Society
Greater London Fund for the Blind
Guardianship Society
Guild of Aid for Gentlepeople
Guinness Trust

Halifax Council of Social Service
Hastings and St. Leonard's Civic Society
Hearts of Oak Benefit Society
Heritage Craft Schools and Hospital
Hillcroft College
Holiday Fellowship
Home of Comfort for the Sick, Southsea
Home for Confirmed Invalids
Home for Orphan and Friendless Girls, Scarborough
Home Workers' Aid Association
Homes for the Aged Poor
Homes for Motherless Children, Ealing
Homes of Rest for Gentlewomen
Homes of St. Barnabas
Homes for Working Boys in London (Inc.)
Hospital Saturday Fund
Hospital Savings Association
Hostel of God (The Free Home for the Dying)
Hostels for Crippled and Invalid Women Workers (Inc.)
Housing Centre
Hull and Yorkshire Institution for the Deaf and Dumb
Hyelm Movement

Ideal Benefit Society
Incorporated Soldiers', Sailors' and Airmen's Help Society
Incorporation of Carters in Leith Friendly Society
Indefatigable and National Sea Training School for Boys
Independent Order of Oddfellows, Manchester Unity, Friendly Society

v

Independent Order of Rechabites, Salford Unity, Friendly Society
Industrial Welfare Society
Institution of Gas Engineers' Benevolent Fund
Invalid Children's Aid Association
Invalid Kitchens of London

James Murray's Royal Asylum
John Groom's Crippleage, Inc.

Kendal and District Guild of Service
King Edward's Hospital Fund for London
King George's Fund for Sailors
Kingsdown Orphanage
Kingston and Surbiton Central Aid Society

Ladies' Home, N.W.8
Lambeth Borough Council
Lancashire Community Council
Lancashire Standing Conference of Voluntary Youth Organisations
Land Agents' Society Benevolent Fund
Langford Cross Children's Home
League of Remembrance
Leeds Council of Social Service
Leeds Incorporated Institution for the Blind and Deaf and Dumb
Leicester Charity Organisation Society
Leicester and County Mission to the Deaf and Dumb
Linen and Woollen Drapers' Institution
Liverpool Home for Incurables
Liverpool Personal Service Society
Liverpool Sailors' Home
Liverpool Seamen's Friend Society and Gordon Smith Institute for
    Seamen
Lloyd's Patriotic Fund
London Association for the Blind
London Council of Social Service
London and County Permanent Benefit Society
London Federation of Boys' Clubs
London Hospital
London Marriage Guidance Centre
London Shipowners' and Shipbrokers' Benevolent Society
Lord Mayor Treloar's Orthopaedic Hospital
Loyal Order of Ancient Shepherds, Ashton Unity, Friendly Society
Luton Youth Council

Maghull Home for Epileptics
Manchester City League of Help
Manchester and Salford Boys' and Girls' Refuges
Manchester and Salford Council of Social Service
Manchester and Salford District Provident and Charity Organisation
    Society
Manchester Royal Residential Schools for the Deaf
Marine Society
Marriage Guidance Council
Meath Home of Comfort for Epileptics
Memorial Centre of Help for Service Babies
Mental After-Care Association
Methodist Church Youth Department
Methodist Local Preachers' Mutual Aid Association
Metropolitan Clerks' Provident and Benevolent Society
Metropolitan Public Gardens' Association
Middlesbrough Community Council
Middlesex Hospital
Midland Counties Institution
Ministers' Benevolent Society
Missions to Seamen
Morning Post Embankment Home
Muller's Orphan Homes

National Adoption Society
National Association of Boys' Clubs
National Association of Discharged Prisoners' Aid Societies
National Association of Girls' Clubs and Mixed Clubs
National Association of Maternity and Child Welfare Centres
National Association for Mental Health
National Association for the Prevention of Tuberculosis
National Catholic Youth Association
National Children's Adoption Association
National Children's Home and Orphanage
National Conference of Friendly Societies
National Council of Associated Children's Homes
National Council of Evangelical Free Churches—Women's Council
National Council of Labour Colleges
National Council of Social Service
National Council for the Unmarried Mother and her Child
National Council of Women of Great Britain
National Deposit Friendly Society
National Federation of Community Associations
National Federation of Housing Societies
National Federation of Old Age Pensioners' Associations

National Federation of Permanent Holiday Camps
National Federation of Women's Institutes
National Federation of Young Farmers' Clubs
National Foundation for Adult Education
National Free Church Women's Council
National Hospital
National Institute for the Blind
National Institute for the Deaf
National Old People's Welfare Committee
National Playing Fields Association
National Society for Cancer Relief
National Society for Epileptics
National Society for the Prevention of Cruelty to Children
National Trust
National Union of Holloway Friendly Societies
National Union of Townswomen's Guilds
New Birmingham Friendly Society
New Tabernacle Friendly Society
Newspaper Press Fund
Newsvendors' Benevolent and Provident Institution
Norfolk and Norwich Deaf and Dumb Welfare Association
Northern Counties' Institute for the Deaf and Dumb
Northumberland and Tyneside Council of Social Service
Nottingham Institute for the Deaf
Nottinghamshire County Council Sherwood Village Settlement
Nuffield Foundation
Nursery School Association
Nurses' Fund for Nurses

Officers' Families Fund
Old People's Homes Committee
Order of Druids Friendly Society
Orphan Homes, Leominster
Out-of-Doors Fellowship
Outward Bound School
Over Thirty Association
Oxford and Bermondsey Club
Oxford Preservation Trust

Papworth Village Settlement
The Peak District and Northern Counties Footpaths Preservation
    Society
Peckham and Kent Road Pension Society
People's Entertainment Society
Personal Service League

Perth Association for Improving the Condition of the Poor
Pharmaceutical Societies' Benevolent Fund
Pilgrim Trust
Poor Clergy Relief Corporation
Presbyterian Church of England Welfare of Youth Department
Provident Clerks' Benevolent Fund

Queen Adelaide Naval Fund
Queen Elizabeth's Training College for the Disabled, Leatherhead
Queen's Institute of District Nursing

Ramblers' Association
Reading and District Council of Social Service
Reedham Orphanage
Reed's School
Registry of Friendly Societies
Rhodes Trust
Rotary International
Rowntree & Co. Ltd.
Rowton Houses
Royal Albert Institution, Lancaster
Royal Albert School
Royal Alexandra School
Royal Association in Aid of the Deaf and Dumb
Royal Commission for the Great Exhibition of 1851
Royal Cornwall Home for Girls
Royal General Theatrical Fund
Royal Hospital and Home for Incurables, Putney
Royal Masonic Benevolent Institution
Royal Medical Benevolent Fund
Royal Midland Counties Home for Incurables, Leamington
Royal Military Benevolent Fund
Royal National Lifeboat Institution
Royal Naval Benevolent Society
Royal Naval Benevolent Trust
Royal Naval Fund
Royal Naval and Royal Marine Maternity Home, Portsmouth
Royal Naval and Royal Marine Orphan Home, Portsmouth
Royal Sailors' Rests
Royal School for Deaf and Dumb Children, Margate
Royal Seamen's Pension Fund
Royal Surgical Aid Society
Royal United Service Home for Girls
Rural Music Schools' Association
Rural Reconstruction Association

Sailors' Home and Red Ensign Club
Sailors' Orphan Society of Scotland
St. Andrew's Society, Swanage
St. Basil's Home for Aged Women
St. Dunstan's
St. Edmundsbury and Ipswich Mission to the Deaf and Dumb
St. John Ambulance Brigade
St. Loye's College for the Training and Rehabilitation of the Disabled
St. Margaret's School, Croydon
St. Marylebone Housing Association Ltd.
St. Nicholas Home for Mothers and Babies
Salisbury Diocesan Association of the Deaf and Dumb
Salvation Army
Save the Children Fund
Scapa Society for Prevention of Disfigurement in Town and Country
Scarborough Council of Social Service
Scottish Churches Council
Scottish Council for the Care of Spastics
Scottish Council of Social Service
Scottish Girls' Friendly Society
Seafarers' Education Service
Seamen's Friendly Society of St. Paul
Searchlight Cripples' Workshop
Selborne Society
Shadforth Annuities
Shaftesbury Homes and *Arethusa* Training Ship
Shaftesbury Society
Sheffield Council of Social Service
Sir Josiah Mason's Almshouses
Sir Josiah Mason's Orphanage
Social Survey
Spelthorne St. Mary
Society for the Protection of Ancient Buildings
Society for the Relief of Aged and Infirm Protestant Dissenting
  Ministers
Society for Relief of Distress
Society for the Relief of Distressed Widows
Society for the Relief of the Houseless Poor
Society of St. Vincent de Paul
Solicitors' Benevolent Association
S.O.S. Society
Southend Civic Guild of Health
Southern Railway Servants' Orphanage
South Lambeth Committee F.W.A.
S.S.A.F.A.

Standing Conference of National Voluntary Youth Organisations
Stationers' and Papermakers' Provident Society
Stroud Holloway Original Benefit Society
Student Christian Movement
Surrey Voluntary Association for the Care of Cripples
Sussex Diocesan Association of the Deaf and Dumb

The Thistle Foundation
Titford's Charity
Toc H (Women's Section)
Town and Country Planning Association
Town Planning Institute
Tyne Mariners' Benevolent Institution

Union of Girls' Schools for Social Service
United Law Clerks' Society
Universal Beneficent Society

Vellum Binders' and Machine Rulers' Pension Society
Voluntary Unofficial Aunts

Wandsworth Committee F.W.A. and C.A.B.
Warrington and District Deaf and Dumb Society
Welsh League of Youth
West Ham Home and Hostel for Girls
Westminster Diocesan Education Fund
Widows' Friend Society
Women's Co-operative Guild
Women's Employment Federation
Women's Group on Public Welfare
Women Teachers' Thrift Association
Women's Voluntary Services
Woodlarks Camp Site Trust
Workers' Educational Association
Workers' Travel Association
Working Men's College
Worthing Council of Social Service
Wright-Kingsford Home for Children

Young Christian Workers
Young Men's Christian Association
Young Women's Christian Association
Youth Hostels Association

PART VII

SELECT BIBLIOGRAPHY ON VOLUNTARY ACTION

THE following list comprises in the main the books found most useful in preparing the Report, excepting Annual Reports of societies and like material. It does not, of course, profess to be a complete bibliography of voluntary social service.

The bibliography is arranged in sections corresponding generally with the chapters of the Report. Books relevant to more than one section have, however, been listed only once.

I. FRIENDLY SOCIETIES

A—*Sources*

I. THE REGISTRY OF FRIENDLY SOCIETIES

(a) The REPORTS of the Registrar were commenced in 1876, and were carried down to 1938 ; they were suspended during the last war. Statistically, the issues for the nineteenth century are a little unreliable, but the Reports as a whole are essential for the student.

(b) THE GUIDE BOOK OF THE REGISTRY OF FRIENDLY SOCIETIES AND THE OFFICE OF THE INDUSTRIAL ASSURANCE COMMISSION (last edition 1933). A handbook of the law relating to Friendly Societies and to the other bodies with which the Registry is concerned.

(c) Societies registered under the Friendly Societies Acts must furnish an annual return to the Registrar. These returns are filed and the files may be inspected by the public on prior application to the Chief Registrar. The files contain the rules of all Friendly Societies, together with their annual returns for a period of ten years back, and valuation reports. The early rules of many old societies are preserved here.

II. THE LIBRARIES OF THE UNIVERSITY OF LONDON, particularly the British Library of Political and Economic Science and the Goldsmiths' Library, contain a large collection of literature relating to early Friendly Societies. (See "London Bibliography of the Social Sciences," s.v. "Friendly Societies.")

B.—*Official Reports*

Report from the Select Committee on the Laws respecting Friendly Societies. (B.P.P., 1825, IV), pp. 177.

Report from the Select Committee on the Laws respecting Friendly Societies. (B.P.P., 1826-7, III), pp. 135.

Report from the Select Committee on the Friendly Societies Bill . . . with minutes of evidence. (B.P.P., 1849, XIV), pp. xvi, 266.

Report from the Select Committee on Friendly Societies. (B.P.P., 1852, V), pp. x, 132.

Report from the Select Committee on the Friendly Societies Bill. (B.P.P., 1854, VII), pp. xviii, 148.

Reports of the Commissioners appointed to enquire into Friendly and Benefit Building Societies. (B.P.P., 1871-4), four vols.

Report from the Select Committee on Friendly Societies, etc. (B.P.P., 1888, XII), pp. viii, 93.

C.—*Other Publications*

(i) *Directories, etc.*

ANCIENT ORDER OF FORESTERS. Directory of the A.O.F.F.S., Wolverhampton, etc. 1868 to date.

ANCIENT ORDER OF FORESTERS. Foresters' Miscellany and Quarterly Review. 1871 to date.

INDEPENDENT ORDER OF ODDFELLOWS, MANCHESTER UNITY. Deputies' Guide, London, A.M.C., 1934. (This contains some account of the history and financial progress of the Order.)

INDEPENDENT ORDER OF ODDFELLOWS, MANCHESTER UNITY. Oddfellows' Magazine. Manchester : 1829 and onwards.

(ii) *Law of Friendly Societies*

FULLER, *Frank Baden*. The Law relating to Friendly Societies. 1st Edn., London : W. Clowes, 1896, pp. xxii, 280 ; 4th Edn., London : Stevens, 1926, pp. xlvii, 684.

PRATT, *John Tidd*. The Laws relating to Friendly Societies. 1st Edn., 1829. 15th Edn., edited by M. Mackinnon. London : Butterworth, 1931, pp. xxxvi, 242, 25.

(iii) *Friendly Societies' Accounts*

JONES, *E. Furnival*. Friendly Societies' and Trade Unions' Accounts. London : *The Accountant* (Accountant's Library, vol. 28), 1901, pp. vii, 154.

LINGSTROM, *G. L.* A Lecture on the Duties and Responsibilities of Lodge Auditors. Manchester : I.O.O.F., M.U., n.d., pp. 22.

LINGSTROM, *G. L.* A Manual of Bookkeeping for Lodges of the Independent Order of Oddfellows, Manchester Unity, Friendly Society. Manchester : I.O.O.F., M.U., n.d., pp. 43.

TURNBULL, *F.* Friendly Society Accounts. Manchester : Independent Order of Rechabites, 1939, pp. 152.

(iv) *Actuarial Works*

BLAKE, *W. T. C.* "ABC of a Friendly Society Valuation." J.I.A. Students' Society, IV, pp. 1-30.

BRODIE, *R. R.* "The Effect of a Change in the Rate of Mortality upon the Value of Sickness Benefits." J.I.A., vol. LXIV, Pt. 11, p. 207, 1933.

BROWN, *C. H. L.* and TAYLOR, *J. A. G.* Friendly Societies (Institute of Actuaries Consolidation of Reading Series). Cambridge University Press, 1933, pp. xii, 96.

HARDY, *Sir George F.* "Essay on Friendly Societies." J.I.A., XXVII, 1887, and reprints.

MOORE, *J. M.* "Dividing Friendly Societies." J.I.A., Vol. LXIX, Pt. III, 1938, p. 228.

WATSON, *Sir Alfred W.* An Account of an Investigation of the Sickness and Mortality Experience of the I.O.O.F., Manchester Unity, during the five years 1893-1897, etc. Manchester: I.O.O.F., M.U., 1913, pp. xv, 489.

WATSON, *Sir Alfred W.* Friendly Society Finance considered in its Actuarial Aspect. London: C. & E. Layton, 1912, pp. vi, 132.

WATSON, *Sir Alfred W.* "The Methods of Analysing and Presenting the Mortality, Sickness and Secession Experience of Friendly Societies, with examples drawn from the experience of the Manchester Unity of Oddfellows." J.I.A., Vol. XXXV, Pt. IV, 1900, p. 268.

WATSON, *Sir Alfred W.* "Some Points of Interest in the Operations of Friendly Societies, Railway Benefit Societies and Collecting Societies." J.I.A., Vol. XVIV, Pt. II, 1910, p. 168.

(v) *Historical and Descriptive*

ANCIENT ORDER OF FORESTERS. The A.O.F.F.S. Centenary, 1834-1934.

BAERNREITHER, *Joseph M.* English Associations of Working Men. London: Swan, Sonnenschein, 1889, pp. xv, 473.

BRABROOK, *Sir Edward W.* Provident Societies and Industrial Welfare. London: Blackie, 1898 (Victorian Era Series), pp. 224.

BURROWS, *Victor A.* "On Friendly Societies since the Advent of National Health Insurance." J.I.A., Vol. LXIII, Pt. III, 1933, p. 307.

CAMPBELL, *Richardson.* Provident and Industrial Institutions. Manchester: Independent Order of Rechabites, n.d.

COOPER, *Francis R.* Facts about Friendly Societies. Dealing with Reserve Fund, Holloway, Deposit and Dividing Societies. London: Co-operative Printing Society, 1907, pp. 9.

CREW, *Edwin.* The Loyal Order of Ancient Shepherds, Ashton Unity, Centenary Souvenir (1826-1926). Manchester: L.O.A.S.A.U., 1926, pp. 112. Portraits and Illustrations.

CUNNINGHAM, *John W.* A Few Observations on Friendly Societies and their Influence on Public Morals. London: 1817.

EDEN, *Sir F. M.* Observations on Friendly Societies. London: 1801.

EDEN, *Sir F. M.* The State of the Poor. London : 1797, three vols.

HARDWICK, *Charles.* Manual for Patrons and Members of Friendly Societies.

HARDWICK, *Charles.* The History, Present Position and Social Importance of Friendly Societies. 3rd Edn. revised. Manchester : Heywood, 1893, pp. xiv, 170.

HARDWICK, *Charles.* The Provident Institutions of the Working Classes Friendly Societies : their history, prospects, progress and utility : a lecture. London : 1851.

HEWART, *Archibald.* "Friendly Societies" (Transactions of the Actuarial and Insurance Society of Glasgow, Series 2, No. 4).

HINE, *Reginald.* "Dorset Friendly Societies and their Emblems." Proceedings of the Dorset Natural History Club, Vol. 49.

HOLLOWAY, *George.* Prize Essay on Superannuation and Old Age Pensions. (Forster Prize Essays on Friendly Societies.) Manchester, 1879.

INTERNATIONAL LABOUR OFFICE. Voluntary Sickness Insurance (I.L.O. Studies and Reports, Series M, No. 7). London : P. S. King, 1927, pp. xlviii, 470. (Contains a brief account of British Friendly Societies.)

MOFFREY, *Robert Wm.* A Century of Oddfellowship. Manchester : I.O.O.F., M.U., 1910, pp. 200.

MOFFREY, *Robert Wm.* Rise and Progress of the Manchester Unity of the Independent Order of Oddfellows, 1810-1904. Manchester : Taylor, Garnett & Co., 1904, pp. 85.

NEWMAN, *Tom S.* The Story of Friendly Societies and Social Security. London : Hearts of Oak Benefit Society, 1945, pp. 39.

NEWMAN, *Tom S.* History of the Hearts of Oak Benefit Society. London : Hearts of Oak Benefit Society, 1942, pp. 203. Portraits and Illustrations.

ROSE, *Rt. Hon. George, M.P.* Observations on the Act for the Relief and Encouragement of Friendly Societies, 1794.

SMITH, *R. G.* "Progress and Position of Friendly Societies." (Trans. Actuarial and Insurance Society of Glasgow, Series 6, No. 7.)

SPRY, *James.* History of the Oddfellowship. London : Pitman, 1867.

SPRY, *James.* Manual of Oddfellowship, for the use of the initiated : being an attempt to explain the origin, degrees and emblems of the Independent Order of Oddfellows, Manchester Unity. London : 1862.

THORNLEY, *John.* History of the Grand United Order of Oddfellows. Manchester : J. Heywood, 1911-13, 4 parts.

WALLER, *W. C.* "Early Huguenot Friendly Societies." (Trans. of the Huguenot Society of London, 1901.)

WILKINSON, *J. Frome.* The Friendly Society Movement. London : Longmans, 1886, pp. xvi, 229.

WILKINSON, *J. Frome.* Mutual Thrift. ("Social Questions of Today" series, ed. H. de B. Gibbins.) London : Methuen, 1891, pp. xii, 324.

WILLIAMS, *David.* Friendly Societies. London : Published by the author, 1903, pp. 36.

(vi) *Industrial Assurance*

WILSON, *Sir Arnold* and LEVY, *Hermann*. Industrial Assurance : an historical and critical study. Oxford University Press, 1937, pp. xxxiii, 519. Bibliography.

(vii) *Approved Societies*

HARRIS, *R. W.* National Health Insurance in Great Britain, 1911-1946. London : Allen & Unwin, 1946, pp. 224.

LEVY, *Hermann.* National Health Insurance : a critical study. (National Institute of Economic and Social Research : Economic and Social Studies, No. IV). Cambridge University Press, 1944, pp. x, 366. Bibliography.

II. BUILDING SOCIETIES

Official Publications

Reports of the Chief Registrar of Friendly Societies. London : H.M.S.O. (last issue 1938).

Guide Book to the Registry of Friendly Societies and the Office of the Industrial Assurance Commisioner. London : H.M.S.O. (Last ed. 1933).

Building Society Statistical Summary. London : H.M.S.O. (Annual).

The Provision of Houses for Owner-Occupation in Scotland. (Report by the Scottish Housing Advisory Committee.) London : H.M.S.O., Cmd. 6741, pp. 74.

Other Publications

BACON, *R. K.* The Life of Sir Enoch Hill. The Romance of the Modern Building Society. London : Nicholson & Watson, 1934, pp. 160.

BELLMAN, *Sir Harold.* "Building Societies : some Economic Aspects." (*Economic Journal*, March, 1933.)

BELLMAN, *Sir Harold.* Building Societies : Retrospect and Prospect. London : London General Press, pp. 24.

BELLMAN, *Sir Harold.* The Thrifty Three Millions. London : Abbey Road Building Society, 1935, pp. xii, 357.

BUILDING SOCIETIES ASSOCIATION. The Building Societies Gazette (monthly magazine of the B.S.A.). London : Franey & Co.

BUILDING SOCIETIES ASSOCIATION. The Building Societies Year Book. London : Franey & Co.

COHEN, *J. L.* Building Society Finance. London : Reed & Co., 1933, pp. 227.

COLE, *G. D. H.* Building Societies and the Housing Question. (Design for Britain Series No. 28.) London : J. M. Dent, 1943, pp. 31.

ELKINGTON, *George.* The National Building Society, 1849-1934. Cambridge : Heffer, 1935, pp. x, 79. Plates.

FAIRCHILD, *Edwin C.* Building Societies : their Reform and their Future. London : J. M. Dent, 1945, pp. 90.

LEAVER, *J. B.* Building Societies, Past, Present and Future. (Design for Britain Series, No. 19.) London : J. M. Dent, 1942, pp. 31.

MANSBRIDGE, *Albert.* Brick Upon Brick. London : J. M. Dent, 1934, pp. xxii, 236. (A History of the Co-operative Building Society.)

THE TIMES. British Homes : The Building Society Movement. (Reprinted from the Building Societies Number of *The Times*), 1938, pp. 109.

WEBB, *Arthur.* Signposts of Building Society Finance. (Design for Britain, Series No. 1.) London : J. M. Dent, 1942, pp. 29.

WURTZBURG, *E. A.* The Law Relating to Building Societies (9th edn., ed. G. W. Knowles.) London : Stevens & Sons Ltd., and Sweet & Maxwell Ltd., 1946, pp. xxx, 393.

III. CONSUMERS' CO-OPERATION

CARR-SAUNDERS, *A. M.,* FLORENCE *P. Sargant,* and PEERS, *Robert.* Consumers' Co-operation in Great Britain : an examination of the British Co-operative Movement. London : Allen & Unwin, 1938, pp. 556.

COLE, *G. D. H.* A Century of Co-operation. Manchester : Co-operative Union, 1944, pp. iv, 428.

HALL, *E.* and WATKINS, *W. P.* Co-operation : A Survey of the History, Principles and Organisation of the Co-operative Movement in Great Britain and Ireland. Manchester : Co-operative Union Ltd., 1937, pp. 408.

WEBB, *Sidney* and *Beatrice.* The Consumers' Co-operative Movement. London : Longmans, 1921, pp. xv, 504.

IV. HOSPITAL CONTRIBUTORY SCHEMES

BIRMINGHAM HOSPITAL SATURDAY FUND. Sixty-five Years of the Birmingham Hospital Saturday Fund, 1873-1938. Birmingham : 1938, pp. 48.

BRITISH HOSPITALS CONTRIBUTORY SCHEMES ASSOCIATION. Directory of Contributory Schemes (latest issue refers to 1943). Birmingham : 1943, pp. 35.

CAN, *Gerald.* Twenty-one Years of Service : The History of the H.S.A. London : H.S.A., n.d., pp. 22.

POLITICAL AND ECONOMIC PLANNING. Report on the British Health Services. London : P.E.P., 1937, pp. 430.

V. HOUSING AND HOUSING SOCIETIES

MINISTRY OF HEALTH. Management of Municipal Housing Estates. London : H.M.S.O., 1946, pp. 44.

MINISTRY OF HEALTH. Rent Control in England and Wales. London : H.M.S.O. (C.133), 1946, pp. iv., 15.

MINISTRY OF HEALTH. Report of Interdepartmental Committee on Rent Control ("Ridley Report"). London : H.M.S.O. (Cmd. 6621), 1945, pp. 63.

MINISTRY OF HEALTH (CENTRAL HOUSING ADVISORY COMMITTEE). Private Enterprise Housing. London : H.M.S.O., 1944, pp. 56.

BROWNE, *Reginald.* Housing Societies. (Design for Britain Series, No. 35). London : J. M. Dent, 1944, pp. 31.

BROWNE, *Reginald.* The Housing Society Movement in Great Britain. (Reprinted from *Architectural Design and Construction,* 1943.)

DEWSNAP, *E. R.* The Housing Problem in England and Wales (Manchester University Economic Series), 1907.

NATIONAL FEDERATION OF HOUSING SOCIETIES. Official Bulletin. London : N.F.H.S.

VI. SAVINGS BANKS

HORNE, *H. Oliver.* A History of Savings Banks. Oxford University Press, 1947, pp. xvi, 407. Illustrations and Bibliography.

VII. THE DEVELOPMENT OF PHILANTHROPY

BARNETT, *Samuel* and BARNETT, *Dame Henrietta.* Towards Social Reform. London : Fisher Unwin, 1909, pp. 359.

BOSANQUET, *Helen.* Social Work in London, 1869 to 1912 : A History of the Charity Organisation Society. London : John Murray, 1914, pp. xii, 420.

CHARITY ORGANISATION SOCIETY. Charity Reform Papers. London : T. Scott, various dates.

FAMILY WELFARE ASSOCIATION. The Family Welfare Association. London : F.W.A., n.d., pp. 10.

GRAY, *B. Kirkman.* A History of English Philanthropy. London : P. S. King, 1905, pp. xvi, 302.

VIII. THE RED CROSS

BEST, *S. H.* The Story of the British Red Cross. London : Cassell, 1938, pp. xv, 275.

GUMPERT, *Martin.* Dunant : The Story of the Red Cross. London : Eyre & Spottiswood, 1939, pp. 311

INTERNATIONAL RED CROSS COMMITTEE AND LEAGUE OF RED CROSS SOCIETIES. The International Red Cross. Paris-Geneva, 1937, pp. 28.

MORRAH, *Dermot M.* The British Red Cross. London : Collins, 1944 (Britain in Pictures Series), pp. 47. Plates, etc.

IX. THE ORDER OF ST. JOHN

BECKWITH-SMITH, *Mrs.* A Short History of the Grand Priory in the British
Realm of the Venerable Order of the Hospital of St. John of Jerusalem.
London : St. John Ambulance Association, pp. 24.

KINNAIRD, *The Hon. George.* "The Order of St. John of Jerusalem."
Quarterly Review, October, 1946.

X. RURAL AND URBAN AMENITIES

MINISTRY OF TOWN AND COUNTRY PLANNING. Conservation of Nature in
England and Wales : Report of the Wild Life Conservation Special
Committee. London : H.M.S.O. (Cmd. 7122), 1947, pp. v, 139. Maps.

MINISTRY OF TOWN AND COUNTRY PLANNING. Footpaths and Access to the
Countryside : Report of the Special Committee. London : H.M.S.O.
(Cmd. 7207), 1947, pp. 134.

MINISTRY OF TOWN AND COUNTRY PLANNING. Report of National Parks
Committee (England and Wales). London : H.M.S.O. (Cmd. 7121),
1947, pp. vi, 134. Maps.

ABERCROMBIE, *Patrick.* The Preservation of Rural England, etc. Liverpool :
University Press, and London : Hodder & Stoughton, 1926, pp. 56.

COMMONS, ETC., SOCIETY. The Journal of the Commons Society.
London : 1927 to date.

COUNCIL FOR THE PRESERVATION OF RURAL ENGLAND. Annual Reports (to
date) and Quarterly Reports (to date).

EVANS, *Richardson.* An Account of the Scapa Society. London : Constable
& Co., 1926, pp. xviii, 374.

EVERSLEY (*G. J. Shaw-Lefèvre, 1st Baron*). Commons, Forests and Footpaths. London : Cassell, 1910, pp. xxiv, 356.

GEORGIAN GROUP. The Georgian Group : Its Origin and Purpose. (Georgian
Leaflet No. 1.) London : 1947.

NATIONAL TRUST. The National Trust : A Record of Fifty Years' Achievement (ed. James Lees-Milne). London : Batsford, 1945, pp. xii, 132.
Plates.

NUFFIELD COLLEGE SOCIAL RECONSTRUCTION SURVEY. Britain's Town and
Country Pattern : A Summary of the Barlow, Scott and Uthwatt Reports.
London : Faber & Faber, 1943, pp. 111.

XI. COMMUNITY AND COMMUNITY CENTRES

MINISTRY OF EDUCATION. Community Centres. London : H.M.S.O., 1946,
pp. 40.

HARRIS, *E. Sewell.* Community Centres and Associations (with a Foreword
by Sir Wyndham Deedes). London : N.C.S.S., n.d., pp. 52.

MANCHESTER AND SALFORD COUNCIL OF SOCIAL SERVICE. Community Centres
and Associations in Manchester. Manchester : M.S.C.S.S., 1946,
pp. 87.

NATIONAL COUNCIL OF SOCIAL SERVICE. Village Halls and Social Centres in the Countryside. London : N.C.S.S., 1945 (5th Edn.), pp. 85.

STEPNEY RECONSTRUCTION GROUP. Living in Stepney. London : Pilot Press, 1945, pp. 64. Illustrations.

STEPHENSON, *Flora* and STEPHENSON, *Gordon*. Community Centres : A Survey. London : Housing Centre, 1946, pp. viii, 117. Diagrams.

WHITE, *L. E.* Tenement Town (Foreword by Dr. G. F. Macleod, M.C., D.D.) London : Jason Press, 1946, pp. 77.

XII. YOUTH

BOARD OF EDUCATION (NOW MINISTRY OF EDUCATION). The Challenge of Youth (Circular 1516). London : H.M.S.O., 1940, pp. 4.

BOARD OF EDUCATION (NOW MINISTRY OF EDUCATION). The Provision of Facilities for Recreation and Social and Physical Training (Circular 51). London : H.M.S.O., 1945.

BOARD OF EDUCATION (NOW MINISTRY OF EDUCATION). The Service of Youth (Circular 1486). London : H.M.S.O., 1939, pp. 4.

BOARD OF EDUCATION (NOW MINISTRY OF EDUCATION). The Youth Service After the War. London : H.M.S.O. 1943 pp. 32.

BOARD OF EDUCATION (now MINISTRY OF EDUCATION). Teachers and Youth Leaders : Report of the Committee appointed by the President of the Board of Education to consider the Supply, Recruitment and Training of Teachers and Youth Leaders. London : H.M.S.O., 1944, pp. 176.

BOARD OF EDUCATION (now MINISTRY OF EDUCATION). Youth in a City : An Account of an experiment of Youth Service in its initial stages. London : H.M.S.O., 1943, pp. 10. (Board of Education, Educational Pamphlet No. 117.)

YOUTH ADVISORY COUNCIL. The Purpose and Content of the Youth Service : A Report. London : H.M.S.O., 1945, pp. 16.

CENTRAL ADVISORY COUNCIL FOR EDUCATION (ENGLAND). School and Life : A First Enquiry into the Transition from School to Independent Life. London : H.M.S.O., 1947, pp. 115.

ANON. One Hundred Years, 1844-1944 : The Story of the Y.M.C.A. London : Y.M.C.A., 1944, pp. 58.

BARBER, *D. H.* Voluntary Work with Boys : A Handbook for Youth Leaders. London : Vawser & Wiles, 1946, pp. 70.

BOY SCOUTS' ASSOCIATION. The Road Ahead : Being the decisions of the Council of the Boy Scouts' Association, based on the recommendations of the Commission on Post-War Scouting. London : B.S.A., 1945, pp. 48.

CLARK, *Edith M.* Youth and the Village Club. London : Nelson, 1946, pp. viii, 96.

COOKE, *Douglas* (*ed.*). Youth Organisations of Great Britain. London: Jordan & Sons (second issue), 1946, pp. xii, 344.

EDWARDS-REES, *Desirée*. The Service of Youth Book. Wallington, Surrey : Religious Education Press (3rd edition), 1945, pp. 148.

GRUBB, *Dermot (ed.)*. Youth Service Handbook, 1945-46. London : W. Walker & Sons, 1945, pp. xxx, 145. Illustrations.

JEPHCOTT, *Pearl*. Clubs for Girls : Notes for New Helpers at Clubs. London: Faber & Faber, 1943, pp. 68.

LUTON YOUTH COUNCIL. Report on the Leisure-Time Facilities for Young People in Luton. Luton : Y.C., 1947, pp. 24. Illustrations.

NATIONAL COUNCIL OF Y.M.C.A.'S. Our Message is Jesus Christ : Being the Official Report of the British Convention . . . 1936. London and Edinburgh : National Council of Y.M.C.A.'s, 1936, pp. 213.

STANDING CONFERENCE OF NATIONAL VOLUNTARY YOUTH ORGANISATIONS. The Selection and Training of Youth Leaders. London : N.C.S.S., 1945, pp. 8.

TYNEMOUTH YOUTH COUNCIL. Youth Survey Report. Tynemouth : Youth Council, 1947, pp. 42.

XIII. SETTLEMENTS

STOCKS, *M. D.* Fifty Years in Every Street : the Story of the Manchester University Settlement. Manchester University Press, 1945, pp. xii, 126. Frontispiece.

UNION OF GIRLS' SCHOOLS FOR SOCIAL SERVICE. Fifty Years of the U.G.S., 1896-1946. London : U.G.S., 1946, pp. 40. Illustrations.

XIV. FAMILY CASE WORK

Final Report of Committee on Matrimonial Causes (Denning Committee). London : H.M.S.O. (Cmd. 7024), 1947, pp. 37.

HORDER, *The Rt. Hon. Lord, and others*. Rebuilding Family Life in the Post-War World. London : Odhams Press, n.d., pp. 136.

XV. CHARITABLE TRUSTS

ASSOCIATION OF CERTIFIED AND CORPORATE ACCOUNTANTS. Some Legal Aspects of Charities, with a Foreword by the Rt. Hon. Lord Latham. London : Fiscal Press Ltd., 1947, pp. xx, 122.

CARNEGIE TRUST. Centenary of the Birth of Andrew Carnegie : The British Trusts and their Work, with a Chapter on the American Foundations. Edinburgh : Pillans & Wilson, 1935, pp. x, 155. Plates.

COMMITTEE ON THE SUPERVISION OF CHARITIES. Report of the Home Office Departmental Committee on the Supervision of Charities. London : H.M.S.O., 1927 (Cmd. 2823), pp. 47.

HOBHOUSE, *Sir Arthur*. The Dead Hand : Addresses on the subject of Endowments and Settlements of Property. London : Chatto & Windus, 1880, pp. xiv, 240.

MILL, *John Stuart*. Art. "Endowments" in *Dissertations and Discussions*, Vol. IV. London : Longmans, Green, 1875.

ROYAL COMMISSION FOR THE EXHIBITION OF 1851. An Outline of its Activities Past and Present. London : Royal Commission, 1924, pp. 12.

SURVEY COMMITTEE ON THE PROBLEMS OF AGEING AND THE CARE OF OLD PEOPLE. Report of a Survey of Charitable Trusts. London : Nuffield Foundation, 1947, pp. 56.

XVI. THE HANDICAPPED

(i) *Old People*

BRITISH MEDICAL ASSOCIATION. The Care and Treatment of the Elderly and Infirm : Report of a Special Committee of the British Medical Association. London : B.M.A., 1947, pp. 28.

HOUSING CENTRE. The London Almshouses : Six Centuries of Housing for the Aged. London : Housing Centre, n.d., pp. 29.

NATIONAL OLD PEOPLE'S WELFARE COMMITTEE. Old People's Welfare : A Guide to Practical Work for the Welfare of Old People. London : N.C.S.S., 1946, pp. 64. Bibliography.

NUFFIELD FOUNDATION. Old People : Report of a Survey Committee on the Problems of Ageing and the Care of Old People, under the Chairmanship of B. Seebohm Rowntree, C.H., LL.D. Oxford University Press, 1947, pp. viii, 202. Illustrations.

THOMAS, *Geoffrey*. The Employment of Older Persons : A Survey carried out in mid-1945. London : Social Survey, 1947 (NS/60/2). (Draft Report, duplicated), pp. 62, and Appendices. Tables.

(ii) *Children*

HOME OFFICE. Report of the Care of Children Committee ("Curtis Report.") London : H.M.S.O., 1946 (Cmd. 6922), pp. 195.

NATIONAL COUNCIL OF ASSOCIATED CHILDREN'S HOMES. The Care of Children Deprived of Home Life. London : N.C.A.C.H., 1947, pp. 8.

NATIONAL COUNCIL OF SOCIAL SERVICE. In *Loco Parentis* : A Report with recommendations prepared by a Committee under the Chairmanship of His Honour Judge Gamon on existing legislation governing the adoption of children. London : N.C.S.S., 1947, pp. 20.

PARR, *Robert J*. The Baby Farmer : An Exposition and an Appeal. London : N.S.P.C.C. (2nd Edn.), 1909, pp. 77.

REDWOOD, *Hugh*. Harvest : The Record of the Shaftesbury Society, 1844-1944. London : Shaftesbury Society, 1944, pp. 68. Illustrations.

WOMEN'S GROUP ON PUBLIC WELFARE. Children Without Homes : Proceedings of a Conference . . . London : N.C.S.S., 1945, pp. 40.

(iii) *Prisoners*

HOME OFFICE. Report of Commissioners of Prisons and Directors of Convict Prisons for the year 1945. London : H.M.S.O. (Cmd. 7146), 1947. pp. 120.

(iv) *The Tuberculous*

TRAILL, *R. R.* The Problem of Phthisis. (Paper read at the Medical School, Aberdeen University, April 15th, 1947), pp. 22.

(v) *The Unmarried Mother*

FISHER, *Mrs. H. A. L.* Twenty-one Years and After. (A History of the National Council for the Unmarried Mother and her Child.) London: N.C.U.M.C. (2nd edn.), 1946, pp. 23.

(vi) *The Deaf*

ROYAL RESIDENTIAL SCHOOLS FOR THE DEAF, MANCHESTER. Centenary of the Founding of the Schools, 1823-1923. (A History.) Manchester: Taylor, Garnett, Evans & Co., 1923, pp. 71. Illustrations.

WELLS, *Arthur G.* "An Attempt to Estimate the Incidence of Defective Hearing in England and Wales." *British Medical Journal*, July, 1937.

XVII. PROBLEMS OF LEISURE

National Income and Expenditure of the United Kingdom, 1938-1946. London: H.M.S.O., 1947 (Cmd. 7099).

MINISTRY OF LABOUR AND NATIONAL SERVICE: CATERING WAGES COMMISSION. The Staggering of Holidays: A Report. London: H.M.S.O., 1945, pp. 24.

MINISTRY OF LABOUR. Report of Committee on Holidays with Pay. London: H.M.S.O. (Cmd. 5724), 1938, pp. 79.

MINISTRY OF EDUCATION. Further Education: the Scope and Content of its Opportunities under the Education Act, 1944. (Ministry of Education Pamphlet No. 8.) H.M.S.O., 1947, pp. 200.

ABRAMS, *Mark.* "Britain Off Duty" in *World off Duty* (Contact Publications). London: 1947.

BARNA, *Tibor.* The Redistribution of Incomes through Public Finance in 1937. Oxford: Clarendon Press, 1945, pp. xi, 289.

BOX, *Kathleen.* The Cinema and the Public: An Inquiry into Cinema-Going Habits and Expenditure made in 1946. London: Social Survey, 1946 (N.S. 106), pp. 17. Tables.

BRUNNER, *Elizabeth.* Holiday-Making and the Holiday Trades. Oxford University Press: 1945, pp. 65.

INDUSTRIAL WELFARE SOCIETY (INC.). Holiday Savings, 1938, pp. 15.

LANCASHIRE STANDING CONFERENCE OF VOLUNTARY YOUTH ORGANISATIONS. Gambling Among Young People. Manchester: Lancashire Community Council, 1946, pp. 10.

LEONARD, *T. Arthur.* Adventures in Holiday-Making. London: Holiday Fellowship, 1934, pp. 220.

LITCHFIELD, *R. B.* The Beginnings of the Working Men's College. London: Working Men's College, 1902, pp. 12.

NATIONAL FOUNDATION FOR ADULT EDUCATION. Voluntary Agencies in Adult Education. (Foundation Papers, Supplement No. 1.) London: N.F.A.E., 1947, pp. iii, 32.

NATIONAL COUNCIL OF SOCIAL SERVICE. Holidays : A Study of the Post-War Problem. Oxford University Press : 1945, pp. 84.

SLATER, *Patrick*. First and Supplementary Reports on the Demand for Holidays in 1947. London : Social Survey, 1946 (N.S. 86). (Draft Reports, duplicated), pp. 12 and Appendices ; 19. Map, Graphs, Tables.

SEERS, *D.* The 1947 National Income White Paper. (In "Bulletin of the Oxford University Institute of Statistics," Vol. 9, No. 7) July, 1947.

WOLFE, *Lawrence*. The Reilly Plan—a New Way of Life. London: Nicholson & Watson, 1945.

NATIONAL COUNCIL OF SOCIAL SERVICE. Citizens' Advice Bureaux in Britain and Advice Centres in Liberated Europe. London : N.C.S.S., 1944, pp. 59.

XVIII. STAFF PROBLEMS

BRITISH FEDERATION OF SOCIAL WORKERS. The Practice of Social Work : A Report of an Experimental Course of Training in the Practical Work—Supervision of Students . . . London : B.F.S.W., 1946, pp. 60.

NATIONAL COUNCIL OF SOCIAL SERVICE. Salaries and Conditions of Work of Social Workers : A Report by a Joint Committee under the chairmanship of T. S. Simey, M.A. London : N.C.S.S., 1947, pp. 85.

YOUNGHUSBAND, *Eileen L.* Report on the Employment, Training of Social Workers. Edinburgh : T. and A. Constable, 1947, pp. viii, 180.

XIX. FINANCE OF VOLUNTARY SOCIAL WORK

BRANDER, *J. P.* The Community Chest and Chest Council System : Central Financing and Planning of Charities. London : Allen & Unwin, 1941, pp. 64.

HUNT, *G. Vivian.* Memorandum on Finance of Voluntary Organisations. Sheffield : Council of Social Service, n.d., pp. 10.

XX. PIONEERS

ANON. Charles Booth : A Memoir. London : Macmillan, 1918, pp. viii, 176. Portrait.

BARNETT, *Henrietta.* Canon Barnett, His Life, Work and Friends. London : John Murray, 1918, two vols.

BEGBIE, *Harold.* Life of William Booth. London : Macmillan, 1920, two vols. Portraits.

BELL, *E. H. C. Moberly.* Octavia Hill : A Biography. London : Constable, 1942, pp. xvii, 297. Illustrations.

CAMPBELL, *John.* Memoirs of David Nasmith. London : John Snow, 1844, pp. xx, 476.

CHAMBERS, *Robert*. A Biographical Dictionary of Eminent Scotsmen. London : Blackie, 1868-70, three vols.

FRY, *Katherine* and CRESSWELL, *Rachel*. Memoir of the Life of Elizabeth Fry . . . edited by two of her daughters. London : Hatchard, 1848, two vols., pp. xxii, 521 ; viii, 540. Illustrations.

HALL, *Sophy*. Dr. Duncan of Ruthwell, founder of Savings Banks. Edinburgh : Oliphant, Anderson and Ferrier, 1910, pp. 156. Portrait.

HAMILTON, *Cicely*, and BAYLIS, *Lilian*. The Old Vic. London : Jonathan Cape, 1926, pp. 285. Illustrations.

HAMILTON, *Mary Agnes*. Sidney and Beatrice Webb : A Study in Contemporary Biography. London : Sampson Low, Marston, 1933, pp. x, 314.

HOGG, *Ethel M*. Quintin Hogg : A Biography. London : Constable, 1904, pp. 419. Illustrations.

HODDER, *Edwin*. The Life and Work of the Seventh Earl of Shaftesbury, K.G. London : Cassell & Co., 1886, two vols., pp. xx, 525 ; x, 527. Portraits.

MAURICE, *Frederick Denison*. The Founder of the Working Men's College and his Objects : two hitherto unpublished papers by the Rev. Frederick Denison Maurice, with an Introduction by his son, Major-General Sir Frederick Maurice, K.C.B. London : Working Men's College (1906), pp. 11.

REFFOLD, *A. E.* The Audacity to Live : A Résumé of the Life and Work of Wilson Carlisle. London and Edinburgh : Marshall, Morgan & Scott, Ltd., 1938, pp. 95.

REYNOLDS, *E. E.* Baden-Powell : A Biography of Lord Baden-Powell of Gilwell. Oxford University Press, 1942, pp. 283.

SOLLY, *Henry*. These Eighty Years. London : Simpkin & Marshall, 1893, two vols.

WAUGH, *Rosa*. The Life of Benjamin Waugh. London : T. Fisher Unwin, 1913, pp. 320. Portrait.

WHITNEY, *Janet*. Elizabeth Fry : Quaker Heroine. London : Harrap, 1937, pp. 328. Illustrations, Bibliography.

WILLIAMS, *J. E. Hodder*. The Life of George Williams. London : Hodder & Stoughton, 1906, pp. xvi, 356. Illustrations.

WILLIAMSON, *David*. Ninety Not Out : A Record of Ninety Years' Child Welfare Work of the Shaftesbury Society and R.S.U. London : Hodder & Stoughton, 1934, pp. 190. Illustrations.

XXI. GENERAL WORKS

BEVERIDGE, *Sir William*. Report on Social Insurance and Allied Services. London : H.M.S.O. (Cmd. 6404), 1942, pp. 299.

BEVERIDGE, *Sir William*. Report on Social Insurance and Allied Services. Appendix G (Memoranda from Organisations). London : H.M.S.O. (Cmd. 6405), 1942, pp. 244.

BOURDILLON, *A. C. F. (ed.)*. Voluntary Social Services. (Nuffield College Social Reconstruction Survey.) London : Methuen, 1945, pp. xi, 322.

CLARKE, *John J.* Social Administration. London : Pitman (4th edn.), 1946, pp. x, 774.

FAMILY WELFARE ASSOCIATION. The Annual Charities Register and Digest. London : Longmans and F.W.A. (54th edn.), 1947, pp. vi, 501.

HORDER, *Rt. Hon. Lord (advisory editor)*. Health and Social Welfare (an annotated directory of welfare and kindred organisations). London : Todd Publishing Co., 1947, pp. 527.

ROBSON, *W. A. (ed.)*. Social Security. London : Allen & Unwin (2nd edn.), 1945, pp. 472 (includes articles on Blind Welfare and on Industrial Assurance).

For Product Safety Concerns and Information please contact our
EU representative GPSR@taylorandfrancis.com Taylor & Francis
Verlag GmbH, Kaufingerstraße 24, 80331 München, Germany